Yale Readings in Insurance

FIRE INSURANCE

Edited by
Lester W. Zartman, Ph.D.

William S. Hein & Co., Inc.
Buffalo, New York
2003

Library of Congress Cataloging-in-Publication Data

Fire insurance / edited by Lester W. Zartman.
p. cm. -- (Yale readings in insurance)
Originally published: New Haven : Yale University Press, 1909.
Includes index.
ISBN 1-57588-779-7 (alk. paper)
1. Insurance, Fire. 2. Insurance, Marine. I. Zartman, Lester W. (Lester William), 1878-1909. II. Series.
HG9665.F47 2003
368.1'1--dc21

2003047758

This acid-free reprint was digitally archived under the strict quality control guidelines established by William S. Hein & Co., Inc.'s "Preservation Program" This program was established to preserve the integrity of legal classics for future generations of legal researchers.

This paper meets the requirements of ANSI/NISO Z39.48-1992 (Permanence of Paper).

Printed in the United States of America.

YALE READINGS IN INSURANCE

FIRE INSURANCE

EDITED BY

LESTER W. ZARTMAN, PH.D.

ASSISTANT PROFESSOR OF POLITICAL ECONOMY, YALE UNIVERSITY

NEW HAVEN, CONNECTICUT
YALE UNIVERSITY PRESS
LONDON
HENRY FROWDE
OXFORD UNIVERSITY PRESS
1909

Printed in the United States

PREFACE

The "Yale Lectures on Fire and Miscellaneous Insurance" appeared five years ago. Although a considerable edition was printed, the unexpectedly large demand soon exhausted it, and as the plates were destroyed, for two years the lectures have been out of print.

It seems desirable that either a new edition of the lectures should be printed, or that something new should be published in their place. The latter alternative has been chosen, and instead of simply reprinting the old lectures, the plan has been adopted of selecting special readings, partly from the "Yale Lectures," partly from other sources. This plan was preferred because the literature of fire and miscellaneous forms of insurance has been developing so rapidly that a much more comprehensive textbook can now be prepared than was possible a few years ago. By not confining this volume to a reprint of the old lectures, it has been possible to take advantage of the advance which has taken place in this literature. Only seven of the lectures in the old volume are reprinted, and all but one of these have been extensively changed. Some of the matter now published has never appeared before, and much of the remainder has been revised.

The major part of this volume is devoted to the subject of fire insurance. The general principles involved in fire insurance are typical of those found in all forms of insurance other than life insurance. The miscellaneous forms of insurance, such as marine, steam boiler, employers' liability, and workingmen's insurance are discussed to the extent that each introduces new methods and new principles into the business. In selecting these readings, the aim has been to avoid those authors who treat the subject in technical language, as well as those who make the subject more simple than it really is, and thus conceal its real problems. The broad selection of material would not have been possible without the coöperation of others. It is a pleasure to record the fine spirit of publishers in permitting reprints from copyrighted books, and the willingness of authors to revise articles where changed conditions made revision desirable.

LESTER W. ZARTMAN.

NEW HAVEN,
August, 1909.

CONTENTS

YALE READINGS IN INSURANCE

CHAPTER I

HISTORY OF FIRE INSURANCE IN EUROPE [1]

FIRE insurance as now commonly practised is usually considered to have begun after the great conflagration of London in 1666. While marine insurance — the oldest form of insurance in existence — had been steadily developing and extending with the great expansion of trade and navigation which followed the discovery of the New World, and although merchants and ship owners from very remote times clearly foresaw and provided against the perils of navigation, very little specific attempt was made by property owners to secure indemnity for loss caused by fire prior to the date above mentioned.

It is true that some forms of provision for the aid of those suffering from loss by fire and other calamitous causes apparently existed in very remote times, as the following quotation will evidence:

"The earliest application of fire insurance known to us was in connection with communes of towns and districts. These communes flourished in Assyria and the East more than 2500 years ago. Judges, priests, and magistrates were appoineed for each town and district with power to levy contributions from each member of the commune to provide a fund against sudden calamities such as drought and fire. If the judges were satisfied that the fire was

[1] By Richard M. Bissell, Vice-President of the Hartford Fire Insurance Company, Hartford. Reprinted from pages 13–24 of the "Yale Lectures on Insurance, Fire and Miscellaneous."

accidental they empowered the magistrates to assess the members of the commune either in kind or in money, and in the event of any member being unable through poverty to meet his share of the contribution, the deficiency was made up from the common fund. These communes still exist in a modified form in China."

As early as 1240 A.D. the laws of Count Thomas of Flanders provided that the members of a community as a whole should make good a loss which fire might cause to an individual, unless the incendiary who caused the fire could be discovered, in which case the loss was to be made good from his property and he was to be banished.

It will be noted that the plans outlined above contemplated an assessment by the state and that all property owners were protected. We may discover here, therefore, the beginning of state fire insurance, which will be later more fully described and which continues in Germany and elsewhere to this day on a large scale.

Another method for protection and security against loss by fire, water, robbery, or other calamities, arose during the Middle Ages in connection with the various Anglo-Saxon and German guilds, the members of which made regular contributions toward a common relief fund.

In 1609 a plan was suggested by one of his subjects to Count Von Oldenberg, wherein it was proposed that he individually should consent to insure those of his subjects, who might so desire, against the loss of their houses by fire upon an annual payment to him of a fee or premium of one dollar for every one hundred dollars of valuation. This suggestion was declined by the Count, though not without some hesitation, and, though he suggested that such a plan might well be undertaken by a company of private individuals, no action on his suggestion seems to have been taken. This, so far as I have been able to discover, was the first suggestion ever made looking toward the formation of a company or association for fire insurance purposes only.

In England various fire insurance schemes were proposed in 1635, 1638, and 1660, but for one reason or another — largely owing to the great Civil War — none of them was fully organized, and as late as 1667 there is evidence that fire insurance as we know it did not exist.

In 1666 came the great fire of London, which burned for four days and nights and spread over 436 acres of territory. This was an alarming and appalling calamity. Over 85 per cent. of the buildings in London were destroyed, while the property loss is estimated to have been about ten million pounds, — a sum which has been calculated to equal over three hundred million dollars at present values. In the absence of insurance this was a blow from which London was slow to recover, as is shown by the fact that in 1673, seven years later, about one thousand buildings were yet to be replaced. Relatively, this London fire was the greatest in the history of the world, and the date of it — September 2 — was observed as a Fast Day for more than one hundred years thereafter.

Immediately after the fire various plans for the protection of individuals against loss by fire began to be devised. In 1667 the first regular system for insuring buildings against fire began. In that year, one Nicholas Barbon opened an office where he individually proposed to insure houses and buildings. A few years later, in 1680, after having had some success, he formed a partnership known as "The Fire Office." This company, for a given consideration, engaged to pay the assured the amount of indemnity declared in the policy, or contract, should his house or building be destroyed by fire, or to repair it should it be only "damnified" — *i.e.*, damaged. No liability, it will be noted, rested upon the assured beyond the payment of the premium.

In 1681, a few years after this first company was established, an attempt was made by the city of London to establish an insurance account, or business, and funds and property were put aside and dedicated for that purpose.

Houses were insured for any term up to one hundred years. But the enterprise did not prosper and was abandoned in 1683.

Then followed, in the same year, what was called the "Friendly Society." This concern, which had an existence of nearly one hundred years, conducted its business upon an entirely different plan, as follows: First, the assured paid yearly a small sum, varying according as the building to be insured was brick or frame. This charge was to cover the expenses and, we may presume, the profits of those who operated the company. Second, the assured deposited with the company a sum equal to five annual payments as a guarantee that future payments and assessments would be met as required. This money could be appropriated by the company if the assured failed to keep up his payments. Third, the assured signed an agreement to contribute his share toward the payment of any and every loss which the company might sustain up to an amount not exceeding thirty shillings for every one hundred pounds of insurance carried by him. It will be seen that all losses were to be paid from the contribution of the assured, upon whom, also, rested all liability and for whom the operators of the company or the "undertakers," as they were termed, acted only as collectors and distributors.

This was a form of mutual insurance, as it is now called; that is to say, insurance where the policy-holders are directly liable for one another's losses. This company was also fairly successful.

Another purely mutual company was organized in 1696. This company proposed a deposit to be paid back, less expenses, when contracts should terminate; also that profits from interest on invested funds over and above losses and expenses should be divided among the members or policy-holders, and that each year a rate of assessment should be declared by the directors, according to which levies should be made on the policy-holders for payment of losses or for the distribution of profits to them. It was assumed that the interest or earnings from the accumulated deposits would pay all losses, and this seems to have been the case, for the company prospered and grew and is in existence to-day, having greatly developed in size and scope, being the oldest insurance company in existence. Its operations are limited to London and its suburbs. The original title of this company was "Contributors for Insuring Houses, Chambers or Rooms from Loss by Fire by Amicable Contribution." This was afterward changed to "Amicable Contributionship," and in 1776 the name of "Hand in Hand" — taken from an emblem used by the company in marking and designating buildings which it insured — was adopted.

The companies heretofore mentioned all confined their operations to buildings and mostly to dwellings only, but the need for insurance upon goods and stocks of merchandise was very great. About 1706, one Charles Povey opened an office for insuring such property in London. He was without backing or support of any kind and furnished merely his promise to pay in event of loss. This venture was apparently greeted with ridicule and the proposal to insure personal property seems to have been commonly considered impractical. Nevertheless Povey persisted and soon began another enterprise designed to insure personal property throughout Great Britain and Ireland, but finding his first venture unprofitable devised the scheme (which would seem to be quite in accord with some very modern methods of corporate finance), of organizing a third institution to take over the other two. This was accomplished. The new concern was at first called the "London Insurers," but almost immediately after its formal inaugury in 1710 it adopted the name of the Sun Fire Office, and under this name began its successful career which still endures, making that office the oldest non-mutual company in existence as well as the first company which ever undertook the insurance of movables or personal property. It has continued to be a partnership, *i.e.*, not a corporation, and is almost unique among insurance companies in that respect. The first contracts of the Sun provided for payment of losses out of a reserve to be made up of one-half the premiums paid, the liability of the company ceasing when that reserve should be exhausted. Later the company, doubtless under stress of competition, made its promise to pay absolute, and in 1726 a capital fund of 48,000 pounds was created as additional security for policy-holders.

Another curious feature of the contracts made by this first company doing general business was the proviso that in case of loss, 5 per cent. should be deducted from claims for defraying the expenses of the company's officers in investigating and settling the loss. This was reduced to 3 per cent. in 1716, and abandoned altogether not later than 1794. This feature seems to have been quite common among insurance companies during the early history of the business, but was too obviously open to objection and criticism to endure after serious competition arose.

Between 1710 and 1720 numerous insurance schemes were launched, modeled after one or the other of those described above. Some succeeded, more failed or were wound up. In 1720 the first chartered companies or corporations made their appearance. In that year two companies — the Royal Exchange Assurance Company and the London Assurance Corporation — were granted charters, first to do a marine insurance business, and in the following year to transact also fire and life insurance business. This date then, 1720, marks the advent of modern stock companies in fire insurance. One of the first announcements, or "broadsides" (as such notices were then styled) of the Royal Exchange Assurance contains the following as one of the arguments which should persuade insurers to patronize it rather than the mutual associations or contributionships theretofore doing most of the business:

"For the security of all persons insured by this Corporation, their capital stock or fund is by their charter established and made liable and shall always be ready to pay and make good to the assured the amount of all losses by fire."

Later in the same paper appeared the following:

"And whereas persons assured by other societies not incorporated, are subject to calls in case of a loss or a deduction out of the money due to the sufferer, those that are assured by this Corporation are not liable to any calls (*i.e.*, assessments), or deductions whatsoever."

These considerations — namely, freedom from all personal liability on the part of the assured beyond payment of a fixed premium and the fact that in the case of stock companies their entire capital stock and accumulated funds are pledged to the payment of losses — have no doubt chiefly caused the commercial world to favor stock companies or corporations up to this date, when such companies do a very large proportion of all the fire insurance business.

This may be said to bring the history of fire insurance in Great Britain down to modern times. During the last three-quarters of the eighteenth century fire insurance companies, both mutual and stock, but chiefly the latter, were organized in very considerable numbers and for the most part copied the methods, contracts, and practices of the earlier companies. Many of these companies still survive; indeed, some of the largest English companies in existence date from that period.

The early histories of these first ventures in fire insurance contain much curious and interesting matter, but time and space do not permit a study of their plans and methods. One feature of their early operations, however, has developed to such great proportions and has become of such great importance as to demand mention here, namely, the protection of property against fire. It was a natural and immediate outcome of the first attempt at fire insurance by Nicholas Barbon that his interest in fires and their prevention should be greatly augumented. Accordingly his and the other early offices devised metal house plates to be securely fastened to those buildings which might be covered by their policies, and then hired men and provided some simple apparatus for extinguishing the fires which might arise in or near the buildings so marked. These house plates were also considered as a mark of acceptance and assumption of liability by the companies. Some offices even stipulated that liability should not begin until their plate had been affixed to the building which the policy was to cover. This it was thought tended to hinder fraud and prevent disputes. Moreover, because they brought a building under the protection of the company's firemen and because they evidenced to the public the fact that the property owner would not be ruined by fire, these plates were esteemed as desirable and valuable by policy-holders. They became in fact a sort of basis of credit, and the custom of using these plates endured, especially in smaller places, long after their original use had disappeared. In fact, such plates are used in some foreign countries today. In America their use was very common until about twenty-five years ago; they may still be seen over the door of many New England homes and are not yet entirely obsolete among the farmers in some sections of the country.

The ordinary method of preventing the spread of fire at that period seems to have been by blowing up buildings by gunpowder, and this work was commonly done by the artillery, or Royal Gunners. The early insurance companies used also bucket brigades and hand-pumping engines. Each company had its own liveried firemen, who were expected to guard its interests. Later some of the companies organized corps of watchmen and patrolmen who should discover fires in their incipiency, give the alarm and summon the firemen of the company for whom they worked. Still later, when the practice of insuring personal property began, it was found advisable by the Sun office — the first, it will be remembered, to transact that class of business — to provide a body of men for the purpose of removing insured goods from burning buildings and for protecting them when so removed from thieves and pilferers. As companies multiplied, so did their private fire and salvage corps increase in number, until in 1808 fifty fire engines were kept up by the companies in London alone. In 1825 a number of these companies consolidated their fire brigades. In 1833 all were united, but not till 1866 was the establishment turned over to the city. It seems very strange that private corporations should have so long been allowed to control and direct this important branch of civic administration.

Inasmuch as modern fire insurance had its genesis and early development in Great Britain, whence also American ideas and practices were derived, we have devoted most of our limited time to the early history of the business there and can give but slight and incidental attention to the subject in other foreign countries. This course has seemed to be proper, not only for the reason just mentioned, but because English fire insurance companies have developed more rapidly and, following the track of English ships and commerce, have carried their operations throughout the world to a far greater extent than the companies of any other country. There is no quarter of the globe where fire insurance may not be obtained from English offices. The insurance companies of other countries for the most part confine their operations to their own country, with the exception perhaps of Germany, the companies of which country have in later years also embarked in the world-wide business.

In the various kingdoms and provinces which now constitute the German Empire, as has been mentioned before, the various communal guilds had provided some crude form of insurance for their members, and in many places this function was transferred to the various municipalities as the guilds disappeared. One writer describes this process as follows: "As the absolute monarchical police-state constitutes the bridge between the middle ages and modern times, so too the transition from the mediæval guild plan of mutual help to the modern system was bridged by state insurance. The guilds of the middle ages lost their importance and private industry was not rapid enough to supply the void left by them, and so the state was forced to step into the breach." [1]

Such public fire insurance outside of Germany is still to be found in German-Austria, Denmark, Switzerland, and Scandinavia. At a comparatively recent date about 40 per cent. of the outstanding insurance in Germany was carried by the institutions conducted by the government or by various municipalities. Throughout Germany and Switzerland to-day all buildings of ordinary occupancy are assured by the government as soon as built. Each owner is assessed pro rata, according to the appraised value of his own insured buildings, for the losses within the state. Money payments are not made by the state in event of loss, but the damage is repaired or the building replaced by the government. The necessity for insurance on other classes of property than buildings caused the formation of the first stock company in Germany in 1812, since which time many companies, both stock and mutual, have arisen, also various local associations similar to the old guilds and perhaps descendants from them.

In France, while various insurance companies were set on foot during the second and third quarters of the eighteenth century, all perished during the general financial collapse which accompanied the French Revolution. The first regular stock company organized thereafter seems to date from 1818.

In other European countries fire insurance seems to have had even a later development — thus in Austria the first stock company was organized in 1822, and the first

[1] J. S. Bloomingston, Ph.D., "Fire Insurance."

mutual company in 1825. In Russia the first company appeared in 1827.

In all civilized countries there are now fire insurance companies, even in China.

Methods and plans vary in different parts of Europe. In France, under the Code Napoleon, every individual is liable for loss or damage which may happen to others through his fault. In case of fire the law holds that the fault rests with the tenant or owner on whose premises the fire originates, unless he can prove himself without fault; in other words, the burden of proof is on him. Hence a tenant, for example, takes out insurance first on his own personal property; second, to protect him against possible claims to be made by his landlord, and third, to protect him against possible liability to his neighbors for damages resulting from fires attributable or attributed to his carelessness or negligence. It would be highly instructive to compare more completely the varying conditions and methods under and by means of which the business of fire insurance is conducted in different parts of the world, but we cannot attempt it here.

CHAPTER II

HISTORY OF FIRE INSURANCE IN THE UNITED STATES [1]

In a history of fire insurance in this country one must of necessity consider whence the business came, the stage of its development, when it came and, to some degree, its originating cause. Only enough can be said on these points to identify its origin, establish the line of descent, and set forth how and when it came to be brought to this country. Furthermore, the consideration of so large a subject in a brief paper can only be of a skeleton character with a fair emphasis upon some of the formative factors.

One of the results of the great fire of London in 1666 was the devising of plans for the protection of individuals against loss by fire. The great fire of London was relatively the greatest in the history of the world, over three-fourths of the buildings in the city having been destroyed, and the estimated loss aggregating about ten million pounds sterling. So great indeed was this loss that, ten years later, the buildings had not all been replaced. Quite a number of plans were tried, and before the close of the century a company, which finally became the Hand-in-Hand, was established. In 1706 Charles Povey opened an office in London for insuring property owners in that city against loss from fire, but his plan merely involved his promise to pay. Shortly after this first attempt he started another enterprise for the purpose of insuring

[1] By F. C. Oviatt, late Editor of the *Philadelphia Intelligencer.* Reprinted from pages 335–358, Volume XXVI of the *Annals of the American Academy of Political and Social Science.*

against loss from the destruction by fire of personal property throughout Great Britain and Ireland, and in 1710 organized a proprietary or stock company which took over these two institutions, and which was named the Sun Fire Office, though commonly referred to at present as the Sun, of London, which still exists as one of the leading fire insurance corporations of the world, and is as familiarly known in this country as at home. In 1720 two more companies were chartered, which still exist, and both of which maintain branches in the United States, namely, the Royal Exchange and the London Assurance.

Fire insurance may be said to be due to an idea born of necessity and only existing at the beginning of the eighteenth century in a crude and experimental form. The period being the colonizing one, the Englishmen who came as settlers to this country brought the idea with them, so that the development of the thought of making the fire loss less burdensome to the individual is as much, if not more, American than British. Originating in England, two separate lines of fire insurance development have been carried forward, each influenced by local features of indemnification, but with remarkable fidelity to type, and from these differing lines of development has grown up an international business factor of large importance.

Having noted its origin and traced the line of descent, let us now follow the fortunes of the younger branch of the fire insurance family as developed in this country. In doing this it may be noted that fire insurance and the more employed marine insurance became early factors in the commercial development of the colonies. They grew with the growth of the business of the country, and have been part of the bone and sinew of material prosperity of the American people.

The first forms of insurance in this country were marine. In 1682, as we are informed from records, vessels engaged in trade between England and the colonies were insured against the perils of the sea, and as early as 1721 an advertisement appeared in the *American Weekly Mercury* announcing that John Copson, of High Street, Philadelphia, would open an office for insurance on "vessels, goods and merchandise." For a long period the insurance business of the colonies continued to be marine; part of it being written by agents of English companies, and the remainder being issued in American ports. In 1762, at the London Coffee House, at the southwest corner of High and Front Streets, Philadelphia, John Kidd and William Bradford announced that they would underwrite risks in general, and before the close of the century a considerable number of such offices had been established. In Philadelphia the first steps toward the protection of property took the form of organizations for the extinguishment of fires and regulations concerning the nature and location of buildings. In 1730 the city authorized the purchase of three more engines, four hundred buckets, twenty ladders, and twenty-five hooks, and in 1752 with approximately 2,076 dwelling houses (not including churches, public buildings, warehouses, and workshops), the city possessed seven fire extinguishing companies.

In this same year the *Pennsylvania Gazette,* under date of February 18, contained an advertisement of proposed articles of insurance of houses from fire in or near the city. The plan had the approval of the lieutenant-governor of the province and of Benjamin Franklin, and on April 13 directors were elected, and the Philadelphia Contributionship was thus formally organized, being the first fire insurance company to be organized in the United States. Its plans were an adaptation of those of the Hand-in-Hand of London; in fact, the company became quite generally known as the Hand-in-Hand, and its first house mark was four hands clasping wrists. One curious incident should be noted. The directors of the Contributionship in 1781 decided that houses having trees planted before them should not be insured, because the trees made it difficult to fight fires. This policy created considerable friction and opposition, out of which grew, in 1784, the Mutual Assurance Company. The house mark of this new company was a green tree, cast in lead, fastened to a shield-shaped board, affixed to the front of the insured property. Both of these companies are still in existence and continue to transact business along the same general lines as at first, namely, what is known as perpetual insurance. This, in brief, is a deposit of a certain percentage of the face value of the policy which is paid once for all, the interest on it proving sufficient to provide for the losses sustained. In 1794 the Baltimore Equitable Society, operating upon the same general plan, was established.

In December, 1792, the General Assembly of Pennsylvania was petitioned for permission to incorporate the Insurance Company of North America, and on April 14, 1794, the incorporation of the company was authorized, and almost immediately thereafter that of the Insurance Company of the State of Pennsylvania. Both of these companies were organized to transact marine insurance, but during the first year of the North America's existence, the directors concluded to add the business of fire insurance, and the proposals for insurance were completed in the latter part of the year. The proposals were for insuring full value. Two general hazards were provided for; the first class including common insurances and providing for brick or stone houses, stores and furniture or merchandise therein, while the second included those houses which were not wholly brick and stone and such extra hazardous goods as pitch, tar, turpentine, etc. For the first class the rate was thirty cents per hundred on an eight thousand dollar policy and forty-five cents on a policy not exceeding sixteen thousand dollars; while in the second class the rates were seventy-five cents per hundred dollars.

The earliest company in New York, of which we have any record, was the Knickerbocker Fire, organized April 3, 1787, under a deed of settlement. The original title, however, was that of the Mutual Insurance Company, the name Knickerbocker not being assumed until May 12, 1846. The company was by its charter permitted to transact fire, marine, and life insurance, and in less than a month the New York Insurance Company was organized with practically the same privileges. Three years later, March 21, 1801, the Columbian Insurance Company of New York was organized, and on April 4, 1806, followed the incorporation of the Eagle Fire with a capital stock of $500,000, and now the oldest New York stock fire insurance company. Most of the companies in New York organized during the latter part of the eighteenth century, and the first forty years of the nineteenth century, were what are known as special charter companies and, following the development of the day, most of them were organized for the purpose of writing marine insurance. Another of the early New York companies which is still in business is the Albany Insurance Company, which was organized in March, 1811. The charters of most of the companies of this day were what are known as limited charters. Some of them were for twenty years, some for thirty, but the principle of limitation was quite generally and distinctly recognized.

Commerce early became an important part of New England development, and most of the towns were seaports or situated at the head of navigation on the more important rivers. As soon as the New Englander began to trade, he recognized the hazards which attended the transportation of merchandise. No sooner was this recognized than marine insurance in its earlier forms made its appearance. The marine companies in New England, as in other parts of the country, issued fire insurance policies as soon as there was a call for them. Fire insurance, however, did not seem as important as marine insurance, and the stronger of the early insurance companies devoted more of their attention to water-borne merchandise. In 1799 there was organized at Providence, the Providence-Washington, which still continues to do a prosperous business.

The early underwriting in Connecticut, as in the other colonies, was generally of a personal or partnership character. It should be remembered that the country in the last decade of the eighteenth century was poor. Its capital had been very largely exhausted by the Revolutionary struggle, and enterprises which had been prosperous had been completely disorganized, and during the whole period of the confederacy the uncertainty of the future paralyzed to a large extent the commercial life of the colonies. The industrial life of Connecticut was simple; coarse articles for necessary use were manufactured, and the surplus products of agriculture and merchandise of home manufacture were exported to the West Indies. In 1792 the Hartford Bank and the Union Bank of New London were organized, and with the business development which followed the organization of these institutions insurance partnerships came. Thus, in 1794, Sanford and Wadsworth opened an office in Hartford for insuring furniture, merchandise, etc., against fire, and the next year associated with themselves Jeremiah Wadsworth, John Caldwell, Elias Shipman, and John Morgan in a copartnership under the title of the Hartford and New Haven Insurance Company for the purpose of insuring vessels, stock, merchandise, etc. In 1797 Elias Shipman established a separate office in New Haven which was chartered as the New Haven Insurance Company, but which retired in 1833. The men interested in these insurance ventures, for they were ventures, were the merchants of the leading cities, Hartford taking and holding a commanding position. Jeremiah Wadsworth, one of the leading spirits in the mercantile and financial life of Hartford, was well known outside of that state, since, for example, he was one of the founders of the Bank of North America of Philadelphia in 1781, holding one hundred and four shares of the original stock. In 1785 he was elected president of the Bank of New York, and was also interested in the organization of the Hartford Bank. This note of Colonel Wadsworth is given so that the character of the men who engaged in early Connecticut underwriting may be understood, and the reason seen why Hartford has always held such a prominent position in the underwriting world. It is because men of brains, means, and faith established the business.

As these partnership policies involved a great deal of labor the organization of a corporation seemed a very natural step, and in 1803 a charter was procured for the Hartford Insurance Company. The business of this company was marine and the capital was $80,000 in shares of $40 each. Twenty-five per cent. was paid in notes and 75 per cent. in notes secured by mortgages. But in 1825 the company was merged in the Protection Insurance Company. About this time also, a group of companies was organized for the purpose of writing marine insurance, but most of them were obliged to go out of business on account of the depression in marine commerce consequent upon the War of 1812. Some idea of the paralysis of commerce of the United States caused by the embargo and non-intercourse acts is to be gathered from the fact that exports fell from $110,084,207 in 1807 to $22,430,960 the following year. Duties on imports at New London shrunk from $201,838 in 1807 to $22,343 in 1810. Most of the marine companies were killed as a result of the depression. The Norwich was saved by changing its business to fire insurance in 1818 and, as noted above, the Hartford was transformed into the Protection.

The oldest fire insurance company in Connecticut is the Mutual Assurance of the city of Norwich, which was organized in May, 1795, under a deed of settlement. The company has never attempted to do a large business, being largely a neighborhood affair. In 1810 the Hartford Fire was organized and is thus the oldest stock fire insurance company in the state. The original capital was $150,000, with privilege of enlargement to $250,000. The subscribers were obliged to pay in 5 per cent. in thirty days and 5 per cent. more in sixty days, the remaining 90 per cent. to be secured by notes and mortgages. There was not a great deal of money to be had in those days, consequently notes and mortgages had to form the principal basis of corporate organization. The organizers of this company had everything to learn, because they knew nothing about fire insurance, for there was not much to be known. It was chance, pure and simple. There were no data by which the cost and the charge could be brought into anything like proportionate relations. Some idea of rates may be gathered from the charges on a few of the early policies. Number one was a builder's risk of $4000 for three months at twelve and a half cents. Number five was $10,000 on a gin distillery at 1¼ per cent. Numbers twenty-one and twenty-two were $20,000, being respectively on a stock of drygoods and hardware, the former at seventy-five cents and the latter at twenty-five cents. The year after the company organized, it began to plant agencies, but without any system. For instance, there was one agency at Canandaigua, N. Y.; another at Middlebury, Vt., and by 1820 an agency had been established at Cleveland, Ohio. As showing the relative importance of cities and towns, it should be noted that it was not until 1821 that an agency was established in New York City. The compensation was a sort of graded commission, determined by the importance of the town. Three of the agents were given 10 per cent. on all premiums received exceeding $1000 for any one year, while in the early years some gratuities were voted by the directors to those who had rendered special services. The president received no salary until 1823, when he was paid $200 per annum, voted semi-annually after the work had been done.

The first secretary of the Hartford Fire, Walter Mitchell, did not live in Hartford, but in Wethersfield, and appears to have suited his own convenience as to office hours. His convenience was not exactly the convenience of the citizens of Hartford, and so in 1819 the Ætna was organized, with a capital of $150,000 with the privilege of increasing it. The first policy of the Ætna was issued August 7, 1819, and about a month later the first reinsurance known in this country was entered into by the Ætna when it assumed all of the outstanding risks of the Middletown Fire. It rather liked the experience apparently, because three years later it was willing to reinsure the New Haven Fire, which reinsurance, however, was secured by the Hartford. In the beginning of the fire insurance business, the matters which are now sent to trained experts were considered by the board. The vital portions of each policy with the survey were read to the board of directors before delivery. The officers and directors did quite a little traveling or exploring, and on these trips, made from time to time, agents were appointed, which was the principal work of a fire underwriter when traveling in those days. In 1822 the directors of the Ætna voted the secretary two dollars per day and his expenses when he went out to establish agencies; while he was drawing his per diem allowance, however, his salary as secretary was suspended, since they did not believe in paying for work which was not performed. The secretary, however, did not do all of the pioneering work, much of it being done by the directors.

The pluck of these early underwriters is well illustrated by the action of the Ætna directors in the matter of settling the losses incurred by the great fire of 1835 in New York. The Ætna's losses amounted to $115,000. The directors were notified that the fire would probably exhaust the entire resources of the company, and one of the directors asked President Brace what he intended to do. "Do?" he replied, "go to New York and pay the losses if it takes every dollar there," pointing to the securities of the company, "and my fortune besides." The directors pledged him their support and the losses were paid. The premium receipts increased so rapidly that in twelve months the Ætna had as much cash as before the fire. It was the same spirit which led the shareholders to contribute $2,500,000 to maintain the technical solvency of the company after the Chicago and Boston fires. The success of institutions with such men in charge is assured when they take hold.

Until the close of the century there had been about ten mutual and four stock companies, organized in the country, while by 1820 this number had increased to seventeen stock companies in New York, six in Pennsylvania, two in Connecticut, and one each in Rhode Island, New Jersey, and Massachusetts. Of these, twelve are still doing business. It should be noted here that very early in the history of the business an attempt to exclude foreign insurance companies was made. Statutes were enacted in Pennsylvania and New York in 1810 and 1814 respectively, forbidding foreign companies to transact business in this country. These prohibitory statutes continued in force until after the great fire in New York in 1835, which rendered necessary the enlargement of the sources from which fire insurance indemnity might be secured. Most of the early companies transacted both fire and marine insurance. As the business of the country developed, the people began slowly to recognize the importance and necessity of fire insurance, though for many years the growth of public recognition was slow. The burden of the fire loss in the smaller communities was quite largely borne by voluntary contribution. A man's house or barn was burned and the owner's neighbors made up a purse which should enable him to rebuild, or help him, at least, to get a new start; and in some portions of the country this practice obtained until past the middle of the nineteenth century. In some of the municipalities, ordinances were enacted which compelled owners of property to have and keep in repair leathern buckets.

Some idea of the slow development of the business can be gathered from the fact that while the Insurance Company of North America decided on its form of fire insurance policy in November, 1794, it had, one year later, issued only seventy-three policies. In 1796 this company decided to accept risks in any part of the United States, if the premiums were adequate to the risk in the opinion of the officers, and in that year it had risks on its books in Western Pennsylvania, New Jersey, New York, Massachusetts, Delaware, Maryland, Virginia, North and South Carolina. In 1798 it declined an application from an agency in Charleston, S. C., but in 1807 the company decided to authorize agents. There was quite a rapid growth of companies during the first thirty years of the nineteenth century, which companies, as a rule, were purely local, there being only one here and there which transacted any business to speak of, outside of the cities where it was located. There was but little security behind the policies issued beyond the current receipts and the good faith of the men who managed the companies.

The great New York fire of 1835 swept out of existence most of the New York companies. This fire closes what may be termed the first period of American fire insurance, a period devoted almost wholly to pioneering. While many of the corporate ventures were failures, still the lessons of the period pointed the way to the more perfect development which was to follow. Mistakes were discovered and steps taken to correct them. A question asked of Edwin G. Ripley, for example, led to the classification of risks. One of the patrons of the company, noticing the frequency of fires in certain lines of business, asked Mr. Ripley if the Ætna made money on paper mills. The question was a poser, but he straightway began to get ready to answer the next man, and so started the classification of risks several years in advance of his competitors. At this time, also, fire insurance in the large cities had become a recognized factor in commercial life. Outside of the cities, however, it was looked upon with more or less distrust, or perhaps it might be said was considered unnecessary.

Turning our attention to the second period we find new factors entering the buisness. The public demanded more certainty in the matter of the contracts and greater provision for the stability of the companies, so in 1837 the first step was made in the direction of reservation. The State of Massachusetts provided that companies should maintain a fund to insure their contracts being carried out, and this was the beginning of what is known as the unearned premium fund. The start toward this is an important factor in development as it marks the beginning of two things: First, making sure that the policy-holders shall be protected in the contracts they have entered into with the companies; and second, the entrance into the fire insurance field, of the state, which, from this modest beginning as will be seen later, has gradually developed the extensive system now known as state supervision.

The development of this idea of reservation is interesting, especially in view of the fact that it is recognized to-day as one of the corner-stones of successful fire underwriting. In 1853 the New York legislature enacted a law providing for what is known as the unearned premium reserve. By the terms of this law, a reinsurance fund ranging from about 30 to 60 per cent. of the unexpired premiums was required to be maintained. The sum thus set aside, which became a liability, was assumed to be sufficient to reinsure in a solvent company the unexpired risks of a company which desires from any reason to retire from buisness. The legislature tinkered with the law in 1862, providing for the reservation of the full amount of the unexpired premiums in all cases where dividends exceeding 10 per cent. were paid. The companies considered this a burden and sixty companies petitioned the legislature to change the law requiring 100 per cent. reservation to one fixing the percentage at 50 per cent. of the premiums. The New York insurance department opposed this request, and justified its opposition by figuring out from the loss record that a 50 per cent. reinsurance fund was inadequate. This subject of reservation and dividends was also discussed by the Massachusetts supervising officials, and in the ninth annual report of the Massachusetts insurance department it was proposed to establish what was known as a "state guarantee" by which the companies should pay an annual tax. There were to be three classes under this scheme; the first, where less than two million dollars of risks were insured, the dwelling-house tax was to be five cents on every hundred dollars insured and ten cents per hundred on other buildings and personal property; the second class, where the amount at risk was between two and six million dollars, was to pay a tax of two cents and four cents per hundred at risk; and the third class, where the amount at risk was over six million dollars, the tax was to be one-half cent and one cent on each hundred dollars insured. This shows the experimentation indulged in by state departments for the purpose of getting the business upon a sound loss-paying basis. In these early days of state supervision, companies desiring a license were examined by special commissions. The requirements were slight, and not infrequently the companies of this period were obliged to go out of business within a few years after organization. When the conditions which existed in the fifties and sixties are compared with those of the present day, it will be seen that the evolution of the business has been steadily toward certainty so far as the policy-holders are concerned, though no means have been devised to prevent the capital invested from being dissipated through bad management and excessive losses.

Another feature of the second period was the development of the mutual idea. The New York fire of 1835 destroyed a great majority of the New York companies. This created a feeling of distrust in the public mind, and the organization of mutual companies became the order of the day, and by 1853 sixty-two companies reported to the comptroller of New York, having an aggregate capital of over eleven million dollars. The mutual plan commended itself to the people of that day as correct theoretically and economical in operation. In practice, however, these companies proved unsatisfactory for the reasons that they were based upon incorrect principles and because of a lack of staying power. One of the weaknesses of the mutual plan in practice is admirably stated in the report of James M. Cook, comptroller of New York in 1854, in which he says: "The formation of a mutual insurance company upon a proper and sound basis never contemplated the taking of risks in other states than our own."

The mutual companies had attempted to operate upon the same basis as the stock companies did. The mortality among the mutuals, however, was excessive. A general insurance law was enacted in 1849, and during the succeeding four years over fifty-four mutual companies were organized. By 1860, however, only seven of these survived, and Superintendent of Insurance, Barnes, of New York, estimated that the losses to the people through the failure of these forty-seven companies averaged at least $50,000 per company. These companies were organized with premium notes as capital in amounts far exceeding the ordinary and legitimate premiums to be charged in the regular course of business. The second error was that of permitting mutual companies to issue both mutual and cash policies. These mutual waves have gone over the country at irregular intervals ever since, and in each instance the original experience has been duplicated to a greater or less extent.

Two forms of mutual companies have persisted. One, township mutuals, which as long as they confine their operations to a small territorial area, where every person knows every other person, aid in the distribution of the fire loss of a given country community and serve their purpose well. Where they branch out and attempt to do a village and city, or general business, failure is inevitable. The second form of mutual development is that typified by the mill mutuals. These are based upon knowledge, inspection, and improvement. They have, however, in all cases ultimately failed as mediums for transacting a general fire insurance business.

The companies gradually recovered from the blow of the New York fire and in a few years additional companies had started so that the number of companies was in a measure commensurate with the growing business of the country. There were a large number in New York, Philadelphia, and Boston, and there were companies in other cities where there was enough local business to warrant. These companies served the business of the country well, as a whole, and only began to retire as the development of the country's business interests, consequent upon the development of the railway system and the telegraph, gave the company doing a general business a decided advantage over the one doing a local business. In this period also state supervision took a definite form in the shape of the establishment of departments by New York and Massachusetts and gradually by other states. Attempts were also made to devise a more nearly uniform fire insurance policy. Up to this time, and for a considerable time thereafter, each company devised its own policy contracts. It took what seemed to be good out of the English policies, clipped from its neighbors, and as one man with much experience said, this was, so far as policies were concerned, the period of scissors and paste pot.

The agents and the companies, principally the companies, in some of the large cities, formed local boards during the fifties. These boards, dominated mostly by local companies, were the forerunners of the present system of organizations of local agents, but were materially different because they were largely experimental. Out of this local board movement also grew an agitation for better fire protection, and thus while in the early history of the country nearly all the fire departments were volunteer, paid departments gradually became the rule, and the companies established protective departments for the protection of damaged stocks so that the loss might be lessened through care. The successors of these departments are the fire patrols of to-day. Some facts concerning these early local boards may be of interest. In 1819 an organization was formed in New York, known as the Salamander Society, the members of which were pledged not to deviate from established rates of premium. New companies were invited to join and, if they refused, were to be specially considered, which appears to have been understood and acted upon as a threat. This organization was of little practical significance, and was followed by another organization in 1826 and another in 1857, which formed the fire patrol or fire police in 1859. Some few attempts were made in the late thirties and in the forties towards standard rating, but merely amounted to a faint foreshadowing of the system which is being striven for to-day. The record of the New York board is typical of most of the local boards of the earlier day.

Another step in the progress of this period was the employment of special agents, better known as field men, owing to the spreading out of companies which did business in other places than the immediate vicinity of the home office. The strictly local company could supervise and care for its business through employees of the home office. When distances, however, became too great for this class of employees, men had to be employed for this special work of looking after the field. At first, the greater part of the work of special agents was the adjustment of losses, though they paid some attention to the agencies, at times inspecting risks and authorizing rates. The period under review was one when the West was being settled, and the foundation laid for the magnificent development of the latter half of the nineteenth century. These pioneers with their poorly constructed and rapidly-growing villages and cities, soon felt the need of fire insurance. Yet the Middle West, or as sometimes termed, "beyond the Alleghanies," was almost an unknown land, and the ignorance of the East persisted long after the canal boat, river steamer, and railway had begun to open this region.

In the history of the early days of insurance in Connecticut, attention was called to the fact that the Hartford Insurance Company, organized in 1803 to write marine insurance, was merged in 1825 with the Protection, organized to write a fire insurance business. The secretary of the Hartford became the president of the Protection, while the secretary of the Protection, Thomas Clap Perkins, had much to do with the pioneering work of the Protection. Ephraim Robins, a merchant of Cincinnati, saw a notice in a Hartford paper that the Protection had been formed. Having lost most of his property in a cyclone, the importance of insurance was presented in a very forceful way to the mind of Mr. Robins. He came to Hartford, presented the claims of the West in such a way that the company authorized the establishment of a western department with Mr. Robins as general agent. This was in 1825, and the task of planting the agencies of the company in Ohio and other western states was immediately started. The company's office was a sort of headquarters for prominent Whig politicians, and also proved to be a training school for some of the brightest and most successful men in western fire insurance. The western department of the Protection was the beginning of the American agency system on anything like a large and comprehensive scale. The business grew rapidly and when Mr. Robins died in 1846, the premiums collected by the agency amounted to three million dollars. From the western office of the Protection went the forerunners of the modern special agent or field man. The Protection eventually failed because it did not build up a large enough surplus, and its officers did not really know where the company stood owing to a lack of systematic knowledge.

Following the Protection, the Insurance Company of North America and the Ætna made the venture into the territory west of the Alleghanies, the former locating at Erie and the latter at Cincinnati. The failure of the Protection gave a great impetus to the development of the western department of the Ætna, as it was in the field and ready to make the most of the opportunity offered. In 1853 J. B. Bennett became general manager of the Ætna and took charge of the western business. The same year that he took charge of the Ætna's affairs, J. B. Bennett prepared a blank proof of loss. Before this time these proofs had been written out on the occasion of each adjustment. This was a waste of time from Mr. Bennett's standpoint and so he prepared a form which, in its essential features, has not been changed since. The Hartford began to send out numbered policies in 1864. These companies employed special agents, who, working under conditions hard to realize to-day, went up and down the country, appointing agents, inspecting towns, and settling losses. Indeed the fire insurance business is greatly indebted to these men for their faithful labor. Many mistakes were made in this period, because there was little coöperation, but still there was a gradual approach toward better conditions and a larger and more comprehensive development. Nearly, if not all, of the companies organized during the first period made the mistake of dividing too large a proportion of the profits, and thus not leaving enough money to meet the drain of heavy losses. When a big fire occurred the companies found themselves in a difficult situation and several times it was only by guaranteeing by the directors of their personal fortunes that a company was enabled to survive. This tendency of keeping up dividend payments at the expense of surplus continued well past the middle of the nineteenth century, and the importance of maintaining a good working surplus was not fully realized until after the Chicago and Boston fires. In 1864 the superintendent of the New York insurance department, in his annual report, declared that several companies were accustomed to declare dividends without making any provision at all for outstanding risks. Legislative provision was made in New York to prevent this, as in 1849, it was enacted that "no dividend should ever be made by any company when its capital stock was impaired or when the making of the dividend would have the effect of impairing its stock, and any dividends made in violation to such section subjected the stockholders to an individual liability to the creditors to the extent of the dividend so received." Still they continued the practice of declaring such dividends until forced by the hard school of experience to transact their business upon business principles.

The third period of fire insurance development begins practically with the close of the Civil War. This may be termed the period of coöperations. Conditions were very unsatisfactory, rates were low, and prosperity for the companies was not very apparent. Hence, in 1866, the fire insurance companies of the country organized the National Board of Fire Underwriters, and for the next ten years it was the controlling factor in fire underwriting, and marks the most important change which had so far been brought about in the fire insurance business. Its purpose was to bring about a coöperation between the companies upon matters of common interest and to insure adequate rates and proper forms. At this time there were a very large number of local companies and quite a number of what are best classified as agency companies.

Three new factors came into the fire insurance business about this time: First, the daily report, devised in 1867 to facilitate the transaction of business, gradually took the place of the old monthly statement, but was slow in win-ning favor with underwriters since some of the managers preferred the old form of reporting as being more satisfactory. The original form of the daily report, devised by Alexander Stoddart, has not been materially changed with the passing years. The idea was to select good men in the different towns as representatives, have them examine the property upon which insurance was sought and send in a daily report, containing the written portion of the policy and diagram of its exposures, the rate, terms, etc.; in fact, a practical reproduction of the descriptive part of the policy. This was sent to the home office, the agent at the same time, writing and issuing the policy. If the company did not care for the risk, it notified the agent and the policy was withdrawn. This departure placed a very great responsibility upon the local representatives since they virtually passed upon the business of the company and most of them, be it said to their credit, served their company most faithfully. This plan was popular and was gradually adopted by all the companies. It is one of the great foundation stones of the modern agency system.

Out of this idea of a daily report grew two others. The first one was to have some means of keeping the home or branch office in touch with the agents, and also affording the company an independent source of information concerning the character of the business written. For this purpose, the special agent had the scope of his employment widened beyond the mere adjustment of losses. He traveled around among the agents, appointed new agents in desirable territory, secured an idea of the larger risks and special hazards of the towns he visited, saw to it that the agents kept their monthly accounts paid up and, generally speaking, was the hand of the company in the field. Soon the incompleteness of the information furnished the home or branch office as to the physical character of the risks and their environment presented a problem which had to be solved. To solve this, the special agents made diagrams of the towns they visited and marked upon them the risks of the company. Originating in the Ætna's western office, but antedating this period a little, was the business of making maps. On the first of May, 1856, William H. Martin, a civil engineer, was employed by the Ætna to make maps of important points where the company was transacting business, and in June of the same year the first map was copyrighted in the name of the Ætna Insurance Company. One of Mr. Martin's assistants, D. A. Sanborn, saw the possibilities of the map business. He removed to New York and tried to induce Mr. Martin to join him, but the latter preferred to remain with the Ætna and did so until his death in April, 1903. These maps made it so much easier to transact the business of the company that a considerable demand was created for them, resulting in the almost universal use of what are known as the fire maps. The large towns and cities are mapped, and the map company keeps them up to date, supplying the insurance company with all the changes. The map department of the modern fire insurance company is one of its most important adjuncts. It enables the daily report examiner or manager in the office to know accurately about the character of the risk he is to pass upon. The amount which the company has in any block is marked on the map, so that at a glance it is possible for the company to decide whether it desires to increase its holdings. Before the use of maps, however, all of the risks of the company were marked, and a record of the company's holdings were kept on what are known as block sheets. These enabled the company to know the amount it had at risk, though they did not furnish information as to environment such as the modern fire map gives at a glance. These three devices gave the business a wonderful impetus. An old underwriter, for example, states that one of the great advantages secured through the use of the daily report was that the frequency of the knowledge prevented stealing on the part of agents through writing short-term insurances which were not reported. This underwriter estimated that his office saved at least 12 per cent. through the increased frequency of knowledge concerning the writings of the local agents.

Belonging to this third period, but really beginning with the closing years of the second period, was the opening of the Pacific coast to the business of fire insurance. The Phœnix, of Hartford, was the pioneer. The officers of the Phœnix visited the Pacific coast, looked over the ground and on May 1, 1862, established a Pacific coast department in charge of R. H. Magill. At this time, all the fire insurance business of the coast was written at San Francisco through correspondents. The company had a correspondent in a town, information concerning the risk and the amount desired was sent in, the policy issued and forwarded. This was rather cumbersome and slow, so in 1863 Mr. Magill began the establishment of local agencies in the towns of the coast. His success was so great that other companies were obliged to follow his example.

The National Board of Fire Underwriters was just beginning to wrestle with some of its difficult problems when along came the Chicago fire and wiped out many of the insurance companies of the country. Many of the purely local companies were caught through the surplus lines they wrote or the reinsurances which they secured from the agency companies. The companies had only partially recovered when along came the Boston fire and completed the wrecking of a large number of the fire companies which had been struggling along in a crippled condition during the year intervening between the two fires. The National Board now promptly took hold of the situation, and rates were sharply advanced. State boards and local boards in smaller towns were organized and an elaborate system of control was worked out; in fact, in the long run, it was too elaborate. These fires imposed upon the National Board not only revision of rates, but also problems of construction. Chicago had been a wooden city, Boston had also much wood in its construction, and the dangerous mansard roof was then in the heyday of its popularity. A determined crusade was therefore made against these forms of construction, and the preparation of a basis or schedule for rating was attempted at this time. There was also a large influx of new companies as a result of the increased rates following the Boston and Chicago fires.

In 1874 the companies doing business in New York were compelled to report their unearned premium liability, and to this period also belongs the adoption of the safety fund law in New York. The increase in the number of companies, and the profit which attended the business because of the increased rates, induced a period of demoralization which extended from 1874 to 1880, during which numerous irresponsible companies were formed. To make matters worse, the National Board, in April, 1877, stopped making rates and relegated this subject back to the local boards, with the result that the high rates could no longer be maintained. Every company was a law unto itself; there was no profit, and it was apparently a struggle for the survival of the fittest. The fire insurance business, however, had become so large that this demoralization could not be permitted to continue. Some method of coöperation had to be found, and this begins the last period of this study. It should be noticed here that fire insurance had been going through an evolution, and step by step the scope had become broader and better calculated to assist the business development of the country. New ideas and new doctrines had come to the front as necessity compelled. The rating by the National Board, through its state boards and local boards, had been so much of an improvement over the former conditions that things could not be permitted to go backward. Something new, however, had to be devised.

In the eighties, the field man proved the way out. He

had been doing his work quietly and unobtrusively, and the main difficulty had been lack of numbers and too large territory to oversee. The abdication by the National Board of its rate-making powers threw a large amount of additional work upon his shoulders. Accordingly, in 1872, the New York State Association of Supervising and Adjusting Agents was organized; in 1881, the Underwriters' Association of the Middle Department; in 1883, the Underwriters' Association of New York State and the New England Insurance Exchange; in 1882, the Illinois State Board of Fire Underwriters — all of which may be considered as pioneers in the attempts at coöperation. Into the hands of these associations the detailed work of rate-making was given. Upon them also fell the work of readjusting the local boards, so that the chain of coöperation might be complete. The local agents, then the special agent, and the problems which they could not individually adjust, were sent to the field men's organization and the residue of problems was sent up to the organizations of the companies. Two of these organizations were formed about this time, namely, the Western Union in 1879, and the Southeastern Tariff Association in 1882, while the Fire Underwriters of the Pacific had been in existence since 1870. The Western Union and the Eastern Union are now the managing underwriter's medium of coöperation in the territory east of the Rocky Mountains, while the Pacific coast is under another organization. An outgrowth of the National Board should be mentioned here, namely, the Fire Underwriters' Association of the Northwest. When the National Board gave up its rate-making function the Northwest Association became simply a social and educational association of the western field men, and has increased from year to year in power and influence, until it is the leading social and educational association of the field men in this country.

One of the first practical problems of this period was that of policy forms. There had gradually grown up a fairly satisfactory policy in some sections, but it was purely a local policy. Every city and every section used one that was a little different. Then again, the companies did not cling as closely to one form as they might and, as a result, in adjustments there were conflicting forms. In reality it was difficult under those various forms to determine the liability of the corporation. The National Board adopted a standard policy, but it did not make much progress, and finally, in 1873, Massachusetts provided for a standard policy, which was made obligatory in 1880 upon all companies operating in that state. In 1886 New York adopted a standard form of policy which became mandatory in January of the following year, and which is now in use in all the states where there are not special forms provided by statute.

The next step in the evolution was in the matter of inspections. The mill mutuals, as certain New England companies are styled, were organized under the theory that it was cheaper to prevent fires than to pay losses. Therefore they developed a very thorough system of inspection and the use of fire preventive appliances. Chief among these fire preventive appliances are what are known as automatic sprinklers. The early sprinklers were not particularly satisfactory, but out of the evolution of experience came the modern heads, most widely known of which is the Grinnell. The stock companies found it necessary to meet the competition of these mill mutuals, and so there arose what is known as the Factory Insurance Association, organized in 1890. This was followed soon after by a similar organization in the West, and these organizations make a special feature of inspecting property and writing large policies upon such protected and inspected risks. In line with this idea is the spread of fire preventive methods. This fire prevention idea includes not only sprinklers, but construction, water supply, electrical wiring, and numerous other provisions for the prevention of fire. The National Fire Prevention Association, organized in 1896, has done more to lessen the number of fires by means of proper construction than all other agencies put together. It has enlisted science, architecture, and chemistry in the prevention of fires.

The rating problem has been and still is one of much difficulty. It is hard to build up a system of rates for fire risks which shall be equitable and easily comprehended by property owners. The physical character of risks varies so, and there is so little harmony in the matter of water supply and fire protective appliances in the different cities, that the rating problem becomes and is many sided. The first systematic plan was devised by a committee of which F. C. Moore was chairman, and the schedule, known as the Universal Mercantile Schedule, was promulgated in 1893. It is the main basis for fire insurance rates at the present time. In the late nineties, A. F. Dean, of Chicago, who had been making a careful study of rates, prepared a tariff known as a "Mercantile Tariff and Exposure Formula for the Measurement of Fire Hazards." It is based upon a diffierent theory from the Moore schedule. It is more scientific and flexible and has come into quite general use in the Middle West, and bids fair, as regards principles at least, to become the basis of fire insurance rate-making.

Legislation affecting fire insurance has grown from small beginnings to one of large proportions. Legislation touches the fire insurance business at many points. In 1885 the State of New Hampshire enacted what is known as the valued-policy law. This law prevented any questioning of the value of the buildings insured and the companies promptly withdrew from the state for several years. Laws similar to this have been enacted in a number of states, with the result of increasing the cost of insurance to the buyer. Then adverse legislation has also attempted to prevent coöperation between the companies through the enactment of anti-compact laws and the prohibition of certain clauses in policies. The men who levied taxes began soon after the war to realize that the insurance business was a good field for their activities, so they began to tax premiums, impose fees for filing statements and devise other taxes which aggregated a large amount and have always been a very material burden. As the needs of the states have increased, so the burdens imposed upon the companies have increased. In the later development of fire insurance, legislation and taxes have been among the most serious of the problems to be faced. Despite adverse legislation and the disintegrating tendencies of prosperity, coöperation has progressed. The companies have more and more found themselves unable to stand alone. There were so many points where their interests touched, so many ways in which they could help each other, that coöperation has become a powerful factor in the business.

Another feature of this period was the foundation of organizations for adjustment of losses whereby a company, when it was not convenient to employ the special agents, could secure the service of trained and expert adjusters. These organizations do good work and fill a want long felt. This was followed in due time by a plan for minimizing the expense and increasing the efficiency of adjustments. This originated in New York and makes for progress in the matter of systematic work. Still another advance has been that of salvage wrecking or the handling and sale of damaged stocks, an advance which has manifested itself both in the form of company organizations and private corporations.

Despite the many lines of progress, however, there has been from time to time the recurring mutual wave and the Lloyds craze. The latest of these waves, that of Lloyds, has only recently receded. It followed a high tide of mutual experiment, neither of these waves evidencing any advance in the direction of sound underwriting. After the Lloyds wave began to recede, legislation was invoked, and only last winter the New York legislature enacted legislation against the vanishing Lloyds form of underwriting. Duplication of company power was also attempted in 1897 and 1898 in the form of underwriters' agencies or the attempt to form two companies out of one. They created some discussion and friction, but only a few remain and it is questionable how successful they are. The latest phase of the business of insurance to be noted is that of the organization of the local agents into coöperative relations. The agents, like the companies, have found that they have many interests in common, and that one agent standing by himself does not amount to more than one company standing by itself. Having come to the conclusion that certain things of vital interest to them might be improved, they have formed a national association as well as state associations, whose work, as a whole, has been a benefit to the business.

From this historical study the reader will, no doubt, have noted the very great advance made in fire underwriting since the period when trees were not permitted in front of insured property. The evolution has been fragmentary, it is true, and not altogether in an orderly manner, but it has been a steady evolution nevertheless. Starting in ignorance of method, only having an object in view, the business of fire insurance has gradually reached out, and has more and more found a sure footing. The managers have noted where the relations of the business demanded changes; conflagrations have brought home to them certain truths; and when a form of organization or a method of doing buisness has broken down, men have been found to come forward to try something new, generally an advance over that which had been discarded. These men soon realized that the sole business of fire insurance was not simply to pay losses. The evolution has naturally been gradual up to the point where the skilled and capable underwriter recognizes that his business, being a part of public progress, should subserve the public interest best by preventing fires. Therefore, he has made concessions in rates for the men who will take the extra precautions in the line of building and fire prevention. His horizon has broadened and he sees that fire fighting and construction are closely related in the prosperity of his business. He has learned, but slowly it is true, but nevertheless he has learned, that what the public desires above everything else is certainty, and while he has grumbled many times at the intervention of the state in his business, to-day he recognizes that intervention, as a rule, makes for the certainty which both he and the assured desires. There are many incidents and events in the century and a half of fire insurance in this country which might have been wisely different, but taken as a whole, it has been a sound and progressive development, comparing favorably with that of any other line of business.

CHAPTER III

FUNCTION OF FIRE INSURANCE [1]

THE term insurance has been used in describing the fund accumulated to meet uncertain losses. It is evident that in a static state all producers who are exposed to risk must accumulate such funds. While it is uncertain whether the accumulation of any individual producer will be enough to meet the loss he suffers, that of the entire body of producers in any industry must be large enough to cover the losses of the group as a whole. Otherwise there would be in the long run a great diminution in the amount of capital in hazardous industries, and a serious disturbance of the static adjustment. Such a phenomenon is inconsistent with the notion of the static state. A fruit-dealer who at irregular intervals suffers loss through decay must add to the price of his fruit enough to cover such uncertain loss. A ship-owner has to increase his freight rates more or less, if his ships occasionally lie idle in port. In this sense, then, every producer, in the absence of all opportunity of transferring his risk, must insure himself. Such insurance would be defined as the accumulation of a fund to meet uncertain losses. From the point of view of economic theory, as has already been shown, the insurance fund includes only that part of the accumulation that is intended to cover the uncertain part of the loss; it is that part only whose amount is affected by the influence of uncertainty.

This individualistic method of providing for uncertain

[1] By Allan H. Willett, Instructor in Economics in the Carnegie Technical Schools, Pittsburg. Reprinted from pages 387–408, Vol. XIV of the Columbia College Studies.

loss is spoken of sometimes as *latent* insurance,[1] and sometimes as *self*-insurance. The latter term is usually applied to such conduct on the part of large concerns with many risks of kinds commonly transferred to regular insurance companies; the former is more frequently used of the preparation to meet risks of kinds which insurance companies do not assume. While it may be impossible to avoid the use of the term insurance in referring to these forms of economic activity, it is evident that in common usage the word is ordinarily employed in a different sense. It is used to denote the transfer of risk. Any person who guarantees another against accidental loss of any kind is said to insure him. It is in this sense that the capitalist-entrepreneur insures the capital of those from whom he borrows. This use of the term insurance, however, like the preceding, fails to bring out its real significance. To apply it to all individualistic preparation for uncertain loss extends it too far in one direction; to apply it to every transfer of risk extends it too far in another. To form a complete conception of insurance, it is necessary to add to the notions of accumulation of capital and transfer of risks the idea of the combination of the risks of many individuals in a group. We should define insurance, then, as that social device for making accumulations to meet uncertain losses of capital which is carried out through the transfer of the risks of many individuals to one person or to a group of persons. Wherever there is accumulation for uncertain losses, or wherever there is a transfer of risk, there is one element of insurance; only where these are joined with the combination of risks in a group is the insurance complete.

[1] "Partout où il y a un risque à courir, une assurance latente protège la valeur ou même le gain menacé par ce risque. On la retrouve dans la commission prélevée par le banquier, dans les prix surélevés du marchand qui livre à crédit, dans les taux parfois usuraires de certains prêts." — Michel Lacombe, "Assurances," Say and Chailley's *Nouveau Dictionnaire d'Economic Politique*, Vol. I, p. 101.

In many respects the increase in the number of distinct risks that an individual producer carries is analogous to the combination of the risks of many individuals. Other things being equal, a ship-owner who has a hundred ships, and who carries his own insurance, is in the same economic condition as any one of a hundred ship-owners, each possessing one ship, who have combined their risks in a group through a system of insurance. The gain from the combination of risks is due solely to the increase in the number of risks in the group; and if that increase takes place through the growth of a single industry, the same advantage is obtained. It is partly because of this fact that large industrial concerns are able to carry their own insurance. With the increase in the number of distinct risks to which they are exposed, the cost of carrying the risk relatively diminishes. This gain is one of the influences that foster the growth of large industrial organizations. In the absence of all other conditions affecting their size, it would lead in the end to the concentration of each line of industry, or even of all lines, in the hands of a single organization; and in the presence of these other conditions, the size that would finally be found most advantageous would be affected by the increase in the number of risks.

It is time to point out the exact nature of the gain under consideration. It is evident that it will not be due to any reduction in the actual amount of positive loss. What the increase in the number of separate risks in the group does bring about is a reduction of the uncertainty for the group as a whole, a substitution of certain loss for uncertain loss. As is well known, the probable variation of the actual loss in any year from the average for a series of years increases only as the square root of the number of separate chances of loss included in a group. Now, as we have seen, it is through the accumulation for meeting uncertain loss that the special reward for risk-taking is obtained. Competition will not cut the accumulation for this purpose down to the average amount of loss; it leaves a margin of safety. It is evident, therefore, that anything that diminishes the degree of uncertainty reduces the cost of risk to society. As the uncertainty diminishes, the accumulation to meet the uncertain loss is brought nearer to the probable loss as estimated by the law of averages. If all the uncertainty could be annihilated, the accumulation would be limited to the exact amount of the foreseen loss, as in the case of any other fixed element in the cost of production.

The application of this principle to the institution of insurance is evident at a glance. The risk that an insurance company carries is far less than the sum of the risks of the insured,[1] and as the size of the company increases the disproportion becomes greater. It is primarily through this reduction of uncertainty that a static society would be benefited by the existence of insurance. The cost of commodities would be reduced through the diminution of that part of the expense of producing them that is involved in the necessity of paying for the assumption of risk. The nature of this gain may be made clear by a simple illustration.

Let us assume that there are 10,000 capitalists of the same reluctance to incur risk, each owning a house valued at $5000; that all the houses are exposed to the same danger of destruction by fire; that the average annual loss for a period of years has been 50, and the average variation 20; and that the rate of interest in safe investments is 3 per cent. If each owner makes an allowance of 3 per cent. a year for the amortization fund, what annual rental will he demand for his house?

The uncertainty to which each investor is exposed is the resultant of two factors, the average loss and the prob-

[1] "The aggregate danger is less than the sum of the individual dangers, for the reason that it is more certain, and that uncertainty of itself is an element of danger." William Roscher, *Principles of Political Economy*. Translated by J. J. Lalor. New York, 1878, Vol. II, p. 261.

able variation. What would be the reluctance of an investor to incur the risk in the case assumed, and what reward would be necessary to overcome the reluctance, are empirical facts that we have no means of discovering. It is a conservative estimate that on account of the risk each capitalist will demand an extra 1 per cent. on his investment. The annual rent will then be at the rate of 7 per cent., that is, $350 for each house. At the end of a decade, if the favorable and unfavorable years just offset one another, the group will have suffered a loss of 500 houses, valued at $2,500,000. This gives an average annual loss of $25 for each of the 10,000 investors. Meantime each of them has received $50 a year on account of the risk. In the group as a whole the destroyed capital has been replaced, and each investor has received a net reward of $25. The hirer of the house, who has had to pay this additional rent, is not at all concerned with the way in which the income has been distributed among the different owners. Some of these have suffered losses which the $50 a year was not enough to cover; others have escaped loss, and the entire $50 represents a net gain for them. Each consumer, in this case each house-renter, has had to pay $25 a year more than he would have had to pay if it had not been for the uncertainty.

Now let us examine the situation of the same persons after a system of insurance has been introduced. We will leave out of consideration the incidental expense of the insurance itself, and for the sake of simplicity it will be assumed that the reluctance of the insurer to assume risk is the same as that of the house-owners, and that the fact that the houses are insured has no effect upon the probability of loss. What is the uncertainty to which the insurer is exposed when he is carrying the risk of the entire group, and what reward can he obtain for assuming it?

As the average variation of the annual loss has been 20, we may assume that a minimum loss of 25 houses for the group is certain to occur each year. The insurer, then, has to face a certain loss of 25 houses a year, and a probable loss, as determined by past experience, of 25 more. For the former, the competition of other insurers will prevent him from obtaining more than enough to replace the loss. That will be $125,000 for the group, or $12.50 for each house. For the uncertain loss we will assume that he will be able to obtain a return of twice the probable amount of loss, just as the single investor did, though there are reasons why he would probably demand rather less. That will make this part of his income $250,000 for the group, or $25 for each house. Each house-owner, therefore, will have to pay the insurer $37.50 a year, and their competition with one another will prevent any one of them from obtaining more than that from the person to whom he lets the house. The entire rent will now be $337.50 a year. Each consumer saves $12.50 a year, and each capitalist is still rewarded at the same rate as before for carrying risk. If these 10,000 houses had been joined with a large number of others, so that there were, let us say, 1,000,000 in the group, a similar calculation would show that the cost of the risk to each hirer of a house would be reduced to $26.25 *per annum*, or only $1.25 more than enough to cover the actual loss in a series of years.

That this gain is in no way dependent on the combination of the risks of different investors in one group, and that it could equally well be obtained by a single concern with an increasing number of risks, is manifest. It is equally manifest that it would be advantageous for a person with a large number of risks to join them with as many others of the same kind as possible. While so-called self-insurance becomes cheaper as the number of risks increases, it would never be as cheap as regular insurance if the insurance business were rightly managed. If it is cheaper for a concern to carry its own risk than to pay premiums to an insurance company, it shows either that the company considers the risk higher than the concern thinks is right, or that the insurance business is so expensively managed that the cost of the management more than offsets the gain from the increase in the number of risks. The prevalence of the custom of self-insurance against risks such as the regular insurance companies assume is a serious reflection on the management of the companies.

The effect of the principle that we are considering on the size of insurance companies is the same as that already noted in speaking of independent industrial organizations. It is a force working towards large companies. The larger an insurance company is, the cheaper it can afford to give insurance. It might be impracticable, but it would not be economically unjustifiable, to require small companies to carry higher reserves in proportion to the amount insured than large companies are compelled to carry. In the absence of conflicting influences each branch of insurance would finally be concentrated in the hands of a single company. Nor is there any reason why the process of centralization should stop here. There is the same economic advantage in combining risks of entirely different kinds, provided they are correctly estimated, as there is in combining risks of the same kind. The difficulties in the way of such general combinations are all of a practical nature. Whatever may be said on the ground of expediency for the laws passed by some of our states restricting the freedom of insurance companies in the matter of assuming different kinds of risks, economic theory affords no justification for such policy. The more risks the cheaper the insurance, is a universal economic principle. One enormous company carrying all risks would be the ideal organization of insurance

The gain due to the combination of risks and to the consequent reduction of uncertainty is not the only economic benefit of insurance. There is another advantage resulting from the transfer of risk, which is of the same kind as the one previously noticed in speaking of the capitalist-entrepreneur. It is desirable for society that risks should be correctly estimated. Men differ much in their ability to judge them. The segregation of the work of estimating risks leads to a differentiation of capitalists, as a result of which those who are especially adapted to that task will be the ones who will undertake it. Moreover, their natural ability will be further developed through the experience and training of the work itself. On the other hand there are many men capable of rendering good service to society in comparatively safe industries, who are so constituted that the necessity of running any great chance of loss seriously diminishes their efficiency. The possibility of transferring the risks of their business to others for a fixed premium frees them from the paralyzing influence of uncertainty, and enables them to make the best use of their powers in other directions. The gain to society from the transfer of risks is obtained partly through the reduction in the cost of carrying the risks when they are borne by those who have the most ability to estimate them and the most confidence in their own judgments about them, and partly through the increase in the efficiency of those who are abnormally sensitive to the influence of uncertainty.

The gains of which we have been speaking are partly offset by the cost of carrying on the insurance business. This cost consists of interest on the capital and wages for the labor employed in the actual performance of the work. What that cost ought to be, if insurance companies were economically conducted, and how far the actual cost exceeds that amount, we need not stop to inquire. There is a generous margin between the price for which a large insurance campany can afford to assume a risk and the price which an individual producer would demand for carrying it. That this margin is not exhausted even by the extravagant methods of management that characterize existing insurance companies is proved by the almost universal prevalence of the custom of insurance. That it is more nearly exhausted than it ought to be is proved by the persistence of the custom of self-insurance. It must not be forgotten, however, that insurance companies carry on many other forms of activity besides their special work of furnishing insurance. Investment is a prominent feature of so-called life insurance, and preventive measures of various kinds are carried out by insurers of property. Insurers of boilers have their inspectors, fire insurance companies have their patrols, burglary insurance companies their private watchmen, and so on through the list. The part of the premium which is used in carrying out these protective measures ought not to be considered as part of the cost of insurance. It is work that would have to be done in some form by individual producers or by society, if it were not performed by the companies. The fact that the companies do it is an indication that it is accomplished more cheaply or more efficiently by them than it could be by the insured themselves. Another legitimate form of expense that ought to be recognized is the cost of securing the services of experts in appraising property and estimating risks. This work would also have to be performed in some way by individual producers if they carried their own risks. It might perhaps be accomplished more cheaply by them, but it would certainly be done more crudely and inaccurately. The gain from the accurate valuation of risks by experts more than counterbalances the necessary increase in the expense.

There is another form of loss of serious proportions which must not be left unnoticed in comparing the advantages and disadvantages of insurance. It is an essential feature of a perfect system of insurance that the occurrence of the event for whose economic consequences compensation is guaranteed shall never be a source of gain to the insured. In an ideally complete system the payment by the insurance company will just equal the loss of the insured. Now it is a matter of common observation that insurance is often obtained in excess of the actual value of the property insured. As a consequence there is considerable wilful destruction of property for the purpose of obtaining the insurance. Moreover, it is doubtful whether it is practically desirable that the amount of the insurance equal the full value of the property, since no incentive would be left to the insured to guard against the destruction of his property. Over-insurance leads to fraud, full insurance to carelessness, and even partial insurance to some diminution of watchfulness. Whatever increase may occur in the amount of positive loss either through fraud or through carelessness must be deducted from the diminution in negative loss in estimating the net gain which insurance brings to society.

The economic significance of insurance in a state is connected with its influence in reducing the burden which the existence of risk imposes on society. So far as the degree of risk is lowered, and the reluctance to assume it is diminished, so far is society benefited by the institution of insurance. How great the gain is, even under existing imperfect conditions, it is impossible to estimate, since it is difficult to conceive how the large enterprises of the present day could be carried on without the possibility of transferring to insurance companies many of the risks involved in them. It could certainly be done only on a much larger margin of safety than is now considered necessary.

The essential features of economic insurance as we have defined it are the accumulation of capital to meet uncertain losses, and the transfer and combination of risks. Many other conceptions of insurance have been held by various writers on the subject. Some originated in an over-emphasis of a comparatively unimportant phase of the institution, others in a wrong interpretation of some feature of it. As an example of the former kind may be mentioned the conception of those writers who find the significance of insurance in the diffusion of positive losses over a large group of persons.[1] That the insured in the

[1] "Considerée dans son principe même, l'assurance est une associa-

long run pay all the losses is undoubtedly true, but the distribution of the losses is only an indirect result of the insurance; it is neither the purpose of it nor the immediate consequence. The purpose of securing insurance is to avoid uncertainty. The insured buys security by the payment of a fixed premium, and after he has bought it his condition is not affected by the number of losses which the insurer may have to make good. If the number of losses increases, the premium rate may be raised; but in all cases of complete insurance the cost of it is a definite element in the expense of production, the amount of which is fixed before the occurrence of the losses. Only in the case of mutual assessment companies is there a direct distribution of losses over a group. A member of such a company is not in the same economic situation as one insured for a fixed premium. He has not transferred his risk and purchased security; he has exchanged one risk for another, usually a small chance of a large loss for a larger chance of a smaller loss. Where there is a mere diffusion of loss there remains some degree of uncertainty as to the amount of loss that each member of the group will suffer; where there is complete insurance the insurer has taken upon himself the entire chance of loss, so far as concerns the risks covered by the insurance. To define insurance, then, as the distribution of losses is to make too prominent an indirect and comparatively unimportant result of it,

tion qui a pour objet de répartir entre tous ses membres les pertes occasionnées à quelques-uns d'entre eux par certains événements fortuits, de telle sort que chaque membre supporte sa part de l'indemnité due aux victimes du sinistre." — Ch. Dumaine, "Assurances," Say's *Dictionnaire des Finances*, Vol. I, p. 220.

"Versicherung im *wirthschaftlichen* Sinne ist diejenige wirthschaftliche Einrichtung, welche die nachtheiligen Folgen (zukünftigen) *einzelner*, für den Betroffenen *zufälliger*, daher auch im *einzelnen Falle* ihres Eintretens unvorhergesehener Ereignisse für das Vermögen einer Person dadurch beseitigt oder wenigstens vermindert dass sie dieselben *auf eine Reihe von Fällen* vertheilt, in denen die gleiche Gefahr droht, aber nicht wirklich eintritt." — Adolph Wagner, "Versicherungswesen," Schonberg's *Handbuch*, 4te Auf, 2 Band 2, s. 359.

and to leave entirely out of the definition the elements in which its ecomomic significance really lies.

The other erroneous conception of insurance to which reference has been made is even more indefensible than the one just noticed. Instead of arising from an over-emphasis of a comparatively unimportant feature of the institution, it is based on an essentially false idea of its nature. Because each insurance contract considered by itself is a contingent contract, and because the event upon which the payment by the insurer to the insured depends is uncertain, many writers have regarded insurance as a form of gambling.[1] But the resemblance is in reality of the most superficial kind. It is not difficult to discover the mark of distinction between the two transactions. Insurance involves the transfer of an existing risk from one person to another; gambling involves the creation of a new risk to which neither party to the transaction was exposed before the contract, and to which they are both exposed after it. If a man insures his factory, he frees himself from uncertainty, and the other party to the con-

[1] "Let us now contrast the workings of insurance. In this case also the contract is a wager. A house-owner pays an insurance company fifty dollars, in return for which he is to receive five thousand dollars in case his house burns down within a specified time; just as he might pay a book-maker fifty dollars and receive five thousand in case a specified horse wins a race." — Arthur T. Hadley, *Economics*, p. 99.

"Le contrat aléatoire est une convention réciproque dont les effêts, quant aux avantages et aux pertes soit pour toutes les parties, soit pour l'une ou plusieurs d'entre elles, dépendent d'un événement incertain. Telles sont le contrat d'assurance, . . . le jeu et le pari, . . ." — Code civil français, Art. 1984. Quoted in Charles Berdez, *Les Bases de l'Assurance Privée*, p. 56, note.

"Wenn also der unorganisierte Spiel des Schicksals den Menschen in Gefahr bringt, so begreifen wir, dass das Mittel, welches er ihm entgegensetzt, ein organisiertes Glückspiel sein wird. Er erreicht dadurch die Wirkung, dass er zur selben Zeit, wo er von eineme Verlust betroffen wird, durch das Glückspiel einen Gewinn erhalt, der gerade den Schaden deckt." — R. Schlink, *Die Natur der Versicherung*, Wurzburg, 1887, s. 13.

tract assumes it; if he makes a wager with another, his own uncertainty and that of the other person are both increased at the same time. Undoubtedly in the past many transactions which wore the virtuous guise of insurance were no better than gambling contracts. If a person takes out a policy on property in which he has no insurable interest, he virtually makes a wager with the insurance company that the property will be destroyed. Such contracts are clearly against public policy, and legislation has done much to limit their number. The courts on the other hand have frequently given a liberal construction to the phrase "insurable interest," and many contracts of doubtful legitimacy are still tolerated. A legitimate insurance contract, however, may always be distinguished from a gambling contract by the principle pointed out. Insurance is the transfer of risk, gambling the creation of risk.

After a system of insurance against any class of risks has been established, an entrepreneur has a choice between three methods of meeting such a risk, in an industry that he has decided to enter. He may adopt preventive measures, he may obtain insurance, or he may carry the risk and pay a higher price for the capital he borrows. His selection among these different modes of conduct will depend upon their relative cost. Expenditure for any one of them is to him an item in the cost of production, and he will naturally adopt the one that is cheapest. As a matter of fact, in nearly all cases it is necessary to combine the three methods. Preventive measures are adopted by which the total amount of risk is somewhat reduced; a part of the remaining risk is transferred to insurance companies; the rest is borne by the capital in the industry. The amount of the expenditure for each of these purposes is determined according to the principles already established. The payment for the capital exposed to risk contains an element of reward for risk-taking, which is large in proportion to the degree of risk; the payment for insurance contains a relatively smaller element of the same kind; the payment for prevention contains none at all.

The entire sum paid by the insured to the insurance company is called the insurance premium. As the companies carry on many forms of activity which are not an essential part of their business of furnishing insurance, and the expense of which is paid out of the premiums they receive, the cost of the insurance itself is less than the amount of the premium. In a strict economic sense the insurance premium includes only that part of the payment to the company that would have to be made to induce it to assume the risk. Expenditures for preventive measures, whether made directly by the entrepreneur himself, or first incurred by the insurance company and then recovered from the insured, are no part of the cost of insurance. This distinction, however, is not observed by all writers.[1] Because the entrepreneur has a choice between prevention and insurance, it seems to be inferred that the two forms of expenditure are essentially alike. It is evident, however, that if all expenditures for the purpose of preventing accidental loss are to be regarded as insurance premiums, a very considerable part of the cost of production must come under that head. Such an extension of the term, insurance, utterly destroys its economic significance. Nor is the situation much improved by limiting its application to the expenditures for those preventive measures that make it possible to obtain insurance from organized companies at a lower rate. The distinction does not depend on any such accidental circumstance as that. It goes back to the fundamental difference between the

[1] See, for example, Alfred Marshall, *Principles of Economics*, Vol. I, p. 469, note. "Again, certain insurance companies in America take risks against fire in factories at very much less than the ordinary rates, on condition that some prescribed precautions are taken, such as providing automatic sprinklers, and making the walls and floors solid. The expense incurred in these arrangements is really an insurance premium. . . ."

methods by which the amounts of the two kinds of payments are determined. One includes an element of reward for risk-taking, which in the case of insurance goes to the insurer, whose capital is bearing the risk; the other is determined by the direct cost of introducing the preventive measure, whether the work is done by the entrepreneur himself or by the company. Prevention and insurance are complementary methods of preparing to meet uncertain losses; only confusion can result from the attempt to make them identical.

Not only do insurance companies carry on many forms of activity that are no part of their peculiar functions as insurers, but not all their activity as insurers has any direct bearing on the productivity of capital. The insurance of consumption goods is almost as common as the insurance of capital goods. It would not be difficult, in the light of the principles already discussed, to discover the laws that determine the adoption of insurance by the owners of consumption goods, or the nature of the social service that such insurance renders. A study of that sort would not be without interest, but it is outside the range of our investigation. We are concerned only with the insurance of capital, that is, with insurance as a method of lowering the cost of producing commodities.

Insurance is primarily a method of making accumulations to meet uncertain losses. Attention has already been called to the gain that accrues to society through the reduction in the amount of such accumulations which insurance brings about. There are one or two other points in connection with this aspect of the institution that deserve consideration. Capital alone can insure capital. The guarantee of security by one who had no means of making good the losses that occurred would be a fruitless proceeding. The amount of capital necessary to give security evidently depends on the amount of risk that the capital assumes. As the number of risks carried by an insurance company increases, the amount of its accumulations also must increase. Stock companies start with a certain amount of capital contributed by the members of the company, and make additional accumulations out of the contributions of the insured. Mutual companies, if they are to perform their functions perfectly, must also make accumulations of the same kind, but these funds are all contributed by the insured themselves, who virtually constitute the company. From the point of view of economic theory the difference between the two kinds of companies is of no significance. One form of insurance is not necessarily any cheaper than the other. If the entire business of insurance were on a strictly competitive basis, and if the accumulation of the companies were in all cases limited to the amounts necessary to give security, it would be a matter of no importance by whom the funds were contributed. Capital is invested in the business of insurance for the same purpose that any other investment is made — in order to obtain reward. If the insuring fund of the mutual companies is made up out of the current contributions of the insured, the owners of the capital thus invested will require in some form the same return on their capital that they could obtain in any other investment with the same degree of risk. The members of the mutual company are carrying on the business of insurance with a part of their capital, which acts as a guarantee fund for the capital that they have invested in more hazardous enterprises. The gain accrues to the insured as insurers instead of accruing to the members of a stock company. As there is no reason why the accumulations of mutual companies should be any less than the accumulations of stock companies, of which the capital stock forms a part, there is no reason why the return to the capital thus invested should be any less in the former than in the latter. Whatever gain can be secured under competitive conditions by insuring in a mutual company rather than in a stock company is due to the fact that the insured themselves have invested capital in the insurance business.

How large the accumulations of insurance companies ought to be in proportion to the risks they carry can be determined only by experience. The prime requisite of such an institution is security. Therefore the accumulations must be large enough to cover the probable losses, with a margin of safety for unexpectedly large ones. It is safe to say, however, that the accumulations of many companies are in excess of the amount thus determined. I do not refer here to the accumulations made by life insurance companies, which combine entirely different functions with that of insurance, and a large part of whose funds represent simply investments of capital by the insured. Nor do I include that part of the funds of insurance companies which is used for other purposes than insurance, such as the expenditures for preventive measures. That part of their accumulations which is strictly an insurance fund is often larger than it needs to be. The possibility of making such unnecessarily large accumulations is due to imperfect competition, which does not force the cost of insurance down to the competitive level. If, however, it were necessary for these funds to lie idle in the vaults of the company, it is evident that there would be no motive for making accumulations larger than the conditions of the business demanded. Any excess would be distributed as dividends among the stockholders of the company, or, in a mutual company, would result in an immediate lowering of the insurance premium. That this distribution of the entire surplus does not take place is explained by the fact that capital which is insuring the other capital is not prevented on that ground from participating in other forms of industrial activity. We have already seen in the case of the capitalist-entrepreneur that while his own capital acts as a guarantee fund for the capital that he borrows, it at the same time performs its part in the direct productive activity of the industry in which it is invested. The fulfilment of the insurance contract does not require the creation of new capital; it requires merely the transfer of the ownership of existing capital. Therefore the accumulated funds of insurance companies, even that part of them which is economically necessary, instead of remaining otherwise unproductive, are invested in such ways that they earn an income for the company. Of course there are certain restrictions as to the forms in which such investments should be made. For practical reasons it is desirable that the funds should be invested where there is the least danger of loss, and where the difficulty of realizing on the investments is at a minimum. But the important point is that capital which is insuring other capital may at the same time be directly employed in the production of wealth. The unnecessarily large surpluses of insurance companies are allowed to accumulate, not for the sake of the reward they can obtain in the insurance business, but for the sake of the interest paid for their use by those to whom they are lent.

It is evident that the possibility of using productively the reserve funds of insurance companies reduces the cost of insurance. Under competitive conditions the return that capital invested in the insurance business can secure will be fixed. In the long run it will consist of pure interest plus the reward for carrying the risk to which it is exposed. All other income that the companies receive will operate to reduce the payments of the insured. If it were necessary for reserve funds to remain unproductive, the income that they now earn would have to be obtained from the insured in the form of higher premiums.

One question in this connection remains to be answered: In what sense is the employment of capital to insure other capital a productive function? The difficulty in answering this question is due to two circumstances. On the one hand, capital which is insuring other capital may at the same time be productively employed in other ways and create the same amount of physical product as any other capital so employed. On the other hand, the reward which capital obtains for insuring other capital is entirely created by the capital that is insured. It is evident, therefore, that insuring capital, as such, is not directly creating physical product. Its service is to create a condition which increases the productivity of the capital that is insured. In return for this service a part of the product of the insured capital is handed over to the insurer. But this is not to deny the productivity of the insuring capital. In an economic sense the product of a unit of capital is the part of the total product whose creation is due to the presence of that particular unit. If, then, the insuring capital, by virtue of its service in guaranteeing safety, increases the total product of the insured capital, the additional part must be attributed to the insuring capital as its product. If there were a monopoly of the privilege of granting insurance, the entire increase in product might be appropriated by the insurers. Perfect competition, on the other hand, would bring about an influx of capital into the insuring business which in the end would reduce the total return to capital in it to the same proportions as the return to capital in any other industry involving the same degree of risk. The remainder of the economic gain due to the existence of the institution of insurance would then accrue chiefly to the consumers of the commodities created in the industries in which the insured capital is employed. There is no fundamental difference in kind between the reward for risk-taking which accrues to capital employed directly in a hazardous enterprise and the reward which insuring capital obtains for the risk it assumes. In both cases there is an increased productivity of industry on account of the assumption of the risk, and in both cases the capital exposed to risk obtains a part of the increased product as its special reward. In both cases, moreover, the amount of the extra reward which capital can obtain by assuming risk is fixed by the sacrifice of the most reluctant investor whose capital is needed to meet the demands of society. The only difference between the two kinds of income is the comparatively unimportant one that in the former case the extra product is created directly by the capital that receives it, while in the latter case it is created by other capital and handed over to the insuring capital as a reward for creating the conditions which make possible the increased productivity of the capital which is insured.

The statement is sometimes made that all insurance is mutual insurance.[1] It is evident from a consideration of the facts already established that this is only partially true. All insurance is mutual in the sense that all the losses are in the long run paid by the insured. Obviously an insurance company could not long survive if it systematically made good the losses of the insured out of its own capital. To the company the payment of losses is an element in the cost of carrying on its business, and in the long run consumers necessarily pay all the expenses of production. This mutual aspect of insurance, however, does not bring out its fundamental significance. This lies in the reduction of the cost of producing commodities through the relief of producers from the disagreeable feelings aroused by uncertainty, and the substitution of security for insecurity. The burden of insecurity, which would rest upon individual producers in the absence of a system of insurance is in no way borne by the insured as a body after insurance has been introduced. A large part of it is entirely annihilated, and the remainder rests upon the insurers whose capital has assumed the risks of the insured. Even in the case of so-called mutual companies, while the surviving uncertainty is still borne by the members of the company, the real significance of the institution does not lie in this fact, but in the reduction of the uncertainty as a result of the insurance. The overemphasis of its importance in causing a diffusion of loss is due to an imperfect analysis of its economic effects.

Insurance is evidently far from being a gratuitous gift

[1] See, for example, H. C. Emery, "The Place of the Speculator in the Theory of Distribution," *Publications of the American Economic Association*, 3d Series, Vol. I, No. 1, p. 105.

to society. The component parts of its cost are the wages of the labor employed in the insurance business, interest on the capital invested in it, and any increase in the amount of positive loss through fraud or carelessness, which the existence of insurance induces. This cost first falls upon the entrepreneurs who choose to insure their capital rather than to pay capitalists a higher price on account of risk. To the entrepreneurs, therefore, it is a part of the cost of production; it will be embodied in the price of the commodities, and will thus be shifted to the shoulders of consumers. It is in the end the consuming public that pays the entire expense of insurance. This does not by any means imply that the condition of consumers is not benefited by the existence of insurance. The comparison lies, not between the cost of insurance and no cost, but between the cost of insurance and the cost of risk without insurance. The gain to the consumer comes through the reduction in the price of commodities, and the amount of the reduction is determined by the difference between the interest which the entrepreneur would have to pay for capital exposed to the entire risk of the industry on the one hand, and the lower interest on the capital when it is insured, plus the cost of the insurance itself on the other hand.

There has been a singular lack of unanimity among writers on political economy with regard to the division of economic theory in which the treatment of insurance ought to be placed. Some have considered it in connection with production, others have regarded it as a phenomenon of consumption, while still others have found it inexpedient to bring it under any of the recognized divisions, and have put it at the end of their works along with other subjects of a more or less dubious economic character. There seems to be little occasion for such uncertainty. If the old divisions of production, distribution, exchange, and consumption are to be maintained, there is no doubt that the proper place for the discussion of insurance, at least so far as insurance of capital is concerned, is in the department of production. With regard to the insurance of consumption goods the case may not seem so plain at first sight, since there is not the same direct relation between such insurance and the productivity of industry. Nevertheless, it undoubtedly belongs in the division of production. It belongs there, not because it affects the productivity of other capital, but because the creation of security is in itself a form of production. If the owners of consumption goods are willing to pay a price for the sake of having them insured, it is evident that they are obtaining something in exchange which is of more value to them than the money with which they part. What they obtain is security, and whether or not it seems best to consider such security as a consumption good, or as any form of wealth, it cannot be questioned that the capital and labor engaged in creating it are serving mankind in the same way as that employed in the creation of any commodity for which consumers are willing to pay.

The conclusions reached in the present chapter are in part as follows: Complete insurance, in the economic sense, is the accumulation of funds for uncertain losses, and the combination of the risks of individuals in a group. The advantage of such an institution in society is the result of its influence in reducing the burden of risk. To call all insurance mutual, or to define it as the distribution of losses, is to put the emphasis on a comparatively unimportant aspect of it; to call it gambling is to confuse forms of activity fundamentally different both in their purpose and in their consequences. Capital employed in insuring other capital is productive, and the reward it receives is a part of its product. Capital employed in insuring consumption goods is creating something for which the owners of the goods are willing to pay. It, therefore, is also productive. The treatment of insurance naturally belongs in the division of economic theory that deals with the phenomena of the production of wealth.

CHAPTER IV

ORGANIZATION OF COMPANIES[1]

In a general way it may be said that fire insurance is transacted through three different agencies, the first and most important of which is the stock companies; the second, the various forms of mutual companies, and the comparatively unimportant third, the association of individual insurers known as individual underwriters, and Lloyds. Mutual companies again may be divided into three classes — first, the local county or town mutuals; second, the state or general mutuals, and third, the manufacturers mutuals commonly known as the factory mutuals and their imitators.

The local or county mutuals are by far the most numerous of any class of companies in the United States. Their number is approximately 1500. There are 125 in New York State alone.

The laws which govern their organization and operation are very dissimilar in the different states. In some states, notably in New York, they are prohibited from operating in large cities. This is, in New York at least, a result of the great fire of 1845, when all existing mutual companies doing business in New York City were bankrupted. Usually their operations are limited by law to a few non-hazardous classes — such as farm property, dwellings, churches, and stores — in a given limited district. Often their operations are comfined to a town or

[1] By Richard M. Bissell, Vice-President of the Hartford Fire Insurance Company, Hartford. Reprinted from pages 66–85 of the "Yale Lectures on Insurance, Fire and Miscellaneous."

county, though in New York State a local mutual company may operate throughout five counties.

As a rule they must have, before organization is perfected, applications, *i.e.*, promises for a certain amount of insurance, usually somewhere between $50,000 and $200,000, already on file, and a portion of the premiums therefor — commonly 25 per cent. — paid in advance in cash.

Having secured the necessary applications, those who are organizing the company — usually a group of farmers, who think the charges of the stock companies are exorbitant — secure from the state authorities the proper papers of incorporation; then a meeting of the applicants or members is called and officers are elected. Business is then begun by issuing their policies to the original applicants. In most cases all the work of the company is done by the secretary, who very likely is the village postmaster, store-keeper, or bank cashier, and who receives a fee for each policy issued, or who may be compensated by a salary. Those interested in the company urge their friends and neighbors to join them, appreciating the necessity for a considerable number of policy-holders amongst whom the losses may be divided. The applications thus secured are usually passed upon as to valuations, desirability, etc., by the executive committee or board of directors. If an application is approved a policy is issued by the secretary, and perhaps signed by one or two of the committee. These policies are issued in consideration of a small cash payment, equal to about one-fourth the price commonly charged by stock companies, and a note given by the applicant for an amount equal to three or four times the cash payment. These notes are subject to call if the needs of the company so require. Each policy-holder is liable for the losses of the company, according to the articles of agreement or incorporation or the by-laws of the particular company in which he is insured, or perhaps according to an agreement assented to when the policy is issued. Sometimes the limit of liability is stated in the policy. In some cases each policy-holder is liable for his fractional share of any or all liabilities which may come to the company. More often, however, this liability is limited to a certain percentage of the amount of insurance the individual carries or to some multiple of the amount for which he has given premium notes. The policies are usually issued for five years.

Since the executive committee and all the applicants are neighbors and acquaintances, the personal and financial qualifications of every applicant, as well as the value and condition of his property, are well known, and thus the danger from dishonest losses or over-valuation is reduced to a minimum. No man with a bad reputation can secure insurance in one of these institutions, if it is properly conducted. Moreover, every policy-holder is constantly, as it were, under the surveillance of his neighbors, who are members — many of them — of the same company; consequently the opportunities for the successful perpetration of fraud are not good. Furthermore, while in many rural communities it is considered a very clever business stroke to get the better of one of the large stock companies, who, like the railroads, are looked upon as natural enemies, it is an entirely different matter when a man's desire to realize on his policy results in an assessment upon his neighbor. An attempt to do so, whether successful or not, usually results in ostracism for the offender.

These companies, when wisely and honestly managed, succeed or fail according to the burning record of the districts where they operate. A few heavy losses in the earlier years of their existence usually finish them. Farmers and villagers quickly tire of assessments. On the other hand, in those districts which have had favorable records as to fires — and there are many such — these little companies live and prosper for years. Often they accumulate assets of considerable value and in such cases furnish indemnity to their members at very low cost.

Having no expense of any kind save the fees of the secretary and the cost of their few supplies, they can be very economically operated. Whether their record as a whole has been one of profit or loss to their members cannot be said with any degree of certainty. Large numbers are organized and equally large numbers fail every year, and while many are short-lived, some exist to-day which are fifty or more years old. Their strength and their weakness alike are largely due to the fact that they transact business in a very limited field, where every risk is known and watched, but where a few losses make insurance very costly owing to the limited number of those among whom the losses are distributed. They are usually free from the heavy burden of taxation which rests upon stock companies, being thus favored by that policy of discrimination on the part of the legislator which so often is in evidence where the farmer or laboring man is concerned.

Concerning the formation of the mutual companies which do a general business throughout one or more states, and which are usually called state mutuals to distinguish them from county and town mutuals, the laws of the different states vary to an extreme degree. In New York and some other states there are no laws whatever governing or controlling such companies. In others, as for instance Wisconsin, the laws are specific and minute. On the whole, the most marked difference between these laws and those which govern the town mutuals concern the amount of applications for insurance which must be secured before a charter can be had. In Wisconsin this amount is $750,000 as compared with $50,000 for a local mutual company. In some states the classes of business which these state mutuals may write are limited by law; in others the maximum amount of liability which may be assumed on any one risk is so fixed. The Wisconsin law is remarkable for providing specifically for five kinds of mutual companies which may transact business over an extended territory. Among them are companies formed by retail lumber dealers, hardware dealers, church societies, and finally a class unique in insurance history so far as I know, viz., mutual companies formed by the treasurers of county insane asylums and poorhouses.

These general or state mutuals have not on the whole been successful, for, having ordinarily no great strength of assets, they cannot command business in districts remote from their place of domicile, except by quoting dangerously low prices. Moreover, they are compelled to delegate to agents or others the power to select risks and do not always get the best service. Those who operate the company lack the incentive of profit, a most important factor.

Such companies commonly do not possess and cannot acquire the highly trained staff, the complete organization and concentration of authority necessary for the successful prosecution of a general business under competitive conditions throughout a wide territory, and when such powers are given to some official of a mutual company, too often the trust is abused. As long as the business grows rapidly and heavy assessments are avoided — for the loss ratio on a rapidly growing business is always small — the members are not likely to interest themselves in the methods pursued, and when, after a time, the assessments become heavy it is usually too late to apply a remedy. The fact that there were seventy-four such mutual companies in New York State alone in 1853, and but two or three to-day, is sufficient commentary on their experience, to which it is perhaps permissible to add the following from the first annual report of the Insurance Department of the State of Pennsylvania, issued in 1863:

"Not a few mutual companies have been shipwrecked because of the ambition of officers to accumulate a large business; going far from home; trusting to agents, and measuring prosperity by the amount at risk and gross cash receipts.

"Near home, within the limits of half a dozen counties,

the officers and members are more or less intimately acquainted with the character of those composing the partnership and the property at risk; but far from home, in this or other states, they are necessarily, to a great degree, ignorant. There the agent acts for them. His interest is to do as much business as possible and he is not always so critical as to the risks he assumes as he ought to be. In time, loss after loss is followed by assessment upon assessment, until the home members of the company find that the insurance which ought to have been cheap has turned out very dear. The cause of the disaster is very plain. The laws essential to cheap insurance have been set at defiance. Hazardous and special risks have been written at rates far less than the stock companies could afford, as if the mutual system contained within itself an exemption from the inevitable laws of hazard. The officers of the company attribute their misfortunes to an unprecedented run of ill luck. Mere chance played the smallest part in producing the catastrophe; want of knowledge and judgment the largest. Then comes the trouble. The policy-holders rebel against the payment of the large assessments. The company resorts to litigation to compel payment. It is pressed to pay losses and is compelled, in turn, to press the payment of assessments. The practical usefulness of the company is at an end and its career is terminated amid the execrations of all parties interested."

It is true that there are throughout the country a number of fortunately prosperous old institutions of this kind which have been conservatively managed, have transacted a selected business only of the non-hazardous classes, and have confined their operations almost invariably to limited territory. These institutions have had honorable careers, and have furnished cheap indemnity.

In life insurance the policy-holder looks to the company for a certain definite payment at some time in the future, and, so far as experience shows, runs little if any risk of personal liability by becoming a member of a mutual company. In fire insurance, however, the policy-holder contracts for indemnity against an extraordinary and even unlikely loss, and yet by joining a mutual company he exposes himself to the possibility of a serious personal liability, in the event of a conflagration, or if the bad selection of risks results in heavy losses. Instances have occurred where former policy-holders have been assessed as late as five years after their own policies had expired, and long after they supposed their connection with the mutual company of which they had been members had ceased.

We now come to the consideration of the most interesting, and, so far as their influence on the methods of fire insurance companies and on the fire loss of the country is concerned, by far the most important class of mutual companies, viz., those known as the factory mutuals.

Edward Atkinson, LL.D., one of their most eminent officials and advocates, is authority for the statement that this class of companies was devised for the *prevention* of loss by fire, the payment of indemnity for losses sustained being a secondary matter.

Theoretically speaking, insurance companies pure and simple have nothing to do with the prevention or extinguishment of fires, or with the reduction of the fire waste. Their province is merely to distribute the losses which fires cause. Despite this truth, it was a short-sighted business policy which prevented the stock companies from actively coöperating with factory owners, especially with cotton and woolen manufacturers, who, when the burning ratio, and hence the cost of indemnity, had risen to an unbearable extent, sought so to improve their property as to reduce the number and amount of losses and so indirectly the cost of insurance. It seems to be true, however, that the failure or absence of such coöperation was largely responsible for the origin of this class of factory mutual companies, whose methods as first practised by themselves, later by the stock companies, have fairly revolutionized methods of protection against fire and made possible greatly reduced rates for risks of all classes when properly protected.

The first of these companies was organized in 1835 by Zachariah Allen in Providence, Rhode Island, and was called the Providence Manufacturers' Mutual Company. In 1850 there were three of these companies, and the number had increased to seven by 1860. There are now in Rhode Island and Massachusetts eighteen such companies in active operation, and others in Pennsylvania and other parts of the country. These companies are carrying insurance amounting to over one billion of dollars on factory property.

The activity of these companies was greatly increased, and the expansion of their operations greatly aided, by the material advances in rates which were made by the surviving stock companies after the Chicago and Boston conflagrations. These advances, amounting to 56 per cent. or more, compelled factory owners to look about for less costly sources of indemnity, with the result that many of them adopted factory mutual methods of protection and secured the low-cost insurance resulting therefrom.

From the outset these companies have endeavored, first, to ascertain and eliminate the causes of fires, and, second, to provide such ample protection that any fire which might occur should be extinguished with but slight loss.

In these particulars the record of the Associated New England Factory Mutual Companies has been quite wonderful. Their method is to charge a cash premium based upon the class of work done, construction of the building in question, the extent to which dangerous processes are eliminated, and the extent and efficiency of the apparatus for extinguishing fires. No factory can secure the protection of this system unless in respect to all these matters it comes up to a prescribed standard of excellence. In addition to this cash payment, a liability for assessments equal to five times the cash premium is assumed by the policy-holder. As a matter of fact, however, since 1850 no assessment has been found necessary by any of the New England companies. On the other hand, the cash premiums have not only paid losses and expenses, but have enabled a division of profits to be made at the close of each year. In this way the actual cost of indemnity is reduced to a small amount.

Mr. Atkinson ascribes the success of these companies to recognition of the following principle: "The only persons who can prevent loss by fire are the owners or occupants of the insured premises. Upon them rests the responsibility for heavy loss, if any occurs, in nearly every fire. All that the insurance company can do is to pay indemnity for loss which, if large, in nine cases out of ten, is due to the lack of apparatus for preventing loss or to the lack of care and order in the conduct of the work."

In their efforts to ascertain and eliminate the causes of fire, these companies have investigated and endeavored to safeguard all processes used in manufacture. They have investigated methods of illuminating, heating, lubricating; have devised elaborate plans for the safe construction and arrangement of factories in order that the spread of fire might be retarded and that especially dangerous processes might be isolated, and, finally, have tested and applied the most modern and approved apparatus for extinguishing fires. Moreover, when a factory comes into their membership they not only see to it that in all respects its condition is brought up to their requirements, but by frequent inspection they secure the constant maintenance of such conditions. They are, indeed, hardly to be called insurance companies at all, but rather associations of manufacturers with experienced inspectors and engineers, whose work it is to eliminate the possibility of loss or serious damage by fire. The insurance feature only comes into play when, despite their precautions, a damage is incurred. It will be realized that, though the number of fires and the loss resulting therefrom have been very greatly reduced by these methods, a large expenditure is necessary to construct, arrange, and equip a factory in such a way as to bring it up to the standard of their requirements.

While to these factory mutuals must be given the chief credit for inaugurating such plans for safeguarding property, the stock companies have for a number of years been pursuing methods of coöperation with the owners of factories, and other classes of property as well, similar to those briefly hinted at above, and now are as well equipped as the factory mutual companies to make suggestions to property owners for the proper construction, arrangement, care, and protection of their property.

The properties thus equipped in accordance with the views of experts are called "protected" or "equipped" risks, and there exists the keenest rivalry between the factory mutual companies and the stock companies to secure the control of this class of business. Thus far the efforts of the mutual companies have been more successful, especially in New England, though the stock companies are gradually reducing their rates to a point where they approximate the low cost at which the factory mutuals have been able to furnish indemnity.

There is no reason why this class of mutual companies should not combine to prosper if they continue to confine their field to isolated and thoroughly protected factories, the hazards of which have been properly provided for.

Mr. Atkinson, in regard to this matter, says, "The method of granting contracts by the factory mutual companies must of necessity be limited to special establishments, each carefully guarded from the other and fitted with its own apparatus for the extinction of fire. The mutual contract cannot safely be adopted in the crowded districts of large cities for the reason that the owner or occupant of one building may have a very dangerous neighbor in the next, over which he has no control."

There are two factors unfavorable to this class of companies; first, the possibility that too extensive liability, as compared with the income, may be assumed on individual risks, owing to implicit reliance on the experience already gained, in which case dangerously large losses may be incurred; and, second, the growing competition of the stock companies for the protected risks, which is constantly becoming keener. The stock companies have two important advantages to offer their patrons; first, that their policies are issued at net cost instead of in consideration of a cash payment to be later reduced by dividends; second, that no liability whatever is assumed by the policy-holder.

Insurance organizations of another class have flourished in great numbers during the past ten or fifteen years. These are known for the most part as Lloyds of one kind or another. They are voluntary partnerships for the purpose of insuring property. As a rule each partner is liable for a certain portion of every loss which occurs. The name Lloyds is, of course, taken from the famous English institution, and is too often used in order to convey the impression that these new American concerns are comparable in point of resources and reliability with that office. As a matter of fact very few indeed of the so-called Lloyds in this country are in a position to offer reliable contracts of indemnity. They furnish the combined promises of a number of private individuals, and the value of the contract in most cases is entirely dependent upon the financial strength of these individuals, though in a few instances a guarantee fund is paid in, which is liable for claims. Some of these concerns are responsible and have honestly and promptly paid their losses. Most of them, however, are without any of the qualities which a company transacting an insurance business should possess, and not a few are operated solely in order to get possession of premiums, which are not by any means designed to be accumulated for the benefit of their foolish patrons. One very frequent feature of their contracts, which makes them without particular value in the congested sections of large cities, is the provision that in case of a general conflagration the liability of each partner under all outstanding contracts shall be limited to a certain fixed amount. These policies are usually issued through some one agent acting for all the partners, who, as a rule, know nothing about the transactions in which their names and credit are involved.

While these Lloyds are most of them new institutions — recent phenomena in the insurance world — their operations have been so general and the results so unsatisfactory to the public, that in ten states laws have been passed which require a cash deposit or capital to be paid in by every such partnership as security for the fulfilment of their contracts. One state — Pennsylvania — prohibits them altogether. In seventeen states there are as yet no laws applicable to them. In the rest of the United States they are, by the wording of the insurance laws, subject to the same restrictions and requirements as ordinary insurance companies. There are from sixty to seventy of these Lloyds now in existence operating in a more or less general way in the United States, of which number perhaps less than half a dozen are responsible and worthy of a limited recognition. There is no way of ascertaining the volume of business which these institutions transact.

We now come to the consideration of the methods of incorporated stock companies, which, as before stated, form altogether the most important class of insurance companies, both as to the business transacted and as to solidity of assets and reserve, and which transact 90 per cent. of all the business done in the United States.

In the case of American companies, at least, it is usual for the directors to concern themselves chiefly with the financial or banking department of the company's business, largely because insuring property against fire is a business requiring technical training and one which must be conducted by men well versed in its numerous details. Therefore the business of insuring property is commonly left to the officers of the company and their assistants.

The whole country is usually divided into districts or departments and an officer, or more than one, placed at the head of each. These departments in some cases are all under the immediate supervision of the chief executive and located in the head office of the company. It is believed by some company officers that a more consistent policy, a more uniform method of procedure and greater economy of operation can be secured in this way. The majority of companies, however, establish departments in various large cities, each department having jurisdiction over the states naturally tributary to the city where it is located. These departments are usually called general agencies. The companies which maintain them do so because of the belief that in this way they can get in closer touch with their various agents and with the insuring public, and therefore can secure the best obtainable results, both as to the amount of business obtained and in the matter of closely supervising it. The cities usually selected for department offices are New York, Chicago, and San Francisco, and, to a smaller extent, Boston, Philadelphia, Atlanta, New Orleans, and one or two others.

The head office of the company contains the department for the states adjacent thereto. These departments are intended to work thoroughly the territory under their jurisdiction according to the general scheme of operations adopted by the company. Some companies endeavor to secure business from the larger cities only, but, both for the sake of a larger income and because of the safety and steadiness which can only be secured from a widely distributed business, most companies endeavor to get business from all possible sources where a profit is likely.

The business is secured by means of agents residing in the various towns and villages where the company operates. These are called local agents. In large cities, such as

Cleveland, Rochester, Louisville, etc., these local agents usually devote their entire time to securing and handling the business, and often the same man or firm in such a city will act as agent for anywhere from one to a dozen insurance companies. In the smaller places, however, the amount of business to be done is so small and the number of companies desiring it so large that the business usually demands only a portion of the agent's time, and is, therefore, combined with banking, the practice of law, store-keeping, or some other occupation. Moreover, the agent in such little places acts for as many companies as he will consent to represent.

It will be seen that local agents are the means by which a company comes into direct contact with the insuring public. The local agents are the ones who secure for the company the business on which it feeds. They are, therefore, a factor of supreme importance in the business, and companies endeavor through their special agents and in other ways to maintain cordial and friendly relations with them. In order to insure success, popularity with local agents is quite as important as popularity with the public in general. In order that there may be an intimate knowledge of the business at each agency, that new agencies may be secured and unsatisfactory ones discontinued, and to the end that all matters concerning the transactions between local agents and the department office may be properly supervised, men called special agents are employed, whose duty it is to travel constantly over the field to which they are assigned, locating agencies at all available points, carefully inspecting and securing accurate information concerning all the risks which the company insures, collecting overdue payments, endeavoring to secure from local agents as much desirable business as possible, and in general to further the interests of the company in every legitimate way. To them also is assigned for the most part the duty of arranging with claimants for the settlement and payment of the losses which occur in their particular territory, though some companies doing a very large business have so many losses to settle that expert adjusters, as they are called, are employed for this purpose only. The local agents are equipped by the company with the various forms, books of record, and other supplies necessary for the transaction of business; also with blank, unsigned policies.

When a contract is secured by an agent, from some property owner a policy is at once filled out, executed, and delivered to him, and as soon as possible thereafter an abstract of this contract, containing a full description of the property and all the details of the contract, is made out by the agent on a blank provided for that purpose, called a "daily report." This report is thereupon at once mailed to the department office which has jurisdiction over the territory in which the agent is located, and at the end of each month an account or statement of all the contracts made during the month is sent by the agent to the same department office, accompanied, or to be followed, by a remittance for the premiums collected.

The local agent is compensated by a commission, usually 15 per cent. on the amount of premiums secured or renewed by him. He is presumed and required to protect the interests of the company or companies he represents by carefully selecting desirable business and by following out their instructions in all matters. Companies endeavor to provide their agents with complete instructions as to their desires and methods concerning the conduct of business, so that agents may properly care for their interests.

When the daily reports of policies issued reach the office of the company they are carefully examined and reviewed by trained men called examiners. If the wording of the contract (the form, so-called) is found to be faulty, if the price is deemed to be too low, or if any other error is discovered, the agent is promptly requested to amend the contract in the necessary particular. If the property insured is deemed to be an undesirable subject for insurance he is requested to cancel or terminate the contract at once.

The duties of the examiner are extremely important. They demand an intimate acquaintance with the hazards usually incident to various kinds of property; also familiarity with the conditions affecting the district or town where each risk is located. Moreover, in judging a risk, the character of the ownership, the nature of the inherent and adjacent or exposing hazards due to the various occupants in the vicinity, the amount and quality of the protection against fire, the record of the locality as to fires, the rate, *i.e.*, price obtained, and numerous other factors must be considered and investigated with considerable thoroughness by him. To facilitate this work the general offices are equipped with maps showing the construction and size of every building in the business districts of all towns of importance; also with commercial reports indicating the financial standing and business records of all merchants and manufacturers, inspection reports of important risks made by special agents and trained experts as well, and various other tables, books of reference and of rules, which aid the examiner in passing judgment upon the numerous reports which come before him. A successful examiner, however, must have a clear head, quick perceptions, cool, careful judgment, and a very considerable knowledge acquired by experience. The examiner has usually two or more assistants who help him in matters of detail.

The monthly accounts or statements before referred to are also carefully gone over by auditors or bookkeepers. When the work of examining and auditing is done, the daily reports and the accounts pass on into the hands of a large force of clerks, who from them make up the elaborate records and statistics which the insurance companies are required to keep, partly for their own guidance and partly to comply with the laws of the different states.

In addition to the daily reports and accounts, canceled policies are also forwarded in large numbers by agents to the general offices; also notice of changes in contracts, called indorsements. Those must all pass through the same intricate and complicated process as the original daily report.

In another part of the office the losses are handled. Every loss is at once reported to the general office in whose territory it occurred. It is then assigned to the proper man for settlement — usually a special agent. As soon as possible he visits the scene of loss and arranges a settlement with the property owner. The completed reports of these settlements are forwarded to the general office and are very carefully tabulated, classified, and compared with the record of premiums received, the premiums and losses of each class being grouped by themselves in order that the experience of the company, that is, the profit or loss arising from transactions with each class of risks, may be ascertained. A large department office in the course of one year will receive, perhaps, 125,000 daily reports from its agents, who will be located in, say, 2500 cities, towns, and villages. These daily reports will carry premiums averaging about $20 each, or amounting to $2,500,000 in all. Such a department will also have to adjust and pay from 3000 to 4000 losses each year. To keep the elaborate records and tables of statistics concerning all these transactions, to watch them throughout the life of the contracts, to collect the moneys due and to pay carefully and justly the losses — all these tasks involve an amount of detailed, arduous, and technical labor which is formidable to contemplate. They also render necessary the services of well-trained men — high-priced, many of them — and a very large expenditure for proper equipment and maintenance. At the head of such a department is a manager, or general agent, as he may happen to be called. He is responsible for the results obtained in the territory under his jurisdiction. He must see to it that the numerous and troublesome details of the general office work are kept up, exercise general supervision over the examiners and their work, direct the movements of the traveling special agents and inspectors, decide all important questions arising in loss settlements, and last, but not least, utilize all these various factors in such a way that the company may secure its fair proportion of desirable business. A large department as indicated above will have on its rolls from 2000 to 3000 agents and perhaps one hundred or more salaried employees.

At the head of the company the president and other officers exercise a general oversight over all the departments. Usually monthly tabulated reports of all transactions are made by the departments to the head office. Any profits are also remitted to the head office for investment. On the other hand, if losses exceed the receipts of any department, advances are made to that department.

The officers are also charged with the duty of deciding upon the general policy and methods of the company for the guidance of the various departments. The amounts for which liability may be assumed on different kinds of risks are also determined by them. In other words, the plan of campaign is laid out and managed by the officers and executed by the department managers through their special and local agents. In the case of those companies which do not make use of separate departments located in different parts of the country, a large staff of officers is customary at the head office, where the junior officers perform the duties usually devolving upon department managers.

In the large cities where values are great and congested and where consequently the amount of business to be done is very large, another class composed of middlemen or brokers, as they are called, has arisen. These men secure from property owners orders for insurance which they then place with the local agent and in return receive a portion, usually one-half or more, of the agent's commission. These brokers usually take entire charge of the insurance affairs of their patrons, acting as their agents in all matters relative thereto. In New York City so universal is this method of transacting business that there are practically no local agents who solicit or secure business direct from property owners, and most companies maintain their own offices with salaried managers, with whom the brokers deal.

CHAPTER V

RATES AND HAZARDS [1]

In the language of fire insurance, the name "risk" is applied to any piece or kind of property which an insurance policy may cover. The hazards of a certain risk (as for instance a building), or of a certain class of risks (such as flour mills), are the peculiar or particular circumstances or characteristics pertaining to or affecting it which favor or make for its destruction by fire. The extent to which these hazards endanger a given risk theoretically governs its rate, *i.e.*, the price, per cent., which must be paid for insurance. A brief examination of the subject of hazards, therefore, will naturally precede and lead up to the subject of rates.

Hazards may be divided broadly into two classes, — physical and moral, or personal, as they are sometimes called. The physical hazards are inherent in the risk itself and in its surroundings. Moral hazards arise from personal factors. Physical hazards may be partially measured, appraised, estimated, and to a certain extent controlled. Moral hazards are hidden, presumed rather than known, not to be measured or scheduled.

The causes of fires are of far greater variety than is commonly known. They are indeed almost infinite in number, for practically every substance and almost every process of labor, manufacture, or commerce is under cer-

[1] By Richard M. Bissell, Vice-President of the Hartford Fire Insurance Company, Hartford. Reprinted from pages 92–126 of the Yale Insurance Lectures, Fire and Miscellaneous.

tain circumstances or in certain relations to other articles or processes productive of danger from fire.

Physical hazards may be divided into two classes, as external and internal, which are sufficiently distinguished by their names. The external hazards include lightning, conflagrations, sparks, bonfires, forest and prairie fires (which are sometimes very serious hazards), and exposure, the greatest of which by far is exposure, — *i.e.*, the danger to which a risk is subject from the burning of other risks or substances. To this cause is due 28 per cent. of all losses, both as to number and value. Property valued at $50,000,000 was destroyed by exposure fires in 1902. We speak of exposures as a hazard and attribute 28 per cent. of all losses to exposure, meaning thereby that as to 28 per cent. of all risks that are destroyed or damaged, the losses are caused by fires the origin of which is exterior to the risks embraced in the 28 per cent. It is an obvious truth, however, that the original cause of an exposure loss is usually to be found in some physical hazard and, ordinarily, an internal physical hazard pertaining to an adjacent risk. The following general rule may be laid down: The degree of exposure hazard to which any risk is subject is determined, first, by its own combustibility and ignitibility, *i.e.*, the readiness with which it will ignite and the rapidity and completeness with which it may be destroyed by fire; second, by the distance which separates it from the buildings or substances from which the exposure hazards arise; third, by the inherent hazards of the risks adjacent to it or within burning distance, and fourth, by the extent of protection which it receives from water works, fire department, or private apparatus. Under especially dangerous conditions there is hardly any limit to the burning distance. In the summer of 1894, during a drought, accompanied by high winds, there were extensive forest fires in northern Wisconsin and Michigan, and risks were burned by exposure arising from fires twenty miles or more distant. Sparks and embers fell on the decks of vessels many miles from land on Lake Superior. The exposure hazard constitutes a factor in the total of a risk's hazards, which is highly susceptible to reduction by efficient fire protection. In case of frame mercantile buildings, it frequently constitutes the most important factor in determining the rate.

The most important of the external hazards are, in their order, — after exposure, sparks, which cause about 4 per cent. of the entire number of fires (locomotive sparks alone caused over 600 out of 1500 cotton fires during 1902, of which the average loss amounted to over $5000), and lightning, which is responsible for nearly 3 per cent. of all losses, or three and a half millions in 1902.

The internal hazards are much more numerous and, leaving out exposure, much more productive of fires. They may be sub-divided into five classes, which, however, are not absolutely distinct. The first class, according to our arbitrary division, is spontaneous combustion. This, while ordinarily not an imminent hazard, becomes one whenever vegetable or animal fiber is handled or stored, as in cotton and woolen mills, cotton warehouses, ice houses, etc. It is a characteristic of these substances when more or less saturated with any oily substance (more especially if it be an animal oil or grease), that rapid oxidation or spontaneous combustion ensues. Two hundred and three out of 1683 fires in cotton mills, and 151 out of 1630 fires in woolen mills, were due to this cause.

The next general division comprises the hazards due to the operation of machinery. These include friction of machinery, heated bearings, accidents and breakages, overheated boilers and stacks adjacent to inflammable substances, and the presence of foreign substances in fast-running machinery. For example, in the pickers used in cotton and woolen mills and in cotton-ginning machines, sparks caused by the presence of stones, buttons, cartridges, etc., caused a great many fires. In cotton mills, 984 out of 1683 fires were caused by friction and the presence of foreign substances in machinery, and in flour mills, 477 out of 2616 fires were caused by friction in machinery.

The third division comprises the hazards incident to processes. Among these are hazards arising from dry kilns, roasting furnaces or ovens, use of inflammable mixtures for painting or japanning, the compounding of combustible and explosive chemicals in drug and paint mills, the improper or careless handling of heated substances, such as molten metals or the dried fertilizer just from the dry kilns, the use of fire heat under kettles, etc., and the production of various explosive gases or mixtures, as, for instance, dust in flour mills and starch factories or benzine vapor in furniture factories or japanning ovens.

The fourth and, so far as the number of losses and value of property are concerned, by far the most important of internal physical hazards, is due to the various processes and kinds of apparatus used for purposes of heating and lighting. It is quite natural that the process of heating — which usually means the actual use of fire —should make more losses than any other cause, yet it is a sad commentary on American methods of building, and on American laws concerning building, that defective flues should be responsible for twice as many fires as any other one physical or known moral hazard. This cause also is responsible for a greater property loss than any other. Flues may be defective in construction, as when wooden joists or timbers are allowed to pierce their walls, or when unprotected holes are left by careless masons, through which sparks or flames may escape. They may become defective by settling or cracking, due to insufficient support, or because the building is moved or shaken in consequence of a tornado or wind storm or if struck by lightning. In 1902 over 14,000 fires, or 13 per cent. of the total number of fires, were attributed to defective flues, and the total property loss resulting was over $11,000,000. Other fires due to methods of heating were caused by hot ashes and coals improperly deposited in dangerous places (barrels for example), or through carelessness or defective apparatus allowed to come in contact with combustible substances. Still other fires were caused by hot stoves and furnace pipes and by overheated stoves and furnaces, and the list includes the fires caused by steam pipes passing through or adjoining unprotected wooden surfaces. In all, about 20 per cent. of the total number of fires are directly traceable to the use of fire for heating purposes.

The fires due to methods of illumination included in 1902 over 400 caused by candles, over 3700 from accidents to lamps, resulting in more than $2,000,000 of losses, 970 from gas jets, and over 1000 from electric wires, which are classed with the methods of illumination for convenience, though electric wires are often used to convey power. The losses due to the use of electricity are larger by far in amount than those due to any of the other means of illuminating, chiefly, no doubt, because electricity is now so generally used in buildings and localities where large values are collected, while candles, lamps and even gas are now principally used in dwellings, small stores, and small factories; furthermore, fires of electrical origin are often not discovered until they have gained considerable headway. The value of property destroyed by fires of electrical origin in 1902 was $12,000,000. Fires due to other methods of illumination were more than four times as numerous as the fires of electrical origin, yet the ensuing loss was slightly below $5,000,000 or less than one-half the amount due to use of electricity.

The fifth general division of internal hazards includes everything not already classified. The various fires due to accidents and carelessness find a place here. The list includes oil stove accidents, fires from matches, which caused in 1902, 4000 fires, with a loss of over one and a half millions of dollars, children playing with fire, cigars, cigarettes and tobacco pipes, with a record of 1100 fires in 1902, and the numerous other causes of comparatively smaller importance which have not already found mention.

All of these classes and sub-classes of hazards might still be almost indefinitely re-subdivided, for new hazards and new manifestations of old hazards are to be met with daily. If the causes of the 76,000 fires which occurred in 1902 could be ascertained with accuracy, each would be found to differ in some respects from every other. When all ascertainable hazards have been classified and the causes for fire set forth so far as we can ascertain them, there yet remains about 16 per cent. of all fires for which the causes cannot be discovered. It is not strange that the causes of many fires escape detection. In the first place many incendiary fires, if fully successful, destroy all traces of origin. The same is true of fires caused by electric wires, defective flues, spontaneous combustion, sparks, and many other obscure or hidden causes. In fact, whenever fires acquire such proportions before their discovery as to prevent subsequent inspection of the points of origin, or when the amount of destruction is sufficient to obliterate any indication of the cause (in cases when the origin is not witnessed) that cause will usually remain a mystery. It will be readily seen that this very considerable percentage of fires of unknown origin renders anything like an exact estimate of the effect of the various hazards impossible, and one of the difficulties of making a scientific and accurate apportionment of rates is therefore at once obvious.

The foregoing must be considered to be merely a rough general index of the numerous heads included in the very important subject of physical hazards. As the profession of fire underwriting progresses and develops, the investigation and safeguarding of these hazards is more and more passing into the hands of experts, and, indeed, the subject is one sufficiently comprehensive and complex to afford a life work to students of the best technical training.

In this discussion we must now pass on to the consideration of the other grand division of hazards, usually called moral hazards. Moral hazards arise from the personal (including the financial) circumstances which affect risks. They are indefinite, incapable of analysis, separation, or estimation, yet they are of the greatest importance in fire insurance. Some authorities believe that more fires are attributable, directly or indirectly, to moral or personal causes than to physical, and, while any such attempt to estimate the results of moral hazards must be largely conjectural, it is quite certain that they are accountable for a very large percentage of the fire waste. Moral hazard is said to exist in regard to a particular risk whenever a benefit, real or supposed, direct or indirect, would ensue to any one, especially the owner, by reason of the destruction of the insured property; also, and nearly as important, whenever for any reason no one has a strong interest in its preservation.

In other words, not only the desire to destroy, but also the lack of a strong desire to preserve, creates moral hazard, so called, and it is hard to say which condition is the more dangerous. The prospect of a profit from fire or the absence of a financial incentive to preserve a risk make it impossible for an insurance company to rely upon the exercise of that due care and diligence for its protection which is essential, if business is to be transacted at a profit.

There are various ways in which moral hazards may arise which can be named and described. The possibility of their occurrence is patent to every one as soon as they are named, but to find out or know in advance that any of them exist in connection with a given risk is often beyond our powers. Hence losses due to such causes cannot be avoided. Any cause which seriously injures the value of a risk or diminishes its productivity is likely to create moral hazard, if the risk be well covered by insurance. Therefore insurance companies avoid risks where for any reason there is doubt as to value or productivity, — summer hotels which have not succeeded, buildings which are likely to be condemned, mines where paying quantities of ore have not been found, flour mills where the water power has failed, etc. All of these are pertinent examples. Any man would prefer money equal to the cost of such properties to the properties themselves. So, too, experimental properties, — temporary branch stores and new ventures of every description which have not demonstrated their earning power, must be handled with greatest caution. The mere fact that capital has been invested does not always indicate that value exists, and the rule of prudence and of indemnity as well, viz., "no profit to the assured from fire," points the way to the wise rejection of risks where this question of value is involved. Such risks are not only likely to be wilfully fired by a dishonest insured owner, but, even in the hands of honest men, are not likely to receive that assiduous care and watchfulness which men give to their successful enterprises. Indifference and carelessness differ only in degree from the actual desire for the destruction of property so far as the probability of its accomplishment is concerned.

In view of the considerations mentioned above, insurance companies look with disfavor upon those risks where the amount of insurance carried exceeds the value of the property and are inclined to fear a moral hazard in connection with them. It goes without saying that such a condition would be dangerous where the owner is dishonest, and where he is honest the fact that no personal loss can come to him from a fire is likely to induce that carelessness and lack of precaution which constitute one species of moral hazard.

Financial embarrassment and the pressing necessity for ready cash often create the most serious kind of moral hazard. A merchant with notes overdue or who sees failure ahead, or a farmer who cannot pay interest on his mortgage, is often in a position where the ready money obtainable from his insurance policies, even if not equal to the value of his property, would nevertheless help him tide over a pressing emergency.

Another situation which frequently involves moral

hazard is when property of any kind becomes involved in litigation or where there is dispute as to ownership. In such cases divisible cash is much more available than property which must be liquidated, and everybody interested might well be benefited by a fire which would simplify the settlement of a dispute. Moreover, the enmities aroused in the course of litigation are themselves a source of danger.

The foregoing remarks apply to moral hazards which arise in connection with the owners of property, but there are species of moral hazard which do not involve acts or neglect of the owner, but spring from the acts or desires of others. These chiefly arise from the ill-will of those to whom the property owner or his property is in some way objectionable, or who have been or are likely to be injured by the nature of the property itself or the kind of work carried on therein. Any building, such as a fertilizer factory, contagious hospital, dance hall or saloon, which interferes with the peace and enjoyment of a neighborhood or hurts the value of surrounding property, offers a constant temptation to those who may be injured by it. Its destruction would be a distinct benefit to them. Similarly, any property owner whose disposition and practices are such as to make numerous and bitter enemies is likely to feel the results of the hostility thus aroused through the burning of his property.

It will be seen from the preceding pages that the elements which go to make up hazards to which insured property is subject are numerous, complicated, and varied. We will now endeavor, briefly, to survey the methods used by insurance companies to measure these hazards, *i.e.*, to fix rates or prices.

Moral hazards may be dismissed at the outset; they cannot be measured or charged, for usually they cannot be ascertained till after a fire. Their existence, however, greatly increases the fire waste and is responsible for the greater part of what are known as basis rates, to be later described, *i.e.*, the irreducible foundation, incapable of analysis, upon which all systems and every schedule of rates are based.

In the early part of this course the principle was laid down that fire insurance is a tax, — a tax levied for a specific purpose, — to repair the fire waste. All agree that taxes are necessary evils, but there is anything but unanimity as to methods for imposing and collecting them. No other function of government causes such bitter debate, acrimonious dispute, public clamor, and individual discontent as this matter of taxes. There is perhaps no other obligation resting upon citizens that is so constantly and ingeniously evaded.

Now it is by means of a graduated scale of rates or charges that insurance companies collect the enormous sums required to recoup the provident among the losers by fire, and there is the same diversity of opinion, almost the same intensity of debate, among those who devise these rates as exists between protectionists, free-traders, and single tax theorists. Moreover, from the public which is taxed arises the same clamors of discontent, the same charges of inconsistency, the same endeavors to lessen the individual burden, which are to be noted in the process of collecting ordinary taxes, and too often, as in the case of such taxes, these complaints have some reasonable foundation. Also, as in the case of ordinary taxes, it frequently happens that the most clamorous objectors and the most enterprising in securing relief are to be found among that number who, if the truth were known, are taxed at too low a rate rather than too high. From the very nature of things these clamors and this discontent are inevitable, though as the process of making rates becomes more and more scientific and therefore more equitable, we may hope that both the discontent and the reason for it may be greatly lessened. That there is some ground for the discontent, all underwriters will agree, for the task of apportioning with absolute correctness and fairness the fire loss among the various classes of risks and to each individual of a class, according to the hazard of each, is an absolutely impossible one. Even to approximate fairness is enormously difficult. This is partly because of the absence of reliable data and the impossibility of obtaining them. There are, broadly speaking, no constant factors in the rating problem. In life insurance, rates to-day are frequently based upon a mortality table constructed from the experience of seventeen companies in 1838, and these tables are still found to be substantially reliable, but there are no unchanging mortality tables in fire insurance experience.

The proper basis for a table of rates, constructed on scientific principles, might well be thought to be the combined experience of a number of companies carrying similar classes of hazards during a period sufficiently long, and over a field sufficiently wide, to justify generalization. Such data have been hitherto unobtainable for various reasons, viz.; lack of uniform system of classification, lack of coöperation owing to the furiously competitive conditions under which the business is carried on, and finally and chiefly, the difficulty of properly classifying those most numerous losses which result from fires communicated from one building to another, known as exposure losses, and those other numerous losses, the causes of which are unknown. Even were the necessary data obtainable and could they be properly segregated, their value as bases for rate tables might be open to question. In the last analysis the basis for the rate on any risk must be largely determined by the hazards, *i.e.*, possible causes of fire, inherent in risks of the class to which it belongs. For example, the rate on a flour mill must be based upon the known dangers inherent to all flour mills, with such additions or subtractions as the peculiarities of the individual mill may make proper; but during the last forty years the process of milling flour has been revolutionized; instead of the old heavy millstones revolving slowly, we now have small steel rollers operated at a very high speed.

Formerly, owing to the imperfect apparatus used, flour mills were so filled with dust that the air in them was very like a dry fog, impenetrable to the eye in many parts of the mill. This dust was inflammable to the extent of being explosive. The best modern mills contain machinery which practically eliminates dust. It would be hardly too much to say that all processes, from the time the wheat enters the mill till the flour is packed in bags or barrels, differ from those in vogue forty years ago. Probably it would also be within the bounds of truth to say that each year brings a new change in some part of the machinery or process. What is true of flour milling is true of most other manufacturing industries. One of the causes of the success of American manufacturers has been their willingness to discard old machines long before they are worn out for new ones better designed for their work, while foreigners cling to their old machines, both from unwillingness to change and from motives of false economy. A flourishing rubbish heap is often a sign of real progress.

Again, the various processes and machines which have come into existence in the effort to make valuable the waste product of various industries have entirely altered the nature of many factories. For instance, in the case of packing houses, — in addition to the work for which such buildings were originally designed, viz. — the slaughtering, cutting, curing and keeping of beef, pork, ham, sausage, etc., there have been added the manufacture of fertilizer, of cooked, canned meats and vegetables, the manufacture of medicinal extracts, and other processes too numerous to mention, each of which brings a new hazard to be estimated and accounted for in the rate.

Furthermore, there are certain changes in methods of heating and lighting and of using power, involving the use of gasoline, electricity, etc., which have greatly altered and are constantly, to a large extent, altering the hazards of the buildings where they are used. Every new machine, every new process, makes a change in the sum total of hazards and therefore the carefully collected data showing the experience on any particular class of risks may at any time, by the invention of new machinery or by the discovery of a new process, chemical or otherwise, be rendered absolutely valueless, and the underwriter may be compelled to make new rates to cover hazards which have not endured long enough to furnish any experience whatsoever.

Difficult as the accumulation of proper data and the ascertainment of the fire cost of each class might be, and despite the necessity for frequent revision and reconstruction, owing to the changing nature of the factors involved, insurance companies might well undertake the task and endeavor to ascertain more closely the necessary basis of fire cost for each class of business as a foundation upon which to build a proper system of rates, were it not for the hostility of legislatures, and of the people as well, to any kind of combined or associated endeavor to fix or maintain such rates. Such hostility, we must hold, arises from a failure to comprehend the true nature of insurance, and the further failure to apprehend the principle that a properly constituted rate is chiefly made up of factors which are not in the control of underwriters and which cannot be correctly ascertained and formulated by them except through associated effort and combined experience. The attempt to cure inequalities and injustices which occur in the making of rates by legal process springs from the same mental astigmatism which induces men to attempt by law to prevent fluctuations in the purchasing value of silver or of any other commodity. Fair, equitable, and adequate rates are a prime necessity, not only for insurance companies, but for the insuring public, for in the long run the premium income must pay the losses. In other words, adequate security demands adequate rates. Impairment of security, an undoubted loss to policy-holders, must result from inadequate rates.

The foregoing remarks apply to the difficulties which attend the making of proper rates for various classes, but even greater difficulties are met when the attempt is made, as it must be made, to fix an appropriate rate for each individual of a class. In life insurance no such differentiation is attempted. Every man insured at age twenty-nine under the same kind of contract pays the same rate, and it is assumed that every insurable life at age twenty-nine has the same expectation. In fire insurance, however, no two risks are exactly alike and every detail of every risk must be examined and its contribution to the total hazards of the risk estimated. Moreover, in fire insurance many, if not most risks, undergo frequent changes and must therefore be re-examined and re-rated from time to time. It is this necessity for determining the proper charges and allowances for the numerous differences which characterize the construction, occupancy, location and exposure, methods of heating and lighting and extent of fire protection, not only for every class of risks, but also for every individual of each class, which constitutes the greatest practical difficulty to be overcome in making a fair assessment of the fire cost.

Without trying to investigate the history of the various methods of classification which have characterized the business, or to give any account of the differing processes for making rates which have been attempted from time to time by insurance companies, interesting and instructive as those subjects are, we will now proceed to take up a few of the systems and methods by which rates are to-day made.

Rates may be said to be made to-day by two processes: First, by what is known as the personal inspection or judgment rate system; and, second, by carefully prepared and more or less scientific schedules.

The judgment system of rating is rapidly giving way before the use of highly complex and specialized schedules. It is open to serious and obvious criticism, yet has in times past served a very useful purpose and is not without its good features. A few words will sufficiently describe it. By means of a more or less complete system of classification, companies ascertained in a rough way the average cost of many kinds of risks, and this information was put into the hands of their special agents or gradually absorbed by them in the course of their work. Formerly special agents did practically all of the work of making rates in company with local agents. When a town was to be rated, these average cost figures were used as basis or foundation rates. Usually towns were rated by committees of from two to five special agents who acted for all companies. No rule or regular method of procedure governs the making of rates under this system. The rates so made simply indicate the opinion or judgment of the rate-makers. Little attempt was made to analyze the factors which determined the judgment of the committee as to each risk. Nevertheless, since that judgment was usually the result of the experience and observation of many years spent in such work, the rates made were in many cases quite satisfactory and equitable to a moderate degree. No attempt was made to take account of minor differences, but all good features or defects of construction and exposure, and also all the hazards of occupancy and processes, were lumped together, and if, as a whole, to the mind of the raters, they were sufficient to appreciably differentiate the particular risk from the average risk of its class, a penalty was added to, or an allowance was made from, the average rate which experience had shown to be about adequate.

Such a system was fairly satisfactory during the years when buildings as a rule were in point of construction very much alike, but with the growth of improved methods of building, and with the increase and improvement of the apparatus for protection against fire, to say nothing of the great changes in business methods, such a system fails to discriminate properly between risks of the same class which may differ widely in many important respects. Moreover, the personality of the raters under the old system was a highly important factor — to such an extent, in fact, that different committees might produce quite different results when rating identical risks. The system of schedule rating which attempts to take into account the various features of construction, exposure, internal hazards, and protection against fire, which are peculiar to each risk, obviates these objections, though itself, as will be shortly seen, open to criticism of another nature.

As already hinted, no perfect system of apportionment of the fire tax can be devised. On the whole, the system by schedules applicable to each class gives promise of development into a means of fixing rates which will be much more equitable and satisfactory than any other method which has yet been followed, and there is reason for hope, with more perfect statistics and a better appreciation of the relative potentialities of the different hazards, that the various schedules will ultimately develop until they come to be universally recognized by the public, as well as insurance officials, as satisfactorily solving, so far as it may be solved, the complex problem involved in making rates.

In the early days of insurance history two rates only were known, — one for buildings of brick construction, another for frame, and these rates applied regardless of occupancy. Gradually, as the hazards of the different kinds of business came to be appreciated, a system of classification was begun which has been growing and enlarging until to-day, nor has its growth or enlargement by any means reached its limit. At the present time many companies divide their risks into over a hundred classes and further sub-divide each class according to construction, *i.e.*, whether brick or frame, and according to the class of the town or city, viz., whether protected or unprotected, in which the particular risk may be located. From their experience with these classes approximations are made by companies of the actual average cost of insuring each class, but in order to fix the prices for the individuals of a class there is required a mass of diagrams, statistics, and other data, showing the particular features of each risk, which are almost infinite in number. This will be apparent from the statement that these data include more or less complete descriptions of practically all buildings in the central portions of all cities, towns, and villages of any size in the United States.

Companies as a whole are estimated to expend over a million of dollars per annum for rating purposes. Single companies expend as much as $20,000 per annum for maps alone.

The prime requisite for a system of rates is that it shall so far as possible be uniformly equitable; that is, it must compel each class of risk and each individual of the class to pay its proper proportion of the fire tax. To approximate such a result, however, not only are the data before mentioned necessary, but the amount of insurance to be carried on each risk must be known. At least nine-tenths — Mr. Dean says nineteen-twentieths — of all losses are partial. The great majority are small as compared with the value of property insured. It is evident that, in case of a partial loss destroying less than one-half the value of an insured property, a man who carries insurance to, say, 50 per cent. of the value of his property, secures the same amount of indemnity as the man who carries insurance amounting to 80 per cent., though the latter has paid a much heavier tax. It follows that where, as is usually the case, there is a fire department and water works, the man who carries insurance amounting to 80 per cent. of the value of his property is entitled to a lower rate than the one who carries insurance amounting to but 50 per cent. of that value. For this reason all properly devised schedules or tariffs for making rates are based upon the use of a co-insurance clause, usually the 80 per cent. co-insurance clause, which compels insurance equal to 80 per cent. of the value to be carried, and penalties in the shape of higher rates are imposed where a lower percentage of insurance is carried. No other means has ever been devised, or is likely to be devised, which so fairly and automatically apportions the insurance tax according to the value of property, just as ordinary taxes on real estate and personal property are supposed to be apportioned. One way of stating the principle involved is to say that the expectation of salvage is one of the factors involved in making rates.

The schedule system, as its name implies, makes rates by applying to classes of risks and to individual risks certain predetermined charges and credits based upon the various factors of construction, occupancy, exposure, and protection against fire. In practice, in the several states or districts of the country, many different schedules for all classes of risks are used, though more than one attempt has been made to evolve a system of rating which might be everywhere applicable. We shall not be able even to mention many of these numerous systems, nor is it necessary, since for the most part they differ in detail rather than in principle.

In the case of such simple classes as dwellings, schools, and churches, where the hazards are practically the same for each individual, the class rate is applied to every risk, differences being made only as between brick and frame and those under or beyond the protection of an efficient fire department.

The schedules used in rating the different manufacturing classes, such as wood-workers, packing houses, flour mills, etc. (usually called special hazards), are made up substantially according to the following general plan:

First. The standard or ideal building of the class in question is described. This building is standard, not only in arrangement and construction, but often as to its equipment for extinguishing fire. A basis rate is then assumed for a risk equaling the standard. This basis rate, while arbitrarily fixed, is nevertheless the expression of the judgment of expert raters as to irreducible foundation of hazard incapable of analysis and made up of the numerous intangible and incalculable things (including moral hazard and an allowance for unknown causes), which is thought to be inseparable from any risk of the particular class under consideration, no matter how perfect its structure and arrangement may be.

The basis rate having been determined, the various defects in construction, dangerous or improper factors of arrangement, and deficiencies in the nature and extent of the apparatus for fire protection are listed with a table of, usually fixed, charges for each; usually, too, there are some credits mentioned for extraordinary features of equipment or construction too infrequent to be conveniently included in the description of the standard. Provision is also made in such a schedule for a further credit or charge for the presence or absence of the 80 per cent. co-insurance clause, or some other percentage co-insurance clause, in the contracts. When a flour mill, for example, is to be rated, the assumed basis rate for flour mills is used as a starting point, and to it are added the various deficiency charges which may be found on inspection to pertain to the particular mill to be rated. From the rate thus obtained a deduction is made for any credits to which the mill is entitled. When the rate thus made up is ascertained, the price to be charged is fixed by the allowance or charge for the use of the co-insurance clause above referred to.

Many of these schedules are so minute and intricate as to require the services of an expert rater for their application, and therefore, and also for the sake of economy and uniformity, these schedules are applied to special hazards by men skilled in their use acting for associations of companies in the various districts. The factor of exposure (sometimes of great importance) may be covered by more or less elaborate charges; or more frequently in the case of special hazards, together with other additional objectionable features, is left to the judgment of the rater. This is because special hazards, as a rule, are more dangerous to their surroundings than endangered by them.

Moreover, they are usually more or less isolated as to location, hence their chief hazards are internal. While, on account of the numerous and often hazardous processes involved and because inflammable material is frequently handled, these risks might be supposed to present unusual difficulties to the rater, they are on the contrary easier to rate with a reasonable degree of satisfaction, both to the companies and the owners, than the apparently more simple mercantile risks, which so far exceed them in number and value. The different processes and dangerous materials are, in the case of special hazards, conspicuous, and their hazards comparatively obvious, hence their appraisal or estimate may be the more easily made. In these schedules many of the more serious defects are often penalized by very severe charges in order to compel property owners to remedy them; indeed, one of the chief merits of the schedule system of rating as a whole is that it encourages safe methods of construction, arrangement and protection, and recognizes them in the rates.

Another and the chief argument usually advanced in favor of schedule rating is that, since it lists the various defects of each risk and the charges made for the same, property owners may know why the price which they are compelled to pay for insurance differs from that which may be paid by their neighbors, and hence may realize that they are not suffering from the effects of arbitrary discrimination or of personal judgment of the rater, since it is evident that the rate on their own property is governed entirely by its own faults or merits.

In some states or districts as many as thirty different schedules for different classes of risks are in use.

The rating of mercantile property, which comprises by far the most important class, both as to the number of risks and value, with which insurance companies have to deal, is the most difficult technical task which confronts the underwriter.

There are many schedules in use for this purpose in

various parts of the country, most of which, however, have many points of resemblance. The following may be taken as a description of the average schedule of this kind used in towns and cities of moderate size — those used in the largest cities are more elaborate.

In most states and districts the cities, towns and villages are divided into classes — commonly from four to six in number — according to the amount of protection afforded by the water works and fire department of each. Two basis rates — one each for brick and frame mercantile buildings — are then adopted for each class of towns. The basis rate is usually in the case of brick buildings predicated upon an assumed type of building adopted for that purpose and described in detail in the schedule. In order to determine the rate on any one building or its contents the proper basis rate is taken as a foundation, and to it are added the fixed additional charges made necessary by its structural defects, which are usually listed with more or less minuteness in the schedule, a stated charge being made for each defect. To the rate of the building thus determined additions are made for the exposure hazards from adjacent risks according to the table or rule provided in the schedule. From the figure thus obtained a deduction is made on account of credits allowed for those features of construction, or of individual fire protection, which may be permitted by the schedule. The resultant rate is called the unoccupied building rate. It is then further increased by a charge made on account of the nature of the occupancy, such, for instance, as a drug store or a dry goods store, and thus becomes the final building rate.

The rate on the contents is then made, frequently by an addition to the building rate, named in the schedule itself as applying to the particular kind of contents under consideration; but more often all kinds of contents are classified roughly into from two to four or five classes, and an additional charge, over and above the building rate, to be applied to the contents, is provided for each class, and is used in every case where contents which may be embraced in that class are found.

The foregoing applies to the rating of brick mercantile buildings and their contents. Rates on frame mercantile buildings are usually made by a more simple process.

In the first place, all frame mercantile buildings are esteemed to be substantially alike for the purpose of insurance, the differences in point of construction which are recognized being confined to metal roofs and brick or iron coverings for side walls. A basis rate is agreed upon for frame buildings in each of the various classes of towns into which a district may be divided, and charges are made for occupancy and exposures. These charges, so far as occupancy is concerned, are usually very few in number. Where frame buildings are concerned the rate on contents is seldom, if ever, higher than the rate on the building itself, and very often less than the building rate, because a high rate on such a building is usually due to a heavy exposure hazard, which, so far as the contents are concerned, may be overcome by their hasty removal when the danger of fire is imminent.

The treatment of exposures in these numerous schedules shows great variety of practice, especially as regards brick buildings. In fact, for the most part this important feature in the rating of mercantile buildings and contents has had very inadequate treatment. When brick buildings are exposed by other risks, one method, very frequently used, is to make a fixed charge for unprotected openings in side walls without regard to the character of the exposure. Another is to add to the rate of the exposed risk, where there are unprotected openings, some percentage of the rate of the exposing risk, according to its distance from the risk to be rated.

Many tariffs, however, leave the question of exposure charges to the judgment of the rater, for it is difficult, especially in the case of brick buildings, to provide a satisfactory and workable rule for such charges in a schedule designed to be comparatively simple. For frame buildings there are usually definite rules in the shape of a heavy fixed additional charge over and above the basis rate for each frame building within a given distance — usually 20 feet — of the building to be rated. Thus, if a frame building unexposed carries a basis rate of $1\frac{1}{2}$ per cent., $\frac{75}{100}$ of 1 per cent. will be added for every frame building exposing it within 20 feet, and also for every frame building which goes to make up a continuous row of wooden buildings up to some arbitrary limit, such as 8 per cent., which is assumed to cover the most dangerous hazard which can be created by a combination of frame mercantile buildings. It will, of course, be understood that the basis rates, as well as the increments of charge made for exposures, vary in the schedules used in different parts of the country.

As hinted before, two attempts have been made to evolve systems or schedules for rating mercantile property which might be universally used. The first of these schedules was prepared by a committee of eminent underwriters under the chairmanship of Mr. F. C. Moore, then president of one of the largest American insurance companies, and is called the "Universal Mercantile Schedule." It, or some modification of it, is used in many of the large cities of the country to-day, including New York, Cleveland, Denver and many others, and it is, so far as results yet obtained are concerned, the most important of any of the tariffs which have ever been issued. It is also, of all rating schedules, the one which has been most carefully and minutely elaborated and adjusted to meet the almost infinitely varied combinations of the factors of construction, occupancy and protection which are to be found in the mercantile buildings of a large city.

This schedule was a great advance beyond anything before known in the history of scientific rating and has exercised a very important and growing influence upon the framers of other schedules subsequently made, many of which are but imperfect adaptations of the Universal Mercantile Schedule. It is an extremely complicated and intricate schedule and cannot, therefore, be described or discussed in detail in the limits of this paper. A few extracts from the writings of Mr. Moore in regard to it will be given, which, in connection with what has already been stated in regard to schedule rating, will enable some idea of its purpose and scope to be formed: (It is suggested in this connection that the student consult Mr. Moore's book "Fire Insurance and How to Build.")

"The mere fact that there are more than a hundred features of construction in a single building which should enter into the consideration of its rate, irrespective of nearly forty features of its city or environment, nearly forty more different features of fire appliances, to say nothing of more than a thousand possible hazards of occupancy; and the further fact that no individual knowledge is equal to the task of putting a price upon so many items, nor any individual memory capable of remembering them, proves, without further demonstration, the necessity not only of conference to secure combined knowledge for fixing prices, but, also a printed record or schedule, to prevent omissions or mistakes."

"In 1891 a committee of four underwriters was appointed to prepare a schedule for rating mercantile risks which should be universal in its application throughout the country. Early in their deliberations they reached the conclusion that such a schedule should be formulated upon the following lines, and that it should recognize:

"*First.* A key-rate — as to which various cities and towns differ.

"*Second.* Charges for variations from standards of construction — which ought to be the same everywhere.

"*Third.* Charges for hazards of occupancy — which ought to be the same everywhere.

"*Fourth.* Charges for insuring contents according to

their susceptibility to damage — which ought to be the same everywhere.

"*Fifth.* The variation of these charges, according to the construction of the building. Clearly the same amount should not be added, even for the same stock, to two different buildings where one is an exceptionally good building and the other an exceptionally poor one; there should be more difference between the building and stock rate in the one case than in the other.

"*Sixth.* The treatment of fire extinguishing facilities, proximity to hydrants, etc., for the particular risk rated, according to circumstances; it being clear that if the risk is within reach of hydrants, steam engines, etc., and on an eight-inch or larger water main, it should rate differently from another of like kind, even in the same town, if the other risk be not so fortunately located."

"So in other items or features of the schedule, the committee found it necessary to go into every detail of hazard, leaving as little as possible to the judgment of a rating expert, so as not only to save his time and thought at every stage of the rating process, but to prevent, also, those inconsistencies of rating in risks of one and the same hazard, resulting from fluctuations of judgment, which so often produce dissatisfaction on the part of owners and result in appeals for legislative interference with rating organizations."

"*First.* A standard city was conceived and described. It involved level and wide streets, gravity water works, adequate pipe service and other features fully explained.

"*Second.* A standard building was described, which may be regarded as a model of ordinary construction, not fire-proof.

"*Third.* A key-rate.

"The basis rate or starting point for rating a standard building in a standard city was fixed at 25 cents, after careful consideration of the experience tables of the companies."

Since buildings of this class are to be found rarely, this was of course pure assumption.

"From this starting point or basis rate of 25 cents, and to obtain the key-rate of any city, or that figure at which a standard building in the city should be rated, additions were made according to the deficiencies of the city as to water works, fire department, building laws, inaccessible or narrow streets, etc., etc. This key-rate, so determined, is thereafter used to obtain the rate of any building in the city to be rated by adding to it charges for its deficiencies from the specification of a standard building."

For the purpose of rating contents of buildings and in order to make occupancy charges, no fewer than 1287 varieties of contents are listed, each with its appropriate fixed charge to be added to the building rate; and also a different charge to apply to the contents themselves, over and above the final building rate. Moreover, a separate application for credits for fire protection is provided for the contents as compared with the building.

"No schedule should be framed upon a basis which does not recognize a certain named percentage of insurance to value."

"The universal schedule, however, does not enforce or require any particular amount of insurance, but simply adjusts itself (by reductions from ascertained rate according to stipulated account of co-insurance) to whatever amount the property owner elects to carry."

The chief objection to this, or in fact to any system of schedule rating, is the necessity for the constant use of assumptions, not only in determining the basis rates, but in making the charges, for each defect of the construction, or for occupancy, which go to make up the final rate.

A great deal of time and a vast amount of comparative research has been expended in the endeavor properly to appraise the dangers incident to all the various features of construction, protection, occupancy and exposure, yet it is manifestly impossible from any obtainable record of experience to assert that a retail drug store, for instance, will make proper an addition of exactly 10 cents to the building or an addition of exactly 50 cents to the rate on contents over and above the building rate in all cases.

A tariff has been devised by Mr. A. F. Dean, of Chicago, called by him a "Mercantile Tariff and Exposure Formula for the Measurement of Fire Hazards," which differs radically in many respects from the "Universal Mercantile Schedule," and which has come into very general use in the western states. This tariff is intended to render some of the defects just mentioned less important, and is, moreover, founded on a different conception of the problem of rating. Instead of endeavoring to establish a basis rate for a standard risk in a standard city, Mr. Dean's tariff divides cities into six classes, beginning with villages which have no protection whatever and which are known as towns of the sixth class. This is a very suitable basis for such a classification since its definition is simple, its existence real and unchanging; while on the contrary our ideas of a standard city are likely to change from time to time. From this as a starting point towns are graded according to their protection up to the first class, which includes all cities having protection in the way of water works and fire department of exceptional completeness and efficiency, and better than those classified under sections 2 to 6 inclusive. Moreover, for the purpose of rating, provision is made for the adoption, as a starting point, of a one-story, brick building of ordinary construction located in a town of the sixth class. This kind of building is fully described in the tariff. Such buildings are common in towns of that class. However, this tariff does not attempt to name the basis rates. They are supposed to be adopted or selected in each state or district by raters who have had experience therein. This does away with the necessity for making ideal standards and estimating basis rates therefor. Concerning this matter of adopting basis rates, Mr. Dean holds that the experience of underwriters enables them to estimate more readily a proper rate for an ordinary building, such as may be found in great numbers, than for an ideal standard, which represents a class with which insurance companies have had very little if any experience. Nothing more simple could be thought of as affording a starting point or basis rate than the one-story building selected by Mr. Dean; nor could any risk be found for which experienced underwriters could more readily or intelligently name a proper rate.

This basis rate having been decided upon, additions or deductions are made for good or bad features of construction, occupancy, protection or exposure, but since the average building is taken as a starting point these charges and credits will be fewer in number than where a standard building is taken as the foundation, and charges made for the numerous deficiencies which every ordinary building has. Moreover, instead of making these charges and credits by means of arbitrarily fixed amounts, the additions and subtractions are made by the percentage method. For example, in the "Universal Mercantile Schedule," ten cents is added to the rate of a building having a retail drug store therein, whereas in Mr. Dean's tariff a percentage of the previously ascertained building rate is added for this occupancy, and a similar method is used in making charges and credits for various features of construction. The system employed for estimating the proper percentage additions to the rate on account of occupancy is especially ingenious and logical — two additions are made for most occupancies, one for the causative hazard of the contents, *i.e.*, the danger which their presence begets, the other for the extent to which the contents are likely to aid the spread or intensity of a fire.

Similarly, the percentage plan is followed for establishing basis rates for one-story brick buildings in towns of the other classes; that is, the basis rate for a town of the third or fourth class would be ascertained by deducting a certain percentage from the basis rate selected for a similar risk in a town of the sixth class.

The chief object in adopting the percentage system for variations in the factors affecting rates is that it preserves the relativity of charges and credits which are made in rating. It is manifest that where a basis rate, for example, is 40 cents, an additional charge of 10 cents for occupancy on account of a drug store is much more severe than where the basis rate is, say, 80 cents. With the charge for a drug store occupancy of 10 per cent. on the basis rate, however, this inequality would be obviated. Again, the charge of 12 cents for open, unprotected elevators in a building of moderate area and, say, three stories in height, and which, in consequence of these features, enjoys a low rate, is relatively very much heavier than the same charge in the case of a large six or seven-story building of great area which bears a high rate. In the latter case 12 cents would probably be about one-tenth of the total building rate, while in the smaller building it would be at least 20 per cent. Moreover, an open elevator in a building of unusual height or area is a much more serious defect, and is likely to be responsible for much greater destruction of property than a similar elevator located in a small building of moderate height. The same reasoning might be applied to the credits or deductions made for favorable features. In support of his views on this subject Mr. Dean says:

"If, under the law of averages, a thousand buildings of given construction, occupancy and protection will show a given ratio of loss to value during a given period, under the same law a thousand flues, hatchways, skylights, well-holes, wooden ceilings, or other parts of the building, of given construction, will each contribute its unvarying quota of this ratio, hence the several parts stand in a position of unchanging relativity, not only to the whole but each to the others. Fire hazard is, by nature, a network of relativity. In constructing a basis schedule we necessarily select certain features of hazard as separable and attach to each of these a charge, while to the residue consisting of unanalyzable parts we attach a lump charge and call it a basis rate. There is no intrinsic difference between the charge we call a basis rate and the other charges excepting that it includes all things too obscure, indefinite or unimportant to schedule. If under the law of averages the relativity between the whole and its parts does not change, and the relativity among the several parts themselves is constant, it follows that each charge bears an unvarying relation to the basis rate, or, conversely, the basis rate a constant relation to the other charges. This being the case, it is false logic to treat the basis rate or any of the charges as a dissociated element of hazard, for every change in basis rate or charge involves a disturbance of their mutual relativity. The real question in establishing every charge is, what ratio of the total loss will this feature of hazard under the law of average probably contribute? When this ratio has been established by judgment and experience, it should take its place in every schedule as a fixed ratio bearing a constant relation to the whole and its several parts."

Under this tariff the rates on the contents of brick buildings are established through a differential added to the occupied building rate. This differential is based upon the damageability of the contents by water, smoke, heat, breakage, etc., as the result of fire, and represents the relative value of fire department protection to contents as compared with its value to the building itself. The tariff contains a table of differentials referring to about four hundred different kinds of contents, and further graded to correspond with ten different sets of basis rates, each set including a basis rate for a town of every class. These differentials are also arrived at by the percentage method, by averaging the differentials contained in many previous tariffs made for unprotected towns, and then subjecting these differentials to an ingenious scale of percentage comparisons with the building as affected by the various grades of fire protection, according to the theory that the greater the damageability of the contents the less valuable to them — as compared with the building — is the protection against fire afforded by water works and fire departments.

A separate schedule based upon similar principles is devised for frame buildings, by which rates for frame buildings and their contents in a city or town of any class may be readily ascertained when once a basis rate has been adopted for an ordinary shingle-roof, frame building in a sixth class town. One important difference between the brick and frame schedules to be noticed is, that the differential for contents in the case of exposed frame buildings depends upon their removability instead of their damageability, and a table of contents graded according to their removability is provided.

The matter of exposure charges and hazards is treated in a separate department of the tariff called the exposure formulae. These formulae enable the rater to make additions to the rates of both brick and frame buildings and their contents on account of exposure hazards by means of a highly ingenious exposure table, graduated with reference to the construction of buildings, the distances between risks which affect each other, the amount of fire department protection, and the hazards of the exposing risks. This table is also made up on the percentage system, each risk radiating a percentage of its own rate or absorbing a percentage of the rate of the adjoining risks. The theoretical considerations upon which this table and its applications are based are given below in Mr. Dean's own language:

"External exposures are classified under three heads:

"*a*. Radiated exposure, consisting of the proportion of its own hazard a risk radiates toward exposed risks.

"*b*. Absorbed exposure, consisting of the proportion of radiated hazard absorbed by an exposed risk.

"*c.* Transmitted exposure, or the proportion of the hazard a risk absorbs from one side, that is transmitted by it to a risk on the other side.

"Under the above classification, it is proper to bear in mind:

"*First.* That every exposing risk radiates some ratio of its own hazard towards exposed risks.

"*Second.* That every exposed risk absorbs some ratio of this radiated exposure.

"*Third.* That every risk transmits some ratio of the hazard it absorbs.

"*Fourth.* That radiated, absorbed, and transmitted exposure are all modified by structure, clear space and fire department protection.

"In view of the numerous ratios and *ratios of ratios* found in the problem of measuring exposures, the necessity for some fixed standard of comparison is clear, because a standard is the first essential in all measurement — it is equally clear that as ratios are to be measured the standard must be a ratio and not a quantity. Again, if we view exposure from the standpoint of cause and effect, it is evident that radiated exposure is to be taken as cause; hence it is necessary to select some ratio of the hazard of the exposing risk as a standard.

"In selecting any standard of measurement, it is proper to choose that which is most generally available and most free from change. These qualities are found in the greatest degree, perhaps, in the exposure of frame buildings by frame buildings. In existing tariffs, there is substantial agreement in granting that a frame building transmits all the exposure radiated towards it by other contiguous frames, and while there is a considerable diversity in the ratio of radiated exposure in the several tariffs, they approach nearer to uniformity in this ratio than in any other feature of exposure. An examination of different state tariffs shows a range of exposure charge in unprotected frame rows from about one-third to one-half the hazards of the exposing risk. The average of all tariffs approximates closely to 40 per cent., while under the different grades of protection this ratio decreases in proportion to the protection.

"It can hardly be disputed that, under like protection, like buildings radiate like ratios of their own hazard, and if this be true the standard of radiated exposure under any given grade of municipal protection should be the same everywhere; hence all tariffs should agree in the adoption of a common standard."

Whatever may be thought of the brick and frame schedules, and though founded upon scientific principles and worked up according to scientific methods they will, undoubtedly, be criticised as to details, it is the writer's belief that the exposure formulae, at least, will come to be recognized as exhibiting the most satisfactory, logical and adequate treatment known up to this time, of this highly complex and hitherto maltreated department of the science or business of making rates for mercantile risks. A detailed explanation of them is impossible within the limits of this paper, which, indeed, must be considered as an introduction to the study of rating systems rather than an exposition of their methods and practice. Moreover, some little study is required in order to understand the use, or to appreciate the great value of these exposure formulae. Nor would it be possible for any one without large experience to realize the difficulties which must be overcome in any successful attempt to construct a logical and workable scheme for the proper measurement and distribution of exposure hazards. Mr. Dean's tariff formulae as now published are intended for use in towns and cities of ordinary size and would require additional elaboration for use in the largest cities. There is no reason why tariffs or schedules based upon the same principles should not be made for all kinds or classes of risks, manufacturing as well as mercantile.

CHAPTER VI

FIRE-RATING [1]

FIRE-RATING, as a science, must consist of an accurately verified body of knowledge, and an activity based upon this body of organized knowledge, which has for its end the measurement of fire hazard in conformity with the principles established by the science itself.

"A science teaches us to know, an art to do. Science gives us principles, while an art gives us rules. In art, truth is a means to an end. In science, it is an end itself. Historically, art has often preceded science." [2]

The activity of measuring fire hazard based upon this organized body of knowledge might be called an art, and the real question is, whether this activity can be intelligently guided by a basic science consisting of an organized body of knowledge of the phenomena of fire destruction.

There is an interesting contrast and resemblance between the evolution of fire-rating and the evolution of gunnery. Gunnery has for its end the concentration of destruction, while fire-rating has for its end the dispersion of destruction. Gunnery seeks to send destruction with the greatest possible certainty to a given spot. Fire-rating seeks to apply relief for destruction by fire with the greatest possible accuracy through the equitable distribution of assessed loss over areas of time and space. Gun-

[1] By A. F. Dean, Assistant Manager, Western Department, Springfield Fire and Marine Insurance Company. Reprinted from pages 47–60, 73–80, of "Fire Rating as a Science;" J. M. Murphy. Chicago, 1901.

[2] Sphere of Science, Hoffman.

nery started from the established fact that gunpowder is explosive; fire-rating, from the fact that fire is destructive. From its established fact, gunnery provisionally assumed that gunpowder, exploded in a tube open at one end, would eject a missile; next, that by pointing the tube in a given direction it would send the missile in that direction; next, that the projectile would go farther with a larger charge of powder and the elevation of the open end of the tube; next, that it would go farther if round than if of irregular shape, and still farther if conical rather than spherical.

All these assumptions were qualitative, and the further progress of gunnery as a science demanded quantitative prevision, in order to send the projectile as nearly as possible to any given spot within the widest range. It was found that by rifling the gun to impart a circular motion to the projectile it would go straighter, but this circular motion was found to develop a lateral tendency, known as windage. The possibility of quantitative reasoning started with the invention of graded sights to measure the exact degree of elevation and deviation in the gun necessary to correct windage and gravitation. Through the investigation of explosives and initial velocity, the gradual evolution of a variety of collateral apparatus followed, until it has become possible to send a projectile to any desired point within a radius of fifteen or twenty miles with marvelous accuracy; and out of the original fact that gunpowder is explosive many sciences, or more properly arts, have been evolved. Among these we find the construction of guns, projectiles, range-finders, sighting apparatus, explosives, fortifications, and armored protection. In addition to these allied activities, applied mathematics has been pressed into service in the investigation of force and resistance, and in determining the relations between initial velocity and the parabola of two directions, caused by windage, gravitation, etc.

During the slow evolution of gunnery and its collateral

sciences, it was assumed that a hollow projectile, filled with explosive material, could be made to explode either within a given time or in contact with its target, and that the explosion of the projectile would create greater destruction than a solid projectile.

Quantitative prevision paused, however, with this secondary explosion of the shell, and it remains for the future to determine the possibility of ascertaining how many sub-projectiles will be created by this explosion, and in what direction and how far each fragment will go.

So, in the problem of fire-rating, starting from the known fact that fire is destructive, we seek to disperse the disaster through assessments on specific property, in proportion to its specific liability to destruction, under the general law of average.

By keeping a record for a year we can determine at the end of the year the ratio between receipts and disbursements necessary to make good the destruction, and through a comparison of the total amount insured with the total premiums received we are able to determine the average rate for a given period on all property. By similar comparisons we are able to determine the ratios of loss and expense. Experience has further shown that certain species of property have so many points of resemblance that they can be grouped in classes, and that the record of any of these classes, for any given period, will show similar ratios for each class. So far we are able to establish exact measurement, from which we are enabled to determine intelligently our selling price for indemnity as a whole, or for any class of which we have kept a separate record. With equal precision we can, by classifying the different grades of fire department protection, or construction of buildings, determine the average for each standard of protection for each character of building; or by keeping a record of any or all of these features we can determine the averages for one or all in any given state.

So far our reasoning has potentially the accuracy of mathematics. We now reach a secondary degree of accuracy in the specific features of each risk, as found in its methods of lighting, heating, occupancy, structural features, private devices for preventing fires, and its exposures from other buildings. It is clearly within the possibilities of statistical science to determine the relative degrees of hazard between lighting a building by candles, coal oil, gas, or electricity, or heating it by open fire-places, stoves, hot air, or steam furnaces, and it would be equally possible to determine the same relations with all the more important features of structure, occupancy, and exposure, provided it were possible to locate in every case the cause of the fire, but it would require a vast and expensive system of statistics based upon data impossible to obtain, for the reason that the origin of fires is very often unknown. This difficulty has been met by utilizing a system of analysis of the individual risk, through which we estimate by charges and credits the relative hazard of its parts, as far as analyzable. In adopting this plan of avoiding a tremendous expansion of statistics for a comparatively unimportant end, fire insurance has followed the usages of the industrial world and all governments in determining value relations by estimate; hence, as an expedient, it is identical with the expedient adopted from time immemorial by governments and peoples for similar conditions. In thus adopting the economic law of common sense instead of searching for obscure and innumerable laws of causation in the effort to obtain more exact relations among unimportant factors, reasonable equity is obtained so long as personal favoritism is abolished, and every man accorded the same charge or credit for the same item of hazard.

We now reach a third phase of fire-rating, in the nameless, numberless, and often remote causes of fire which are not only unanalyzable, but often undiscoverable.

In this stage, analysis and prevision are as uncertain

as in the post-explosion stage of gunnery, in which it is impossible to foretell the specific consequences which will result from the bursting of a shell. In this remote region which lies outside the borderland of inductive observation, however, fire underwriting experience has brought forth from the crucible of conference and competition some nuggets of pure metal, by establishing fixed usages which appeal to common intelligence. Mercantile occupancies have been analyzed, classed, graded, and valued; the permanent features of industrial processes sorted, estimated, and labeled with their relative hazard value, and the residuum of irreducible slag left in the crucible has been estimated as a whole for each class of property under the name of "basis rate." This basis rate, arbitrarily assumed as the residuum of hazard, after it has been purged of all measurable factors, is the nucleus on which each rate estimate is built, and when so built we have a synthesis of artificial relations between the analyzed and unanalyzed factors of hazard as a sort of working hypothesis. By a singular reversal of ordinary reasoning methods, these artificial relations, established by reasoning purely hypothetical, constitute the basis of the ratios on which fire insurance must establish its sequential relations.

In ordinary reasoning, the individual rate should come last instead of first, but necessity has compelled a reverse process of reasoning — a good deal like it would be in gunnery if we should begin with the pieces of an exploded shell, and calculate the trajectory of each irregular fragment back to the place it occupied in the shell before explosion, then figure the gravity, windage, elevation, initial velocity, and all that sort of thing necessary to replace the shell intact in the gun whence it started. This perplexing reversal is, however, a logical necessity imposed upon fire insurance by its relations with policyholders, and the fact does not necessarily render the solution of its problem less accurate on that account. It is this blindfolded orientation that creates most of the prevailing skepticism as to the possibility of scientific rating. This confusing necessity of backing into the shafts before we start, originates from the following sequence of usage.

The ratios of loss and expense are found by comparing amounts disbursed with aggregate premiums; but this aggregate is composed of a large number of premiums from individual risks, and a condition precedent to the collection of these premiums is that there must be a relation established between each individual hazard and its premiums, satisfactory to the buyer of indemnity. This makes the first act that sets the wheels in motion an estimate of the individual premium; for it is the aggregate of these individual premiums which constitutes the standard that enables us to sight back and determine the relative accuracy of the original assumptions, and the determination of this relative accuracy enables us to tell not only whether these assumptions were too high or too low, but how much too high or low — in other words, to establish the quantitative reasoning through which we can accurately estimate hazard in dollars and cents. In this reciprocal process, established rates must be made through an endless cycle of reasoning in which it is as immaterial which comes first as it is in the cycle of causation between the chicken which lays the egg and the egg which hatches the chicken. The essential point is that a series of provisional assumptions through an unending process of readjustment tend to become more and more exact, provided we are faithful to the assumptions.

In its present status, fire-rating as a science might be compared with the science of gunnery, as it would be if reasoning had simply amused itself with wagering on the probable trajectories of the fragments of exploding shells. We gather up the *disjecta membra* of provisionally assumed charges and credits, and patch them onto a provisionally assumed nucleus, known as a basis rate, and then call this thing of provisionally assumed shreds and patches an individual rate. When a local tariff of these assumptions has been formulated, it is turned out to the mercy of the elements. Contention within and without is allowed to work its own sweet will in changing artificial relations of coexistence into relations of sequence, and the structure of artificial relations we have erected with so much travail begins to disintegrate almost before the paint is dry. This local tariff of individual rate estimates, constructed with more or less regard to a basis tariff of hypothetical assumptions, is, up to date, the furthest reach of fire-rating as an activity. It would be a work of supererogation to point out the lamentable results of the arrested development which has checked further growth at the primary stage of reasoning, where we simply recognize coexistent relations in hazard, which we arbitrarily alter, apparently without the slightest conception that in so doing we are essaying the impossible task of changing space into time. Viewed as coexistent relations only, there is no lack of inconsistency in our rates, but by constant tinkering with these relations in the attempt to make them sequential we violate a fundamental law of all science. We construct a basis schedule of each state, but cannot show that it bears any logical relation to the schedules of other states. We say that each individual rate is the sum of a basis rate combined with certain charges and credits, but cannot show whether this basis rate is relatively correct when compared with others, nor can we show that the charges and credits which permeate many classes are consistently imposed upon each class.

This naive disregard of relations crops out not only in the comparison of every existing basis tariff with other tariffs, but in the comparison of parts of the same tariff with other parts; selecting for example the following:

Illinois State Board Minimum Tariff	1894
Minnesota and Dakota	1895
Southeastern Tariff Association	1895
Indiana Mercantile Schedule	1893

Missouri, Kansas and Nebraska Minimum Tariff.... 1886
Missouri Minimum Tariff 1894
Illinois Mercantile Schedule...................... 1895
Western Mutual Underwriters' Association Minimum Tariff 1882
New England Insurance Exchange Schedule 1894
Universal Mercantile Schedule 1896

In the following table [1] the upper figures show the number of times the same charge appears in all the above tariffs, and the lower figures show the different charges made for the same thing:

Awnings, wood on one-story building, $\frac{4}{5}$, $\frac{4}{10}$, $\frac{1}{20}$.
Boiler in frame boiler-house, $\frac{17}{25}$, $\frac{3}{30}$, $\frac{10}{35}$, $\frac{56}{50}$, $\frac{1}{60}$, $\frac{1}{65}$, $\frac{29}{75}$, $\frac{3}{85}$, $\frac{18}{100}$, $\frac{2}{150}$.
Shingle roof boiler-house, $\frac{8}{10}$, $\frac{2}{15}$, $\frac{10}{25}$, $\frac{1}{50}$.
Shingle roof on brick boiler-house, $\frac{5}{10}$, $\frac{6}{15}$, $\frac{29}{25}$, $\frac{1}{30}$, $\frac{3}{50}$.
Cornice, wood, $\frac{1}{5}$, $\frac{5}{5}$, $\frac{4}{10}$, $\frac{2}{25}$.
No casks or pails of water, $\frac{7}{5}$, $\frac{46}{10}$, $\frac{13}{20}$, $\frac{59}{25}$, $\frac{19}{50}$.
Dipping in building, $\frac{16}{25}$, $\frac{12}{50}$, $\frac{1}{100}$.
Heating by furnace, $\frac{1}{3}$, $\frac{1}{5}$, $\frac{4}{10}$, $\frac{15}{15}$, $\frac{3}{25}$, $\frac{1}{40}$, $\frac{3}{50}$.
Heating by wood stoves, $\frac{16}{10}$, $\frac{9}{15}$, $\frac{4}{20}$, $\frac{25}{25}$, $\frac{3}{30}$, $\frac{1}{40}$, $\frac{2}{50}$.
Heating by coal or oil stoves, $\frac{5}{5}$, $\frac{36}{10}$, $\frac{13}{15}$, $\frac{6}{20}$, $\frac{27}{25}$, $\frac{1}{40}$, $\frac{1}{50}$.
Lighting by other than by gas or electricity, $\frac{2}{5}$, $\frac{27}{10}$, $\frac{5}{15}$, $\frac{26}{25}$.
Lighting by kerosene, standard metal lamps, $\frac{8}{5}$, $\frac{1}{10}$, $\frac{1}{20}$.
Lighting by kerosene, glass lamps, $\frac{1}{10}$, $\frac{1}{15}$, $\frac{1}{20}$.
Lighting by kerosene, lamps filled by daylight only, $\frac{2}{10}$, $\frac{4}{15}$, $\frac{5}{25}$, $\frac{1}{30}$, $\frac{1}{35}$, $\frac{2}{50}$.
Ladders, stationary (none), $\frac{1}{5}$, $\frac{16}{10}$, $\frac{2}{15}$, $\frac{1}{20}$, $\frac{1}{24}$.
Planer, each machine, $\frac{5}{20}$, $\frac{8}{25}$, $\frac{11}{50}$, $\frac{2}{75}$, $\frac{4}{100}$.
Planer, without blowers or conveyors, $\frac{3}{20}$, $\frac{2}{50}$, $\frac{2}{100}$, $\frac{3}{150}$.
Picker in mill, $\frac{1}{15}$, $\frac{1}{25}$, $\frac{1}{50}$, $\frac{2}{75}$, $\frac{9}{100}$, $\frac{1}{120}$.
Roof, shingle, $\frac{4}{5}$, $\frac{14}{10}$, $\frac{98}{25}$, $\frac{11}{30}$, $\frac{44}{50}$, $\frac{2}{65}$, $\frac{8}{100}$.
Spittoons, sawdust, $\frac{8}{5}$, $\frac{1}{15}$, $\frac{1}{50}$.
Shavings vault, wood, $\frac{5}{50}$, $\frac{8}{80}$, $\frac{4}{100}$, $\frac{1}{125}$.
Shavings vault (not cut off), $\frac{19}{10}$, $\frac{3}{15}$, $\frac{7}{25}$, $\frac{1}{30}$, $\frac{2}{40}$.
Shavings vault, standard (cut off), $\frac{7}{10}$, $\frac{7}{15}$, $\frac{1}{50}$.
Shavings vault, standard (not cut off), $\frac{1}{10}$, $\frac{7}{15}$, $\frac{8}{25}$.
Metal stack through metal roof, $\frac{8}{5}$, $\frac{1}{15}$, $\frac{9}{25}$, $\frac{8}{50}$.
Metal stack through shingle roof, with collar, $\frac{1}{10}$, $\frac{54}{25}$.

[1] The author is indebted to the late L. H. Ticknor, Esq., of Peoria, Ill., for the above list.

Metal stack through roof or floor (no jacket), $\frac{7}{25}$, $\frac{2}{35}$, $\frac{14}{50}$, $\frac{3}{75}$.
Metal stack through shingle roof, $\frac{6}{10}$, $\frac{3}{25}$, $\frac{52}{50}$.
Varnishing, $\frac{2}{10}$, $\frac{1}{20}$, $\frac{29}{25}$, $\frac{1}{30}$, $\frac{2}{40}$, $\frac{1}{100}$.
Watchman and clock (none), $\frac{2}{5}$, $\frac{9}{10}$, $\frac{2}{15}$, $\frac{45}{20}$, $\frac{70}{25}$, $\frac{4}{30}$, $\frac{1}{35}$, $\frac{19}{50}$.
Watchman (no clock), $\frac{3}{5}$, $\frac{91}{10}$, $\frac{12}{15}$, $\frac{1}{18}$, $\frac{19}{25}$.
Wood-work, not whitewashed or painted, $\frac{23}{5}$, $\frac{32}{10}$, $\frac{1}{15}$, $\frac{2}{25}$.

One might go on indefinitely pointing out incongruities of this kind in our coexistent relations, and it needs no argument to show that every attempt to cobble these into relations of sequence makes confusion worse confounded.

It would be a truism to say that in the face of inconsistencies so glaring, explanation or defense is impossible. The public contention that rates are made "by guess and begad" is susceptible of proof from the documentary evidence contained in our own tariffs. It matters not that under the leveling force of self-interest among brokers, agents, companies, and the public, receipts and disbursements come out almost exactly even, if taken for decade periods; in other words, that indemnity as a whole is practically sold at average cost. Our failure to make a profit does not concern the public, but our failure to maintain reasonably true rate relations offends the sense of relation which is instinctively the basis of every reasoning process. Even low rates that are inequitable are an offense to common intelligence.

In the past, expediency alone has fixed the price of fire indemnity. The seller has fought for high prices, and the buyer for low prices, and between these two contending influences, rates have been kept in an irregular and spasmodic motion similar to the atmospheric wave known in music as cacophony. Fire destruction, too, like every other motion resulting from contending influences, has created its own wave. We have thus two irregular waves — the loss wave occasioned by the countless elements of fire hazard, and a sort of "rough and tumble" zigzag (which might be dignified by the name of rate wave) caused by the football tactics of buyers and sellers of indemnity, and further complicated by the arbitrary decisions of an umpire, known as the local agent, who has a stake up on the game.

While we know that rates must be constantly changed, we construct our tariffs, in theory at least, on the assumption that we can maintain them permanently at an unvarying level. When contending influences force this level into a rate wave, it is invariably a cacophonous wave, not in harmonious relations with the wave of fire destruction, because it is largely the product of contending personal motives beyond quantitative analysis. In making rate changes, in obedience to the law of expediency, we not only observe no system, but *cannot* observe system. At one time we make a so-called percentage change, at another a flat rate, at another a competitive rate, at another a suspended rate, and after a series of these changes has completely obliterated established relations we are again compelled to construct new basis tariffs, and re-create hundreds or thousands of local tariffs of coexistent relations, which, before we can place them in the hands of our agents, are fly-blown with the germs of dissolution, because they furnish our only available material for establishing sequential relations.

Under such influences, a new departure in rating methods is a crying need, and the first necessity is the fundamental rule of action essential to every scientific activity. This rule must be an accurate definition of the function of fire-rating in its broadest sense as an activity. That fire insurance meets a public need, aside from being a mere means of earning salaries and dividends, must be admitted, else it could not exist. We have been accustomed to define this utility as the distribution of fire destruction from the individual to the community, but in this distribution it is necessary to consider something more than the individual, for each property group, community, state, and year may justly claim relief from an excessive burden of fire destruction with the same logic as the individual; and even the nation at large may stagger under the burden of a single year's losses, and justly claim that these losses shall be spread out through a period of years. This makes it an essential part of the duties of fire insurance not only to distribute, but to redistribute and re-redistribute, in order to avoid oppressive taxation. While the above definition may answer as a broad statement of the ethical obligations of fire insurance to the community, it is not a definition applicable to the needs of a physical science. If the measurement of fire hazard can be done scientifically we must admit that the activity of fire-rating legitimately belongs to the family of physical sciences, and all physical sciences deal with the properties of waves. What we need is a generalization defining the function of fire-rating as a physical science.

An unbiased consideration of the phenomena of fire rates during recent years ought to convince any sane man that in our refusal to permit rate waves to vibrate in harmonious sequence to cost waves we have been floundering about in the vain attempt to adapt an inflexible system to flexible conditions. Like the African who ties up his hair with cotton twine to take the "kinks" out of it, we have long struggled against nature in the attempt to take the kinks out of a thing which stubbornly refuses to remain straight.

Our persistent efforts to flatten loss waves into unvarying rate lines have been a long and irritating struggle against the inexorable physical law of rhythm, and our indisposition or inability to recognize this law has caused endless trouble and misunderstandings among ourselves and with the public.

If it were possible to conceive of a sea-going vessel so constructed as to be unresponsive to the wave motion of the ocean, and started on a voyage from New York to Liverpool, we should find it in heavy weather buried half the time under mountains of sea-water, and the other half paddling through space. Could we trace the ordinary motion of sea-going vessels, we should find a profile view of their line of progress to be invariably a modified form of the surface wave. It is as illogical to ignore the necessity of rhythm in fire rates as it would be in navigation to ignore the law of wave motion.

The ocean surface when relieved from atmospheric disturbances settles down to a dead level. This level is the exact mean between the sum of the wave protuberances and hollows, so that in a dead calm the track of the vessel and water surfaces would be at all times exactly parallel. In the same manner, between any two given points of time there is an average cost of fire underwriting to be found, which is the true mean between the crest and trough of the annual cost wave of each class.

It is this average cost which is the real straight-line, the unchanging sea-level, of every property class, and it is this which we should seek to establish as a fixed basis for our coexistent relations, and our rates should be permitted to fluctuate above and below this mean line in intelligently modified waves, as determined by the greater wave found in the annual cost ratio of each class.

The ascertainment of the true level, of average cost of each class, and the continuous control of the rate wave by reckoning from this as a "base line," constitutes the real problem of establishing sequential relations, and the determination of this base line is as purely a question of statistics, and ought to be as free from contending personal influences, as the establishment of a principal meridian in land-surveying, or the determination of a ship's position at sea.

It is the object of this inquiry to learn how this average cost for each class may be determined, and how from this as a base, rate waves may be so regulated as to be in harmony with their loss wave, and at the same time be modified into waves of endurable proportions.

It is a characteristic of all waves that they become

intolerable when the amplitude of vibration exceeds certain limits. Ocean waves beyond a certain magnitude become destructive to sea-going craft. A deafening noise, a blinding light, a withering heat, an intolerable electrical discharge, are one and all results of width of vibration in the media through which they are propagated.

The well-known generalization that the intensity of all wave motion increases in proportion to the square of the amplitude of vibration, might be said to apply not only to matter but to mind and its concerns, for violent change is destructive to all human interests. Wide fluctuations in values create commercial panics, and in lesser degree wide fluctuations in fire rates are intolerable to the community.

This universal characteristic of wave motion leads us to the unavoidable inference that it is the true function of fire-rating in its broadest aspect to transmute annual cost waves into rate waves, modified into proportions that will be endurable to property interests. This is the fundamental rule from which fire-rating as a physical science must start.

. . . .

It is probable that from the earliest days of fire insurance the companies have maintained tabulations of their experience with grouped hazards. These lists have slowly expanded in differing degrees, though some have reached a far more advanced stage of differentiation than others. In the primitive days when each company not only had the privilege of making its own rates, but from lack of association was compelled to do so, when competition was so small that it could make rates which insured a wide margin of profit, these lists served as a crude scale — something like the farmer's fence-rail and stone — for the quantitative measurement of class hazards in their sequential relations as indicated by individual experience; but in these days of competition, when a company is compelled to keep in the swim by carrying all classes of property, of every grade of desirability, in deference to the wishes of more and more exacting agents, these individual classification lists have fallen into a sort of innocuous desuetude, surviving like the coccyx and vermiform appendix, the remains of organs that served their purpose during some earlier stage of evolution. Kept up at a great expenditure of time and money, and carefully guarded among the secret and sacred archives of each company, it would be difficult to determine what intelligent end these lists serve at the present time that would not be as well served by a Roman soothsayer's chicken-gizzard. Their utility as a practical guide in determining the relative profitableness of classes may be inferred form the following tabulation of the comparative experience shown by a number of these individual lists for the same five-year period. The figures in the column marked "low" show the loss ratio of the company having the most favorable experience, and the figures in the column marked "high" show the loss ratio of the company having the most unfavorable experience, with each of the classes designated by numbers. The column marked "combined" shows the combined loss ratio of all the companies on the same class for the same period:

Class No.	Loss Ratios Shown by Individual Experience		Loss Ratios Shown by Combined Experience
	Low	High	
1	.00	1.11	.53
2	.10	2.13	.54
3	.00	1.31	.43
4	.06	1.88	.66
5	.18	1.69	.50
6	.03	.92	.60
7	.05	.91	.60
8	.19	1.05	.67
9	.10	1.37	.65
10	.34	1.73	.58
11	.12	1.32	.74
12	.16	1.79	.63
13	.21	1.35	.44
14	.18	1.29	.77
15	.02	.78	.25
16	.01	2.11	1.21
17	.08	2.46	.53
18	.43	4.95	.97
19	.19	1.11	.72
20	.04	1.02	.43
21	.33	1.50	.61
22	.29	1.05	.57
23	.16	1.04	.50
24	.29	1.76	.62
25	.18	1.03	.46
26	.13	.86	.52
27	.30	2.64	.64
28	.30	1.65	.67
29	.22	4.46	.97
30	.17	.67	.43
31	.03	2.00	.90
32	.10	2.16	.81
33	.11	1.77	.47

These classes, selected from the lists at random, show that with each and every class one company had a very low loss ratio, while another company had a loss ratio that would bring swift ruin had it not had a more favorable experience with other classes. A mere glance down the two columns marked "low" and "high" will show the utter worthlessness of the separate experience of a single company as a criterion to the average loss ratio of each class, while on the contrary, a comparison of these individual experiences with the column marked "combined" shows that there *is* an established mean which, if known, would constitute a reliable standard for determining adequate class rates.

But further examination into these individual lists reveals an inaccuracy and wastefulness of method which would destroy their reliability, even were the experience of each company broad enough to constitute a reliable criterion. At a rough estimate, one hundred and fifty companies maintain these classification lists, at a heavy expense for clerical work. During a single year these companies receive, let us say, a total of five million daily reports of policies issued, each of which contains a verbatim copy of the written portion of a policy. The necessity for determining the proper class of each daily report received requires that it be carefully scanned and its class number noted upon it, in order that it may be properly entered upon the records. This work is necessarily done in a hurried manner by a clerk or examiner who cannot possibly give much time or thought to each daily report. In many cases it is impossible to tell from the written description how the risk should be classed. In thousands of cases, from fifty to one hundred companies receive daily reports covering the same property which, in the hurry of current necessity, are entered haphazard in any one of a dozen different classes on the ledgers of the several companies, and the same work thus manifolded from fifty to one hundred times creates a corresponding liability to error. A loss on a single risk, wrongly classified destroys the value of the records of two classes.[1]

Another important element of unreliability in these individual lists results from the constant fluctuation of rates. The lists contain the total premiums received and the losses paid on each class, a comparison of which is supposed to reveal the loss ratio of the class. This loss ratio, however, is only useful in determining the adequacy of rates; and with rates constantly changing, the standard ceases to be a standard, and tabulated experience without a standard of comparison is worthless.

Let us take for illustration the rates on the dwelling class, which have declined throughout a large portion of the Northwest from 25 to 35 per cent. during the period named, assuming the premiums and losses on the same amount at risk to have been as follows:

Year	Premiums	Losses
1892	$100,000	$50,000
1893	90,000	40,000
1894	80,000	45,000
1895	75,000	60,000
1896	66,000	50,000
Total	$411,000	$245,000

Total loss ratio, 60 per cent.

Assuming the normal loss ratio of the class to be 55 per cent., the average loss of 60 per cent. shown by the above figures would indicate that dwellings ought to be advanced about 5 per cent., but if we compare the last year's premiums with the losses of that year, we find the loss ratio

[1] In the office of a prominent insurance company a five-thousand dollar line was recently classified as a printing-office. When a loss occurred, it was accidentally discovered that the risk belonged to an entirely different class. This single error affected the company's loss ratio with the one class twenty-five per cent., and with the other nearly one hundred per cent.

to be about 76 per cent., and that dwellings should be advanced about 21 per cent. from current rates, hence, any attempt to fix rates from the figures shown would be met with the question, From what point shall rates be modified — from the highest point or the lowest point, or from some intermediate point? In other words, the value of the figures for quantitative reasoning is destroyed by the vacillation of one of the quantities necessary to the comparison.

Another element of unreliability in the lists of individual companies lies in the non-concurrent grouping of classes. In this respect, probably no two agree; and in the constant evolution of hazards (in the absence of any common source of information), lists are in constant course of change, as determined by the judgment of classification clerks under urgent necessity for immediate action.

In view of the uncertainty of grouping, the uncertainty whether a risk, even when properly grouped, will get into the group to which it belongs, and the destruction of the standard of measurement caused by rate fluctuations, the individual classification list as a basis for quantitative measurement is by several degrees more crude and primitive than the farmer's fence-rail and stone; but as the latter contained the germ which has evolved into the chemist's scales which will weigh an eyelash, these individual company classification lists constitute the embryo which must ultimately evolve into a logical, uniform, and combined system for the quantitative measurement of sequential relations.

Ordinary candor compels the admission that the classification of coexistent relations found in our present tariff system constitutes the only feature of fire insurance which gives it the slightest right to claim that it is not a world-wide game of guess. The same degree of candor will not permit us to deny that, as a practical guide in accepting, or rating risks, company classification lists in severalty are worse than useless, because in their limited way they are misleading. It should be borne in mind, however, that these lists show a distinctly different phase of classification from that found in our tariff system, for the reason that they constitute the embryo of a system for establishing sequential relations.

A careful study of these lists shows that, with all their imperfections, they contain no fault that is not easily and inexpensively remediable. To coördinate these lists into a uniform grouping of classes and to combine the individual experience of each company into grand aggregates, showing the annual experience of all companies with each class, would require neither violation of scientific procedure, nor departure from methods suggested rather than established through these individual classification lists. There can be no verification of sequential relations (which are the combined effect of annual fire destruction and the coexistent relations established through basis tariffs) except through uniform and combined classification. This is the statistical basis upon which fire-rating as a science of sequential measurement must rest.

It would seem to be a reflection upon the intelligence and honesty of the fire underwriting community that during the past quarter of a century every effort to bring about uniform and combined classification for the purpose of establishing intelligent sequential relations should have been thwarted by a silent opposition which has seemingly disdained to argue the question. It has been charged that this opposition emanates from a belief on the part of the management of some of the larger companies that, under existing conditions, these companies possess advantages which would be lost by the revelation of class averages. It is hard to believe, however, that the intelligence which has brought these companies to the front could be blind to the compensating advantages which would accrue from the placing of fire insurance among the recognized and legitimate branches of commercial activity. At most, combined classification would simply establish *averages* derived from the experience of all. It would not unseat common sense, nor dethrone the individual judgment, which itself has been well defined as a finer and more discriminating classification. The establishment of these averages would leave even greater advantages to underwriting ability, capital, and established reputation than under existing conditions, which enable unscrupulous and plunging methods not only to upset the possibility of legitimate underwriting, but not infrequently to win a greater financial success. Greater disparities are found in the comparative success of banks, merchants, and manufacturers, than among fire insurance companies, because legitimate enterprise gives ample scope for the qualities necessary for success. Without doubt, selfishness, inertia, and ignorance are largely responsible for the failure of fire insurance to realize the benefits of combined classification, though it would be as illogical to censure the motives of the fire underwriting community generally as to censure the community at large for its inertia in many important matters of reform which do not admit of logical discussion. "Direct complicity with human affairs is not infrequently a hindrance to the scientific investigation of phenomena. Even the axioms of geometry would be disputed or ignored if men's passions or interests were concerned with them."

The English-speaking peoples adhere to an orthography that is the despair and wonder of the world. We boast of our decimal currency, but refuse to adopt a decimal system of weights and measures, while the complacent Briton refuses to adopt the decimal system for either his currency, weights, or measures. During the slow evolution of single-entry and then of double-entry bookkeeping, the English government stubbornly adhered to a primitive system of keeping accounts by cutting notches in sticks. It would probably be using this system yet had not a conflagration in 1884 burned up all its exchequer tallies. Inertia hath its uses, however, "The man who will not look at the new moon, out of respect to that ancient institution, the old moon," was not created in vain. Perhaps it is fortunate that combined classification was not started too soon, for a false start might have brought the system into disrepute, and it is always easier to start anew than to undo and patch up a system full of errors. To-day, however, fire insurance is in the position of the British government when its exchequer tallies were burned. Many states have destroyed our rating system, such as it is, by anticompact laws; many others are threatening to do so, and a new start is inevitable. If we start along lines that cannot be justified by scientific reasoning at every point, so much the worse for us, for we will ultimately be compelled to tear down our system and rebuild from the foundation.

CHAPTER VII

SCIENTIFIC FIRE–RATING [1]

ALL forms of insurance are alike in two things; they indemnify for loss, and they do so by means of an application of the laws of probability. In gambling parlance, insurance is "a hedge." That is to say, it is the direct opposite of gambling. It does not take chances but, instead, cancels them. Man is, by the laws of nature, subject to various uncertainties of fortune, as to health, life, preservation of property, etc. This liability he cannot escape directly, but he may nullify the financial hazard by means of insurance. Thus insurance is to him not a gamble but a hedge.

It is sometimes erroneously said that companies which engage in insurance are gambling. If they took a few risks only, the charge would be true; but we shall see that the fundamental principle of the law of probabilities is that when a large group is considered, chance is very nearly eliminated and the aggregate loss may be estimated within narrow limits, so that the purveying of indemnity is no more a speculation than dealing in sugar or calico, nor indeed so much. Therefore, by means of insurance we find that not merely is the hazard of the individual offset, but also that the hazard when passed over to the company and combined with others, results in a reasonably reliable loss ratio which is transmuted into a moderate tax upon

[1] By Miles M. Dawson, Consulting Actuary, New York City. Reprinted from pages 56–67 of the "Proceedings of the Thirty-Second Annual Meeting of the Fire Underwriters' Association of the Northwest."

all who, being subject to the same risk of loss, have thus sought protection.

The laws of probability were practically unknown to the ancients, though insurance in a very interesting form was practised in Greece and Rome. The form was in loans to owners of vessels and cargoes at rates of interest far exceeding the usual upon safe securities, it being stipulated that the loan should not be repaid at all if the property were destroyed. Insurance, therefore, made its first appearance as the handmaid of commerce, which office has been in later centuries performed by it in a degree that was inconceivable then. Of course, the additional interest upon such a loan was in reality an insurance premium, charged as a consideration for the risk. Indeed, as has been shown in our day, a considerable part of the interest upon loans is in almost all cases really a premium charged because of the risk of the principal. But in those days, while the thing was known, its nature was not fully understood.

The mathematical law of probability may be stated as follows: If in a large group of persons, for instance, to each of whom a certain thing appears *a priori* equally likely to happen, it does actually happen within a certain time to a certain number, then the risk that such will happen to one person in the group within such time may be represented by a fraction of which the number to whom the thing happened is the numerator and the number composing the group is the denominator. This may be stated in another way which may be even clearer, viz.: This fraction will accurately represent the probability that a given man in the group was one of those to whom the thing has happened. For, indeed, the application of this principle to future happenings calls for an additional generalization and also for careful testing to determine whether the group was large enough to furnish a reliable average and whether the classification really admitted none but like hazards. Even then the result must be accepted as a guide for future estimates of the value of a hazard with caution, until repeated testing has proved the correctness of the deductions in every respect.

But, so far as the mere law itself is concerned, it is as well stated when we seek the chance that the event has happened to a particular man in the past as when we estimate the probability that it will happen to a given man in the future. It is this unity of the law of probability that makes it useful as a means of prevision, and, therefore, as a foundation for insurance. We know the law to be reliable and we surmise that this, in turn, is because other laws, causing the phenomena which we are attempting to forecast, are themselves working with even and reliable regularity. In other words, our study of probabilities leads us to the conclusion that, strictly speaking, there is no such thing as chance — though, so far as the power of the individual to control events is concerned, of course there is and must be; but that causes are continually at work which explain all that happens and that, if our knowledge of these causes were perfect, we should find ourselves in a world of certainty. It follows, therefore, that no grouping is or can be perfect, for, if we could know all the forces that are in operation, we should not merely know which in the group were out of place there but we should also know to which alone the event would happen and they alone would be in place there. It follows, therefore, that it is our task to classify and reclassify, knowing that at best the grouping is imperfect and knowing also that if it ever became perfect, not only would our labors be at an end, but that there would no longer be probabilities, but merely certainties, and that insurance would be impossible. It is clear then, that insurance and the science of probabilities are both ephemeral things which will pass away when man's knowledge is all-embracing. Perhaps, however, the time during which this omniscience is evolving, will be sufficient for our purpose; and we have at least this encouraging consideration that, if the grouping could be perfect, as our critics sometimes think or at least say that it ought to be, it would also be useless. Strangely enough, then, its utility depends upon its incompleteness and imperfection. But we are not on that account to neglect grouping things together which seem to us most nearly alike; for, do what we will in that regard, there will be imperfections enough in the selection, you may be sure.

In fire insurance, where the determination of the amount of a premium has been empirical, as a rule, you have seen a remarkable development in classification which, had it been accompanied by a similar evolution of scientific rate-making, would by this time have put you in possession by easy stages of the most wonderfully and perfectly adapted system known. Unfortunately, it was not so accompanied and the work of determining cost ratios, which are hazard ratios, has been deferred until this complexity has been introduced by the necessities of competition. The most serious and important obstacles in the way of at this time making fire-rating a science arise from the great complexity of these classifications, none of which existed in the beginning. We have classifications by construction, by occupancy, by exposures, and each of these has sub-classifications, almost without end. Then, as we shall see, it is also considered desirable to group by territories and likewise by time, measured by terms of years if not by single years. It is this which makes the labor of preparing the ratios seem so great, and, indeed, to many impossible — this, and the enormous mass of data involved in each group. If the work had been entered upon when there was little attempt at classification, it would have been easy; and since it would have kept pace with the complexity which time has introduced, and indeed would doubtless have suggested and determined that complexity, it would not now be difficult to keep the machine in motion.

In life insurance, to digress for a moment, the development has, in this country especially, also been one-sided.

The science of probabilities, together with its application to rate-making and other problems, has been brought to great perfection; but the grouping has been into one class only, viz.: lives, accepted as first-class, while lives which fell below the standard were unable to secure insurance at all. Naturally such a system has resulted in many lives being accepted which were regarded as on the line or very near it; and within the year the American Society of Actuaries has, on the suggestion of Emory McClintock, Actuary of the Mutual Life, and the greatest living member of the profession in this country, begun as its first great work, to construct with the coöperation of the principal companies mortality tables from their experiences for classes of lives, distinguished by heredity, occupation, personal characteristics, and history. This is a great task, comparable only, perhaps, to the work which we are discussing, that of classifying and ordering the statistics of fire insurance companies, so as to determine the ratios of loss as to each class. It is significant, perhaps, that both branches of insurance, which have in the past been so one-sided in the development of their rate-making systems, though in ways diametrically opposite, should now apparently be approaching the same goal of systematized and thoroughly classified statistical tables, showing the cost by classes. Fire insurance should, it seems to me, come out with the most perfect and useful tables; and what is needed in life insurance is, perhaps, not so much further classification of lives that have all along been accepted but information as to rates which would be safe for the one-sixth part of those who have applied that have been rejected. This information the investigation will not develop and consequently the experiments in the field of insuring impaired lives are being made by means of empirical modifications of the rates with eyes open for everything that can guide the classification. The fire insurance companies have, taking all of them into account, embraced about all classes of property that are subject to the hazard of destruction by fire. The one-sided development of the business has not been narrow as has been the case in life insurance to a lamentable degree.

Perhaps a definition of the meaning which is by me attached to the word "empirical" may not be out of place. The fixing of a price, however cleverly and shrewdly done, without actually computing the costs, is an empirical act. Most prices are thus fixed, to a great degree; for, while the sellers are loth to sell for less than cost, circumstances at times compel it and, on the other hand, they are rarely slow to accept large profits over the cost if opportunity offers. But it is another matter for one to be offering his goods in the market without knowing whether the price he names is above or below the cost. This was the condition, however, in railway rates until very recently. There the rule of the markets: "Charge all that the traffic will bear" was and is yet followed; but there is this difference between the old days and these, that then the wisest managers did not know when they were underbidding the cost, while now there is close figuring done continually to determine that very matter. The situation in fire insurance has been similar to this. In both cases, it reflects great credit upon the acumen, skill, and judgment of the men who have directed the business that the consequences have not been more ruinous; for they had nothing but the general result from year to year to guide them.

In railroading, I have been informed, the old system, while frequently bringing out reliable profits from the whole business from year to year, was found to have caused the greatest inequalities and inequities, when it was once thoroughly examined into. It has been reported that the hasty and imperfect investigation of fire insurance experience that was recently made, showed a similar state of affairs. I may add that this was also until recently the fact, in a large degree, in a business so remote from insurance as banking. Bankers, whether making or losing money on the whole business, have not infrequently had little idea which customers, aside, of course, from the largest of them where the facts stuck out, as it were, paid a profit to the bank or even compensated it for services rendered. But in the best and largest banking houses this is now changed and close track is kept of each account by an infallible system, so that the banker knows of a certainty whether the account is profitable. Thus, in leading New York banks, the account is duplicated by entries, showing when the value of deposited paper is actually reduced to possession by collection of the same. Similar investigations also as to the cost of collecting caused the adoption of the charge for collection of out-of-town checks by the New York Clearing House.

You will observe that in all the four great businesses which I have mentioned, fire insurance, life insurance, railroading, and banking, the development has been from dealing with heterogeneous or mixed groups as if they were of one sort, to dealing with smaller and more thoroughly homogeneous groups. It is the mastery of details that counts in business nowadays and, the larger the business, the more imperative is the demand for this classification and study of details.

The more classifications there are to be handled, the larger must be the statistical data from which deductions are made. The reason for this is that each classification stands wholly or in large part by itself and the ratio of loss must be determined for it separately, just as if it were the only class. Laying aside the question for the time, whether one period, on account of improvements or the contrary, is to be considered to have involved more or less risk of fire, the groups can be made up of different years' exposures, the losses for various years in that class being summed also to make a total. In this way, a sufficiently broad basis may sometimes be found for ratios in a class where the exposures in a single year are too few to yield a reliable average. The enormous mass of details which make up the experiences of the fire insurance companies is, in view of these things, seen to be a benefit and advantage, and perhaps well worth all the additional labor which it entails. For, by reason of the great abundance of the material, it ought to be able to attain at least the following desirable ends, viz.: Thoroughly reliable conclusions as to the cost of insurance as to all the larger and more important classifications, including much information concerning the causes of fires in these classes, giving a basis for extra charges and for credits as well; reasonably definite measurements of the hazards in all the less important classifications, the data being in each case much more plentiful than could otherwise have been expected.

The value of a broad basis is well known to you all, and yet I am sure that an illustration will not be out of place. Common sense teaches us that, for instance, in tossing a cent the chances are even whether it shall turn up head or tail. But if it be thrown but once, it must have turned up one or the other, and if a judgment were based upon that throw only, we would have a certainty. And experience, as well as reason, teaches that there is no certainty that it will turn up once one way and once the other in two throws; nor just half the time one way and just half the time the other way in four throws or any other small number of throws. But what we mean by saying that the chances are even, is that in a very large number of throws the number of heads and the number of tails will be nearly the same, and that in an infinite number of throws they would be just the same. We expect the ratios found by actual throwing the coin, to correspond more closely to the chances which we determined by reasoning about the matter, the larger the number of throws. In the same way, the average fire loss which is drawn from a very large number of exposures will more accurately correspond to the real probability; and, other things being equal, it will be more reliable, the more exposures it is drawn from.

In order to get this broad basis, several companies, indeed many companies, will need to pool their statistics. This has been a stumbling-block in the past, but is not likely to be such in the future, when the advantages and the safety of such procedure are fully understood. I well remember the expression of disgust with which the suggestion was received by a friend of mine, high in the fire insurance world, more than ten years ago. The feeling was at the time that such a thing could be accomplished only by so exposing the experience of the individual company, that all its underwriting mistakes would be an open book to its rivals. In addition to this humiliation, the managers also saw the possibility that their underwriting successes would give such indications to their rivals, that the advantage which they had enjoyed would soon be lost.

Of course, the statistics of the experiences of the companies could be pooled in a manner to involve just such disadvantages. Each company might digest its totals by classes and give in the results, exposing its own mistakes and successes. But if it were done in this way, in addition to this objection, there would be the further objection that the grouping would have to be wholly predetermined, the data could not be rearranged as occasion seemed to demand, and the persons charged with responsibility for the results could not know certainly that the grouping had been made in precisely the form desired, so that their conclusions were drawn from just the facts they assumed to be true. The experiences of life insurance companies could have been collected in a similar manner to make mortality tables; but they never have been, and few actuaries would be willing to assume responsibility for the result, if they were. The form in which the material is collected is, instead, in individual risk histories on cards. And, as soon as the cards come in, they lose their identity so far as the company is concerned, and, in any event, they are not combined so as to show to anybody what that company's individual experience has been. Of course, in collecting the data for the pool, a company may and, indeed, should put the same together for its own guidance and advice. But it will not be known to other companies and, moreover, will be of greater value to the company itself, when it can compare its own experience with the experience of all. The task of reporting this mass to a central body in such a manner may seem gigantic, but it is really no more labor than to digest the data before sending it in. It is better and more economical to have the sorting done by one set of clerks, and under the supervision of the committee in charge. The same individual cards, too, are likely in such case to be employed successively for different purposes, falling into new groups one after another until all the information which they give is extracted.

Mention has already been made of the desirability of having the material fluid, so to speak, so that it may be grouped into new and unexpected classifications, instead of being required to fall into predetermined classes. All fire insurance men have preconceptions as to what the statistics, when thus brought together, will demonstrate. In order to deal with the subject at all, it will be necessary for the committee in charge to recognize these preconceptions, as a means of determining the first forms of classification. But the first grouping, however skilfully made, is never likely to prove wholly correct. Many of the preconceptions are sure to be erroneous; and, when this is shown, the material should be in such form that new groupings, suggested by the facts as they develop, may be adopted.

There is one sort of hazard which deserves to be put to one side for separate consideration; that is the conflagration hazard. Two things appear to be clear about it from the outset, viz., first, that to get any sort of measurement for it, many apparently unlike hazards in all other regards must be grouped together and, second, that in order to get an average, periods much longer than one year must be employed. When the method of properly measuring this hazard has been arrived at, it will also involve the necessity for recognizing, that reserves to cover it must take into account a period of much more than one year. Then the truth will come to light, that much of the funds which are now held as surplus, are really reserves against this conflagration hazard, and that it is wisdom to accumulate such and folly to fail to do so. The liability on this account reminds one of what the actuaries call "suspended mortality" in life insurance. This means that the company which assumes that, because at younger ages it shows a great saving on the mortality estimates, the same salvage will apply straight through, forgets that the men who failed to die at forty, are merely reserved to make a larger number of deaths at the higher ages. Thus conflagrations are not expected every year, and such portion of the premium as represents this hazard is not released when the year has passed, unless the risk is wholly off the books.

This reference calls to mind the safety fund law of New York, which is, in a way, a recognition of this necessity for a special conflagration reserve. Its defect seems to me to be that instead of being a provision directly to cover the conflagration risk, it is only indirectly so, since it acts as a special protection of other policy-holders against their reserve values being swallowed up by the conflagration.

The inquiry is surely pertinent, in view of the trouble and expense which such an undertaking as this investigation would occasion, what is the good of the ratios anyhow? Many consider that rates are made by competition, and that the idea of securing uniform rates without combination is a foolish dream. And they reason that, since combination is necessary in order to sustain rates, and since by means of combination it is already demonstrated that they can be kept high enough to pay a good profit, the expense and labor to ascertain costs would be wasted.

Much of this contention is justified. Too much must not be expected of the mere ascertainment of the costs. In manufactures, for instance, the cost is usually perfectly well known to all parties. Yet undue competition has often brought about absolutely ruinous conditions, and the excuse which is most frequently offered for trusts and combinations, is the practical impossibility of carrying on the business at all under free competition. Yet it is even worse to compete without knowing what you are losing when a certain price is made. In these very periods of cut-throat competition, the manufacturer who has most completely in hand the information about costs, is enabled to inflict far worse injuries than he receives, while his adversary strikes in the dark and often injures himself instead of his antagonist.

Surely it is irrational to carry on a business in such a manner. Moreover, the fact that it is thus carried on, cannot be hidden from others and it creates unusual resistance to rating schedules. Men resent changes in their rates, anyhow, but yet more do they fight against them when they can set their judgment up against the underwriter, knowing that the latter cannot assign a reason for his opinion, and is, in fact, in doubt whether the rate should be so much or so much. Well do I personally recall the effect of a rating upon the property owners in the country town where I was brought up — a rating which involved doubling many premiums. It was not comprehensible to the business men that these risks were good at the old rates the day before, but required the new on that day. It takes good grounds to justify such to the mind of the average man. And the resentment and ill-feeling occasioned in this manner and fomented by the surmise that the rate-makers do not know that the new rates are correct, result in movements against the companies, in laws against combinations and the like.

But it is not merely as a means to avoid this sort of prejudice that accurate information as to costs would be useful. The fact that rates were thus determined would gain the good will of many. This information in simple form, would satisfy men that their interests were guarded in the working out of these problems, and that care was taken to make rates in proportion to the value of the protection. In my own short experience as a fire insurance man, I remember that a little talk about the underlying principles of insurance more than once disarmed prejudice. If these fundamental principles were strictly regarded, as they would be under a system of scientific rating, it is difficult to see how a business man could offer a fair excuse for objecting to pay what experience showed to be his just share of the losses and expenses of the business.

If the tariff associations were abandoned, it is true that the mere fact that the costs had been accurately ascertained might not restrain undue competition. It would, however, be likely to have a steadying effect upon rates and might serve ordinarily to confine the competition within narrow limits. Such, in any event, has been the effect in life insurance, so far as the regular companies are concerned. Moreover, since the purchaser of fire insurance buys a promise, instead of a commodity, rates that are cut too much might, if the fact could be shown, create such fear of the security of the company as would cure the evil or keep it within bounds. It would be foolish to say that this effect can be depended upon, for we have the fact to face that for many years assessment life insurance has been liberally patronized, although charging rates so insufficient that the safety of the insurance was imperiled. You also have known many instances where doubtful fire insurance has readily been accepted in order to save a little on the premiuns. While this is true, however, the fact that most of the fire insurance is in companies that decline to meet the competition of notoriously unsafe concerns, shows that most business men do value security above a saving in rates. When the facts concerning the cost of fire insurance have come to light as to èach classification, companies that for a time seek to do business at rates that are below cost can be made to appear notoriously unsafe very readily, because they really would be so. Such would rarely be backed by substantial capital and would not be feared.

Another most important advantage that should flow from this determination of the costs of fire insurance is that it ought to contribute very much to the solution of the commission problem. It is well known that the difficulties concerning commissions had their origin in the fact that certain classes of hazards were known to be more profitable than others, and this, not because of the superior skill of one company over another in selecting risks of that class, but because of the fact that the rates were higher in proportion to the hazard. These classes came to be known as preferred, and, while the Western Union companies were doing nothing to show their preference for them, the non-union companies were emphasizing their choice by offering much larger commissions for preferred risks. With the costs accurately ascertained, the gross premiums may be made to accord with the net, with the same margin for expenses and profits, or with a different margin, as is thought wisest, and level or graded commissions will be provided for, precisely as the companies prefer. Moreover, it will be in their power to make any class of risks more or less profitable by changing the margin, and thus to take it out of the possibilities that larger commissions shall be offered than all are able and willing to pay.

Reference has already been made to the steadying effect which the mere fact that the costs have been ascertained, will be likely to have upon rates. This steadying effect, however, would be greatly increased if this cost were made the basis of reinsurance reserves as reported to the departments instead of such reserves being based upon gross premiums as at present. By "gross premiums" I mean the actual premium receipts for the year, "net" in the sense that cancellations and the like have been deducted. At the present time a company gets off with a smaller reserve charge, the more insufficient its premiums have been. Thus, if it accepts business for half rates, its reserves are half as much as if its rates were full. In this manner insolvency is sometimes concealed for a time and the state's certificate of solvency becomes vain. In a recent annual report of the Massachusetts department, public attention was called to the fact that by means of reinsurance an insolvent company might transfer its business to a concern that was not more solvent in point of fact, but that made an appearance of solvency, if charged under the rules with a reserve liability for only one-half the reinsurance premium, however inadequate that might be.

The question is pertinent whether the cost schedules would be likely to be accepted by state legislatures as standards of solvency. As to this nobody can surely say; but we do know that a scientific reserve was adopted as to life insurance companies and that the presence of this legal standard has had a wonderful steadying influence upon life insurance premiums in the regular companies.

In this connection, it is worthy of remark that the legal reserve rules as to the valuation of life policies have not brought about absolute uniformity as to life insurance premiums. There are many variations; but these are kept within reasonably narrow limits. In consequence, there is not much complaint about these differences. It must be conceded, though, that the problem in fire insurance is different; for in life insurance considerations as to the profit-earning power of the various companies influence the choices, as also do personal preferences and especial confidence in particular institutions. In fire insurance, on the contrary, so long as the company is safe, there is never much choice, and so the cheapest bidder gets the risk as a mere matter of business. But, on the other hand, it does not follow that because in life insurance an equilibrium of rates has not been the result of scientific reserve systems, it would fail to be the consequence of the adoption of such a system of fire insurance reserves.

It is possible, too, that the companies might turn to the very device for assuring that they can collect ample premiums that has long been employed by life insurance companies, viz., to make the policies participating. This was tried in fire insurance many years ago, but had little then to recommend it. Now, however, the competition is hard and close and it is possible that often the insured would attest his confidence that the rates should be materially lower by being willing to pay the higher rate, provided the insurance was written, so that his policy would participate in the profits. Life insurance companies have by this means been enabled to collect one-fourth or more over the stock or non-participating rates, every cent of which extra premium is available if needed, to pay losses or expenses. In fire insurance, of course, great care would need to be exercised, and if this excess were subject to the payment of commissions, there might be no possibility of making the plan work. But, operated with caution, it might work all right, giving the insured lower actual cost, while assuring the company against the possibility of coming out behind. This may prove to be the ultimate solution of the problem of providing flexible premiums, in spite of the fixed cost ratios which investigation would discover.

Another benefit that might flow from the establishment of a joint statistical bureau is that, gradually by a process of extension, the indemnity furnished by fire insurance companies might be widened to cover many risks which are now tabooed. Thus the hazard of loss by explosion might be investigated and, instead of excluding this risk of property loss, it might be included. Insurance is more valuable, the more inclusive it is; and, where the risk of loss from one cause is slight, it can hardly be covered except in connection with other hazards to the same property. In a like manner, the risk of the collapse of a building might be covered. As to the subject matter of insurance, there might also be the extension to cover profits which a business man loses through the stoppage of his business when his property is destroyed. Remuneration for such lost profits is nowadays strictly ruled out by all companies; if this could be covered safely, it would be well. In London, according to the press reports, the need for such insurance has become so pronounced, that a separate company has been organized to furnish it.

It has been argued that the ratios which would be arrived at, would be vitiated by the fact that insurances for full value and insurances for only a part of the value would be grouped together. It is, to be sure, well known that both overinsurance and underinsurance have their perils for the company. Thus overinsurance tends to induce incendiarism, and underinsurance results in much protection being furnished for a small premium. Since most losses are partial and, indeed, for small parts of the value, a policy for one-half the value or less often calls for as large a payment on the part of the companies as if it had been for full insurance.

We have already seen that there can be no claim that the classification is perfect and, in fact, that a perfect classification would be useless. In this regard, it must be conceded, I am confident, that the classification cannot be homogeneous. The cost as ascertained, will be higher, by some percentage not yet measurable, than it should be when full but not excessive insurance is carried, and lower than when a very small part of the value is insured or when excessive insurance is taken. But the cost ratios will represent the average, insurance being taken as men desire to take it, some too much, some too little, many approximately the right amount. These are, perhaps, in the present stage of the business and of our knowledge the most useful ratios we could have. Deductions from rates, based upon such costs, might be allowed when full insurance is taken, and this is doubtless the best form for such discrimination to take — much preferable to fining the insured for not carrying full insurance and less likely to arouse resentment and cause retaliation in the form of adverse legislation.

It has been asked again and again, what effect these ratios would be likely to have upon the schedule system which has been so widely introduced and which unquestionably has served a very good purpose. It must be replied that nobody knows in advance. If anybody did know just what the ascertainment of these ratios will reveal and could prove to others that he knew it, much expense and trouble might be spared us. For myself, I have been interested in the Universal Mercantile Schedule from the moment I heard of the idea, and I procured a copy as soon as I could. It seemed to me then and it seems to me now both a step toward more intelligent treatment of the question and also an absolutely necessary precursor of scientific rating, showing the general methods which must be pursued and also the necessity for cost ratios, based upon actual experience, by means of which to construct a schedule, perfect and reliable. It has seemed to me to be a sort of John the Baptist crying in the wilderness, or a schoolmaster to bring us to Christ. There can be no doubt that the results of an investigation will indicate the desirability of schedule rating and nobody, of course, will welcome more heartily the changes in the present schedules, no matter how radical and sweeping, if correct and founded upon substantiated facts, than the able and ingenious gentlemen to whose prevision of the coming conditions and to whose indefatigable labors we owe the present schedule. Scientific rating comes not to destroy the law nor the "profits," let us hope, but to fulfil.

Let us see what the investigation might be expected to yield in the way of information that would throw light upon the schedule. First of all, it ought to be able to determine for each class the loss ratios from various assigned causes, differentiating also by comparing smaller groups, as to risks with and without certain improvements and fire-fighting appliances. By this process a close estimate, first, of the residual, unverified cost, and then of the costs because of deficiencies, etc., might be made. Surely many things, that in the opinions, even of persons who are most favorable to scientific rate-making must yet remain subjects for empirical modifications of the rates, are likely during such an investigation, if properly conducted, to take definite form and in some cases to yield thoroughly reliable ratios for extra charges or allowances.

Naturally the investigation, if attempted, would cover separate ratios for various territorial divisions and also ratios for different periods of time. These, together with the reports as to ratios of loss from different causes of fire, might solve the question which has troubled so many underwriters, whether there really is something in mere locality which affects the fire ratios favorably or unfavorably. The bearing of this investigation upon the Universal Mercantile Schedule, just because it claims to be universal, is manifest.

Proper classifications will also enable the committee in charge of such an investigation to determine the influence upon the fire loss ratios, of single and multiple occupancies, of various sorts of occupancies, of exposures of every sort and nature. Such investigations will be intricate and it will greatly facilitate them if the information comes on cards, in the manner already indicated, so that they may be shuffled about and grouped again and again for different purposes. It ought to be possible to extract all the information that will be useful before the card is cast aside; and, in order to do this, the amount of information contained upon each card will not need to be multifarious. Comparatively simple groupings only should be called for.

The labor of conducting such an investigation will be very great because of the enormous mass of material to be digested and because of the number of classifications that will be needed. But, while arduous, the work will not be difficult and will in the end prove simple and easy. None of the intricate and puzzling mathematical problems which actuaries have to deal with, when handling life insurance statistics, will here be encountered. A perfectly clear head, a firm grasp upon the objects to be attained and unfailing insight into the methods by which the same may be secured, will help over the worst difficulties in classifying such a mass and drawing proper deductions from its statistics. The task would not be regarded formidable by skilled statisticians, except on the ground of the amount of data, and even that is not great when compared with the statistics which are often treated in connection with a national census. There is certainly nothing insuperable in the difficulties of the task; and the work ought not to involve expense at all comparable to the probable value of the results.

CHAPTER VIII

STANDARD FIRE INSURANCE POLICY [1]

1. The............fire insurance company in consideration of the stipulations herein named and of.......... dollars premium, does insure .... for the term of ....from the..........day of..........190.., at noon, to the..........day of..........190.., at noon, against all direct loss or damage by fire, except as hereinafter provided, to an amount not exceeding.......... dollars, to the following described property while located and contained as described herein, and not elsewhere, to wit:..

2. This company shall not be liable beyond the actual cash value of the property at the time any loss or damage occurs, and the loss or damage shall be ascertained or estimated according to such actual cash value, with proper deduction for depreciation however caused, and shall in no event exceed what it would then cost the insured to repair or replace the same with material of like kind and quality; said ascertainment or estimate shall be made by the insured and this company, or, if they differ, then by appraisers, as hereinafter provided; and, the amount of loss or damage having been thus determined, the sum for which this company is liable pursuant to this policy shall be payable sixty days after due notice, ascertainment, estimate, and satisfactory proof of the loss have been received by this company in accordance with the terms of this policy. It shall be optional, however, with this

[1] A copy of the printed conditions of the New York standard fire insurance policy.

company to take all, or any part, of the articles at such ascertained or appraised value, and also to repair, rebuild, or replace the property lost or damaged with other of like kind and quality within a reasonable time on giving notice, within thirty days after the receipt of the proof herein required, of its intention so to do; but there can be no abandonment to this company of the property described.

3. This entire policy shall be void if the insured has concealed or misrepresented, in writing or otherwise, any material fact or circumstance concerning this insurance or the subject thereof; or if the interest of the insured in the property be not truly stated herein; or in case of any fraud or false swearing by the insured touching any matter relating to this insurance or the subject thereof, whether before or after a loss.

4. This entire policy, unless otherwise provided by agreement indorsed hereon or added hereto, shall be void if the insured now has or shall hereafter make or procure any other contract of insurance, whether valid or not, on property covered in whole or in part by this policy; or if the subject of insurance be a manufacturing establishment and it be operated in whole or in part at night later than ten o'clock, or if it cease to be operated for more than ten consecutive days; or if the hazard be increased by any means within the control or knowledge of the insured; or if mechanics be employed in building, altering, or repairing the within-described premises for more than fifteen days at any one time; or if the interest of the insured be other than unconditional and sole ownership; or if the subject of insurance be a building on ground not owned by the insured in fee-simple; or if the subject of insurance be personal property and be or become incumbered by a chattel mortgage; or if, with the knowledge of the insured, foreclosure proceedings be commenced or notice given of sale of any property covered by this policy by virtue of any mortgage or trust deed; or if any change, other than by the death of an insured, take place in the interest, title,

or possession of the subject of insurance (except change of occupants without increase of hazard), whether by legal process or judgment or by voluntary act of the insured, or otherwise; or if this policy be assigned before a loss; or if illuminating gas or vapor be generated in the described building (or adjacent thereto) for use therein; or if (any usage or custom of trade or manufacture to the contrary notwithstanding) there be kept, used, or allowed on the above-described premises, benzine, benzole, dynamite, ether, fireworks, gasoline, greek fire, gunpowder exceeding twenty-five pounds in quantity, naphtha, nitro-glycerine or other explosives, phosporus, or petroleum or any of its products of greater inflammability than kerosene oil of the United States standard (which last may be used for lights and kept for sale according to law, but in quantities not exceeding five barrels, provided it be drawn and lamps filled by daylight or at a distance not less than ten feet from artificial light); or if a building herein described, whether intended for occupancy by owner or tenant, be or become vacant or unoccupied and so remain for ten days.

5. This company shall not be liable for loss caused directly or indirectly by invasion, insurrection, riot, civil war or commotion, or military or usurped power, or by order of any civil authority; or by theft; or by neglect of the insured to use all reasonable means to save and preserve the property at and after a fire or when the property is endangered by fire in neighboring premises; or (unless fire ensues, and, in that event, for the damage by fire only) by explosion of any kind, or lightning; but liability for direct damage by lightning may be assumed by specific agreement hereon.

6. If a building or any part thereof fall, except as the result of fire, all insurance by this policy on such building or its contents shall immediately cease.

7. This company shall not be liable for loss to accounts, bills, currency, deeds, evidences of debt, money, notes, or securities; nor, unless liability is specifically assumed

hereon, for loss to awnings, bullion, casts, curiosities, drawings, dies, implements, jewels, manuscripts, medals, models, patterns, pictures, scientific apparatus, signs, store or office furniture or fixtures, sculpture, tools, or property held on storage or for repairs; nor, beyond the actual value destroyed by fire, for loss occasioned by ordinance or law regulating construction or repair of buildings, or by interruption of business, manufacturing processes, or otherwise; nor for any greater proportion of the value of plate glass, frescoes, and decorations than that which this policy shall bear to the whole insurance on the building described.

8. If an application, survey, plan, or description of property be referred to in this policy it shall be a part of this contract and a warranty by the insured.

9. In any matter relating to this insurance no person, unless duly authorized in writing, shall be deemed the agent of this company.

10. This policy may by a renewal be continued under the original stipulations, in consideration of premium for the renewed term, provided that any increase of hazard must be made known to this company at the time of renewal or this policy shall be void.

11. This policy shall be canceled at any time at the request of the insured; or by the company by giving five days' notice of such cancellation. If this policy shall be canceled as hereinbefore provided, or become void or cease, the premium having been actually paid, the unearned portion shall be returned on surrender of this policy or last renewal, this company retaining the customary short rate; except that when this policy is canceled by this company by giving notice, it shall retain only the *pro rata* premium.

12. If, with the consent of this company, an interest under this policy shall exist in favor of a mortgagee or of any person or corporation having an interest in the subject of insurance, other than the interest of the insured

as described herein, the conditions hereinbefore contained shall apply in the manner expressed in such provisions and conditions of insurance relating to such interest as shall be written upon, attached, or appended hereto.

13. If property covered by this policy is so endangered by fire as to require removal to a place of safety, and is so removed, that part of this policy in excess of its proportion of any loss and of the value of property remaining in the original location shall, for the ensuing five days only, cover the property so removed in the new location; if removed to more than one location, such excess of this policy shall cover therein for such five days in the proportion that the value in any one such new location bears to the value in all such new locations; but this company shall not, in any case of removal, whether to one or more locations, be liable beyond the proportion that the amount hereby insured shall bear to the total insurance on the whole property at the time of fire, whether the same cover in new location or not.

14. If fire occur, the insured shall give immediate notice of any loss thereby in writing to this company, protect the property from further damage, forthwith separate the damaged and undamaged personal property, put it in the best possible order, make a complete inventory of the same, stating the quantity and cost of each article and the amount claimed thereon; and, within sixty days after the fire, unless such time is extended in writing by this company, shall render a statement to this company, signed and sworn to by said insured, stating the knowledge and belief of the insured as to the time and origin of the fire; the interest of the insured and of all others in the property; the cash value of each item thereof and the amount of loss thereon; all encumbrances thereon; all other insurance, whether valid or not, covering any of said property; and a copy of all the descriptions and schedules in all policies; any changes in the title, use, occupation, location, possession, or exposures of said

property since the issuing of this policy; by whom and for what purpose any building herein described and the several parts thereof were occupied at the time of fire; and shall furnish, if required, verified plans and specifications of any building, fixtures, or machinery destroyed or damaged; and shall also, if required, furnish a certificate of the magistrate or notary public (not interested in the claim as a creditor or otherwise, nor related to the insured) living nearest the place of fire, stating that he has examined the circumstances and believes the insured has honestly sustained loss to the amount that such magistrate or notary public shall certify.

15. The insured, as often as required, shall exhibit to any person designated by this company all that remains of any property herein described, and submit to examinations under oath by any person named by this company, and subscribe the same; and, as often as required, shall produce for examination all books of account, bills, invoices, and other vouchers, or certified copies thereof if originals be lost, at such reasonable place as may be designated by this company or its representative, and shall permit extracts and copies thereof to be made.

16. In the event of disagreement as to the amount of loss the same shall, as above provided, be ascertained by two competent and disinterested appraisers, the insured and this company each selecting one, and the two so chosen shall first select a competent and disinterested umpire; the appraisers together shall then estimate and appraise the loss, stating separately sound value and damage, and, failing to agree, shall submit their differences to the umpire; and the award in writing of any two shall determine the amount of such loss; the parties thereto shall pay the appraiser respectively selected by them and shall bear equally the expenses of the appraisal and umpire.

17. This company shall not be held to have waived any provision or condition of this policy or any forfeiture thereof by any requirement, act, or proceeding on its part

relating to the appraisal, or to any examination herein provided for; and the loss shall not become payable until sixty days after the notice, ascertainment, estimate, and satisfactory proof of the loss herein required have been received by this company, including an award by appraisers when appraisal has been required.

18. This company shall not be liable under this policy for a greater proportion of any loss on the described property, or for loss by and expenses of removal from premises endangered by fire, than the amount hereby insured shall bear to the whole insurance, whether valid or not, or by solvent or insolvent insurers, covering such property, and the extent of the application of the insurance under this policy or of the contribution to be made by this company in case of loss, may be provided for by agreement or condition written hereon or attached or appended hereto. Liability for reinsurance shall be as specifically agreed hereon.

19. If this company shall claim that the fire was caused by the act or neglect of any person or corporation, private or municipal, this company shall, on payment of the loss, be subrogated to the extent of such payment to all right of recovery by the insured for the loss resulting therefrom, and such right shall be assigned to this company by the insured on receiving such payment.

20. No suit or action on this policy, for the recovery of any claim, shall be sustainable in any court of law or equity until after full compliance by the insured with all the foregoing requirements, nor unless commenced within twelve months next after the fire.

21. Wherever in this policy the word "insured" occurs, it shall be held to include the legal representative of the insured, and wherever the word "loss" occurs, it shall be deemed the equivalent of "loss or damage."

22. If this policy be made by a mutual or other company having special regulations lawfully applicable to its organization, membership, policies, or contracts of insurance,

such regulations shall apply to and form a part of this policy as the same may be written or printed upon, attached, or appended hereto.

23. This policy is made and accepted subject to the foregoing stipulations and conditions, together with such other provisions, agreements, or conditions as may be indorsed hereon or added hereto, and no officer, agent, or other representative of this company shall have power to waive any provision or condition of this policy except such as by the terms of this policy may be subject of agreement indorsed hereon or added hereto, and as to such provisions and conditions no officer, agent, or representative shall have such power or be deemed or held to have waived such provisions or conditions unless such waiver, if any, shall be written upon or attached hereto, nor shall any privilege or permission affecting the insurance under this policy exist or be claimed by the insured unless so written or attached.

CHAPTER IX

THE NATURE OF THE POLICY CONTRACTS [1]

THE whole theory of fire insurance is logically derived from the axiom that insurance is a means of providing indemnity for loss. This principle as applied to the operations of fire insurance can be illustrated as follows:

"A fire insurance policy is a contract to indemnify the holder thereof for actual destruction, by a certain immediate cause, *i.e.*, fire, of value appertaining to certain specified property owned by him."

The thing to be noticed is that only actual immediate damage is covered by insurance; that is, damage which is attributable directly to the fire, or which is the immediate result of fire. Thus a fire insurance company insuring a stock of merchandise would in case of loss be liable for the value of the property actually consumed, and also damage to the remaining property caused by fire, smoke, and the process of extinguishing the fire. It would not be liable, however, for any loss caused by the interruption or derangement of business and consequent loss of profit.

An insurance policy is a personal contract. It does not follow the property, nor, properly speaking, insure *it* at all, though the language of the day gives a contrary impression. It is an agreement to indemnify a policy-holder for the loss accruing to him personally by reason of the destruction or damage of certain property. Accordingly, no person who is not the owner of the property burned, or who has

[1] By Richard M. Bissell, Vice-President of the Hartford Fire Insurance Company, Hartford. Reprinted from pages 37–65 of the "Yale Lectures on Insurance, Fire and Miscellaneous."

no interest in it, can be a claimant against an insurance company. Nor can an owner make claim on account of any other property than that directly mentioned or logically implied in the policy itself. All policies, therefore, should clearly set forth the description of the property to be insured and the interest of the policy-holder therein. While no one can insure property unless he has a valuable interest therein, any kind of an interest which can be valued in cash may be insured. Accordingly, a man who loans money on a building acquires an interest in it, and he may insure that interest, either separately, or, as is the custom, in conjunction with the owner of the building, both interests being covered by one contract. A purchaser who has paid in part for property which he may not receive until full payment is made, acquires an interest which may be protected by insurance. A life interest in property, also the reversionary interest of the final legatee, may be insured. In fact, any tangible, valuable interest in any kind of property may be made the subject of an insurance policy. It is a maxim of the business, however, that the value of all such interests must not exceed the actual cash value of the property itself.

In addition to the interests already mentioned, it is possible to insure against the loss of almost any ascertainable value which is subject to obliteration or depreciation by fire. Thus, the rental income of a building may be insured by a contract which will make good the loss of rent during the time the building is rendered untenantable by fire. So, also, in certain cases, what is called the use and occupancy of a manufacturing plant; that is to say, its ability to turn out the appropriate finished product in regular quantities, may be insured against interruptions by fire.

The property to be insured must be definitely described. A policy so written as to cover a stock of boots and shoes will not also cover dry goods, nor will a policy insuring a building also insure outbuildings or awnings. The written description forming part of every policy must either specifically mention everything to be insured, or must be couched in such broad terms as to include everything for which protection is desired. Thus a contract insuring merchandise would protect everything kept for sale, the word "merchandise" being very broad in its connotation; whereas a contract, as above, insuring a stock of boots and shoes, would cover nothing else.

In order to appreciate the relations which exist between a fire insurance company and the insured we must bear in mind the following facts, which will also indicate the reasons for the carefully drawn and somewhat stringent contracts by which insurance is undertaken.

In the first place, property covered by insurance is not only for the most part in the custody of the insured, but is usually occupied, operated, or handled by him. Moreover, and this is even more important, the information upon which the insurance is based is furnished by the insured, hence the obvious opportunities for fraud which the stringent policy conditions are intended to prevent — an intention which is only partially accomplished, as the experience of every company will demonstrate. In this connection a comment from a New York court will be appropriate:

"In negotiating a contract of insurance the parties are not upon a level, nor do they deal at arm's length. The insurer, *i.e.*, the company, is presumed to be ignorant, and the insured informed in respect to the subject to be insured. Hence, in forming the contract, the insurer, except he undertake to inquire for himself, does not rely on his own resources, but reposes exclusively on the intelligence communicated by the insured. And hence, further, the parties occupying this unequal position, the law exacts of the party holding the position of advantage — *i.e.*, the insured — the utmost good faith and candor in communicating the facts affecting the risk."

Again, Mr. Hine, in his "Book of Instruction," says:

"In no contract is one party more completely at the mercy of another than the underwriter, *i.e.*, the company, in insurance. He is necessarily ignorant of facts and circumstances that may be vital to the risk and hence open to the fraud of designing men, who may withhold or misrepresent 'material' facts."

Some mention has already been made of the significant features of the earliest insurance contracts, or policies, as they began to be called somewhere about 1700, and did space permit, the history of the development of the fire insurance contract and its attendant clauses would well repay investigation and is recommended as an interesting and highly instructive topic for independent work for any who may care to pursue their studies. The present discussion, however, must be limited for the most part to contracts now in general use, and the history of the development which leads up to them cannot even be briefly indicated here beyond the statement that the simple and brief policies used in the early days of insurance history have expanded into the lengthy and complex documents now in general use by gradual process of development, the numerous changes embodying the results of the experience of the intervening years. Each new clause or provision has a history.

While most of the policies issued during the early years of the nineteenth century were similar, yet divergencies arose at a comparatively early date owing to changes and additions which resulted from the varying experiences and theories of different underwriters. These differences were increased by the efforts of those companies who strove to gain favor by attractive forms of contracts, also by those who endeavored, by cunningly worded and over-stringent forms, to prepare pretexts by which the payment of losses claimed might be avoided. This latter practice has even to this day characterized many contracts made attractive at first sight by their low prices. The swindler in fire insurance, as in other lines of business, endeavors to market worthless wares by quoting prices below those at which valuable and reliable articles can be secured. Since it usually happens that more than one company carries insurance on the same property, the difference in forms of contracts above referred to often produced dispute and confusion when claims arose under them. Until 1867, however, no great degree of uniformity was attempted. The various insurance centers, such as Boston, Hartford, New York, Philadelphia, and New Orleans, each had its characteristic form, some companies doing a widely extended business using various forms in different parts of the country.

In 1867 and 1868 the National Board of Underwriters, an organization comprising most of the leading fire insurance companies of the country, and which has had a very important influence upon the development of the fire insurance business, devised and adopted a form of contract or policy designed to be used universally. However, few companies outside of the city of New York adopted the form in its entirety, and the annoyance to which the public was subjected by the varying kinds of contracts, brought about in 1873, in the State of Massachusetts, a law providing for a standard form of policy, and in 1880 the Massachusetts standard policy was made obligatory upon all companies operating in that state.

In 1886 the State of New York also adopted a standard form of policy which became mandatory January 15, 1887. This policy was devised by the superintendent of insurance in consultation with various eminent insurance officials and organizations. It was carefully prepared and is, on the whole, while not altogether beyond criticism, the most useful and satisfactory fire insurance contract yet brought into anything like general use. It has been made mandatory by seven other states, and is commonly used by all insurance companies doing a widely extended business throughout the United States wherever the laws of individual states do not forbid.

Other forms of standard policies have been adopted by the States of Maine, Massachusetts, New Hampshire, Michigan, Missouri, Virginia, and Wisconsin, but are all inferior to the New York form, which we will accordingly adopt as the basis of our discussion. The standard policy is a form with the conditions and stipulations printed in a certain size type, prescribed by law so that it may be plainly read. Everything is prescribed by law except the premium, the term, date and amount. A space is left for the proper description of the particular piece of property to be insured.

The first part of the contract (see Chapter VIII), below the name of the company, is the statement of the consideration. Policies, like most other contracts, are not valid without a valuable consideration. The important thing to notice here is that not only the premium paid, but also the printed stipulations of the policy are a part of this consideration. Next follows the name of the person or corporation to whom the contract is issued. Then the beginning, duration, and ending of the period for which the contract is to run are clearly stated. You will note that the contracts begin and end at noon. For some reasons it would be more convenient to have a later hour than twelve o'clock, so that the policies might end at the close of a complete business day. Whether the language used means the solar noon, *i.e.*, the moment when the sun crosses the meridian, or twelve o'clock according to the standard time at the particular place where the policy covers, is not yet definitely settled by the courts. Next, the policy limits the amount for which the company may be liable. Then comes a clause limiting the application of the policy to the property described while in the location mentioned in the policy only. Needless to say, the contract is made and the rate of premium fixed according to the hazard of the location of the property when insured, hence the policy must be confined to that location, unless altered by a new agreement between the parties to it. Next follows a space for the description of the property to be insured; also for a description of its location and for any additional permits, stipulations or agreements (such as a permit allowing other insurance, or for the use of gasoline, etc.), which may be agreed upon by the company and the policy-holder, which additional agreements, however, must not be in conflict with the mandatory legal conditions of the policy. After the description follows a paragraph which defines, briefly and fully, the liability of the company and the method for settlement and payment of losses. The first few lines have already been anticipated, and do not need further comment. The latter portion of the paragraph states the options to which the company is entitled; (*a*) to pay to the assured the duly ascertained value of the property damaged, thereby acquiring ownership of it; or, (*b*) to repair, rebuild, or replace the property destroyed or damaged with other of like kind and quality after the loss or damage has been duly proved. But the assured is not permitted to abandon his property to the company except at its option.

The first option is often useful in cases where an excessive damage is claimed on articles whose value has been fixed during the settlement. For instance; if the assured and the company have agreed that the original or sound value of a damaged stock was $10,000, but cannot agree as to the amount of damage done by fire, water, or smoke, it is of course perfectly fair for the company to pay to the assured the agreed value, namely $10,000, and then to dispose of the stock as best it can. Very often by this means controversy is avoided and the claimant satisfied beyond cavil, while the company escapes with the loss of a much smaller sum than the claimant would have been satisfied to accept without dispute. Where this course is followed the damaged articles are usually cleaned, repaired, and put into the best possible condition and then sold. This process is called wrecking and has grown to be a business by itself. A number of insurance companies have organized a company to do such work, and there are also private concerns which conduct renovating establishments, where damaged goods and wares of every description may be cleansed, laundered, polished, repaired, dyed, or put through any other process that will make them salable, and the salvages thus made are frequently surprisingly large.

The second option — that which gives the company the privilege of replacing — is availed of by companies in extreme cases only. Insurance companies are not traders or contractors. They have no special machinery or opportunities for advantageous buying; in fact, are likely to be unable to purchase at as favorable terms as the assured.

Nor if a building is to be repaired or rebuilt can the work be economically supervised and watched by an insurance company, especially if, as is likely to be the case, the location is at a distance from the head office of the company.

Moreover, the requirement that the company shall furnish articles of like kind and quality involves certain risks, for it may be necessary to prove that this condition has been satisfied.

A noteworthy case of this kind occurred not many years since in Tennessee, where the owner of a hotel which had been destroyed succeeded in establishing what seemed to the companies interested an excessively high valuation, — so high, in fact, that it was thought a new building like the old one could be erected for much less than the amount claimed. Accordingly, the companies elected to rebuild instead of paying the loss, and having called upon the assured for plans and specifications, proceeded to make contracts for the restoration of the building exactly as it was before the fire. It was practically impossible for the companies to watch every detail of the construction, but an easy matter for the assured, who lived where the building was located. When the building was finished the companies tendered it to the assured in lieu of payment, but he was able to prove — or at least did prove to the satisfaction of a jury — that the building was not of exactly the same kind and quality as the old one which had been destroyed. Therefore he claimed the full cash payment, and the court decided that the companies were liable. As a result, the assured received the full amount of his claim, with interest, and since the new building was on his land, he also acquired that. This was a very costly experience for the companies and will suffice to explain why the option to replace is seldom used.

We now come to what are commonly called the conditions of the policy.

Paragraph 3 of the policy provides for the forfeiture of the policy by misleading or fraudulent acts or by concealment of material facts on the part of the assured. The policy is based upon the representations and statements of the insured and therefore it is but fair that the company should not be bound in a case where its contract has been secured by false statements, or because of the suppression or concealment of some material fact affecting the hazard. Most of the provisions in this paragraph refer to the negotiations attending the issuance of the policy.

Paragraph 4 renders a policy, which may have been valid during a part of its term, void in case, during its life, some act of the assured, or within his knowledge, operates to alter materially the conditions of the property insured as to hazard or ownership. Since the contract is a personal one it is obvious that a change in ownership makes it of no effect. Furthermore, the contract was made in view of the hazards existing at the time of its issuance and was determined in several important respects by those circumstances, hence a material increase of hazard cannot be assumed without a rearrangement of the contract — generally as to price, but also often as to the amount which the company is willing to carry. Some of the hazards mentioned in this paragraph, such as vacancy, generating of gas, storage of fire works, etc., are so dangerous that most companies will not assume or continue liability where they exist. All of the changes mentioned in this paragraph are considered to affect the hazards involved. It will be noticed that the saving clause "unless otherwise provided by agreement indorsed hereon or added hereto" makes it possible to alter an existing contract so as to permit any or all of the changes mentioned in the paragraph under consideration, *i.e.*, paragraph 4, and as a matter of fact almost every policy does permit one or more of the hazards or changes prohibited in this paragraph.

Paragraph 5 exempts the company from liability on account of fires caused by war, riot, or public authority. Such losses for the most part can be recovered from the municipality, and insurance would be a double compensation. Moreover, such losses are by their nature extraordinary and unavoidable under prevailing conditions. Even the apparatus for extinguishing fire, the presence of which may largely have reduced the price, cannot be used.

Paragraph 5 also in part exempts the company from losses which may be concurrent with a fire loss, but are not losses by fire itself. If the assured remove his goods endangered by fire to a place of safety, it is no more the province of the insurance company to protect them from theft than before. Often companies do pay for stolen articles, but only because it cannot always be determined whether these were burnt or purloined. So, too, when an explosion, as, for instance, of a boiler, is followed by fire, the company can be held for loss caused by fire only, and must be relieved from claims on account of any damage shown to have been caused by the explosion. The clause freeing companies from liability when an assured has failed to use reasonable means to save the property is rarely effective. The burden of proof is upon the company in such case, and it is practically impossible to establish beyond a doubt that the loss or damage was brought about by the assured's neglect to use reasonable means to preserve and save the property.

Paragraph 6 provides that when a building falls as the result of weakened foundations, or is overthrown by a wind storm, or some other cause, the fire insurance covering it instantly ceases, for the reason that such a building at once loses its value and becomes a heap of débris. Fires usually start in such cases from some overthrown lamp or stove, but the fire burns only the débris of a building already destroyed, — not the building itself.

The first lines of paragraph 7 provide that certain articles, not as a rule inherently valuable, but being the evidence of value, shall not be insured. Money and securities are included in this list. These articles afford such opportunities for fraud, can be so easily concealed, and the amount of them is so impossible to determine, except from the statement of the insured, that to insure them would put the company so absolutely at the mercy of the claimant that companies have never been willing to assume liability on them.

The next lines in the paragraph refer to articles concerning which there might be some dispute as to the application of a policy couched in general terms, or concerning the value of which a difference of opinion might readily arise, and, in general, articles of a class which companies will not willingly insure unless under exceptional conditions. Hence it is provided that, in order that these be included within the scope of a policy, they must be specifically mentioned. They are by no means prohibited from insurance; in fact, they are very commonly insured.

The last lines are intended simply to put the several companies who may happen to insure the same building under different forms of contracts on an equality as to certain very perishable items.

Paragraph 8 merely emphasizes what is said in paragraph 3 as to certain written statements made by the assured, or assented to by him prior to the issuance of policy.

Paragraph 9 is inserted for the protection of the companies, because, under the common law, an insurance contract may be affected or altered by verbal agreement, and because many of the details between agents and insurers must be handled by clerks. A clerk or a middleman may deliver a policy, collect the premium for the agent of the company, or even take an order for him, but cannot act as authoritative agent of the company unless so empowered by the company in writing. Many times claims for special terms, privileges, etc., are based on alleged verbal promises of clerks or middlemen.

Paragraph 10 simply enforces the conditions embraced in paragraphs 3 and 4 as to a policy renewed. In other words, it renews the obligation of the assured, as well as that of the company.

Paragraph 11 permits either party to the contract to terminate it. In case the company so elects, the assured is allowed five days in which to secure other insurance. When the assured chooses to cancel, the company is permitted to retain more than the proportional fractional part of the original premium; that is, in case of a one year policy canceled at six months by the assured, the company is allowed to retain slightly more than one-half of the premium. This is because the company is compelled to expend a considerable part of every premium received in handling the record of the contract so as to comply with the law, and in other ways to consume at the outset a part of each premium in fixed charges. If it is terminated prior to maturity by the assured, the law holds the company to be entitled fairly to recover those fixed charges. If the company chooses to cancel, however, these charges are lost, and the assured receives full return premium according to the time which the policy has run. Hence, contracts are seldom terminated by companies without good cause.

Paragraph 12 refers exclusively to mortgage interests, and provides that, as to such interest, companies may alter the policy conditions as they see fit. There is some plausible reason for this, since mortgages based upon the value of destructible property must be protected, and it is also necessary that such protection shall not be jeopardized by some improper action of the borrower, *i.e.*, the property owner.

Paragraph 13 simply provides that the efforts of the assured to save his property from destruction by removing it from danger shall not result to his harm. Ordinarily a removal without the consent of the company vitiates the policy and this paragraph simply makes an exception to this rule.

Paragraph 14 states very clearly the duties of the assured if fire occurs, and provides, *first*, — that he shall give the company due notice of its occurrence.

Second, — that he shall protect the property saved, whether damaged or undamaged, — at the same time making an inventory of the same, with complete statement of quantities, values, and amount of claimed damages. And,

Third, — that he shall, within sixty days, render a complete statement, under oath, giving in detail a full account of the fire and a description of the property involved, and of the facts concerning its ownership, in accordance with the list to be found in the paragraph under discussion.

The next paragraph gives to the company the opportunity to inspect all that remains of the property, to cross-examine the assured as to claims and statements made, and to verify same by an examination of the books and records of the assured.

It will be seen that these provisions and requirements contemplate the making of a complete proof or statement by the claimant, which the company may thereupon verify, test, and pass upon, and, if the proofs set forth a claim which is satisfactory and correct under the terms and scope of the contract, it is to be presumed the company will, at the proper time, pay it.

Paragraph 18 is very important. It provides for the distribution of loss among the various companies insuring identical property, according to the amount which each company carries. For instance, if there is $20,000 total insurance actually in force on any piece of property and one company carries $5000 of this amount, that company must pay and must pay only one-quarter of any loss occurring to the property up to the amount for which it is liable; and this condition is valid even if one or more of the other companies carrying the same risk are unable to satisfy the claims against them, for the amount of insurance legally in force determines the amount of various liabilities and claims. The collection of those claims is a subsequent operation.

The paragraph permits special agreements between assured and companies as to how policies shall apply. There are several of these agreements in common use, which will be described later in this lecture.

The last lines only apply where one insurance company assumes a portion of the liability of another company, and permit such contracts between companies to be arranged according to the desires of the two companies. This standard form of policy is intended to secure fair and proper conditions between companies and property owners, and such contracts between companies as reinsurances, so-called, are hardly within its purview.

Paragraph 19 is intended, first, to prevent double compensation; that is, a profit to the insured, from a fire; second, to compel those through whose act or neglect the loss occurred to make good the loss they have caused. Public policy as well as equity demands this. It is manifest that I should not be made free of financial responsibility for my criminal or careless act simply because the person I have injured is insured. In such cases companies commonly pay the loss and then endeavor to collect from the person or corporation responsible for the occurrence of the loss, the amount so paid.

Paragraph 20 is a statute of limitation to guard against wilful and vexatious delays in making claims.

Paragraph 21 is merely explanatory.

Paragraph 22 is intended for mutual companies only, and in effect makes the articles of association of such companies a part of the policy.

The remaining paragraph of the policy recites that no conditions of the policy may be altered except those whose language provides for modification, and that no permissible alteration may be made except by written endorsement on the policy. It will be seen that the whole purpose of the contract is to define the rights of the two parties interested so clearly and fairly that disputes may be avoided and injustice or improper claims prevented. Despite the care exercised by its framers to this end, however, there is hardly a clause in the standard form which has not been referred to some court for authoritative interpretation, and a mass of legal decisions have accumulated which in reality are collateral to the contract and might even with propriety be deemed a part of it. With these decisions, curious and interesting as many of them are, we shall not concern ourselves here, the broad outlines of the contract being sufficient for our purpose.

Despite the apparently stringent conditions and technical exceptions contained in this contract, and although these conditions and exceptions are sometimes made the basis of improper attempts to avoid payment of losses by unscrupulous companies, there can be no doubt that on the whole and in by far the greater number of cases, in fact almost universally, the assured secures absolute justice, and more, from the operation of this form of contract. A very liberal estimate of the amount of litigation under fire insurance policies indicates that not over one-half of 1 per cent. of claims result in law suits. When it is remembered that these claims are, in 90 per cent. of the cases occurring, for partial damage to property, concerning which there is legitimate opportunity for an honest difference of opinion, and in view of the fact that the validity, as well as the amount of all claims must be established before payment, the amount of ensuing litigations is seen to be absolutely inconsiderable. Not so in effect, however, for such is human nature that one resisted claim overbalances in public estimation a hundred which have been settled not only without friction, but even with liberality.

As we have seen, there are various portions of the policy which may be modified by special written agreements with the assured, called endorsements. Any of the numerous prohibitive clauses in paragraph 4 may be waived in this way. So also with the excepted articles noted in paragraph 5. The most important alterations in the contract, however, and those most generally in use are the ones which refer to interests of mortgagees and those which, as per paragraph 18, concern the extent of the application of the policy or its measure of contribution. The policy provides that, as to the creditor's interest, the contract shall apply as may be expressed in the written clause referring thereto. The ordinary way of recognizing a mortgagee's or creditor's interest is to issue the policy to the owner and then endorse upon it "loss, if any, under this policy payable to John Smith, mortgagee, as his interest may appear." When a loss occurs under a policy with this clause the amount of it is settled with the owner, but payment must be first made to the payee, *i.e.*, the mortgagee, until his interest is satisfied, or unless he consents to allow payment to the owner, as he usually will do when the loss is small. Since, however, many loaners need and demand absolute security, it is a very common practice to attach a printed mortgage clause which reads as follows:

"Loss or damage, if any, under this policy, shall be payable to .... as............. mortgagee [or trustee], as interest may appear, and this insurance, as to the interest of the mortgagee [or trustee] only therein, shall not be invalidated by any act or neglect of the mortgagor or owner of the within described property, nor by any foreclosure or other proceedings or notice of sale relating to the property, nor by any change in the title or ownership of the property, nor by the occupation of the premises for purposes more hazardous than are permitted by this policy; PROVIDED, that in case the mortgagor or owner shall neglect to pay any premium due under this policy, the mortgagee [or trustee] shall, on demand, pay the same.

"PROVIDED also, that the mortgagee [or trustee] shall notify this company of any change of ownership or occupancy or increase of hazard which shall come to the knowledge of said mortgagee [or trustee] and, unless permitted by this policy, it shall be noted thereon and the mortgagee [or trustee] shall, on demand, pay the premium for such increased hazard for the term of the use thereof; otherwise this policy shall be null and void."

This clause practically waives all rights of the insurance company as far as the payee is concerned. He may collect his due, even if it can be proven that the owner, that is, the assured, has fired the property himself, or if he has violated every condition of the policy. The only protection for the insurance company in those cases where the policy itself has been made void, but where nevertheless payment must be made to the creditor, is a provision that the claim of the creditor becomes the property of the insurance company and may be enforced by it against the debtor if collectible. This right of subrogation, as it is called, is frequently taken advantage of by companies and in some instances enables them to recover a loss which they have paid under such conditions. The mortgage clause also imposes certain responsibilities upon the mortgagee in case violations of policy conditions occur with his knowledge.

The clauses referring to the extent of the application or contribution of the policy are more difficult to explain briefly or to be comprehended readily. Before discussing those clauses at all, it may be helpful to make a few preliminary observations.

Where there is little or no protection against fire, that is, no local means of extinguishing fires, as in the case of village stores or shops, or where, for any other reason, the property to be insured is thought to be subject to great or total loss should a fire once start, the interest of the insurance companies leads them to limit the amount of insurance (as compared with the value of the property insured) which may be carried or recovered in event of loss. This is done in order that the interest of the owner in preserving the property may be so strong that the utmost watchfulness and careful attention will be observed by him. It is evident if, in the event of fire, he is likely to suffer a severe loss over and above his insurance, he will have a much stronger incentive to guard his property from fire than if it were insured for its full value. For a similar purpose companies find it necessary to limit the percentage of insurance to be carried in certain states or districts where conspicuous or abnormally heavy burning ratios indicate unusual carelessness, unsatisfactory protection, or dangerous methods of construction. In other words, the greater the danger of total loss the stronger pecuniary interest the owner should have in the preservation of his property. On the other hand, where there is efficient fire protection, as in most large cities, or where a policy covers in several distinct locations, or on property which is not readily susceptible to damage, as for instance, bar iron, there is a reasonable prospect that fires will be extinguished before a large portion of the property involved is destroyed. In such cases, therefore, insurance companies naturally desire that a large proportion of the value should be covered by insurance in order that a moderate loss of property shall cause only a moderate loss to the insurance company. In the unprotected village any loss is likely to be a total one. In the protected city almost all losses are partial, and insurance companies try to adapt their methods to the varying conditions.

Where it is desired to limit the amount of insurance, the New York law permits the use of the clause known as the "percentage value clause." This prevents the assured from recovering more than a certain, usually 75 per cent. of the value of the property insured. If by mistake he has been carrying insurance exceeding that amount, he is entitled to a return of the premium paid on the excess over the percentage which the clause fixes as a limit to recovery.

However, by far the greater amount of insurable property is located under more or less efficient fire protection and consequently the limitation clauses are not used, but instead, where possible — for in some states the law stands in the way — what is commonly known as the co-insurance clause is used, which reads:

"It is a part of the consideration of this policy, and the basis upon which the rate of premium is fixed, that the assured shall maintain insurance on each item of property insured by this policy, of not less than 80 per cent. of the actual cash value thereof, and that, failing so to do, the assured shall be an insurer to the extent of such deficit, and in that event shall bear his, her, or their proportion of any loss."

It provides in the words of Mr. F. C. Moore, "that whatever percentage of the property is destroyed — one-quarter, one-half, or three-quarters, as the case may be — that percentage of the insurance is payable"; or, as Mr. E. F. Beddall states the case, "it (the clause) leaves the insured free to carry as much or as little insurance as he deems needful, but it fixes the proportion of the loss recoverable from the company in the event of fire, to such as the assured has chosen to pay for. If he insures for one-half of the value he recovers one-half of the loss, be it partial or total; if the whole of the value, the whole of the loss. There is, there can be, no inequity in this."

Still another statement of its effect may be made as

follows: In order that the assured may secure indemnity for the whole of any large or small loss he may sustain, he must carry insurance equal to the full value of the property involved. Usually a percentage co-insurance clause is used, which makes some given per cent. of the value of the property, ordinarily 80 per cent., the amount which the insured must carry in order to secure in all cases full benefit of his insurance. Failing so to do, he can recover only such proportion of any loss amounting to less than 80 per cent. of the value of the property insured, as the amount of insurance he actually carries bears to 80 per cent. of the value. Thus, if the value is $10,000 and the insurance $5000, he can recover but five-eighths of any loss which amounts to less than $8000; that is, of any loss which amounts to less than 80 per cent. of the $10,000. When, however, the assured carries insurance equal to 80 per cent. of the value of the property covered, the 80 per cent. co-insurance clause is of no effect. The assured in such cases will receive the entire amount of his loss, be it large or small, not exceeding, of course, the amount of the policy. This should be carefully noted, for many people labor under the impression that where such a clause is used only 80 per cent. of any loss can be collected.

The co-insurance clause is even more important as a factor in the problem of making rates or prices, as we shall see when discussing that subject. Where this clause is used in a policy a reduction in price is made as compared with policies covering similar property similarly located, but without the co-insurance clause. In fact, this clause is often called the reduced rate clause in states where the law has not given it a name.

In some parts of the country, for instance Indian Territory, Texas, and Arkansas, where fires have occurred with abnormal frequency, and particularly on certain classes in those sections, such as cotton-gins, which are extremely liable to fire on account of the inflammable nature of the cotton and the process to which it is subjected, the percentage value clause is sometimes replaced by what is known as the "three-quarters loss clause," which reads as follows:

"It is understood and agreed to be a condition of this insurance, that in the event of loss or damage by fire to the property insured under this policy, this company shall not be liable for an amount greater than three-fourths of the actual cash value of each item of property insured by this policy (not exceeding the amount insured on each such item) at the time immediately preceding such loss or damage, and in the event of additional insurance — if any is permitted hereon — then this company shall be liable for its proportion only of three-fourths such cash value of each item insured at the time of the fire, not exceeding the amount insured on each such item."

This clause provides that the property owner shall suffer one-quarter of any loss, great or small, which may occur to his property. This, of course, is used for the same reasons that prompt the use of the percentage value clause, but is much more radical. And, as a further precaution, there is embraced in policies covering mercantile and manufacturing property in states with a bad fire history, clauses making the policies void unless the assured shall keep an accurate set of books, take an annual inventory, and either keep both books and inventory in a fireproof safe, or in a place where they will not be endangered by fire in a building where insurance covers. This clause is known as the "iron-safe clause," of which a copy is as follows:

"The following covenant and warranty is hereby made a part of this policy:

"*First.* — The assured will take a complete itemized inventory of stock on hand at least once in each calendar year, and unless such inventory has been taken within twelve calendar months prior to the date of this policy, one shall be taken in detail within 30 days of issuance of this policy, or this policy shall be null and void from such date, and upon demand of the assured the unearned premium from such date shall be returned.

"*Second.* — The assured will keep a set of books, which shall clearly and plainly present a complete record of business transacted, including all purchases, sales, and shipments, both for cash and credit, from date of inventory as provided for in first section of this clause, and during the continuance of this policy.

"*Third.* — The assured will keep such books and inventory, and also the last preceding inventory, if such has been taken, securely locked in a fire-proof safe at night, and at all times when the building mentioned in this policy is not actually open for business; or, failing in this, the assured will keep such books and inventories in some place not exposed to a fire which would destroy the aforesaid building.

"In the event of failure to produce such set of books and inventories for the inspection of this company, this policy shall become null and void, and such failure shall constitute a perpetual bar to any recovery thereon."

This clause is intended to bar out from the protection of insurance policies the shiftless and careless dealers and manufacturers who abound in many of the smaller towns, especially in the Southwest. It also insures a more satisfactory and intelligent loss settlement, should a loss occur, than is possible in those cases where the entire property is destroyed and no record of quantities or of transactions is preserved.

Still another clause used to govern the application of the policy is one known as the distribution average clause, which reads:

"It is understood and agreed that the amount insured by this policy shall attach in each of the above-named premises in that proportion of the amount hereby insured that the value of property covered by this policy contained in each of said places shall bear to the value of such property contained in all of above-named premises."

This clause provides that the amount of insurance shall attach in each of two or more locations according to the value in each. For instance, a merchant may have his merchandise in three locations — in his store where it is to be sold; in his warehouse, where he keeps a surplus stock, and in the freight depot of the railway or steamship line by which he receives it. As business progresses his merchandise is constantly shifted. One day two-thirds will be in his store; on another day one-half in his warehouse; on still other days he may have none at all in the freight depot. If he insures his stock under a policy with the distribution average clause, the policy will automatically divide itself as the stock is divided from day to day. If one-third of the value is in the warehouse so will one-third of the policy cover there. If the warehouse is empty the policy will apply only in the store and freight-house. And also that part of the policy which covers at each location will be equal to the fraction of the total value of the property at each location.

Various other clauses are used by companies to further the convenience of different patrons, or to provide against the contingencies which arise in different parts of the country, but the foregoing are the principal clauses, the others being more seldom used.

Policies are said to be specific when they cover on one kind of property or in one definite location; floating when they cover under one division property located at a number of different locations; general when they cover several kinds of property under different items at one location; concurrent when they agree exactly as to their wording and as to the kind of property covered; perpetual when their duration is without limit, except by cancelation.

These perpetual policies originated in Philadelphia, where they are chiefly, if not solely, used. It will be remembered that one of the earliest companies issued policies for seven years in consideration of a deposit by the assured, and that the deposit was to be returned to the assured at the expiration of the policy. It was a very natural process to agree with the assured to retain this deposit indefinitely, thus extending the term of the insurance and making it perpetual.

As we have seen heretofore, eight other states have prescribed the New York standard policy, and again, seven states have adopted standard policy forms of their own, each differing from the other and all from the New York form. It follows that every company which does a widely extended business must keep in stock at least eight different kinds of policies. Moreover, since some of the states permit any form of endorsement clause which does not conflict with the policy in use in that state, while others, like New York, permit only clauses which have been specifically authorized by law or passed upon by the insurance official of the state, it will be seen that companies are compelled to have and use a very great number of different clauses. In fact, it requires a very considerable amount of study and a good memory for any one person to be able to keep in touch with the widely differing state requirements as to policy forms and their attendant clauses. Such unnecessarily and often injuriously divergent laws entail great expense and labor on the companies, and neither they nor the insuring public benefit therefrom. It cannot be doubted that one simple form of policy and one set of appropriate clauses would be better for all concerned.

CHAPTER X

THE CO-INSURANCE CLAUSE

I[1]

It has always been a condition of marine insurance, as it should always have been a condition of fire insurance, that the principle of average or co-insurance should apply in determining the amount to be paid in case of loss. It would be as unjust to insure the properties of two owners at the same rate, the one insuring for 50 per cent. and the other for 100 per cent., as to assess the values of their properties for the purposes of municipal or state taxation on different percentages of value.

The old French co-insurance clause read as follows:

"If, at the time of the fire, the value of the objects covered by the policy is found to exceed the sum total of the insurance, the assured is considered as having remained his own insurer for that excess, and he is to bear, in that character, his proportion of the loss."

The German clause was as follows:

"If, in case of loss, the insured objects should exceed the sum insured, and they should be partly saved, the assured will be considered as self-insurer for the excess, and is to bear his share of the loss pro rata."

These two clauses met the issue squarely and left no room for mistake as to what was intended; but after the slipshod American methods of nearly a century of insurance it is doubtful if the use of these clauses, which were

[1] By Francis C. Moore. Reprinted from pages 573–580 of "Fire and Insurance and How to Build;" The Baker and Taylor Company. New York, 1903.

perfectly proper and straightforward, would be accepted without the criticism of placing a portion of the burden of insurance upon the policy-holder, overlooking the fact that if his rate is graded according to the amount that he carries, there is no more reason why he should complain than in the case of goods purchased at retail as compared with wholesale prices.

The following is the form of the co-insurance clause of New York State.

"This company shall not be liable for a greater proportion of any loss or damage to the property described herein than the sum hereby insured bears to . . . per cent. (. . . per cent.) of the actual cash value of said property at the time such loss shall happen.

"If the insurance under this policy be divided into two or more items this clause shall apply to each item separately."

The following is a clever illustration of the fairness of co-insurance:

To write a blanket policy upon large manufacturing plants which are composed of divers risks without the co-insurance clause is the equivalent of assessing a tax on your largest buildings at 30 per cent. of their value, while all other property in the city is assessed at 60 per cent. This discrimination, if made by your tax assessor, would be promptly corrected by the board of equalization; and yet by a singular paradox, legislators, who are insisting upon an equitable and equal assessment and collection of the fire tax, have attempted in some states to force us to tax the poor man at double the rate that we tax the rich corporation. To show you how necessary it is to collect a tax based upon about approximately 80 per cent. of the value of the properties, I will use an illustration which the insurance gentlemen present will understand, and which I hope will be perfectly clear to the laymen present.

Take 1000 detached frame dwellings worth $1200 each,

and insured at $1000 each. The premiums at 1 per cent. would be $10,000. Experience in this South Texas field demonstrates that the loss would be approximately $6000, or 60 per cent. of the premiums. Going further into detail, the underwriter who is making the rates finds that at least 60 per cent. of this total amount comes from trifling losses that range from $1.00 to $150; that there will be two or three losses where the damage will be practically 50 per cent., or $500 each, and two losses where we will say the losses are total, $1000 each. We then have the figures:

2 total losses of $1000 each	$2000
2 losses of 50 per cent., $500 each	1000
50 losses in small amounts from $1 to $150	3000

Now then let us suppose that some underwriter new to the business has entered the field, and has an opportunity to scoop these 1000 good detached dwellings. The owner has found out that most of his losses are small, and he concludes to take a small amount of insurance and no co-insurance. The tyro in the business takes $500 insurance on each one of these 1000 dwellings at the same rate, 1 per cent., which would make his premium $5000. The losses are the same as before. Let us see where each one of the underwriters will find himself. The figures in the last case would be as follows:

2 total losses, $500	$1000
2 damage losses of $500 each (but as the policies are for only $500 each there are two total losses to the company under these policies	1000
50 losses same as in first example, being for small amounts	3000
Total losses paid	$5000

The result of this brilliant feat of underwriting, in which the underwriter insures only one-half the value of the property without co-insurance, will be premiums $5000, losses to the insurance company $5000, and it is minus its expenses, which at 35 per cent. would amount to $1750. The company writing without the co-insurance clause, or at half value, has made a loss of $1750 or about 35 per cent., but this loss does not fall upon the company. Every company recoups its losses by an increased assessment of tax in some other direction, and the result is that the neighbors of the man who had these 1000 dwellings are assessed to pay the $1750 losses made in handling his business, together with a small profit which is needed for the company to continue in business. Is it fair to the owners of property throughout the state, who have been mulcted to pay the loss on this individual because he was improperly assessed?

The following illustration of President Evans of the Continental also shows how unfair is a policy, without the co-insurance clause, issued at the same rate as one containing the clause.

A and B each own a half interest in a building having a present structure value of $20,000. Each insures his half interest separately and in different companies; each company charges the same percentage or "rate" for insuring the property, and that "rate" is 1 per cent. or $10 for $1000 of insurance. A insures his half in the Y company for $10,000 and pays for his policy $100. B insures his half in the Z company for $5000 and pays for his policy $50. A fire occurs and the building is damaged $10,000 only. Company Y, insuring A, is called on to pay but 50 per cent. of the amount of its policy, while company Z pays 100 per cent.; and yet company Y received twice as much premium as did company Z.

It is sometimes impossible for the owner of property of a movable character, changing its location from day to day, and often from hour to hour in each day, as in the case, for example, of the product of a paper-mill, which in the morning may be in the paper-machines at one end of the mill and by evening in the dryhouse, to accept insurance covering specifically. Under such circumstances the distribution form of the average clause may be used, which practically secures specific insurance in that proportion which the insured would fix at the moment of a fire, if he knew the value in each location. In short, the policy applies for such proportion of its amount in any one location as the value in such location bears to the value in all locations.

Of course, the full co-insurance clause, the insurance being equal in amount to the value of all of the property, no matter where located, would take care of the interest both of the assured and of the company, but the property owner is not always willing to have a full co-insurance clause, and under the mistaken legislation of some states the use of any average or co-insurance clause is prohibited. The full co-insurance clause provides that whatever fraction or percentage of the value is destroyed that fraction of the insurance is payable. If one-half the value is insured one-half the loss is collectible from the insurance company. If the whole value is destroyed the whole insurance is collectible.

Let us suppose a merchant having goods stored in two different warehouses, A and B, so located relatively that they could not burn by one and the same fire. In A he has $6000 and in B $3000. If he should take out a policy of $6000 covering in both, without specific amounts and without the average clause, it is clear that the policy would effectually protect him, since a loss in either building would be covered by his insurance, and hence an insurance of $6000 would be almost as effectual as an insurance of $9000 written specifically, the only chance of his losing more than $6000 being in case both buildings should happen to burn at the same time. Any intelligent underwriter would decline to issue such a policy except at double rate; but if the merchant should claim that he could not tell at any one time just what proportion of value would be in each warehouse and for that reason alone could not insure specifically, and is unwilling to pay for insurance in excess of two-thirds of the value, the "distribution form" of the average clause would adjust the matter so that the policy would cover in each in proportion as its value should bear to that in both. This would be better than a specific policy for his purpose and equally as fair for the underwriter, since its effect would be to distribute the insurance at the time of the happening of a fire so as to cover or apply in each warehouse in the proportion that the value in such warehouse bears to the value in both. The insurance on this plan is thus made to follow the value, no matter how often it fluctuates.

Let us suppose the values, then, are $6000 in A and $3000 in B and that a fire occurs doing a damage in A of $4000; as the insurance covers in this building in the proportion that its value ($6000) bears to the value in both ($9000), two-thirds of the insurance, or $4000 would attach in A and in this case be sufficient to pay the loss.

Under the full co-insurance clause, by which the policy pays that proportion of the loss that the whole insurance ($6000) bears to the whole value of the property ($9000), or two-thirds, the owner would only receive two-thirds of his loss of $4000, or $2666.66

If instead of the full co-insurance clause, the 80 per cent. co-insurance clause is used, the policy for $6000 would pay such proportion of the loss, $4000, that $6000 bears to $7200 (80 per cent. of $9000) or five-sixths of it, *i.e.*, $3333.33.

II [1]

Two vital questions confront the fire insurance company with every policy it issues: 1. Is the property insured for

[1] By A. F. Dean, Assistant Manager, Western Department of the Springfield Fire and Marine Insurance Company. Reprinted from pages 119–125 of "The Rationale of Fire Rates"; J. M. Murphy. Chicago, 1901.

too great a proportion of its value? 2. Is it insured for too small a porportion of its value?

In the first instance the owner may become indifferent to the care of his property, or even have a direct incentive to destroy it by fire.

In the second instance the company does not receive sufficient compensation for the risk it assumes, and the owner secures more indemnity than he pays for, thus obtaining an advantage over other people who pay for what they get.

The problem of securing a uniform relation between insurance and value confronts every company in the acceptance of every risk; for it is an established principle in fire underwriting that rates cannot be made intelligently and fairly except on the theory that all property is insured for about the same proportion of its value. It makes no difference what this proportion be if everybody be insured for the same proportion. If all property were insured for only one-fourth of its value, statistical experience would soon reveal the proper rate for property insured for one-fourth value; but if one man has his property insured for one-fourth its value, and another for three-fourths, the former may receive as much indemnity in the event of partial loss as the latter, who paid three times as much for his insurance.

It is impossible for the company or its agent, or even the owner himself, to estimate closely the value of property, and even if it could be estimated, values are constantly fluctuating. The only way to adjust the matter to ensure equity to all concerned must be through a mutual agreement that if the property is not insured for a stipulated proportion of its value at the time of the fire, the assured shall be a co-insurer for the deficit.

This simple plan of adjusting a difficult problem is so fair that the use of the co-insurance clause is world-wide. In France, Italy, Spain, Portugal, Belgium, and the Rhenish Provinces, the co-insurance clause is required by law, and in other parts of Europe the agreement is invariably made a part of the policy contract.

It is singular that what is obligatory throughout Europe is prohibited in this country by law. At the present time ten prominent states of the Union forbid the use of the co-insurance clause. The only explanation ever given for this prohibition of co-insurance is that it encourages over-insurance, but many of the states, while prohibiting co-insurance on this ground, have enacted a valued-policy law which offers an incentive for people to over-insure their property. Besides, a co-insurance clause that makes the agreed proportion between the insurance and value 80 or 90 per cent. does not encourage over-insurance.

Aside from the mathematical necessity for a uniform relation of insurance to value in establishing equitable rates, co-insurance is the safeguard that protects small property owners from the cunning devices of large corporations in their efforts to avoid the payment of their share of the fire tax. If the facts could be once understood, there would be not only a popular demand for the repeal of all laws prohibiting co-insurance, but a demand for the enactment of the European laws which make co-insurance obligatory; because the European laws ensure a just distribution of rates, while the American laws put it in the power of the propertied interests to unload a share of their fire tax upon people of small means. The evasion of the fire tax in this way is no less notorious or unjust than the evasion of state and municipal taxes. It is difficult to make this plain to one not versed in fire insurance. In fact, the vital bearings of co-insurance on rates are not appreciated by the majority of fire underwriters. The importance of the subject, however, justifies the following explanation:

It should be borne in mind that but a small proportion of fire losses are total. Out of twenty claims made against the companies, on a low estimate nineteen are partial losses, ranging from a merely nominal damage up to the nearly full value of the property. This average of partial losses is enormously increased when the property insured is not all subject to one fire. In nearly all large wholesale and manufacturing establishments the contents are located in different compartments, which are separated by brick walls with fire-proof doors and shutters over every opening. Sometimes the property is located in a number of different buildings. When a fire starts in one compartment or building, the fire department, in ninety-nine cases out of a hundred, is able to confine it to that compartment or building, so that in establishments of this kind a total loss seldom or never occurs.

The practice in American fire underwriting, up to about fifteen years ago, was to require a specific amount of insurance upon every building, and when a building was divided by solid brick walls with fire-proof doors, a separate amount of insurance was required to be placed on and in each compartment.

The reason for this was, that if the insurance were spread to cover the entire establishment in one item of insurance, the owners would need only enough insurance to cover the value in one compartment or building, as this would be enough to cover all possible loss. The equity of the regulation regarding specific insurance was so plain that large merchants and manufacturers could not reasonably object to it, and specific insurance was the rule throughout the country, but it was found that specific insurance worked an injustice to property owners in one respect. The owner knew, at least approximately, how much insurance he needed on each building, but it was impossible for him to tell how much he needed on the contents of each building. If a mercantile stock, the value in each compartment or building was constantly changing, and he could not keep his books to show the value in each compartment; if a manufacturing plant, the property in process of manufacture was constantly shifting from one part of the establishment to another, and it was impossible to estimate from the books the value of the property in any one building or compartment. Wholesale merchants and large manufacturers of all kinds began to insist that they must have their insurance arranged to cover any part of their establishment where fire might occur. The companies then proposed to issue policies under a blanket form (that is, covering the entire property in one sum), provided the assured would agree to keep the property insured for 80 per cent. of its value, and if the insurance at the time of the fire should be less than that proportion, the insured should be a co-insurer for the difference between the amount of insurance and 80 per cent. of value.

People readily accepted this equitable arrangement, which relieved them from the care of constantly watching values in each compartment to see that the insurance was adequate. In a short time blanket policies with the co-insurance clause came into general use, and all the large commercial and manufacturing establishments of the country were insured under what became known as "the blanket form, with co-insurance."

In time some schemer discovered that if he could get the co-insurance clause declared illegal, it would be possible to reduce his insurance materially, without impairing the protection afforded by his blanket policy form. To offer any bill that seems inimical to fire insurance is to ensure its enactment in many states, and the anti-co-insurance law has been spreading ever since under the active encouragement of interested property owners.

This law, coupled with the law forbidding tariff rates, creates a condition in fire insurance as absurd as if the state, which requires its tax officials to take oath that they will spread taxes equitably, should at the same time forbid them to fix a uniform tax percentage, or to establish property valuations.

The concession of blanket insurance was obtained on the condition of co-insurance; now the great trusts of the country are claiming the benefits of blanket insurance without co-insurance. Under the anti-co-insurance law there has been a constant reduction of insurance to value on every risk insured under a blanket form, and it is well within bounds to say that, in the aggregate, such risks are not insured for over 40 per cent. of value, and the owners are securing their fire indemnity for about half what they would have to pay for protection under a specific form, thus securing their insurance at an advantage over people of small means whose property is usually located in one building, and subject to total destruction by a single fire.

Co-insurance was not required when insuring dwellings, stores, schools, public buildings, or other similar property. There are thousands of towns throughout the country where the clause was never heard of, and where the people have no direct interest in the subject; but indirectly every small property owner is interested, because the prohibition of co-insurance benefits no one but the great concerns whose distributed property is usually located in cities, or under the protection of private fire departments. Blanket insurance enables these concerns to evade their just share of the insurance tax at the expense of the community at large, because a corresponding increase is made in the loss ratio shown by the statistics upon which rates are established.

It is proper to add that the principle of co-insurance has always been applied to marine insurance, though the reasons are not so logical as in fire insurance, because in the marine risk the property is all exposed to loss, while in a large proportion of fire risks the property is so distributed that it is not subject to total loss. No explanation has ever been given why our laws permit the universal use of co-insurance in marine insurance while prohibiting it, with severe penalties, in fire insurance.

CHAPTER XI

DISCRIMINATION AND COÖPERATION IN FIRE INSURANCE RATING [1]

I. *Discrimination*

DISCRIMINATION in fire insurance rating has two effects. First, substantial injustice is done to competitors, be those competitors individuals, corporations, or cities; second, maladjustment of fire insurance rates has a very serious effect upon the annual fire loss of the country. Not much has been heard of this second effect, but there are reasons for believing that it is of more importance than the injustice which is done to competitors through discriminating rates.

The losses by fire in the United States, direct and indirect, amount to more than half a billion dollars annually. Much attention is being directed to this fire waste, and its causes and remedies are being sought. A great deal is being said about the ignorance of American builders, and of the extravagance of Americans in general in allowing such a tremendous waste to go on, not diminishing in amount, but actually increasing year after year. These accusations are largely unfounded. Nowhere in the world has the art of constructing fire-proof buildings made such progress as in the United States; therefore if Americans build badly, it is for some other reason than ignorance. Americans may be extravagant in their personal expenditures, but better building is a business proposition, and it

[1] By Lester W. Zartman, Assistant Professor of Political Economy in Yale University. Reprinted from the August number of the *Yale Review*, 1909.

would be rather difficult to prove that American business men as a rule are not quick to take advantage of ways of saving money in business. As a matter of fact, a considerable amount of the loss by fire is suffered in the United States because it would be unprofitable to try to prevent the loss. The relative costs of combustible construction and fire-resisting construction have varied so widely that it has been cheaper to build as we have and let buildings, and even cities, burn up occasionally than to attempt to prevent the loss by constructing better buildings.

The principle can be laid down that, in general, if fire insurance rates are properly adjusted, a community will have just that amount of good construction which is profitable for it to have. In other words, the problem of reducing waste by fire is the problem of the cost of fire-proof materials and insurance rates. Prospective builders learn how much different types of buildings will cost; they then find out what the rate of fire premium is on each type and build accordingly. No one can doubt that the rates of fire insurance have a tremendous effect upon the character of construction. If an improvement in construction from the fire standpoint is to be made, it will come as a result of a reduction in the premium rate for insurance. In order to secure the improvement there must be enough saving in the insurance to pay interest upon the additional capital needed for the better construction and enough more to provide a sinking fund to replace the extra capital after a certain number of years. Therefore one of the most important things to consider in discussing the problem of the fire loss is the question of fire insurance rating. If rates measure correctly the various hazards, then the whole attention may be directed to securing cheap fire-proof construction.

Do the rates of fire insurance measure correctly the various hazards? From time to time the charge is made that they do not. Why they do not and what attempts have been made on the part of the companies to make rates conform to hazards, it is the purpose of the present paper to show.

Those who have given the subject of fire insurance rating any thought recognize the extreme complexity of the problem. In life insurance the medical director of each company, in selecting risks, has in mind a standard man — not a physically perfect man, but one who he thinks will live at least a certain number of years. Every applicant who comes up to the requirement of this standard man is accepted; with most companies, all those risks which do not come up to the standard are rejected. Competition among the life insurance companies in the payment of dividends brings them all to much the same standard. How different it is in the fire insurance business! Where is the standard building, the average risk? Frame buildings have one hazard of burning, brick buildings have another; frame churches have one hazard, frame factories have an entirely different hazard. There is one loss record on frame warehouses that are isolated from other buildings, and another loss record on those frame warehouses which are adjacent to other buildings. Each class of buildings has its own peculiar hazards, and every combination of buildings within each class and with those of other classes has a different hazard; the number of combinations, each producing its own risk of fire is infinite. Complicate this situation with the hazards of various kinds of occupancy, and the problem of getting at correct fire rates is apparently insoluble. As if this were not enough to make the problem difficult, there is still the change ceaselessly taking place in methods and materials of construction and in the processes carried on within buildings. Human life has experienced some alteration in 2000 years, but every succeeding phase, at least in modern times, has been marked by a greater longevity. This has made the business of life insurance constantly more secure. In fire insurance the changes in hazards are taking place so rapidly that if the companies had had exact data twenty years ago on which to base rates, they would be nearly useless to-day. The growth of cities, the concentration of population, the building of sky-scrapers, the use of electricity for light and power, the changed methods and machinery in factories — all these have created, within a short period, a new world for the fire insurance business.

Lastly, to complicate the rating situation, there are the conflagrations. The nearest analogy, taking such catastrophes in account, would be life insurance companies attempting to carry on their business under the conditions which prevailed in mediæval times in Europe, when terrible epidemics swept over the country carrying off at times a quarter of the population. To carry on the business of life insurance under such conditions would be well-nigh impossible; yet in the fire insurance field, the conflagrations to-day are almost as disturbing a factor as such epidemics would be in that of life insurance. Feared by all careful managers, subject to no known law of average, they introduce a new complexity into what is already a maze of complexities.

Under such conditions what progress has been made towards securing scientific rating? Space will permit no more than a brief outline of the development which has taken place. In the early history of fire insurance the rating system was extremely simple. All risks were divided into two classes, brick buildings and frame buildings, and the premium on frame buildings was double that on brick buildings. About 1720, risks in England were divided into three classes, and for a century and a quarter this change, with but few modifications, was all the advance made by English companies towards scientific fire-rating. It was in the year 1800 that companies in New York City began first really to classify risks, all risks being grouped under four classes, and a rate fixed for each class. Progress in rating advanced slowly. As late as 1856, more than a century after the establishment of the first fire insurance company in America, a prominent official of one of the companies asserted that nothing more was known about the actual cost of insuring different risks than was known when the first company was established.

Up to 1835 there was not much need for the companies to know the cost of insuring various classes of risks, for up to that time the business of each company had been largely local. Competition was not keen, and the companies simply fixed rates high enough to be sure of a profit. But when the New York conflagration of 1835 and another in 1845 showed the companies that it was fatal to concentrate their business in one locality conditions were seen to have become vastly different; the companies began to spread out in order to get a wide distribution of risks. They thus came in contact with each other, competition became intense, and rates went down. How low they could go and still allow a profit to be made the managers of the companies did not know. As a matter of fact the rates sank too low, and the companies lost heavily. This keen competition for business, with the consequent fall in profits, had an important effect upon the methods of conducting the business. Managers found it necessary to know more about the cost on various kinds of hazards, and classification of risks was taken up in earnest. To-day all the companies are classifying the risks which they insure, though this activity amounts to scarcely anything, inasmuch as no advance has been made over the start given seventy years ago.

After classification of risks, the next step towards better fire-rating was the adoption of the system of rating certain classes of risks by schedules. It is not known exactly how schedule rating originated. So far as information is available, one of the earliest, if not the first, of the applications of the method was made in 1852 by the Philadelphia Board of Fire Underwriters; the schedule adopted was simple and was intended to apply to Philadelphia alone. From that time to this a considerable number of schedules have been worked out by the various underwriting associations; at the present time many different schedules are in use, though there is a gradual tendency towards the adoption of two, the Universal Mercantile Schedule and the Dean Schedule, the latter being at the present time more popular than any other schedule that has ever been devised.

Schedule rating is, in essence, the attempt to secure scientific rating by an elaborate system of classification. Under this schedule system, rates are made by applying to classes of risks and to individual risks certain predetermined charges and credits based upon the various factors of construction, occupancy, degree of exposure to and of protection against fire. For instance, in getting the rate for a specific building there is what is known as the basis rate, which is the rate made upon a certain type of building; in one schedule it is a simple, one-story, brick building; in another it is a well-built, five-story building. The basis rate having been determined, it is applied to the risk to be rated; then the various defects in construction, dangerous factors of arrangement and deficiencies in the nature and extent of the apparatus for fire protection are listed with fixed or percentage charges for each deviation from the standard; credits are then allowed in the schedule for features of equipment or construction better than those possessed by the standard building. Add the charges to the basis rate, subtract the credits, the remainder is the rate upon the specific risk. This is schedule rating.

That the system of rating by schedules is a great improvement over the old method of judgment rating is well recognized. Especially is the adoption of the schedule system of importance in securing better construction. Under the system where the special agent is told that the average premium rate on warehouses for the last ten years has been one dollar and thirty-two cents, with a loss ratio of 43 per cent., and is then sent out to make rates on such buildings, no one can tell what rate his particular building will receive. If a man is contemplating building a new warehouse, or making changes in an old one, and desires, if it pays, to improve the fire hazard by better construction, all that the agent can do is to tell him to go ahead and build, and then a rate will be made. With such uncertainty, no one is likely to consider the fire rates a great deal. Under a system of schedule rating, even one inexperienced in fire insurance matters can take most of the schedules and figure out precisely what reduction in rate will be given for better construction. Will it pay to enclose the elevator wells with brick walls? Look up the schedule and find out; for all is determined beforehand. The schedule system recognizes to a large extent what must be acknowledged, namely, that each building has an individuality of its own. Fire insurance must attempt to measure the hazard of each individual risk, and fit it with a specific rate; and this it does attempt to do through the schedule system of rating.

As has been said, the schedule system of rating is a great advance over the old method of judgment rating; but much remains to be accomplished. If the charges and the credits in the schedule were determined by the known experience of the companies — if shingle roofs, for example, were penalized 10 per cent. because the hazard of burning were known to be increased 10 per cent. by their presence, and these charges and credits were continually revised in the light of new experience — the business of fire insurance would have reached its highest development. Such is not the case. Charges and credits are not based on facts; the schedules so far constructed have simply substituted for the judgment of one rating expert, the combined judgment of a number of experts. This can well be illustrated by the history of the Universal Mercantile Schedule: half a dozen different underwriting associations appointed representatives to formulate a schedule; from the thirty-seven representatives appointed a committee of four was chosen, which made up a tentative schedule representing the pooled judgment of its members;

this schedule was then sent out to all the raters in the various Eastern associations asking for suggestions and criticisms, in the light of which the committee went over all the suggestions, combining them as best it could. This process was repeated five times, so that the final schedule is the result of the combined judgments of a considerable number of men experienced in fire insurance matters; but while this method produced a good schedule, the schedule lacks the authority which one based on statistical data would possess.

This explanation of the ways in which rates are determined has been given in order that the following discussion of rate discriminations may be better understood. The fact to be kept in mind regarding all rates, schedule or otherwise, is that they have no statistical basis. To show that the fire insurance companies do not have a scientific foundation for the rates which they charge does not, indeed, prove that the rates are inequitable; unfortunately, however, for the companies, when under charges of discrimination, they cannot prove that their rates are just, save in the aggregate. Such lack of knowledge is bad for the business, for it causes much hostility on the part of the public and results in much unwise legislation.

Most fire insurance experts will readily admit that discriminations abound in fire insurance rating. In fact the very terminology of the business shows that all classes of risks are not rated according to the risk of loss; almost since the beginning of the business there have existed what are known as preferred classes of risks and others known as special hazards. This could not be if all risks were rated according to the risk of loss, for under such conditions there would be just as much profit in insuring mills, warehouses, and stores, as in writing policies on dwellings and churches. The fact that this terminology of preferred and special classes is not merely the result of a traditional distinction of earlier times, is betrayed by the effort on the part of the companies to secure the preferred classes of risks to-day. In many agencies, 10 per cent. more commission is given for preferred business than is paid for premiums on special hazards.

Two interesting questions immediately arise; why is it that the discriminations in rates are made, and how is it that in such a business as freely competitive as is fire insurance, the distinction between preferred and special risks can be maintained year after year? It will help us in answering the former query to distinguish various kinds of rate discriminations. First, there is the discrimination between large classes of risks such, for instance, as dwellings on one hand and factories on the other; second, there are discriminations between localities; and, again, there are unjust rates as between specific risks.

Taking up in order these varieties of rate discrimination, we first ask why there are preferred classes of risks. These classes exist because of the desire on the part of the companies to assess rates in such a way as to arouse the least opposition. There are many analogies between fire premiums and taxes; as with governments, — which have always found it necessary to levy taxes not so much with regard to the question of their being ideally just, as to the question of whether they can be imposed without raising a storm of opposition, — so is it with the fire insurance companies. They have found that they can levy high rates on dwellings, on contents of dwellings, on churches, schoolhouses, public buildings and kindred risks without causing much opposition. The reason is not far to seek. The rates on dwellings as a class are low, absolutely speaking; few people have large values, so that the premium on each risk is moderate and usually causes little objection to be made. Suppose there is some opposition to the dwelling rates; it may result in a man complaining to his neighbor that the rates on dwellings are too high, and the neighbor may agree with him; but this is about as far as the opposition ever gets. In the same way high rates on churches, schools, and similar property cause little opposition, but how different is the situation if the companies make an increase in rates on mercantile or factory risks. Practically every city has its trade organization, a chamber of commerce, or a board of trade, composed of the leading business men of the city. Even a small increase in rates on risks owned by these men makes a great deal of difference to them, for here values are large. An increase in rates on risks owned by these men means opposition — and opposition which counts, for the organization already exists by which it can be concentrated. The influence which these boards of trade and similar organizations can have upon legislation is so powerful that any rating organization thinks twice before it raises rates upon mercantile and manufacturing risks.

The next question which follows from this description of the condition in fire insurance is why in a business so fiercely competitive as fire insurance there can continue to exist permanent classes of preferred risks. If the old companies are in an agreement to maintain rates, why are not new companies organized to compete for the preferred business, thus bringing rates down to cost? Suppose a company were organized to make a drive for the preferred business. It could get it in two ways: it could either establish new agencies, or it could try to enter into already established agencies. Suppose it chose to establish new agencies, and by reducing rates on dwellings attempted to secure business; about the first man who was approached by the agent of the reduced-rate-on-dwellings company would say, "Reduced fire insurance premiums are just what I want. At what rate can you write my factory?" The agent would have to reply that he could not write the factory at all. The dwelling-house owner would answer that, if the agent could not write the factory he would not change any of his insurance, as the old agent who had always handled his business had had a pretty hard time placing the factory, and it would not be fair to take the dwelling away from him. Thus the agent for the preferred class company would have an extremely difficult task in getting much business.

Suppose then our company, instead of establishing new agencies, attempted to get into established agencies which already control many risks. The local agents have no use for a company which writes preferred risks at reduced rates. A local agent usually represents a number of companies, and any of these is perfectly willing to handle all of the preferred business which the agent controls. The problem with the local agent is, as we shall see, to dispose of his specials. He can do so only by shrewdly mixing them up with his preferred lines. If he gave the preferred business to an outside company, he could not place his less acceptable risks. Thus it is that the local agent refuses ordinarily to represent the reduced rate company, and the company organized to specialize in preferred classes must get business in some other way than by reducing rates.

There are companies which make a specialty of preferred business, but their entry into the field and their success in it has not brought about a better adjustment of fire insurance rates. Rather have they made it worse, for, unable to secure business in either of the ways suggested above, they have purchased it by the payment of excessive commissions. While they have found it impossible to get agents to give them the preferred business by offering to write it at lower rates of premium, they have found it possible to get some agents to give them a share of it at the old rates by offering more commission than the other companies are accustomed to give. By doing this they have not benefited the public by making rates more equitable, for rates have not been reduced; rather have they worked harm by increasing the expenses of the business. Thus are explained the existence and continuance of preferred and special hazards in fire insurance.

The second kind of maladjustment of fire insurance rates is that between different localities. Reference is made to the relative rates between those risks which are subject to the conflagration hazard and those which are not so subject. It has been asserted that if the companies would publish their experience in the ten largest cities of the country, it would be shown that in every one the companies have lost money. That rates should be universally too low in the larger cities, thus encouraging poor construction where good construction is most needed, is due to a number of causes. In the first place, there are the conflagrations. A conflagration is of such sporadic occurrence that, under the conditions of competition which have prevailed, it cannot be taken into consideration in making rates; that this is true is lamentable, since the best remedy for conflagrations would be the penalty of high insurance rates upon those cities where a conflagration is possible.

The conflagration, however, is not the only cause of unprofitable underwriting in large cities. Even the cities which have not suffered from conflagrations show a balance on the wrong side from the fire insurance standpoint. Another cause must be sought; and it is to be found in the conditions under which the sale of fire insurance takes place in large cities. The city has evolved the fire insurance broker, who is shrewder in many cases than the underwriters with whom he deals. He takes advantage of the ignorance of the companies in not knowing the cost value of the commodity in which they deal, and, pitting one company against another, is able to drive a hard bargain. Yet, notwithstanding the unremunerative rates, the large cities are to the average manager tempting ground for work; policies can be written for large amounts and a considerable premium income easily secured. The result is that ambitious managers can scarcely refrain from establishing agencies in the large cities; this makes competition for business severe, and where coöperation among the companies is needed most to hold off the broker, coöperation is almost impossible because of the number of companies and the number of agencies. Without coöperation, rates are cut and exorbitant commissions given for poor business. Thus it is that in the places where the heaviest penalty ought to be placed on poor construction, the tendency is to make it light, and the day of fire-proof cities is put further away.

We come now to a discussion of the last kind of maladjustment of rates, namely, those discriminations in rates which are made between specific risks rather than between classes of risks as a whole. There are several causes for these discriminations. In the first place, companies frequently accept risks at rates, which they know to be grossly inadequate for the risk assumed, simply because they do not wish to offend local agents. To understand how this is so it is necessary to explain briefly how the agency system is organized. A local fire insurance agent frequently represents from four to twelve, sometimes even twenty different companies; an agent who controls large risks needs to represent that many companies, else he could not place all his insurance without dividing up commissions with other agents. The amount, or the "line," as it is technically called, which one company is willing to write on one risk is limited. When a risk is so large that all the companies in an agency get as large a line as each one wants on the risk, there is no quarrel between them; the conflict of interests arises with the smaller risks, and every company, through its special agents, is continually urging the local agent to give it a larger proportion of these smaller risks. On the other hand, the local agent has an assortment of risks under his control which no company wants very much at any rate, and a good many risks which none of the companies want at the rate which is offered. And so he takes advantage of the situation and offers to one of his companies a number of choice risks, preferred business, along with a number of risks which are not so choice. The company can take all, or refuse all; for the local agent will not allow it to pick the good and leave the bad. Thus by shrewdly playing one company off against another, and by carefully mixing up his risks, the local agent is able to force the companies to take risks which they ought not to take at the rates which are offered. Of course, if it were not for the existence of the preferred business, the agent could not get the poor risks in, but the preferred business exists, and the manager of the fire insurance company, in order to get his share of it, will accept many risks at inadequate rates.

Another reason why rates on specific risks are not fixed in proportion to the hazard of loss is because the principle of charging what the commodity will bear holds true in fire insurance just as it does in almost every business where there are large fixed expenses. The way in which this element of fixed expenses, with the consequent cutting of rates, enters into the fire insurance business can be shown best by an example. Let us assume that a company has established itself in a large number of agencies all over the country; to carry on the business profitably it must have a well-organized force of special agents, and a highly trained home office staff. Under these conditions let us assume further that a risk, say a factory, is offered to the company; the company wants the business, but competition is keen, and a competitive rate must be named. To find out this competitive rate, it is only necessary to analyze the expenditure of the company. The total premium income, in general, is paid out as follows:

Losses	55 per cent.
Commissions	15 " "
Salaries of special agents	5 " "
Maintenance of home office	15 " "
Taxes	3 " "
Profit	7 " "

If the burning ratio on the class to which the factory in question belongs is $.825 per hundred, in order to get the current rate of profit, to charge the factory its proportion of the fixed expenses and to pay the agent the regular commission, the company would have to name a rate of $1.50 per hundred on the factory. It will not charge that rate if a lower rate is necessary to secure the business from a rival, and it need not in order to make acceptance of the business profitable; as the expenses for special agents and home office force will continue whether that risk is accepted or not, and both of these can be ignored in making the rate. The tax will have to be paid, and some commission to the local agent, though at times the agent is willing to take a smaller commission in order to induce his company to accept the risk. Therefore, the company can fix a rate of $1.00 on the risk and still make a profit as follows:

Expected loss	$.825
Taxes	.03
Commission	.10

which makes a total expense of $.955, leaving a profit of nearly 5 per cent. to the company upon the transaction, even with the heavy reduction in rate. This assumed situation reflects precisely the real condition in the fire insurance world when that business is subject to free competition; it explains the rate wars which formerly occurred frequently, and which some large insurers and legislators would evidently like to have occur again.

Along with these improper adjustments of rates another allied charge is made against the fire insurance companies, namely, that the companies will not reduce rates readily when hazards are reduced by the adoption of better forms of construction or of fire-preventing devices. Some very good fire insurance men have said that they are not interested in reducing the fire loss; that it is the only function of fire insurance companies to take losses as they find them and to assess them on the community. They are right. That is precisely their function; only they must be sure that they take hazards as they find them and not as they do not find them.

It is perhaps safe to predict that the fire insurance companies will never take the lead in encouraging better construction by granting rate reductions for improvements in hazards. There are good reasons for this prediction. In the first place, what reduction in the rate should be given for an improvement in the hazard — say, for example, for the introduction of automatic sprinklers? No one knows until they are tried for a considerable period, and no one is going to try them unless he can get his fire rate reduced; the insurance companies are not philanthropic enough to make the experiment, neither are business men. The result is that only in rare instances are improvements adopted. Furthermore, to one very interested party in fire insurance rating, a reduction in rates means an actual loss in income. Local agents the country over are compensated by means of a commission upon the premiums secured; and reduction in rates means a reduction in their income. As the local agents still play an important part in rate-making, it is contrary to human nature to expect them to become very enthusiastic over rate reductions. Thus it is that neither the companies, nor the local agents, lead the way in encouraging good construction by offering rate reductions for lessening the danger from fire.

In summing up the situation in regard to fire insurance rates, it has been found that in three different respects rates are not adjusted to the hazard of loss. There are preferred classes of risks; cities are not penalized for their liabilitity to suffer conflagration losses; and there are many individual risks taken at improper rates. Such maladjustment of fire insurance rates has two effects: first, it is a serious factor in the business world where competition is severe; second, it has a most important effect upon the amount of the annual waste by fire. That waste alone is becoming so great that strenuous effort should be made to lessen it; and so far as it is increased by improper fire insurance rating, every attempt to secure a better rating system should be eagerly welcomed.

II. *Coöperation*

In the preceding section, it has been pointed out that rate discriminations in fire insurance prevail. Such a showing is no reflection upon the ability or the motives of the managers of our fire insurance companies; it is not a result which any of them desires. In fact, the officers of the companies are more directly interested in stopping these rate discriminations than is the public; they would like very well indeed to have some plan devised whereby the fire loss could be equitably assessed on the different classes of risks. Frequently the impossibility of assessing the fixed charges upon some risks has become so general that the fixed charges are not collected at all, and the companies have ended the year with losses instead of gains to their credit. To prevent this situation from recurring and to secure better conditions in the fire insurance world, the companies have found it necessary to work together, to form what are commonly known as fire insurance compacts or combinations. These compacts are of such great importance in the fire insurance business and are the subject of so much public discussion that it will be well for us to analyze carefully the objects for which they are formed, and to find out, if we can, the legitimacy of each object. The companies have coöperated for the following purposes:

1. To regulate rates.
2. To regulate commissions.
3. To secure effective and economical supervision of risks.
4. To study hazards.
5. To repress incendiarism.

Is it to the advantage of the public that the companies should be allowed to coöperate to secure these objects, or is it to the injury of the public? Let us consider each of the objects in order. Is a system of compact rating better for the public than rates made by competition?

We have just learned that there are three ways in which discriminations in rates are made. These evils are almost entirely the result of competitive conditions. If the companies could coöperate closely enough they could do away with preferred classes, and increase rates on the special hazards. They do not dare to increase rates on the latter class because they are afraid that the men who own them will go to their legislatures and get laws enacted forbidding all coöperation among the companies. The large cities get relatively low rates because of the competitive conditions; and the third variety of discrimination which has been described is due entirely to competition. If these evils in rating are the result of free competition between the companies then the way to abolish them is to allow the companies to coöperate in making compact rates.

The second object which the companies have sought to obtain through coöperation is the regulation of commissions paid to agents for securing business. There is almost as much necessity for tariff commissions as there is for tariff rates. There are two ways of increasing the business of a company; one way is to cut rates, and the other is to increase commissions. In many cases the latter method is more successful than the former; to understand how this is true it is only necessary to recall the peculiar organization of the agencies. Instead of a company having in a city an agent who represents it exclusively, it has one who may represent a dozen of its most powerful competitors. This is a situation — a number of rivals having a common representative — found in few other businesses, and the result is competition for business within the agency. If this is unchecked, it takes the form of giving larger commissions for business. A local agent controls a certain number of risks; a special agent may stir him up to solicit more risks and thus increase his company's business, or the special may offer more commission to increase his company's business at the expense of the competing companies in the same agency. The competing companies retaliate by likewise increasing commissions, and the war goes on until all, or even more than all, the profits go to the agents in the shape of commissions. A union among the companies to regulate commissions has to be formed, or all will become bankrupt.

From the standpoint of the public this commission demoralization is even more serious than is rate demoralization; if rates are cut the public gets the benefit, while in a commission fight expenses may be so increased as to make a rise in rates necessary. With no commission tariff, an improvement in the hazard means only an increased commission paid by some company to secure the business from another company; while losses are reduced, expenses are increased and the net result is the same to the public. Even from this brief discussion of the commission problem it is safe to conclude that coöperation in the matter of commissions is almost as essential as coöperation in rating.

The third object which the companies seek to obtain through coöperation is effective and economical inspection of risks. If rates are ever to be adjusted to hazards, it will come through better inspection of risks. One of the most serious objections which has been raised to present fire-rating is that good and bad risks are lumped together in one class and given too nearly the same rate; plainly the only way in which the companies can safely discriminate between good and bad risks is by making a careful inspection of all the risks insured. There is nothing to prevent all the companies from making such an inspection, each for itself, except the expense of doing it. But this is an insuperable difficulty; for if each company were forced to inspect carefully each risk that it insured, the expense of such inspection would probably be much greater than the saving in losses which would result from having rates closely adjusted to hazards. And there is a still more serious objection to inspection of risks by individual companies; no matter how thoroughly a representative of a single company may go about the inspection of risks he is not going to accomplish much in the improvement of hazards. Consider the situation as it existed before the companies began to coöperate in inspection. A company's special agent would visit a risk; and though he might see conditions which seriously increased the hazards of fire, yet the knowledge that other companies were anxious to write the risk as it was, and that even a reasonable request on his part would cause ill-will toward his company, would deter him from requiring the removal of defects which he knew to be serious, but which other companies had passed unchallenged. It is the same old story of competition.

How different is the situation when the leading companies coöperated and established inspection bureaus! No matter how many companies are now on a risk, only the authorized representatives of the inspection bureau visit the risk; and since a few men are performing the function hitherto performed by many, experts can be employed, and more efficient inspection is secured. Not only is the inspection more efficient, but the recommendations made, carry with them weight far greater than those made by the representative of the individual company. Under the old system the owner could view with serenity the cancelation of the policy of one company, since he knew that he could get insurance from another; with the companies associated together, the improvements recommended by the inspection bureau must be made, or the policies, not of one company, but of all the union companies, will be canceled. The effect of this coöperation is that improvements have been made; and many classes which were once unprofitable at any rate which competition would allow the companies to secure, have become profitable even at lower rates — a happy situation for the insurance companies as well as for the public.

Very closely connected with the plan of providing for

thorough and economical inspection is the fourth object of associated effort, the study of fire hazards and fire prevention. While it is perhaps true that the stock fire insurance companies are not primarily interested in reducing the fire loss, competition of the mill mutuals and of the preferred class companies for certain classes of risks has forced the companies writing all classes to give attention to the study of hazards. Companies have found that with many classes of risks rates must be closely adjusted to hazards. If they are not, the good mills and factories will go to the factory mutuals, and the better risks in other classes to the non-union, preferred-risk companies which are always looking for profitable business. Therefore in order to forestall competition, actual or latent, the associated companies have found it necessary to establish a laboratory for the study of the hazard of new processes, the value of new methods of fire prevention, and like topics. Here again, it might be possible for one company to make these experiments; but again we may be sure that one company acting alone would not attempt it. It is to the interest of all the companies doing a general agency business to have such studies made of hazards; therefore the companies not only ought to be allowed to coöperate for this purpose, but encouraged to do so.

The last object which the companies have attempted to secure through coöperation is a reduction of losses caused by incendiaries. Each company has to guard itself against the first act of an incendiary; but through coöperation the companies can protect one another from further loss at the hand of the same incendiary. Under the system as carried out at present, whenever a company finds out or suspects that a loss has been due to a desire on the part of some one to sell out to the insurance company at a fancy price, it notifies a central bureau which sends out to all companies a list of all persons suspected of incendiary tendencies.

Besides the effort to keep track of incendiaries, as above

described, the companies' associations seek in other ways to discourage losses due to moral hazard. Rewards are offered for the punishment of incendiaries, suspected criminals are prosecuted, and in other ways a great deal has been accomplished. Since such work is for the good of all the companies, the burden of expense should be borne by all.

What, then, is our conclusion regarding efforts at coöperation among the companies? It is that such coöperation is highly desirable from every point of view.

This conclusion is the exact opposite of that reached by the legislatures of nearly half of our states; twenty-three legislatures have thought that it was detrimental to the interests of the public that the fire insurance companies should be allowed to coöperate, particularly in the matter of rates and commissions. It was in 1883 that Michigan passed the first of the so-called "anti-compact" laws; this measure provided that no fire insurance company should enter into an agreement with another company the object of which was to prevent free and open competition between it and other companies. Michigan's action was followed by Ohio and New Hampshire in 1885, by Kansas, Missouri, Nebraska, and Texas in 1889, by Georgia in 1891, by Iowa, Alabama, and Wisconsin in 1897 and by others until at present (July, 1909), as has been stated, such laws are in force in twenty-three of the states.

There have been a number of motives actuating the state legislatures in passing such laws. The ostensible reason always given has been the fear of a fire insurance trust which would be able to dictate the price of insurance, and which, having this power over rates, would raise them. Admitting for the moment that such a trust is possible, its existence would doubtless be better than a condition of free competition. It is not high rates in fire insurance which cause the greatest evils; the rates which do the most injury are those which do not measure the hazard of loss. Not even the demonstration that a fire insurance trust is possible will justify anti-compact laws.

But there cannot be a fire insurance trust which, because of its ability to dictate prices, is able to secure unusual profits for its members. In order to have a combination with power to dictate prices arbitrarily, such a combination must have a monopoly of some kind. The fire insurance combination, or union, has no monopoly, unless it be the monopoly of experience; and this is the very thing which a compact among the companies makes the common property of any one who wishes to enter into the business. In order to make a rating compact practicable, there must be printed a tariff of rates upon all risks in every community. It is true that the union companies make a pretense at keeping these printed tariffs from outsiders, but such attempts are wholly farcical; the tariffs are printed, they are placed in the hands of a dozen — sometimes hundreds — of agents, and any one can learn without a great deal of trouble the rate upon any risk. This is the rate which the well-established companies deem sufficient for the risk; and thus it is that a new company without experience is able through the printed schedule to take advantage of the experience of the older companies. It has been truly said that instead of a rate union preventing competition, rather is it the nursing bottle for young companies. That it is impossible to establish a fire insurance association or union endowed with dangerous power over rates ought readily to be recognized from the ease with which new companies are organized. No business is easier to undertake than that of fire insurance; no expensive plant has to be acquired as in the case of manufacturing, no expensive right of way secured as for railroading; in most of the states, any one can organize a fire insurance company and begin business as soon as a cash capital of $100,000 has been raised. This fact that companies are so easily organized represents a very effective control over prices. The best-working fire insurance union in the country has never been able to raise the price of fire indemnity high enough to recoup conflagration losses. If the compacts cannot enable the companies to provide for the conflagration hazard, it seems as if there were little ground for fearing that a fire insurance trust will exercise undue control over rates.

There is reason for believing that agitation against the compacts because of their monopoly feature is simply a cover of other motives for attacking the compacts. Under conditions of free competition in fire insurance, rates, as we have seen, are demoralized; but this is a desirable state of affairs for some insurers. In the first place, with no compacts, rates will be a matter of bargaining, and the shrewdest bargainers in the community will get their insurance the cheapest. Competition among the companies is the keenest for large risks such as are found in the manufacturing and mercantile businesses; and the men in charge of these large business enterprises are in charge because they possess greater ability than do their smaller competitors. The situation, then, in fire insurance with no compacts, is fierce competition for the large risks on the part of the insurance companies, and shrewd bargaining ability on the part of those controlling the risks; and the result is low rates for the large risks. We discover here the reason why large manufacturers and large owners of risks are always found fomenting anti-compact legislation directed at fire insurance companies; and, to a considerable extent, the reason why that legislation has spread widely over the country.

Perhaps it is unnecessary, in view of what has been said, to describe several periods in our history during which the fire insurance companies were unable to coöperate. We have passed through several such periods. The years 1855 to 1865 were years in which the companies could not get together on rates. There existed that condition of free competition so alluring to the enemies of fire insurance combinations; and what was the result? At the end of 1865, forty-six out of the one hundred and forty-five companies reporting to the New York Insurance

Department had impaired their capitals to the extent of a million and a half of dollars; in other words the stockholders were paying for the privilege of furnishing insurance. Of course such a situation could not continue, for losses cannot permanently be paid out of capital. The crisis was met by a combination among the companies. Supposing such a combination to have been impossible through uniform action of all the states and the life and death struggle must have gone on between the companies until only a few were left. Then the difficulty in securing enough insurance would have sent rates up; then, as rates went up, profits would have increased, new capital would have been attracted to the business, severe competition would have ensued, and the old cycle of events would have been repeated once more. Such a disturbance in business conditions would have been a severe burden upon industry.

Finally it is interesting to recall the nature of the policy pursued by other countries in regard to fire insurance associations. In England there is one tariff association of practically all the companies, which has enjoyed a continuous existence since 1858; this association determines the rates for all important classes of risks, and so well have rates been adjusted to hazards that owners have never found it necessary to organize mutual companies. The same situation is found in the other European countries. In none are the associations illegal, and in all they are recognized as necessary for the best conduct of the business.

CHAPTER XII

VALUED-POLICY LAWS

I[1]

A FIRE insurance policy, in case of a total loss by fire of property insured, shall be held and considered to be a liquidated demand against the company for the full amount of such policy; *provided,* that the provisions of this article shall not apply to personal property.

II[2]

At the beginning of the present century a religious sect existed in the East Indies, governed by a creed which made assassination for gain a religious duty, a holy and honorable profession. This sect had existed for over a thousand years, and for ages was unmolested by the native rulers paying taxes for the privilege of practising its bloody rites until finally suppressed by the British government in 1834.

Exactly forty years after the thug was suppressed in the East Indies, he was reincarnated under his modern name in the good State of Wisconsin by the enactment of a statute, since known as the valued-policy law, which declared that whenever an insured building should be totally destroyed by fire, the amount of insurance in force should be taken as conclusive evidence of the true value

[1] Revised Statutes of Texas, Article 3089.

[2] By A. F. Dean, Assistant Manager, Western Department of the Springfield Fire and Marine Insurance Company. Reprinted from pages 103–111 of "The Rationale of Fire Rates;" J. M. Murphy. Chicago, 1901.

of the property, and the true amount of the loss or damage, regardless of the actual value of the property. In 1879 this law spread into Ohio, Missouri, and Texas, and is now in force in twenty-one states.[1]

The law changes a contract to make good the actual loss by fire into a plain bet (with average odds of one hundred to one in favor of the assured) that his property will not burn within a stated time. With such odds, a bet on almost any future event beyond the control of either party would find many takers; but when a man carries the keys of his own house in his pocket, and the event is wholly under his control, it is not surprising that legalized wagers of this sort should come to be popularly regarded as "a cinch."

In any event, a law which puts it in the power of the average man to strike a bonanza of this sort with a lucifer match must occasionally tempt some one to strike, for "oft the sight of means to do ill deeds makes ill deeds done."

At current dwelling rates, if one policy-holder out of five hundred is tempted by this law to burn his property, it doubles the cost of insurance for the remaining four hundred and ninety-nine policy-holders; if only one man in two thousand is so tempted, it increases the cost 25 per cent. for the remaining nineteen hundred and ninety-nine policy-holders.

That the law has raised the aggregate cost of fire insurance to the American people; that it is the direct cause of an untold amount of arson, perjury, and murder — no one familiar with fire statistics can for an instant doubt. The dangers of the law to life, property, and morals have repeatedly been pointed out by state officials. During

[1] At the present time, the valued-policy law appears upon the statute books of the following states: Arkansas, California, Delaware, Florida, Georgia, Iowa, Kansas, Kentucky, Minnesota, Mississippi, Missouri, Nebraska, New Hampshire, Ohio, Oklahoma, Oregon, South Carolina, Texas, Washington, West Virginia, and Wisconsin.

the past year, on the ground that it offered an incentive to crime, the law was vetoed by the governors of Colorado, Nevada, and Utah, and the governor of West Virginia refused his signature. In his last annual report, the insurance commissioner of Ohio published statistics showing the increase in fire losses in that state since the enactment of the law, and ends with the following comment:

"I have no hesitancy in believing that over-insurance, sanctioned and encouraged by the valued-policy law, is the cause of the greater portion of this increased fire waste, and that this unnecessary waste will continue and grow worse so long as this statute remains a part of our insurance code."

The state insurance commissioner of Michigan, in his last annual report, condemns the law in language equally strong, and estimates the losses from moral hazard, arising from over-insurance in his state, at 25 per cent. of the aggregate fire waste; in other words, that incendiarism is the cause of one fire out of every four.

But how did this legislative lunacy known as the valued-policy law come into being in an enlightened age and country? What was its genesis? Everything must have a cause. If it were possible to go back through the mists of antiquity, it would doubtless be found that there was some apparently logical reason for the birth of thuggism, some fancied wrong to be righted.

The law enacted in Wisconsin in 1874, and since that time by twenty other states, was originally intended to right an existing wrong, and the history of valued-policy legislation throws an instructive side-light upon the otherwise unaccountable antagonism of legislatures to the industry of fire insurance in all states dominated by the farmers' vote.

Thirty years ago farm property formed a much larger proportion of our aggregate national wealth than it does to-day. At that time the tremendous growth of our manufacturing and transportation facilities, and the concentration of population in our cities was just beginning. The fire companies were then deriving a steady revenue from the insurance of farm property, which as a class was considered doubly desirable, because it had been steadily profitable, and because it was free from the dangers of sweeping conflagrations which in every city jeopardized the entire assets of a company.

Every company wrote farm business freely through its local agents, under the same liberal conditions as other classes of property. The volume of farm business and its exceptional desirability led some managerial genius to conceive the idea that he could largely increase the premiums of his company from this source by sending out traveling solicitors through the country districts, after the manner of the lightning-rod, chain-pump, and patent-churn people. As these solicitors were selected for their glibness and push, rather than for their character or knowledge of the business, and as neither their judgment nor honesty could be trusted, the plan was adopted of taking payment in notes instead of cash. An elaborate application containing a cut-throat warranty was prepared, under which the assured surrendered every equitable right, and became responsible for any over-valuation of his property; and to make assurance doubly sure every policy contained a printed stipulation that the company should be liable for only three-fourths of any loss that might occur. This plan relieved the company of any necessity for the services of local agents, selected for their honesty and skill. There was no cash to handle; no danger of defalcations, and (with a policy condition which compelled the assured to carry one-fourth of the insurance for which he had paid) no danger from over-insurance. Under this jug-handle arrangement it became possible to sell fire indemnity, like tinware, by pedling.

The farmer is generally ready to purchase anything he can pay for with a note, and as "a business getter" the plan was a success. In a few years the agricultural regions swarmed with traveling solicitors ready to sell a farmer a patent churn, windmill, stump-puller, or fire policy with the same glib disregard of the truth. These tramp solicitors were, as a rule, ignorant, unscrupulous adventurers. They were paid by a percentage of the premiums, and it was, of course, to their interest to make as large a sale of indemnity to every buyer as possible, regardless of his actual needs. The companies themselves could afford to be indifferent to the amount of insurance a man procured, as misrepresentations in application could be used to deny liability, and in any event, the assured could not collect more than three-fourths of his actual loss. In time, the adjustment of losses revealed the full iniquity of this plan, and in every farming community fire insurance came to be regarded as a swindle. Of the hundreds of fire institutions then doing business, not over four or five at most were implicated. Nineteen companies out of twenty vainly protested at the buccaneering methods of these so-called farm companies, believing they would bring the entire business into reproach and subject it to inimical legislation. These apprehensions were well founded. The industry of fire insurance became *non grata* in every state where the farmers had the controlling voice in legislation, and the entire insurance community has been made to suffer ever since for the sins of a few unprincipled adventurers.

The American farmer to-day is the hereditary foeman of fire insurance; he makes no distinction between companies on account of character, record, or methods; in the words of a popular song, "All coons look alike" to him; the few companies whose solicitors he learned to distrust in the palmy days of farm insurance are typical of the whole body of fire underwriters. In his ignorance of the facts, the readiest remedy that occurred to the agriculturalist was to wipe out the whole iniquity with a sweeping law which required that the amount of insurance should be taken as the real value and measure of loss, regardless of policy conditions or actual loss. The offer of a reward to any one sharp enough to swindle an insurance company was a practical application of the maxim, "Set a thief to catch a thief"; but in resorting to this crude remedy the farmers forgot to consider the possible consequences to either their own or other people's interests.

Probably no more absurd or dangerous means was ever devised to right a wrong, and the farmers themselves have come in for much the largest share of the evil consequences of their own hasty and ill-advised action. The valued-policy law has cost the farmers millions of dollars, to say nothing of other people. In Wisconsin, Ohio, Texas, and Missouri, where the law has been longest in force, farm rates to-day are about double what they were when the law was enacted. At that time, all companies were freely writing farm risks through their local agents under the same form of policy, and at the same commissions that prevailed in other business. Ask any agent to-day, and he will reply that few or none of his companies will insure farm property at any price. The very companies responsible for the valued-policy law have been forced by the unprofitableness of the business, even at present high rates, to discontinue writing farm property in states where the law exists. These companies killed the goose that laid the golden egg, by creating a widespread moral hazard in a class of property that had been notably free from incendiary hazard. With an advance of about 100 per cent. in rates in valued-policy states, farm property to-day appears on the prohibited list of nineteen companies out of twenty, because losses have increased even more than rates.

This is the history of a law born of blind, unreasoning greed on the one hand, and blind, unreasoning resentment on the other.

These conditions are the results of *open competition.* If farm business had been under control of tariff associations, the united intelligence and honesty of fire underwriters would have scotched the disreputable schemes that generated an equally disreputable law.

In states where the law has not already been enacted it is regularly introduced each session of the legislature and voted for by the country members. If asked why, the invariable answer is, that insurance companies systematically encourage people to buy fire indemnity in excess of what they need; in other words, that they take money for which they render no equivalent. This is the stereotyped argument urged in state legislative halls year after year. To say nothing of the poverty of invention that can devise no remedy for an evil except to create a thousandfold greater evil, that can devise no penalty for a few minor evil-doers except to create thousands of criminals, whose crime has been held under every civilization to be worthy of the death penalty, what shall we say to the legislative inconsistency that imposes a penalty for an offense which is common to every walk of life, even to the law-making power that enacts valued-policy laws?

III[1]

Since the last report made to the Board, a large number of bills adverse to insurance interests have appeared in several state legislatures throughout the Union. The Board through its proper committee has given attention to the same as in former years, and circulars and letters have been addressed to companies interested, in states where obnoxious legislation has been proposed. We have in most cases been effectively aided by the influence of the companies and agents local to the respective states, as well as by the general, state and special agents of the agency companies, acting either individually or through underwriters' associations. If not in a majority, certainly in a considerable number of instances, the bills have been defeated largely by the judicious and timely attention

[1] By D. A. Heald. Reprinted from pages 20–24 of the Presidential Address before the National Board of Fire Underwriters, July, 1886.

of companies and their representatives. The pernicious valued-policy law which, since its enactment in Wisconsin, has reappeared each winter in so many of the state legislatures, received in New Hampshire during the summer of 1885 a brand of disapproval most emphatic and decisive on the part of the companies doing business in that state. The bill was to be deprecated not only on account of its valued features, but because it provided for a revocation of the authority to do business in the state, for any company which should enter into any compact with other companies, for the purpose of governing or controlling rates of fire insurance. Having passed both branches of the legislature, the bill became a law to take effect January 1, 1886, by the signature of the governor on August 29, 1885, and, in accordance with a mutual understanding, all of the companies — fifty-eight in number — of other states, and all of the companies chartered by foreign governments withdrew from the state.

Attention is here invited to the following table given by Superintendent Reinmund of the Ohio Insurance Department, in his report for 1885, published in 1886, in which he recommends a repeal of the valued-policy, or so-called "Howland Law," in that state, which has been in force since July 1, 1880.

"The fire insurance business of the joint-stock companies, in Ohio, for the past ten years shows the following results:

Year	Risks Written	Premiums	Losses	Ratio of Loss to Each $100 of Premiums
1876.....	$290,415,146	$3,676,516	$1,549,904	42.20
1877.....	293,020,072	3,231,629	1,337,461	41.40
1878.....	297,243,412	3,337,812	1,399,904	41.90
1879.....	269,334,609	2,772,868	1,295,477	46.70
1880.....	296,154,409	3,127,331	1,395,494	44.60
Totals	$1,446,167,648	$16,146,156	$6,978,240	43.20

HOWLAND LAW, JULY 1.

Year	Risks Written	Premiums	Losses	Ratio of Loss to Each $100 of Premiums
1881.....	$331,701,721	$3,588,931	$2,068,889	57.60
1882.....	369,872,828	4,058,627	2,356,851	58.10
1883.....	402,796,360	4,490,010	2,355,677	52.50
1884.....	495,554,856	4,676,370	3,507,848	75.00
1885.....	398,988,338	4,704,732	2,714,455	58.80
Totals	$1,908,914,103	$21,518,670	$13,003,720	60.40

"From the above it will be seen, that the average ratio of losses to premiums in Ohio for the five years since the passage of the 'Howland Law' has increased 17 per cent."

Ratio of loss to each $100 of risk written 1876 to 1880..48
Ratio of loss to each $100 of risk written 1881 to 1885..68

Thus the destruction of property by fire in that state has increased from 48 cents on every $100 written to 68 cents, an increase of 20 cents for Ohio, while the increase for the same period throughout the whole country has been from 54.14 to 58.36 or only $4\frac{22}{100}$ cents. Ohio has therefore a net increase of $15\frac{78}{100}$ cents on each $100 written, in her losses as compared with the entire country. Here is a loss to the commonwealth of the state of over $3,000,000 in five years as compared with the rest of the country, and of nearly $4,000,000, as compared with the previous five years in her own state. Whence this increase? We must look to some disturbing cause at work in Ohio, which has not existed in other states. We need not go far for the cause. The silent influence of the law, overturning the fundamental idea of fire insurance based upon actual indemnity to the insured, and substituting therefor a fixed and arbitrary value to the thing destroyed irrespective of its real value, is amply sufficient to account for this alarming increase. To the honest insurer this law offers no sufficient inducement for perjury and arson, but to the dishonest it is too often a commanding incentive to crime, and in these figures is the absolute, irrefutable proof of its terrible influence. These three to four millions is the price paid to the dishonest minority of Ohio by the vast majority of her good and true citizens, for a law far more fatal to her morals than it is or ever can be to her material wealth. How long will the statesmen of Ohio permit this law to disgrace her statute book, demoralize her citizens and waste her wealth, as it is here proved clearly and conclusively to have done, by facts beyond dispute.

Wisconsin is the only other state in which a similar law has been in force for a length of time, sufficient for reliable deductions. The increase of the loss ratio in that state is also remarkable. The figures from the official reports of the Wisconsin Insurance Department for eight years previous to the decision of the Supreme Court of the state, holding the law constitutional, and the eight years succeeding when it may be said to have been in full force and influence, will show the following results:

LOSSES FOR EIGHT YEARS PRIOR TO THE ENACTMENT OF THE LAW.

Year	Amount Written	Premiums	Losses	Ratio of Loss to Each $100 of Premium
1870.....	$147,172,955	$1,622,332	$1,175,212	72.44
1871.....	122,084,464	1,436,197	713,080	49.65
1872.....	142,351,376	1,910,677	922,637	48.29
1873.....	157,406,089	2,174,931	993,281	45.67
1874.....	154,795,630	2,271,059	1,010,023	44.00
1875.....	147,440,317	2,110,034	1,877,111	*89.00
1876.....	133,614,294	1,798,428	634,674	34.00
1877.....	146,983,804	1,645,110	973,913	59.00
Totals	$1,151,848,929	$14,968,768	$8,299,931	55.44

* Loss by Oshkosh fire included; the amount of same paid by companies being stated by the Wisconsin Insurance Superintendent at $920,438.

LOSSES SINCE THE LAW WENT INTO FORCE.

Year	Amount Written	Premiums	Losses	Ratio of Loss to Each $100 of Premium
1878.....	$140,411,389	$1,508,955	$965,478	64.00
1879.....	151,731,034	1,589,472	1,037,193	64.00
1880.....	159,110,857	1,766,528	1,143,541	61.50
1881.....	161,574,070	1,997,317	957,816	47.92
1882.....	175,210,508	2,238,463	1,340,372	59.00
1883.....	188,113,382	2,525,690	1,748,180	69.00
1884.....	199,205,324	2,683,737	2,010,901	74.90
1885.....	196,101,759	2,838,815	2,222,631	78.30
Totals	$1,377,458,323	$17,148,977	$11,426,112	66.62

Ratio of losses to each $100 of risks written, for eight years, 1870 to 1877 .... .72
Ratio of losses to each $100 of risks written for eight years, 1878 to 1885 .... .83

Here nearly the same results are repeated as in Ohio. The first period of eight years shows a ratio of loss to premiums of 55.44, the second 66.62, an increase of 11.18 — with this alarming feature that the two last years after adding the ratio of expenses gave results for 1884 — losses 69 per cent., expenses 33.38, total 102.88, or a net loss on the business of the entire state to all the companies, of $2\frac{88}{100}$ per cent. of premiums. In 1885, losses 74.90, expenses 35.82, total 110.72, a net loss of $10\frac{72}{100}$. How long can responsible underwriting stand up under such conditions?

If we come to that which more nearly concerns the people of the state, we find that the ratio of loss to $100 insured, has increased from 72 cents in the first period to 83 cents in the second — a difference of 11 cents on every $100 insured in the state during that time. Here, too, is shown a cause at work that has produced greater loss by $6\frac{78}{100}$ cents on each $100 than that of the whole country. The conclusion is inevitable that $6\frac{78}{100}$ cents on each $100 insured is the contribution made by the honest policy-holder of Wisconsin to the grasping cupidity of such as have taken advantage of a bad law at the expense of conscience and integrity. These tables are here placed on record without further comment, as a verification of the prediction of intelligent underwriters as to the effect of valued-policy laws, and the results exhibited should certainly lead to their unconditional repeal by all the states where they now exist.

A fair presentation of the self-evident arguments against such laws, and a clear statement of the evils wrought by them, as shown by the sworn reports of underwriters doing business in such states, will, we venture to say, lead to their repeal. Business cannot be transacted safely under such laws. The honor, integrity, and moral welfare of the state demand their repeal, and a candid and truthful statement of facts and figures on our part will, in my judgment, secure this most desirable object at an early day.

IV[1]

The valued-policy feature of the law is alleged by the companies as their principal grievance, under which, they declare, they cannot safely and profitably do business. Of their inability to do business successfully for themselves on that basis, I am not persuaded. To adapt their business to the new situation created by the law might, and probably would, occasion inconvenience, expense, and change of habit, but it could be done. I am, however, well convinced they ought not be compelled to, and for solid reasons, apart from their interest or inclination, they should not be permitted to. Nor would the public be content with it. Under the open policy, the property owner may obtain full protection against loss. Under the valued policy, no company could prudently write insurance to the full value of the insured property. A margin would need be

[1] Reprinted from pages XXXVII–XLI of the Thirty-First Massachusetts Fire and Marine Insurance Report.

left, liberal enough to cover surely any excess in original valuation, and also the possible deterioration in value within the insurance term. While in administration, the valued plan might tend, in some degree, to abate the conceded mischief of over-insurance (for which another and better remedy should be found), it would, as surely, create a popular complaint of under-insurance. A judgment entitled to respect, if not conclusive, has already been pronounced upon the relative merits of the two plans. With free and equal chance of competition for public favor and business approval, the valued fire policy has yielded place to the open indemnity form everywhere.

The question is to be considered in its relation to sound public policy, and a recurrence to the essential nature of the insurance contract should be helpful to a just opinion. An eminent authority correctly defines insurance as "A contract whereby one, for a consideration, undertakes to compensate another if he shall suffer loss. . . . It is applicable to every form of loss. . . . Wherever danger is apprehended, or protection is required, it holds out its fostering hand and promises *indemnity*. This principle (indemnity) underlies the contract, and it can never, without violence to its essence and spirit, be made by the assured a source of profit, its sole purpose being to guarantee against loss or damage."

Legitimate insurance cannot overpass the limit of compensation for actual loss. A contract which promises more than that is, as to the excess, a naked wager, condemned by law and hateful to good morals, and, applied to insurance of property liable to destruction by the machination of the assured who would profit by it, offensive to public policy because a temptation to social crime. A valued policy which over-insures is such a contract, and the statute under discussion protects it.

This principle of insurance, as indemnity, is recognized and enforced in the Massachusetts standard form of fire insurance policy, which all companies are required by law to write, in those clauses of the policy which limit the liability of the company to the actual value of the property and provide that the amount recoverable "shall be estimated according to the actual value of the property *at the time when the loss or damage happens.*"

But, the advocate may argue, the valued policy *is* a contract of indemnity only. It simply fixes the amount by agreement in advance. What amount is indemnity is a matter of estimate, and why may not the estimate be made by appraisal and agreement before, as well as by adjustment after the loss? The answer to the argument is not difficult. The true indemnity is the injury by the loss, and that is measurable only by the value of the lost property when the loss occurs. Between the contract and the loss, the value of the property may sensibly diminish, whereby the moral hazard is made greater, and if insured for full value at date of contract, under a valued policy the assured gets profit in addition to indemnity. To estimate value at date of the policy, or at date of loss, is feasible, because the valuation can be made from known facts; but a reliable valuation of what property will be worth at an uncertain future date is not possible. If the company is to be bound conclusively by the policy valuation, however clear the error, it must, before issue of the policy, cause a careful and competent valuation of each parcel of property it insures; and, furthermore, it must establish a system of supervision of all its risks of that class, in order to protect itself by cancelation of policies should the property depreciate. The burden of cost incident to these prudential measures, and chargeable to the valued policy, would fall upon the public.

Companies are obliged to act largely in the negotiation of insurance through agents other than their immediate officers. And in the selection of such agents the company is not always able to obtain the services of wholly trustworthy persons. Yet to these persons would be confided the valuation of the insured property and the amount of insurance based on that valuation. For the protection of the people it is fit and of legal obligation that the company should be held liable and bound by certain acts of these agents in their insurance transactions, yet that liability should be imposed no farther than the necessities and equity of the case. But under the valued-policy law the company is bound by the agent's valuation, however false or treacherous, and unless corrupt collusion with the assured can be proven. True, the statute permits the policy may be voided by proof of fraud in which the assured participates. But such actual fraud is usually extremely difficult and often impossible of proof and this law tempts to its commission. Where the over-valuation is the fault of the agent, from his incapacity, neglect, or corrupt yielding to the temptation of a larger reward from the transaction, the law refuses a remedy and enforces the injustice. Surely that cannot be good legislation which incites to wrong and shelters it, and impairs the customary freedom of private commerce, unless justified by the prevention of some graver injustice not curable by less objectionable means.

The valued clause is defended on the ground that as a matter of equity the company should be liable for the sum of insurance it is paid a premium upon. There can be, however, no lawful equity between gamesters. Companies may be willing to gamble with the owner or other person upon the chances that a piece of property will or will not burn, — and that is essentially what a policy of insurance becomes when it ceases to be a contract of indemnity. But the state should not lend its authority to enforce a contract repugnant to public morals, however willingly entered into by the equally culpable parties to it. Our courts hold that a contract of insurance made with a person who has no interest in the property is a wager and void in law. Why, for like reason, should not a contract which insures for an amount more than the insurable interest be equally condemned as a wager and illegal? If a man insures his property for more than it is worth, he does so, not to protect himself from a possible injury, but for the gambling chance of a possible profit. If, under those circumstances, the law assures that he shall realize the profit if the property burns, does not the law tempt him to destroy it? A contract for a consideration to pay the assured the amount of damage he may suffer is legitimate insurance, whence arise rights the law will protect. But a contract to pay more than the damage, violates the wholesome law of both private and social morality, and the parties who make it acquire no rights which the civil law should respect or honest men sympathize with. There are insurance companies willing to gamble with this sort; and with the valued policy protecting such transactions with its legal shield, legitimate insurance would suffer from the unworthy competition.

The other reason urged in the support of the justice and expediency of the law, is that the companies unfairly and vexatiously dispute the settlement of losses when the amount payable is subject to adjustment. This assumption of fact is not verified, and the argument sought to be built upon it must fall for want of foundation. My observation is that the companies, conscious of their disadvantage in litigation and sensitive to the popular prejudice, injurious to their patronage, which such controversies are likely to excite, submit to claims they might in good faith, and ought, in justice to themselves and the public, to resist. From self-interest, if no worthier impulse, as a rule with extremely rare exceptions, they liberally perform their obligations. No reason is given, or suggests itself, why a party dissatisfied with the proposed adjustment of his loss under an insurance contract, should not be remitted for a redress of his grievance, if he has a real one, to the established tribunals of justice. What is there singular in the nature of the contract, or the rights and obligations incident to it, that should distinguish it, as respects the legal rights and remedies of parties to it, from other contracts which men make in ordinary business intercourse? This law applies solely to insurance upon buildings and real estate, and to cases of total loss. In a dispute as to value in such a case the assured has an equal, if not superior, advantage in the contention, from the friendliness of the tribunal he may resort to, and his knowledge and ability to prove value. If he wants but justice he is sure of that, and often gets more, in the courts. While recognizing the function of government to protect the weak from the oppression of the strong, I perceive no circumstance in the case under discussion for the extraordinary intervention of that power.

The conclusions to which these considerations lead are: (1) that the valued-policy law violates the essential principle of the insurance contract, a principle it is most prudent to cleave to; (2) that it protects no endangered rights since the protection of the courts is ample for the purposes of justice; (3) that its tendency is to promote dishonesty and crime, the burden of which the public must endure.

CHAPTER XIII

THE CONFLAGRATION HAZARD [1]

It did not need the San Francisco fire to call to the attention of insurance men the importance of the subject of the conflagration hazard; it was a vital question already, in fact it had been only a few months before that an elaborate report on the conflagration hazard of San Francisco had been issued by the National Board of Fire Underwriters, being one of a series on the large cities of the country. But to the insured the conflagration hazard was a very vague idea, not definite enough to prevent him from grumbling at paying premiums that were larger than what were needed barely to pay ordinary losses. It seems an opportune time to discuss the subject of the conflagration hazard — what the companies may reasonably do, and what the insured may do to safeguard his rights.

The rate in fire insurance is designed to cover, first, the fire hazard, second, the expense of doing the business, and third, the profit. The fire hazard is of two kinds, first, the hazard of ordinary fires in which one or a few buildings are burned, second, the conflagration hazard. The two things are practically distinct in spite of the difficulty of drawing the line between them. If the conflagration hazard were eliminated not only would a large part of the premium be cut out, but the business of fire

[1] By A. W. Whitney, Professsor of Mathematics in the University of California. Reprinted from pages 42–50 of a "Report of the Special Committee of the Board of Trustees of the Chamber of Commerce of San Francisco, 1906."

insurance would be one of great steadiness. For with a multitude of risks the fluctuations would be relatively small and would be due mainly to general conditions that affect all business in much the same way. It would then be unnecessary for companies to hold large surpluses. Such, for instance, would be the condition of a company which wrote business only in the country.

In spite of the fact that fire insurance is usually a private enterprise there is no more fundamental fact than that the companies stand simply as agents of the insured. That is, instead of the company insuring its policy-holders, the policy-holders really insure each other, and the company simply manages the details of the transaction. In insurance there are no values created, they are only distributed, and whatever the company distributes must be collected.

There could be no insurance if there were not a large number of the insured. There must be a large enough number of the insured to furnish an average that will be free from large fluctuations year by year. For ordinary fires this may be obtained in a small section of the country and even in a single city. For instance, if there were no danger of sweeping fires a company might very safely write business in San Francisco alone.

So much for the ordinary hazard, but the conflagration hazard is of an entirely different character. Here the inhabitants of no one city could constitute the insurers, for a conflagration might sweep them all down. The insurers must be taken to be the inhabitants of many cities, as many in fact as can be found for which the conflagration hazard is nearly the same. But still the average is not obtained, for even in all the large cities of the country together, conflagrations do not occur in any regular way year by year. It is necessary, therefore, to take not any one year but a long series of years in order to obtain the necessary average without which there can be no real insurance. But even then the average is far from stable;

the San Francisco conflagration in three days did more damage than all the other large conflagrations in this country for the last forty years. The only conclusion then is that it is impossible to have any such perfect insurance against conflagrations as against ordinary fires. Insurance is a wonderful institution, but there are limitations to its usefulness.

These considerations have a practical bearing. The part of the premium that is collected to meet the hazard of ordinary fires is expended during the year, the year being in general sufficient to furnish an average, the company being required to hold as a liability the part of the premium that is still unearned. The part of the premium, however, that is designed to meet the conflagration hazard will not in general be expended during a single year, but must be kept perhaps for many years till the occasion arises for its use. This fund is called the surplus, but very unfortunately; it should be called the conflagration reserve and should be treated as a liability, just as is the reinsurance reserve. Surplus is something "over"; this is not "over," it is held for a definite purpose and hence is a strict liability. This is not a quibble over names, it is an attempt to demonstrate the accountability of a company as regards its surplus, the surplus being in reality contributions of the policy-holders against conflagration.

Admitted then to be a liability, what should be its amount? There are two methods conceivable for its determination, the retrospective and the prospective method, just as in life insurance. The retrospective method analyzes the premiums into a charge for ordinary fires and a charge for conflagrations; this would be very good in order to ascertain what the annual increase of the surplus should be. But the prospective method gives the real criterion of its size. The "average" failing to exist in any reasonable time, the size of the conflagration reserve cannot be based upon what is necessary to meet the "average" conflagration, but instead must be based on what is necessary *reasonably* to meet a "worst" conflagration, that is, the size of the required surplus shall be determined by the amount of the aggregate risks that are exposed to a single conflagration.

To summarize then, surplus should be treated as a liability and its amount determined by a reference to the aggregate risks exposed to a single conflagration. A company's business then in a single city must be limited not necessarily to exactly the amount of its surplus, for practically there is not enough insurance to be had to make this possible, but it should have some definite ratio to its surplus. But how is a new company to get a surplus? In either of two ways, start small and grow big, or else put up the surplus in the beginning. And here is the function of the stock company rather than the mutual company. The insurance principle proper breaks down when it comes to dealing with the conflagration hazard and requires a boost from something else, namely, private capital that is willing to assume risk for the sake of gain. Pure insurance, only where there is a proper average, may be entirely mutual as life insurance and fire insurance in the case of well scattered risks.

A new company then which desires to write business exposed to a conflagration hazard must put up a surplus. As the business develops and the surplus grows, the company may take on a growing amount of city business. If the company should desire to write less city business at any time or to retire altogether, part or all of the surplus would be freed from its character as a liability and would be at the disposal of the company.

The result arrived at is no strange thing. It is nothing but what has occurred to every thoughtful person who has known the insurance situation following a conflagration. It is simply an insistence upon some commensurateness between the resources of a company and the amount at risk in a region subject to a single conflagration, an attempt, therefore, to prevent companies with a capital and surplus of $250,000, but with an energetic agent, from assuming the conflagration risk that belongs to a company of ten times that size; namely, in this case the companies that are now able to pay only 30 to 60 per cent.

You may say, leave such companies to perish of their own egregious intemperateness; that would do very well if it were the company only that suffered, but the greatest sufferers are the policy-holders. There is, to be sure, the eventual action of the law of the survival of the fittest, and if insurers were intelligent enough and well-informed enough this would be better than legislation.

Before you go into a theater it would be well if you were able yourself to examine into the safety of the building; since that is out of the question the next best thing is a building law.

It is almost equally difficult personally to know the fitness of an insurance company to assume a risk. In view of the impracticability of doing this, the next best thing is a law regarding liability. There is a law regarding liability for the unearned current premium, there ought to be a law regarding liability for unearned conflagration accumulations.

Now it is only fair when funds to meet a potential liability have been provided in a prescribed manner that this measure of the potential liability should be taken after the loss has occurred as a measure of the actual liability. That is, if a company has maintained its conflagration reserve, its liability in case a conflagration has occurred should be limited to this amount. This being a part of the contract introduces no element of unfairness; the insured, instead of buying insurance with *theoretically* unlimited liability, but *practically* most decidedly limited because of the well-known expense and delay of litigation and the undesirableness of receiverships, buys insurance in which liability is definitely and legally limited; but the protection is standardized.

This again is not a matter of far-away theoretical interest; it is vitally connected with the actual situation in San Francisco. No fact has been more striking than that *practically* the liability of the companies has been limited. In spite of the fact that companies could be brought into the courts and compelled to pay their claims in full or be driven into acknowledged insolvency, in spite of the fact that there is a state law regarding stockholders' unlimited liability, it is a most notable fact that but three companies are in the hands of receivers, that more than half the companies have been able to settle their claims at less than their face value with few lawsuits, that companies which have paid but 50 and 60 per cent. are likely to be able to close out their claims and yet preserve their plants. This is a state of *actually* limited liability. Which is the better, theoretically unlimited liability with such an attendant host of disagreeable features as we have had in San Francisco, amounting as a matter of fact to limited liability, or a legally limited liability with standardized protection?

Nothing is gained by taking the pound of flesh. To drive a company into insolvency and thereby destroy its plant is to kill the goose that laid the golden eggs. Set a reasonable standard of protection against conflagration, then if this has been observed absolve the company from further liability. The company will then have saved its plant and may immediately go on in business on whatever scale its remaning funds or fund to be put up by its stockholders will warrant.

The details of such a plan can manifestly not be given here, but it is perfectly possible to work them out in an entirely practical, consistent way. To sum up, however, the advantages of such a plan are, first, no company could write an inordinate amount of business and so nullify its capacity to indemnify; second, there would be better, and not only better, but standardized, protection against conflagration; third, the business of fire insurance with this element of uncertainty removed would be far more attractive to capital and would appeal to a better class of investors.

This, by the way, might apparently seem to be dictated by a thought of what would be best for the companies. Not so at all. The fundamentally mutual character of insurance is so dominant that the company is almost lost sight of. As a matter of fact what is best for the insured and what is best for the company are in any large matters identical.

One point more; it may be said that a law of the kind proposed would work a hardship upon the small company. No great hardship; a small company may do as much country business as it pleases, and it may take a share of city business proportionate to its size. To attempt to minimize the advantage of size in fire insurance is ridiculous. Nowhere else is it more true that "to him that hath shall be given"; it reads: "to him that hath a large surplus shall be given much city business and from him that hath not shall be taken away (by reinsuring it, if a company can be found to take it) most of that which an over-energetic agent has written."

And now let us come back to the immediately practical business as it is to-day. Massachusetts, which has always been the leader in intelligent insurance legislation, had a law a few years ago limiting the amount of risk that a company might assume in any one of certain districts in Boston. This law was repealed. It was presumably found that with the law in operation it was impossible to obtain enough insurance, the reason of course being that while the legally prescribed limit would have yielded as much insurance as before, as a matter of fact the conservative companies would not write up to the limit allowed. There was, therefore, a deficiency of, to be sure, a very poor type of insurance, namely, one that gave practically no protection against conflagrations, but nevertheless it gave fairly good protection in the case of ordinary losses, and for this purpose, in the lack of anything better, could not be spared.

This, then, apparently disposes of the practical possibility of placing a limit upon city risk. Yes, absolutely, in large cities if the supply of insurance is to be always limited to what is available now. But the one hope of bettering insurance protection against conflagrations is the enlistment of more insurance capital, and the one way of doing this is to make the business more attractive. A limited liability law would do this. As a matter of fact the safety-fund laws of various states, New York among the number, are exactly of this nature, but if the liability is to be limited, the simplest, most natural limit seems to be had by a reference to the aggregate amount exposed to a single conflagration as outlined above.

Still, as a matter of fact, whether liability should be limited to the surplus, the surplus and capital, or to the surplus, capital, and the excess of the unearned premium reserve over the actual cost of reinsuring the outstanding risks is a matter of detail; the important thing is to grant some form of limited liability in case of conflagration that will save the plant; but it should be granted only if there is the proper commensurateness between the conflagration risk and the company's assets.

Is it worth while to think of conflagrations or do they come so seldom that we may go on in sweet oblivion? Is the insurance business to be organized with the possibility of a conflagration clearly recognized or is it to be based on ordinary loss, and Heaven help us if we have a conflagration? A conflagration may be a theory in New York, but it is a fact in San Francisco. The conflagration hazard, basing it upon the three large conflagrations of the last fifty years, excluding the San Francisco conflagration, and spreading it over the twenty largest cities of the United States, can be demonstrated to have been (on the assumption that the rates have been adequate), on mercantile stocks half as large as the ordinary hazard, and on so-called fire-proof buildings several times as great as the ordinary hazard. This does not appear to be a hazard that should be neglected.

CHAPTER XIV

FIRE INSURANCE ENGINEERING[1]

FIRE insurance engineering is the application of the principles of engineering to prevention of fire, to protection against fire, and to arrangement of property so that the least possible damage will result when fire occurs.

As now practised it is the outcome of many years of evolution from the need of fire insurance companies, but principally during the last twenty years. Although there are many capable men in the business who are not graduates of any college or technical school, a large and increasing percentage is composed of graduates, usually of the technical schools, because the studies there deal directly with the application of the principles of engineering and chemistry inseparably connected with this work.

All over the United States and Canada, to speak of the territory to which most of the American companies confine their operations, the companies maintain organizations for estimating rates, or for inspection to improve risks, work which requires the examination of insurable property of every sort by men in their employ who make this a specialty. Entrance to the profession is usually effected by becoming an inspector of this sort at the rate of $50 to $75 a month, more often the latter to a scientific school graduate, well recommended. In two years the average man can earn $1200 a year. After that the salaries vary too much to give any satisfactory average;

[1] By Frederick C. Moore, Superintendent, Special Risk Department of the Hartford Fire Insurance Company, Hartford. An address delivered before the insurance class in Yale University, May, 1909.

with equal loyalty and hard work, much depends on the good judgment, tact, and initiative of the individual, as in other enterprises. Salaries of inspectors commonly do not exceed $2500 a year, except when they have some share in the executive management. From these inspectors are selected those who fill positions at the heads of the various bureaus and of the special departments maintained by large companies, which pay larger salaries.

Although the money reward is not large for the average as compared to those of individuals in successful independent mercantile pursuits, and although the vocation carries with it the disadvantage of absence from home during the greater part of the time, and the necessity for starting at short notice so that the plans of ordinary home life are almost impossible, the employment is very secure, continuous, interesting, and in most associations very pleasant, so that few leave the business.

The novice spends three months or more under the instruction of a trained inspector in the field. Ordinarily at the end of a novitiate of that length he is able to travel alone to do the simpler work, but it is a year before his judgment is trained so that he is of much value, and it is much longer before his experience is sufficiently varied to enable him to work easily and with confidence.

As there are always more applicants for inspector's positions than places, good material for selection is assured, and the choice being governed in most cases by relative merit, the result is a body of men of good character, energy, and intelligence. Each is spurred on to greater effort by the example of some associate with a better record, by the hope of a more speedy increase in salary, but particularly by the possibility, ever present and never forgotten, of being selected by some fire insurance company, large manufacturing corporation, or large insurance agency or brokerage firm for a position of greater responsibility and higher salary. All the manufacturing and mercantile risks which are insured are visited by such men, who are privileged by their mission to examine every part of the property in detail.

To illustrate the training which makes insurance engineers, let us follow the general work of an inspector in the employ of one of the large inspection bureaus which make a business of reporting the condition of insured property to the fire insurance companies.

He is given a list of properties of every sort to inspect, grouped systematically according to locations, and works alone. Generally speaking, his absence seldom exceeds two weeks. If he goes to Pittsburg, his list may contain an open-hearth steel plant, rolling-mill, crucible steel plant, rail mill, distillery, window-glass factory, plate glass factory, pressed glass plant, rubber mill, department store, car works, modern warehouse for general merchandise, packing-house, harness leather tannery and others. This same interesting variety of subjects is characteristic of the work in most places, and is a never-failing source of interest to one who is a student of industrial processes. To the examination of each of these he applies the same principles, prompted to prevent oversight by a printed question blank. It is necessary to consider the character and influence of neighboring property which may expose the risk in question to the danger of a fire without, the construction, the occupancy, and the materials and processes it entails, particularly with reference to the hazards thereof, care and cleanliness, the private and the public protection, and any special conditions influencing the fire risk, all in detail. Usually he draws a ground plan at the first inspection and this is carefully corrected at each subsequent inspection. With a good plan and report a company can decide what line it will carry.

It requires from a few hours to several days to make an inspection, according to the size of the risk. It will therefore be evident that the number of risks inspected in a year is not necessarily a comparative measure of value, because the skilled man will be given more of the long, difficult inspections. For an entire bureau force they will not average one per working day per man; in fact, the actual performance of one of the largest for last year is .73.

A good inspector is essentially a good reporter. Those who receive the reports prefer to draw their own conclusions, which are often very different from those of the inspector, whose criterion is based on physical conditions, while that of the underwriter is probable profit and loss, and includes prominently the question of rate, which the inspector ordinarily does not know, and is usually specifically instructed to disregard in order that any opinions, which, in addition to the facts, he is expected to express, may not be influenced by the knowledge of the rate.

The expense of getting this information has resulted in the organization of the inspection bureaus already briefly mentioned, which have from twenty to fifty companies as members, each of which gets all the information. This concentration of effort has resulted in the employment of a corps of inspectors large enough to have one inspector in each district, so that when the need arises for an immediate examination of any risk the nearest man will be only a short distance away and can be sent at once. In a day or two thereafter the report is in the office and in another two days can be in the hands of the members. It costs from 4 to 5 per cent. of the premiums of the risks inspected to support a large bureau. The companies believe it pays to spend this money, even though there is only negative proof, since no one can tell what the result would be if inspections were abolished. They certainly prevent fires, cause arrangement of risks which diminish the average loss and forewarn the companies of conditions which lead to loss. These inspections are of value to *every* fire insurance company, because they cause the improvement of the risk whatever companies may write it. No less important are the benefits conferred upon the owner of the plant. In most cases he desires to know what to do to protect his business from the disastrous effects of fire, which not only causes immediate material loss, but also serious consequential loss to his established trade, which competitors win away while he is rebuilding his factory. Consequently he welcomes a thorough inspection, and is glad to consider resulting suggestions. Notwithstanding the predominance of owners of this type there are enough of the sort who meet suggestions with the comment, "I suppose you are obliged to find fault to hold your job," a bit of cynicism quite unwarranted, and which the inspector has heard a hundred times before, so that its one-time wit is quite lost. It is noteworthy that inspectors are as a class very earnest and honest in their work and that they have enthusiastic professional appreciation for a risk which is above criticism.

The same inspectors who carry on the work previously described also report on every important fire immediately after its occurrence. Thus we have full information of conditions before and after the fire, and the comparison leads to improved conditions not only in the risk affected, but also in other risks where similar conditions exist.

Most of these men are members of an organization known as the National Fire Protection Association, formed "to promote the science and improve the methods of fire protection and prevention; to obtain and circulate information on these subjects, and to secure the cöoperation of its members in establishing proper safeguards against loss of life and property by fire," the publications of which may be obtained by any one who is interested in the subject by becoming a subscribing member at an annual fee of $5.

This association holds annual meetings which are attended by large numbers of the field men, and at which are presented the rules, specifications, or other findings of special committees among which such work is divided. Therefore, anything promulgated by the association has been subjected to the criticism of men from all parts of the field in an open discussion. The result is standards for the construction, installation, and use of different devices and materials for fire prevention and fire protection and the elaboration of methods of fire insurance engineering generally. These rules and methods are the guides to the engineer in his work with the property owner, who will, we trust, recognize that the basis for the suggested improvements to his risk are principles which are the outgrowth of the consensus of opinion at these representative meetings and not simply the result of local experience.

In order that the relative merit of these devices and materials may be definitely ascertained from tests under conditions which admit of accurate comparisons, the companies maintain the Underwriters' Laboratories at Chicago, where tests and investigations are carried on with the coöperation and advice of committees of the National Fire Protection Association, in consideration of a fee paid by the applicant for the test, which covers part of the expense of the work. The benefit to the applicant, who is practically always the owner of something which he expects to sell to the public, is that if his product is successful under test he receives the approval of the laboratories, which gives the article a better position in the eyes of buyers. To insure that the entire product will be the same as the samples approved by test, a plan to inspect the product at the factory has been put into effect, the theory being that a particular label attached thereto will be conclusive guarantee of the proper standard of excellence.

The tests have been made principally upon electrical devices and materials, fire-extinguishers, hose, fire-doors, and shutters, automatic sprinklers, and allied devices, lighting and heating devices, and structural materials of various sorts, carried on along the lines of physical laboratory testing, but always with an eye to practical conditions. For instance, a fire-door or shutter is set in a brick panel forming one side of a gas furnace capable of generating a temperature, gradually raised to 1800° to 2000° F., about 1000° being reached in the first five minutes. After an hour's exposure the side of the furnace carrying the shutter is slid rapidly to one side into the open yard, and a hose stream directed against the heated side, reproducing the extreme conditions of actual use. The defects of the shutter are certain to show. The thoroughness of this test is indicative of the methods used generally.

The information developed by field work and by the laboratory tests is being applied to bring about better construction particularly, which is probably the most important condition in limiting fire loss.

One of the most serious handicaps to the successful operation of fire insurance companies is the spread of fire from one building to another, developing in the extreme into conflagrations such as those from which the country has severely suffered in the last few years, and in which fire-proof buildings, of construction so good that the fundamental parts of them withstood the fire, offered no real barrier. This is largely due to the absence of protection for the wall openings, and to educate the public to the need for such protection is one of the most urgent duties of the insurance engineer. Obviously, all buildings cannot be fire-proof, but even on brick buildings of ordinary construction the general protection of the exposed windows would result in enormous decrease in the exposure losses, which, leaving conflagrations out of the question, are very heavy in the aggregate. By some fallacious reasoning it has been the unfortunate custom to omit protection on windows which face streets, but ordinary streets offer no effective stop to flames. By giving the fire department time to work before a fire can reach more fuel, the protection of wall openings will do more than any other structural change to prevent conflagrations.

A study of this question of exposure leads an American to envy the condition in France, which is such that a Napoleonic law can exist that compels an owner to pay damages caused to neighboring property by fire originating on his premises, and to admire the construction that makes it possible for insurance companies to insure that liability for a merely nominal rate.

Another axiom of insurance engineering is that openings through the floors of a building should be closed. A fire causes an ascending draft of heated air, and flame naturally follows that course; furthermore, the natural draft in buildings is ordinarily upward. An open stairway or elevator shaft becomes at once a rapid and easy path for fire, often taking a fire from the basement into the comparatively inaccessible upper floors before the fire department can get fairly at work. With all such openings closed there is time to head it off. In constructing modern factory buildings this principle is observed by providing a brick tower or towers for stairs, elevators, and power transmission, with fire-doors at the entrances.

The character of buildings is improving under the influence of the bonus which insurance companies put upon good construction in the shape of low rates, but many are built in which the construction is so light that the benefits of cut-offs at floors can not be fully realized. The question of the saving in insurance which applies to the value of contents as well as to the building, and for the life of the building, is not given sufficient consideration in planning. Many a building could have been far better built and would have been just as good an investment if the owner and architect had discussed the matter beforehand with a competent insurance engineer, as some of them always do.

In addition to points of construction, the safe arrangement of the hazards of manufacture claims an important share of the engineer's efforts. Although the owner knows the processes of his business far better than any outsider, yet he frequently fails to realize the hazards of it. It is natural that in this respect he should not be as well able to pass judgment as a man who sees those same hazards in a hundred other places also, and whose business it is to weigh them and safeguard against them. It is a noticeable fact that the owner usually optimistically believes that he has a better risk than most others and that *his* risk will not burn; an honest opinion which is the result of years of acquaintance with every nook and corner of it, but which blinds him to the real dangers. As a rule, however, he is willing enough to consider such changes, accompanied as they are by convincing examples, and bringing with them a material reduction in the insurance premium.

The cotton-mill presents a fine example of what the separation of the principal hazards can do for a type. At first there was no attempt to do this, and fires caused by the openers and lappers, which are the machines which tear the raw cotton apart and prepare it for carding, burned entire mills and consequently cotton-mills came to be considered as highly hazardous. Now, a modern cotton-mill is considered a good risk and when protected with automatic sprinklers, one of the very best of any sort, because, although these fires frequently occur, the machines which cause them are in a section of the building by themselves, separated by two walls and two fire-doors from all other parts. Consider carefully the money significance of this arrangement. If the picker hazard were in the main mill, the entire insurance would be paid for at the high rate of that hazard, but cut off as it is now the high rate applies only to the value in the picker house. In a mill without sprinklers, suppose 15 per cent. of the insurable value to be in the picker house, to which a rate of $1.50 applies and the other 85 per cent. to be in the mill on which the rate is 50 cents, then the separation of those hazards is saving the owner of that mill 85 cents per $100 of insurance per year, indefinitely, or $1700 yearly on $200,000 insurance, an example not in the least exaggerated of what this study of conditions by the insurance engineer is doing for the owner every day, and any owner can obtain the judgment of a skilled man for the asking from a company which maintains one on its staff, with resulting benefits of the sort quoted, to say nothing of the added security which the improvement gives to his business.

The study of processes with a view to separating the hazardous ones so that they can not endanger the other parts of the risk, and the reduction of the value in these hazardous places to the lowest possible amount so that the high rates will have the least effect upon the average rate, is of absorbing interest to the engineer and of direct benefit to the assured, and much ingenuity is displayed in the solution of such problems. Every industry and business is capable of profiting by this kind of an analysis, and it is the exception to find a property which has not had careful consideration on this basis, the rate of premium on which can not be reduced by improvements at a cost that will be a good investment for the owner. In addition to the engineering information required, the specialist in the employ of a company brings to a consideration of this sort a knowledge of insurance rules and contracts that is of value.

As a result of work of this kind the companies now recognize that a modern risk of almost any sort can be so much improved that the history of risks of similar kind in the past is not a fair basis of judgment, and they consider risks on their individual merits.

In the detection and safeguarding of hazards technical books and papers give very little information, except those written by insurance men, but there is an increasing number of these latter, which are put before the public from time to time and have good educational value. Insurance engineers are continually finding unsuspected hazards of new processes or new machines, which are consequently reduced or removed with the coöperation of the proprietors, which has already been of great benefit.

It remains for the engineer to plan the most practical

means for fire protection after other considerations are finished, to the end that fires may be extinguished. This attention is not confined solely to the individual risks, but is bestowed upon the fire departments and the water supply and distribution of cities as well. For many years inspectors employed by insurance interests have regularly visited the cities and the larger towns, carefully examining fire departments and the conditions under which they work, making suggestions for the improvement of this service. For several years a more complete engineering organization has been in operation, under which a party of engineers, comprising experts in the subject of water supply, fire departments, and construction, visit a city together and stay there till they have carefully examined it, reporting upon the degree of exposure to conflagration, and the ability of the water supply and fire department to cope with local conditions, including in the report the remedies which they deem advisable, with which the officials of the municipality are made acquainted. The protection of individual risks receives the equally careful consideration of other men in the employ of bureaus or companies. The best of advice is to be had for the asking by municipality or private owner.

Although fire insurance engineering has done and is doing much to prevent loss by fire in this country, some idea of how much there is to be done may be gained from a comparison with the low loss ratio in Europe where rates are so low that automatic sprinklers offer so little chance for further reduction that it is very hard to sell them. We quote a loss per capita of 12 cents in Italy, 49 cents in Germany, and an average loss per capita in Austria, Denmark, France, Germany, Italy, and Switzerland, of 33 cents, as compared to a loss in the United States, in 1908, of $3.02.

There are several reasons for the low loss ratio, the principal one being the absence of wood in construction, and another the smaller number of fires. The first reason is easy to understand, because except in Norway, Sweden, and Russia, the centuries of civilized occupancy have used up the timber so that within the life of present buildings it has been cheaper to build of stone, brick, tile, and other incombustible material. There is a very interesting consular report, printed in 1892 by the United States government, entitled "Fire and Building Regulations in Foreign Countries," containing the answers to a set of questions on these subjects from consuls all over the world, that explains much. One may refer therein to the cities in the British Isles and on the Continent, except the countries already mentioned, and find that there are practically no wooden buildings and that such are forbidden to be built, and this means that floors and staircases are incombustible as well as walls. The only use of wood that is noticeable is in the framing of the roofs in some localities. This plainly teaches us that in good construction lies the greatest single safeguard against excessive loss by fire. Contrast San Francisco, a wooden city, simply wrenched by earthquake, half destroyed by fire, with Messina, a city of masonry, leveled to the ground, but unburned.

Certainly the fire protection of foreign cities is not the reason for their safety. In Rome, a city of 427,000 at that time, the department put out the fires with buckets and fire-extinguishers chiefly. They had hand engines for use where the water pressure was unusually low, and for cases of great emergency one steam fire-engine, but the last time it was used it was over two hours before it could be put into condition to draw water. Imagine Buffalo or Baltimore in that condition.

There is one consolation in the impending depletion of our forests, that it may force the adoption of fire-proof construction, and so give back in saving from fire loss the amount lost in forest value. There are signs that the high price of timber and the difficulty of getting it have already started this movement.

The other reason, fewer fires, is not so easy to understand. Hartford, a city of about 100,000, had 300 still alarms and 147 bell alarms last year, representing actual fires. At the time of the consular report, Rouen, France, about the same size, had 29 fires in one year; Roubaix (114,000), the same; Rheims (105,000) 47, the average being less in Spain and Italy. London, 4,250,000 population, reported 2892 fires; the same ratio per capita as Hartford would have called for 14,500 fires. Porta Fayal, population 6790, a stone city, no fires for five years; Asuncion, Paraguay, 25,000 population, brick and stone buildings, no fire loss for seven years; Parimaribo, Dutch Guiana, 28,000 population, all buildings wooden, no serious fire for forty-five years, and only two alarms for seven years, each a small native hut. The almost universal use of buildings of fire-proof materials no doubt accounts for some of the decrease in these foreign countries, but there must be other stronger reasons, perhaps a slower pace, older civilization, the inherited instinct of centuries when fire insurance was non-existent and fire loss was irreparable, or a milder climate and less heating apparatus.

Broadly speaking, the salvation of this country in respect of fire loss lies in the education of the public, beginning in an elementary way with the children, to which fire insurance engineering can contribute a highly important part. When the American people understand thoroughly that there are many lives and over $200,000,000 of money lost every year from this cause, surely the response will be effective and we shall ultimately cease to blush for the comparison with foreign countries. Although there has never been any attempt to make instruction of this sort a part of the education of the young until very recently, through insurance engineering the insurance companies are unreservedly giving the public the best advice to aid in decreasing this drain of men and material. May the time hasten when the people will realize their responsibility and make free use of the benefits so freely offered, for the sake of the general welfare of the country.

CHAPTER XV

FIRE PROTECTION WITH AUTOMATIC SPRINKLERS[1]

An automatic sprinkler is a water valve, held closed by the use of solder fusing at a low temperature, which is intended to open from the melting of the solder by the heat of a fire in order to distribute water as a fine spray to extinguish the fire. Similar devices have been known for many years, but no practical use was made of the principle until the early '80s, and most of the development has been in the last twenty years.

Sprinklers are ordinarily installed eight to ten feet apart, in water pipes of graduated sizes from $\frac{3}{4}$ inch to 6 inch diameter, attached to the ceilings at regular distances all through the buildings to be protected. The piping does not disfigure the rooms, being placed symmetrically with prominent parts of the framing. After a short time it ceases to attract the attention of those who know it is there, and the casual visitor seldom notices it at all, particularly as the pipes are usually painted a color to correspond with their surroundings, although the sprinklers themselves should never be given any foreign coating.

All manner of risks are equipped, including hotels, parts of dwellings, grain elevators, car barns, rolling mills, schoolhouses, and even a few steamboats, to mention some of the unusual sorts, as well as mills and factories, warehouses and stores of all kinds, even the most elaborately finished department stores. When the owner prefers to sacrifice accessibility to the ornamentation of the store, the pipes

[1] By Frederick C. Moore, Superintendent, Special Risk Department of the Hartford Fire Insurance Company, Hartford.

are sometimes concealed behind the ceiling finish, only the sprinklers themselves projecting.

In places which are freezing cold in winter, compressed air is maintained in the pipes, instead of water, by means of a "dry valve," which automatically allows water to enter when the compressed air escapes upon the opening of a sprinkler. Thus the system is maintained operative despite cold.

The ordinary sprinkler opens at 155° or 160° F., but for places where the temperature is too high to use these, special sprinklers are made with solder fusing at 212°, 286°, or 360° F., though the less necessity there is for the use of these the better, because they are slower to open.

With the two methods just outlined, however, the extremes of heat and cold commonly found can be met, so that it is feasible to have sprinkler protection in all parts of any risk.

The business of installing sprinklers is almost entirely in the hands of the companies who manufacture them, as they will in most cases sell the sprinklers to only a few contractors who have long had dealings with them, an attitude based upon the belief that the work requires long experience to avoid errors which lead to expensive changes before the work finally complies with the insurance engineering rules, a doctrine that is quite in harmony with their business interests, and which is true for the average case of a property owner who expects his own mechanics to do the work well. These sprinkler companies will furnish detailed plans in advance to the insurance organization which is to pass judgment upon the work, so that the annoyance of subsequent changes is avoided by having the plan approved at the beginning. As the expense of forming and maintaining an organization that can make plans and estimates and do the work in accordance with the needs of insurance authorities and the property owners is high, and the invention of a sprinkler and the other necessary appurtenances, which will meet insurance approval, is slow and difficult, there are few companies in the business, and it is exceedingly difficult for a new company to start.

It is of great importance, particularly to the insurance companies, that any new sprinkler shall, before approval, be proven to be able to open when it ought, even under the disadvantage of slight corrosion or loading, and that it shall not open when it is not needed. To comply with both conditions is difficult, as the large number of sprinkler patents shows, and it requires about a year to make all the tests, which are all made by the same organization, and are, therefore, comparative. There are only seven different sprinklers in common use to-day.

The customary preliminary procedure to obtain a sprinkler equipment is to apply to the insurance organization, which passes judgment upon improvements for a plan and requirements to show what is necessary, in their judgment, to protect the risk. This information will be submitted in writing and will enable the owner to obtain from contractors the cost of the work. As he can also find out how much insurance will cost under the proposed conditions, a comparison of the cost with the saving can be accurately made, to govern the final decision whether to make the investment. It is highly desirable to advise fully the person who is to make the suggestions of any changes which may take place in the future, so that their influence on the equipment may be fairly considered, which will be well repaid by resulting economies when the necessary extensions to the protection come to be made. If the property owner possesses the necessary information, or can have expert advice, it is an excellent plan to draw up a plan and requirements which can be considered in detail from every point of view at leisure, the perfected result to be submitted to the insurance organization whose approval he desires, which has the merit of enabling the owner to meet the representative of that organization with an appreciation of the matter that will enable him to discuss fully and definitely, ensuring complete understanding on both sides.

It is natural to ask what benefits are given by automatic sprinklers? The most important one is the protection to an established industry by decreasing to the utmost the chance of its being swept out of existence by an internal fire, which is insurance of prosperity. The product of such a plant is worth more to a buyer who is depending on it than that of an unprotected factory. Another is the ability to obtain insurance indemnity to cover fully risks of very large value, which would be impossible without sprinkler protection, upon which insurance companies rely to protect them in the assumption of much greater than ordinary liability; similarly, a risk of even moderate value, which, nevertheless, can not obtain full insurance because physical disadvantages are too heavy, may be so adequately protected by this means that insurance is readily procured.

A complete equipment usually includes hydrants and hose, and various other appliances besides sprinklers, often the protection of important door, window, and floor openings, and sometimes the modification of other physical conditions, because a survey for laying out sprinkler protection considers the improvement of the risk as a whole, to the greatest degree consistent with the governing conditions, for at the low rates under which such protected risks are written, not only must the protection be perfected, but the chance of occurrence of fire must be decreased, and its opportunity to spread, limited. The cost of sprinkler protection is therefore increased by these other improvements, and the whole varies so much that no set rule is reliable, but it is not uncommon to save enough on the insurance premium by reduction in rate, to offset the cost in four or five years, which is excellent interest on the investment, and a better showing may be made under specially favorable circumstances. Considering only the automatic sprinkler system inside the building to the point where the supply mains enter, not including any work on the water supplies, a roughly approximate idea of cost may be obtained, by estimating the number of sprinklers required on the basis of 80 square feet of floor space per sprinkler, and multiplying the number of sprinklers by $3.50. Special conditions will vary the cost considerably, and to the cost for the sprinkler system is always to be added that of the water supplies and other improvements. An ordinary risk will expend $3000 to $5000, and large ones ten times as much.

The cost is not directly proportionate to the insurable value and there are certain essentials for any risk, however small, so that it ordinarily does not pay to equip risks of small value and there are comparatively few equipped carrying less than $40,000 insurance. The average amount of insurance per risk for 126 risks thus equipped was $251,182.

The important reason why automatic sprinkler protection successfully controls fires is because it is automatic. The instant heat opens a sprinkler, water issues on the fire, day or night, work days or holidays, summer or winter, provided conditions are not abnormal. The result is shown by the record of 8942 fires, reported in risks equipped with sprinklers during a period of more than twelve years, of which 5791 were extinguished by sprinklers unaided, in only 483 cases did sprinklers prove practically useless, and in the other fires other apparatus was also used. In 7239 cases, 83 per cent., not more than twelve sprinklers opened, which shows the value of applying the water at the very outbreak of fire. A single sprinkler at 30 pounds per square inch will discharge as a fine spray about thirty gallons a minute. Under most conditions the operation of one or two sprinklers would have 30 pounds pressure. At 100 pounds the impression is created in the mind of an observer that the spray is so dense and forcible that a man directly under the sprinkler would strangle.

Notwithstanding the copious discharge under adequate pressure, it is always necessary to exercise great care to prevent conditions which will cause fire to open many sprinklers. The water supply is not sufficient in most cases to remain effective when the loss of pressure by friction, which very heavy draft occasions, cuts the pressure at the sprinklers down below the 2.5 pounds during operation, which is admitted as the minimum allowable. Because of this possibility the general belief is that sprinkler protection is principally dependable when fires do not gain headway enough to open very many sprinklers, and this is a safe and reasonably true doctrine. When the water supply is very strong, sprinklers will stop a heavy fire which opens many heads.

There are conditions which prevent sprinklers from giving the protection expected, even when properly installed, and their favorable record is at the cost of continual inspection with the coöperation of the owner. In places where corrosive vapors are given off by the processes, such as dyehouses, bleacheries, dry rooms, chemical works, and many others, considerable numbers of the heads become so corroded that they will not open as they should, and this is apt to be the case after a longer time, even with those which have been specially treated by the maker with a protective coating. Their condition can not be reliably gauged from their appearance, but must be determined by an expert test of a representative number of those suspected, such as can be obtained with the aid of the insurance authorities. It is a serious condition, absolutely putting the sprinklers out of commission, and to be remedied only by replacing the sprinklers as often as necessary.

From carelessness or ignorance, sprinklers frequently become coated with paint, whitewash (particularly from spraying machines), bronze or silver gilt, encrustations of soap, sugar, cement, plaster, or other materials, which are very apt to be similarly objectionable.

Another trouble is that frequently an employee of the property owner disconnects or shuts off parts of the system on account of repairs to building or machinery, forgetting to put the sprinklers back into service as soon as possible. It is a too frequent occurrence, and leads to the removal of sprinkler protection from sections of a few heads to the systems of entire buildings. The same owner would require to be told if steam were shut off from the engine five minutes, and he ought to be just as particular about the water for the sprinklers. Similar in effect is the erection of additions, mezzanine floors, racks hung from the ceiling, partitions, or any structures which form unprotected sheltered spaces in or adjoining a building equipped with sprinklers, and the system should be promply extended to cover them.

Enough has been said of the commoner causes of poor sprinkler service to emphasize the important principle that the owner should devote care and attention to the sprinkler system, as he would to any part of his machinery of production, and the greatest aid to such proper supervision is an inspection by some specially delegated employee at regular, frequent intervals, filing a written report. Nearly one-half of the sprinkler failures on record are due in about equal numbers to water being shut off or to defective or partial equipment, the first entirely preventable, and the second to be much reduced when acquaintance with the matter teaches the owner that a sprinkler system, as well as his machinery, has its limitations.

With some conditions a sprinkler equipment can not be expected to cope. It will be overwhelmed by conflagration, long continued exposure from without, which very likely cuts down the pressure of its water supply by heavy draft of fire department. It is apt to be disabled partly or wholly at the start in a risk where the processes give rise to explosion. In hollow walled, hollow ceiled buildings it can not extinguish fire in the hollow spaces. In industries using large amounts of inflammable liquids, particularly those lighter than water, or large piles of articles which shed water, like barrels, lumber, furniture, — it will not extinguish the first or reach the fire in the others.

The life of a sprinkler system put in according to present

rules ought to be at least thirty years, under average conditions and probably longer. Pipe put in twenty-five years ago is as good as ever, but it was wrought-iron pipe, while soft steel pipe is used now. The sprinklers themselves have given no proof that they deteriorate with mere age, if properly designed in the first place. From the point of view of cost of maintenance the present perfection of the methods of designing and installing fire protection is a more important matter than the life of the system, for it practically guarantees that it will be unnecessary during its lifetime to rebuild a system because it is not adequate for the work it was supposed to do. Many of the early systems did not get a chance to wear out, because experience showed they were not dependable and they were remodeled.

Factories and mills constitute the larger number of risks equipped, many of them isolated. To-day the equipment of risks in the congested areas of cities is becoming much more frequent, which is an excellent thing to decrease the chances for conflagration by diminishing the number of risks in which serious fires may occur, because such risks are usually large and therefore troublesome to control if they burn. The growth of automatic sprinkler protection is due to the unquestionable fact that it is the best known method of extinguishing fires inside a building.

CHAPTER XVI

FACTORY MUTUAL FIRE INSURANCE[1]

THE system of factory mutual insurance was established by the late Zachariah Allen, of Providence, Rhode Island, in the year 1835, when he and his associates organized the Providence Manufacturers' Mutual Fire Insurance Company. In 1848 the Rhode Island Mutual Fire Insurance Company was established.

On January 1, 1900, the Boston Manufacturers' Mutual Fire Insurance Company entered upon the fiftieth year of its existence. The first policies issued were dated September 14, 1850. In that and in the ensuing year, 1851, one hundred and eighty original policies were issued to one hundred and ten members in the sum of $3,320,560. The cash premium or deposit subject to losses and expenses amounted to $33,320. The maximum hazard taken on a single risk was $30,000. The rates varied from a minimum of 40 cents on some storehouses to 1½ per cent. on certain mills. These rates had been established by the two older Providence mutual companies, the Manufacturers' Mutual and the Rhode Island Mutual. I am informed that the mutual rates were made on the basis of the schedule of some of the older stock fire insurance companies, at three-quarters the charge made by the stock companies on the same property.

It is evident that the members and directors rested upon the power of assessment more than upon the cash

[1] By Edward Atkinson, late President of the Boston Manufacturers' Mutual Fire Insurance Company, Boston. Reprinted from "The Prevention of Loss by Fire"; Damrell and Upham. Boston, 1900.

payment in the early history of this, and other factory mutual companies, yet, since 1850, there has been no assessment required by this or any other of the associated factory mutual companies.

During the earlier period of their history the picker departments of cotton and woolen factories were not insured by the mutual companies, nor can I find any evidence that they were separately insured. The risk was probably carried by the owners. It was deemed excessive. But immediate measures were taken for protecting pickers in much greater measure than for the protection of mills, and from computations which I have recently made of the proportions of loss in ratio to value of picker buildings and contents, as compared to the main mills and contents, the loss relatively has been less than in the works proper; thus proving again the one rule developed in this work, a rule which must be fully comprehended outside the lines of the factory mutual companies if the terrible losses by fire in the United States are to be reduced. The rule is as follows:

After the insurance company has done its duty by careful selection of risks and thorough inspection, all that it can do is to pay indemnity for loss which, if large, is in nine cases out of ten due either to the lack of apparatus for preventing such loss, or to lack of care and order in the conduct of the work. The only persons who can prevent loss by fire are the owners or occupants of the insured premises. Upon them rests the responsibility for heavy loss, when any occurs, in nearly every fire.

It has always been the practice of the mutual companies and of late, with excellent results, the practice of the stock insurance companies, to instruct owners and occupants upon their duties to their own property, and to keep them up to the mark by constant supervision and by refusing to grant contracts of indemnity to those who neglect their own duty.

The most difficult work of the president of a mutual

fire insurance company is to do away with the antagonism of owners against the underwriters, and to secure that coöperation in preventing loss by fire which ensues as soon as the identity of the interest of the owner and the underwriter is established.

In 1850, when the Boston Manufacturers' Mutual Fire Insurance Company was organized, the Manufacturers' Mutual Fire Insurance Company, of Providence, Rhode Island, had been in operation for fifteen years; the Rhode Island Mutual Fire Insurance Company for three years. Each of the above-named companies issued policies not exceeding $15,000 on a single risk. This company began by issuing policies not exceeding $30,000 on a single risk.

The Firemen's Mutual Fire Insurance Company was organized in 1854, the Worcester Manufacturers' Mutual in 1855, the State Mutual, of Providence, in 1858, and the Arkwright, of Boston, in 1860. Several years elapsed before any other mutual companies were organized.

The losses have never been so great in any one year as to subject either one of these companies to the necessity of making an assessment in addition to the sum deposited at the beginning of each term, during this period of fifty years. Had this property been of necessity insured in any other way than by the factory mutual companies, there would have been two periods, one immediately after the Chicago fire and one immediately after the Boston fire, when a large part of the contracts of indemnity which had been paid for would have become worthless. That danger of great city conflagrations still exists.

The secret of this success is to be found in the fact that when men combine with each other for mutual insurance they very soon learn the one lesson, which I repeat:

The only persons who can prevent loss by fire are the owners or occupants of the insured premises. Upon them rests the responsibility for heavy loss, if any occurs, in nearly every fire. All that the insurance company can do is to pay indemnity for loss, which, if large, in nine cases out of ten is due to the lack of apparatus for preventing loss or to lack of care and order in the conduct of the work.

At later dates eight other factory mutual companies have been organized in Massachusetts and Rhode Island, and are now associated with the ten senior companies for the joint inspection of risks, but as they came in after the greater part of all the older risks had been covered by the senior companies, they extended their service over such large concerns as could not be wholly covered by the senior companies and over other classes in a wider area, in which service they have rendered a proportionate benefit to their members; their earlier dividends exceeding those of the senior companies in their early history; their recent dividends exceeding those of the senior companies down to and including 1879, when great changes were made in the general conduct of the system as will be hereafter stated.

In 1878 the revenue of this company from premiums was $366,000 — the maximum hazard on a single risk, $80,000. The liability to assessment was still created by the execution of notes promising to pay five times the cash premium in any emergency. The giving of these notes was often objected to, and was in fact superfluous. Measures were presently taken for a change of the law by which the acceptance of the policy created the liability, but it was evident to the undersigned that the cash receipts ought to be brought to so large a ratio to the maximum hazard taken on a single risk, as to render resort to assessment so remote a contingency as to be disregarded substantially, and to that status the present condition of the company has been brought.

Before 1878 no customary or regular meetings of the directors had been held. Inspections had been made in a desultory manner by the presidents or secretaries of the several companies about once a year, usually a few weeks before the expiration of the policy. Modern safeguards had not been thoroughly investigated. Automatic sprinklers were known, but had secured little or no attention. There were no experience tables, no classification of risks, and no real comprehension of the relative hazard on different classes. Everything depended on the personal knowledge and the extraordinary memories of Messrs. Manton and Whiting. Losses had been subject to great variation year by year, as will appear from the diagrams submitted with each annual report. It had become manifest to myself and other directors that a very complete change must be made in the conduct of the whole system, and that new safeguards must be found in order to meet the increasing hazard of larger floor areas, mills of many stories in height, higher speed, new dyestuffs, and to anticipate the new hazard of mineral oil, then gradually being introduced as a lubricant, of electricity, etc.

There also existed a feeling among many members such as governs ordinary business, "not to put too many eggs in one basket." Those who did not investigate the subject were governed in the distribution of their insurance by the amount of the policy, and not by the proportion of the policy to the revenue of each company. It did not occur to them, and it does not now occur to many others, especially to applicants, that if the annual income from premiums is three to four times the maximum hazard taken on any single risk, it is as safe for the member to take, and for the insurance company to grant, a policy, say of $200,000 on an income of $900,000, as it would be to grant a policy of $20,000 on an income of $90,000. On the other hand, by such a concentration, the relative expenses of conducting the several companies are greatly diminished.

In 1878 the first duty of the president was to eliminate poor risks; the amount of insurance written was $43,000,000. In that year and the next a large amount of insurance was canceled which could not be brought to a proper standard of safety, but new risks were added, so that in 1879 the amount written was $44,500,000.

Measures were taken to establish a quarterly inspection under the supervision of Mr. William B. Whiting, the secretary of this company. A regular system was organized, the accounts being kept on the books of the Boston company, the charges being shared in proportion to the relative service by all the senior companies and a portion of the junior companies. At a later date an association was formed to conduct the system of joint inspection at the joint expense of all the companies, since which date the accounts have been kept upon a separate set of books. The executive officers now meet in monthly conference.

In 1880 what may be called the science of preventing loss by fire was fairly entered upon, and at that date measures were taken, after careful consultation with the very few manufacturers, who at their own motion put in the automatic sprinklers, for the extension of that service, which has now become practically universal. Without their support and the confidence due to their practical experience, the writer would have had much more difficulty in promoting the adoption of sprinklers, as some of his own insurance associates were skeptical, and two were positively opposed to them. But the writer had become convinced that, unless the hazard of larger and larger factories, higher speed, etc., could be met, the mutual system would break down; and he then told his associates that automatic sprinklers must be made a condition, cost what it might. In ten years more than half the work was done; in twenty years it has been completed.

In 1879 a careful compilation was also begun, by which the combined experience of all the mutual companies could be registered year by year. In this company risks were divided into ten classes; losses were sorted in proportion to risk taken and premium received from the beginning of the company to that date. A very wide variation from the average was disclosed. On one class the loss had been over 60 per cent. of the premium received; on another it had been but 10 per cent. Measures were taken for the more complete protection of the risks in which the heavy losses had been disclosed and rates were raised. On other risks slight concessions in rate were made, but since the number of hazards in each class, with the exception of three, did not suffice to establish a rule, one loss of considerable amount throwing the average out for a number of years, time was allowed to elapse to justify further changes, if any were required.

Various changes have been made in the adjustment of rates, the inclusion of new risks and the exclusion of poor risks, so that the average loss of premium received on each class has been brought to as close an approach to uniformity as it is probable can ever be attained. We are occasionally liable to a large loss in a class in which there is a small number of risks, which of necessity throws the average out for a considerable period of time. The compilation of statistics is very necessary as a guide to the judgment of the underwriter, but the president, especially the mutual underwriter, who should undertake to govern the conduct of the work by giving regard only to the statistics would either fail, or would be subject to a very wide variation from any equitable adjustment of the relations of each member to the other.

There have been variations in the judgment of the different boards of directors in the several companies. To some the so-called conflagration hazard has given fear of an assessment; but both the statistics and the observation of others disclose the fact that in the great factory cities, where what are called the single hazards are so near to each other as to suggest the danger of an extension of the fire by conflagration, the additional safeguards in the supply of water and the aid which one mill can render to another have resulted in a considerably less proportion of loss, either to risk taken or premium received, than is disclosed by the figures of the isolated mills.

No fire in any one of the large factory cities has yet extended in a destructive manner from one risk, deemed a separate hazard to another, either in the same yard or in an adjoining mill yard. There have been but five fires which have extended from the building, or separate risk in which the fire originated, to another building covered by our insurance, to such a degree as to cause a considerable damage in the second building. These fires have occurred in what are called our isolated risks.

There has recently been a fire which passed from one auxiliary building into another in the same yard without substantially doing injury to the main mill, starting in an unsprinkled section (now sprinkled), and extending for want of skill in the use of the fire apparatus; but these two buildings were not considered separate risks according to the construction of that term.

The mutual contract cannot be safely adopted in the crowded districts of cities, for the reason that the owner or occupant of one building may have a very dangerous neighbor in the next, over whom he has no control; he may not therefore expect to reduce the cost of insurance to the lowest standard attained under more favorable conditions.

During the fifty years of the existence of this company there has been no instance of fire intentionally set by the owner or occupant for the purpose of getting money. There has been but one suspicion of such fire, which after some years was disproved by the confession of the incendiary who had no interest in the property. There has been but one resort to litigation. That was in the case of the Pemberton mill, which owing to a defect in a cast-iron post fell down, taking fire after the fall. The question was raised by the underwriters whether this was an alteration in the risk not contemplated by the contract, due to the neglect of the owner. So far as I can learn, the case was submitted to arbitration, and was compromised by the payment of a sum of money, corresponding to the value of the property after the fall and before the fire. What proportion this came to I am unable to say.

I repeat once more, distrust has sometimes been caused by misapprehension or misrepresentation in regard to the risks taken in the large factory cities, of which there are six, in which many mills insured separately are on the same lines of canal and are sometimes held to be subject to a conflagration hazard. The experience of fifty years proves conclusively that the benefit and additional security due to this proximity is much greater than the danger of a fire extending from one mill to another. There has been no such incident. On the other hand, bad fires have occurred in the heart of these cities, with high winds blowing and under conditions which, had they been the ordinary mercantile risks of a city, might have caused an extensive conflagration; but the aid which each mill extends to the other and the enormous flood of water that can be poured upon any single fire from roof hydrants and other vantage points has enabled the well-organized mill fire departments, working in coöperation with the city fire departments, to put out all such fires without any destructive extension from the building in which they originated. I again call attention to this fact because the same precautions and safeguards could be adopted for the protection of city warehouses and blocks, and until they are, the appalling danger of great conflagrations will continue.

One or two other incidents may be named. It was formerly the practice to appoint outside adjusters as well as to compromise on an appraisement; both practices are now ended. Losses are now adjusted by representatives of the owners and of the underwriters as nearly according to the facts as it is possible to appraise them. There has been no difficulty in carrying out this plan to the satisfaction of all parties in interest.

It may be added that, in four instances, losses have been settled to the satisfaction of both parties, when subsequent adjustments or events disclosed the fact that very considerable omissions had been made by the owners in submitting their statement of property damaged, one mistake being discovered many months after the adjustment. In these cases the owners have been requested to submit their additional claims, and the amounts have been paid, the intention of the mutual companies being to pay, in every instance, the exact measure of indemnity that may be justly due. In another recent instance a loss had been settled by the principal owner, the treasurer being away for his health, on the assumption that the goods stored had been taken in the inventory of a few days before at market value. Two months later, on advices from the treasurer, it appeared that these goods had been valued at 20 per cent. less than market value. The case was re-opened and the difference cheerfully paid.

In only two or three instances that the writer can remember has there appeared to be any effort made on the part of the assured to claim more than a just measure of indemnity under such conditions as to disclose an intent to get more than the true amount. These adjustments have then been made according to the facts; but on the expiration of the policies, the representatives have been informed that they could not remain members of the mutual companies.

The general conclusions to which the writer has been led are, that it is necessary for the conduct of mutual insurance to be as well assured of the quality of the management and the men in charge as of the risk itself. Although this discrimination has formed a constant part of the duties of the executive officers, we have reached a general conclusion that there is much less loss from fires intentionally set in order to collect the insurance money or from incendiarism, than is commonly imputed to these causes. I am also well satisfied that when losses that have occurred are taken up by the underwriters with the intention of paying a just measure of indemnity, any effort on the part of the assured to secure a larger payment is uncommon.

I think it never occurred to the founders of the mutual system and I am sure that it had not occured to myself, that we were engaged in developing an applied science, not only of the utmost importance to the economy and safety in the factory system, but which may slowly be of great service in putting a stop to the destructive fire tax of the country. It may therefore be useful to put upon record the gradual growth of our work until its true scope was almost forced upon our minds in the process of working it out.

Careful records had been kept by the late William B. Whiting, of the incidents of each fire which had occurred during his official connection with the company for nearly the whole of the first thirty years, and I was enabled to recover some accounts of the few fires of any importance that had occurred before his time. These fires and their causes were tabulated.

The first fact which was disclosed was the large number of fires and the large amount of losses attributed to broken lanterns. This led to an examination of all the lanterns in mill use, then wholly supplied with animal oils. Not a single safe lantern could be found in use. All were badly made, liable to melt at the joints and insufficiently guarded. On searching for good lanterns none could be found except expensive brass lanterns made for the railway service. Warnings were given, due precautions taken, and, in connection with the firm, now called the F. O. Dewey Company, safe lanterns at moderate cost were invented, but it took five years to perfect this apparently simple device. Many improvements have been made and there are now two or three types of safe and suitable lanterns for mill use, burning either animal oil, mixed oils, or mineral oils. Since that study of the lantern question there has not been a loss of any considerable amount in any of the works insured by this company which could be reasonably attributed to fault in the lantern. Careful attention to lanterns would doubtless save many fires and losses in city risks, but what owner or occupant ever gives his personal attention to this insignificant cause of very heavy losses?

The second great cause of fires was found in the various oils in use both for lubrication and for smearing wool. The mineral oils were largely used for lubrication; mixed oils were also used, but in the finest work, especially in weaving, fine sperm oil was still assumed to be the only suitable oil. In smearing wool, olive oil, lard oil and mixtures under fancy names more or less liable to spontaneous combustion were in use.

The spontaneous combustion of waste had previously been one of the principal causes of loss by fire. This danger has been almost wholly removed from cotton factories by the substitution of the mineral or so-called paraffine oils for lubrication, in place of animal oils, the mineral oils having no affinity for oxygen. Our investigation of oil disclosed the fact that 33 per cent. of mineral oil, mixed with lard oil, would overcome the tendency to spontaneous combustion. But these mixtures do not serve in machine tool work. Therefore, there is still a liability to the spontaneous combustion of waste used in wiping tools in the repair shops of the textile factories, where pure lard oil must still be used on the cutting tools, also in all our machine and metal-working risks. The liability to spontaneous combustion in woolen mills has been very much reduced since methods were discovered for scouring wool, treated with mixed oils, partly consisting of the mineral oils.

Another singular cause of loss was the pitched roof of factories, commonly called the barn roof. When this roof was substituted for the old style factory roof, the practice was common to put vertical sheathing a few feet from the joining of the roof with the floor, making a long hollow space behind the ceiling at the eaves. This was at the time when nothing but animal oils were used for lubrication, when waste was therefore liable to spontaneous combustion. Several roofs were burned. At length one-half of the roof of a mill was burned, the fire being stopped by the tower. It then occurred to some one to investigate the conditions of the unburned part, and behind the sheathing were found large numbers of rats' nests made of oily waste. The cause of the fire then became plain, — the spontaneous combustion of rats' nests. When this fault was discovered all these sheathings were removed, and the space was kept open over the whole area of the attic floor. That barn roof is no longer tolerated.

Many destructive fires had originated from hot bearings, especially on main shafts. The first fire which called attention to this cause occurred in a basement weaving room two hundred feet long, from a hot bearing at one end of the room. The fire jumped from loom to loom, passing many, melting the solder of a gas meter at the further end, without scorching a towel hanging closely underneath. This led to a suspicion of evaporation, it being assumed that the heavy hydrocarbon vapors had been kept in flakes or planes in the atmosphere by the motion of the looms. On examining the oil, it proved to evaporate 24 per cent. in ten hours at a heat of 140°; that being a heat not infrequently attained on a heavy bearing. Samples were called for from various mills. A tabulation was made of nearly one hundred cotton-mills, which proved a very great variation in the cost of oil to a pound of cloth in the quantity of oil used for lubrication, and in the prices paid for the oils.

In fifty-five mills on print cloth numbers, among which there was no good reason for any variation in the cost of lubrication, the average price paid for oil varied from 29 cents per gallon to $1.05. The gallons of oil to a thousand pounds of cloth varied from 1.3 to 2.84. The cost of oil per thousand pounds of cloth varied from 68 cents to $2.58. There was no apparent relation of price, quantity, or cost each to the other. This table was printed without giving the names of the mills, and submitted to all the contributors, each with a key to his own number. The conclusion reached by all was that each knew little about the subject, while the rest knew less, and I concluded for myself that I knew nothing, and that it was time to bring lubrication to a science if it were possible. This was fairly accomplished. The mineral lubricating oils are now made of various qualities more or less fluid and more or less filtered, but the prices range from a minimum of 13 cents to a maximum of 30 cents for such oils as are made use of on ordinary cotton machinery. What the relative quantity used in recent years is I have no means of ascertaining.

The investigation was followed up until it proved that there was but one well-distilled and safe mineral oil for lubrication to be found, that being made under a patent. In all the rest grave faults were discovered, mainly, that of rapid evaporation. Notice was immediately given to the makers of these oils that a warning would be published to all our members not to buy them or to use them under any circumstances. This led to a threat of a suit at law for interfering with their business, which I immediately urged them to enter in court, as I desired to publish the facts; but I advised them to settle the patent rights and to change their methods of distillation, which advice was taken. A year later, wishing to secure some of the volatile oil for experimental purposes none could be found in the market. The price and cost of lubricating oil were very greatly reduced, all oils being brought to a uniform standard; very great benefit in money and increased safety have since ensued. From the conclusion of that investigation to the present time serious losses from hot bearings have been very rare; in fact, there is not one of any moment on our record that I can recall.

Several members reported to me that their saving in the cost of lubricants in the next two years, resulting from this study, had been more than the cost of their insurance in the same period.

A warning was also given on the reckless use of very combustible varnishes on wooden surfaces, over which fire will pass with the speed of a race-horse, and may be ignited by the slightest cause. Care should also be given to the quality of the materials which are used in treating the surfaces of unpainted wood in offices and dwelling houses, which are apt to be rubbed down with rags impregnated with very dangerous materials of which linseed oil is almost sure to be one of the ingredients. Two instances have occurred in dwellings of my personal friends where these rags, put away in the pantry drawers, have set the house on fire.

After testing and rejecting every existing kind of apparatus for ascertaining the coefficient of friction, an instrument was invented by Professor Ordway on which exact results were secured. That was afterward improved in some measure, and is now in the laboratory of the Institute of Technology. We may claim that lubrication has become an applied science from this investigation.

Methods of lighting were taken up at a very early date. Illuminating gas was mainly in use. There had been very serious fires and heavy losses, coupled with the loss of life, from the breaking of gas pipes during fires, throwing large volumes into burning buildings. Attention was immediately given to outside gates or valves and to right methods of cutting off the gas at the outbreak of a fire, which were wholly wanting in many cases.

At one period there were upon our books one hundred and fifty risks or more lighted by kerosene oil lamps. There had never been any considerable loss from this cause, except from bad lanterns, although many of the lamps were unsuitable. Measures were taken to substitute safe lamps and burners for the poor ones. Attention was given to the quality of the oil in use and the very cheap and dangerous tubular lanterns were thrown out, safe ones being substituted. The number of mills lighted in this way is now much reduced, electric lighting having been substituted. But from that time to the present there has been no considerable loss of any kind from this cause, and only one loss, slightly exceeding one thousand dollars, which could be attributed to the use of kerosene oil; that was caused by the breaking of a bad lantern brought into the yard from the outside by a workman without the knowledge of the agent.

The next subject investigated was the fire-door. The record showed that iron doors had failed; one of the heaviest losses previously on record having happened from the warping of the iron fire-door which separated the picker department from the main mill, the fire passing, and the mill being destroyed. Efforts had been made to introduce the tin-clad wooden door, but it was often badly made for want of proper instructions. The sliding door had been put in position by Mr. Byron Weston. The writer invented an automatic method of closing doors, shutters, and hatches in rather a clumsy way, since very much improved; he fortunately used a lever released by the melting of fusible solder in that undertaking and in the construction of a valve for the conversion of a perforated pipe into an automatic sprinkling system.

The next subject taken up was fire hose. The practice of the makers of unsafe hose was to recommend to the owners to hang up cheap hose "in order to satisfy the insurance inspectors." Much of it proved worthless. A thorough investigation was made, and information was given to all members as to whom they could trust in the purchase of hose. This work has been subsequently extended by the establishment of types of hose designated as the "underwriter" hose, which can be readily identified. But incautious persons are still apt to be cheated on low-priced hose offered them at less than any possible cost for hose of a suitable kind. How many owners or occupants of city buildings ever give any attention to their fire hose, except to see that there is enough cheap hose hung up "to satisfy the inspectors of the insurance companies"?

The general question of the proper height and the right construction of factory buildings received very early attention. There were then several examples of the eight or nine-story factory building surmounted by the early type of the so-called factory roof; the roof itself, in some instances, being two stories in height. One large risk in part under these conditions was dropped as soon as circumstances would permit; the worst building, a large one, having soon after burned. In another instance the owners were induced to remove the two-story roof and to put on timber and plank at the level of the sixth story, making place for the machinery previously in the upper stories on the ground. After the work had been done it was justified, not only by increased safety but by the greater economy in the work of the factory.

Many other risks were covered in by the pitched or barn roof, slated — a very bad type. Later came one of the worst inventions in combustible architecture, the so-called Mansard, or French roof. By persistent action we have secured the removal of many of these roofs, with great benefit to owners in the conduct of manufacturing and very much greater safety.

A bad plan for the construction of paper mills had been long in practice, under the assumed necessity of having a long, hollow roof over the Fourdrinier machines in order to prevent condensation of moisture over the machines, which was one of the worst features of these risks. The losses on paper-mills had been far in excess of the average loss on other risks. It therefore became necessary either to induce the owners to remedy the faults of construction, or else to drop the risks. The former course was taken, rates being advanced in the interval, and the Paper-Mill Mutual Company was organized, so that owners could be trained as directors in the right construction and protection of their own risks. This action led to a complete revolution in the layout and construction of paper-mills, and this change has been justified not only by the greater safety of the works, but by very great improvement in the methods of handling the stock. During the last ten years this company has not met a loss exceeding $5000 on any paper-mill.

Fires from the ignition of bituminous coal attracted our attention. It proved that there was but one variety of coal which had not taken fire, and since a preference or condition for the use of that coal would have given the owners a monopoly, costing consumers much more than any possible loss on the coal itself from spontaneous ignition, it was decided, with the assent of all parties in interest, not to insure bituminous coals against their own inherent hazard, maintaining the insurance of the property endangered by this cause of fire. Actual loss of calorific value by the slow coking of a pile of coal is not very great, although it has sometimes made a great deal of trouble in mill yards. Our present system is fully justified and has worked to the mutual benefit of our members. In this connection it may be related that we shall presently be able to present a report on fire retardent materials for wooden surfaces, which can be very cheaply applied to the wooden posts, which have not infrequently burned off in the coal piles, and which will entirely obviate that danger.

Among the earlier lines of investigation was the test of the strength of wooden posts. The common practice had been to turn these posts, tapering from the base toward the top; this was a waste of material and weakening of strength without any sound reason. Our tests proved the superiority of the square posts, chamfered off at the corners, with hole bored through the center, and a crossway hole near the top and bottom to ventilate and season the timber. This was followed by further tests of the strength of timbers, and the layout of plans for the construction of cotton factories consistently with the rather light weights per square foot of floor which are found in this branch of industry. Other general plans for machine shops, paper-mills, etc., are also kept in stock.

What the factory mutual companies have attempted is to give a proper direction to the use of timber, plank, brick, and concrete, so disposed that with proper apparatus fires may be reached in the beginning, or may be controlled before they attain destructive headway. Had we not been enabled to compass low cost and economy in construction with adequate security against loss by fire, we should never have been able to accomplish the work which has been done. I have often asked, what has been the cost of fire protection in buildings rightly constructed according to our plans? It is not possible to give a positive answer to that question because the conditions vary with the different arts. In that branch of industry with which the factory system originated, namely, the manufacture of cotton, the conditions also vary very considerably, although not in so great a measure. We are accustomed to make all our computations of the cost of buildings, the appraisements for insurance and fire protection by the unit of the square foot of occupied floor; that is to say, of floor put to use in the manufacturing operations, in hallways, stairways, elevators, and the like, not including unoccupied basements unfit to be used which ought never to be tolerated anywhere. On this basis a tolerable average may be named. The average cost of adequate pumps, pipes, and hydrants within mill yards, not including outside connections or outside reservoirs, will not exceed 5 cents per square foot of floor, and may often be put in position at less, any excess being due to extraordinary conditions. The cost per square foot of floor of automatic sprinklers may be put at an average of 3 cents. The entire cost will range from a minimum of 6 under favorable conditions to 8 cents under conditions which may not infrequently arise. In ratio to values this average expenditure would stand at not exceeding 1½ per cent.

for the pump, pipe, and hydrant service, and at an average of 1 per cent. for the sprinkler service. The cost per spindle will vary with fine or coarse work.

One of the most useful functions, still continued in the physical laboratory, is the test and warning against fraudulent and dangerous claims or substances. This work has been especially effective in dealing with fancy oils and mixtures, belt dressings, lamps, heavy gases, or mechanical mixtures of naphtha or gasoline with air, claims for improvement in making steam, fire-proof material so-called, and other matters.

The writer may hope that this record of progress in what may now be justly called the science of preventing loss by fire will have some influence outside the lines of the factory mutual companies. The present condition of the country in respect to loss by fire and contracts of indemnity given by insurance companies is somewhat alarming. All insurance, under whatever name, is a mutual contract to pay indemnity. Under the stock system the capital serves only as a guarantee. It must never be impaired in any great measure for the payment of losses and expenses. The losses and expenses must be covered by the premiums put in by the assured, and it is as impossible for an insurance company to give contracts of indemnity on less than cost for any long period of time as it is impossible for a factory to make and sell goods at less than cost without bankruptcy. The sagacious managers of all insurance companies are now seeking for a remedy for the present dangerous conditions of underwriting. The ash heap due to loss by fire, the excessive cost of fire departments due to bad building and bad occupancy, and the cost of sustaining the insurance system of the country combined, coupled with the excessive demands for additional water supplies for fire purposes only, cannot amount to less than $200,000,000 a year, and is probably much more.

I can find no trace of any annual profit on the entire

business of the nation which would warrant us in estimating the addition to the capital or savings of the people of this country, exceeding $1,500,000,000 even in a prosperous year. It is probably less. It follows that the fire tax is certainly equal to 10 per cent. upon any possible profit of the nation, and is probably 15 per cent. It is equal to the normal cost of conducting the government of the United States under normal conditions, aside from pensions and interest on the national debt, that normal rate being $2.50 per head, amounting last year, on a peace basis, to a less sum than this fire tax.

What is to be done to meet this waste? For the last ten years the representatives of the stock fire insurance companies, especially in Boston, have made consistent, intelligent, and determined efforts to bring about a change, and in some cities great progress has been made in preventing loss, notably in this city of Boston. But in some other cities the danger of a most destructive conflagration still exists, and it is probably only a question of time when such a conflagration will occur, rendering a large part of the stock insurance companies bankrupt which may have large lines in such cities. Without those large lines of insurance their business could not be conducted under existing conditions. This danger of most destructive conflagrations can neither be met by legislation nor by insurance companies. The owners and occupants of these dangerous and combustible buildings and districts are responsible for this great danger and must pay the penalty; until they act in combination under intelligent advisers big fires are their own fault.

Although the method of granting contracts of indemnity by the factory mutual companies must, of necessity, be limited to special establishments, each carefully guarded from the other and fitted with its own apparatus for the extinction of fire, yet there are vast fields not yet covered by this mutual method. The more hazardous the work, the more reason for adopting this system of preventing loss. All the wood-working establishments and many other branches of industry might be combined in the same way; the only thing necessary being to overcome the antagonism with which owners usually regard the underwriters, and to bring them together as co-partners, under a sufficient deposit, each sustaining the other in the effort to find out the causes of danger and to remove them.

A mutual insurance company might be organized for the insuance and prevention of fire in church buildings. We burn 11.36 churches per week in the United States. By combination for mutual insurance the church members might be assured against cremation in this world, if not in the next.

A very large part of the great shops and department stores are badly planned, little consideration having been given in their construction to danger of fire, except in some cases in choosing the material of which the buildings are constructed. Fires have spread with extreme rapidity over open stocks, even in fire-proof buildings, so-called, in which there have been many openings or stairways passing from one floor to another, to the complete destruction of the contents. The factory underwriters regard the vertical hazard much greater than the horizontal hazard. They are obliged to deal with very large floor areas, very often of one acre each, sometimes much larger, covered with combustible material. But since the introduction of automatic sprinklers all fires have been stopped with moderate loss from any great horizontal spread. No fire has passed from one floor to another, in any building insured under the supervision of the undersigned, by burning away the thick plank floor in any working department of any mill. In one instance, a fire originating at the bottom of a pile of jute in a storehouse burned through the floor, making a porthole through which a stream of water was thrown to the heart of the fire. The fires which have passed upward or downward from floor to floor have passed either through belt openings which are now nearly abolished, or, getting by the doorways, have passed through the elevator shafts or stairways.

The true model of a great department store may at some future date be a building without any windows in the walls except, perhaps, in the upper story, if a top or roof light does not suffice to show goods for which daylight is needed, electricity serving to give light, and a forced circulation of air warmed and cleansed giving better ventilation than can be attained by opening or closing windows. Such an establishment might be built with passages from floor to floor in separate towers, or stair chambers at each corner, each carefully cut off at each floor by automatic fire-doors and with no other openings from floor to floor. The latest storehouses in cities, where narrow areas make it necessary to construct buildings of many stories in height, have been built substantially on this plan. This may seem a somewhat visionary idea, but what stands in the way? If show windows are needed around the lower story, they can be cut off by fire-proof walls and ceilings from the interior, lighted and protected separately from the main building and entered from the towers.

While it may not be possible to apply all the rules and methods to the miscellaneous hazards of a city, yet a very large part of the safeguards which are required by the mutual companies, as a condition of insuring property, have been brought into use for the protection of the commercial hazards of cities and can be extended rapidly when owners and occupants can be aroused to the necessity.

CHAPTER XVII

HISTORY OF MARINE INSURANCE[1]

In discussing marine insurance one deals with a subject far more technical and complex than any other system of indemnity. Fire insurance provides against loss occasioned by a single occurrence. Life insurance insures against an event, the occurrence of which is inevitable, and the risk concerning which has been approximately measured by the application of the law of average to accumulated data. Marine insurance, however, undertakes to indemnify a person against the loss of ship, goods, freight, anticipated profits, or any other insurable interest, through any of the numerous perils and adventures connected with navigation, such as the perils "of the sea," fires, collisions, pirates, thieves, seizures and restraints, jettisons, barratry of the master or mariners, and all other perils, losses or misfortunes which might be assumed by the policy.

While determined efforts have been made for years, and with success, to place the prosecution of life and fire insurance upon a scientific basis, this can scarcely be said of marine underwriting. Some of our leading marine companies, it is true, do possess a large mass of experience which is used as a basis in computing rates. Yet it is also true that, taking the business as a whole, there is no other branch of insurance in which success is so largely

[1] By Solomon Heubner, Assistant Professor of Political Economy, University of Pennsylvania. Reprinted from pages 421–452, Vol. XXVI, Annals of the American Academy of Political and Social Science.

dependent upon the native sagacity, the keenness for observation, and the general specialized ability of the individual underwriter to know not only men, but the effect of climate, seasons, geographical localities and numerous other considerations upon any of a large number of risks, as in marine insurance. To a very large extent the business is inherently a system of estimates, and the importance of the personal qualities of the underwriter cannot be over emphasized.

It is this complex nature of the business which is no doubt responsible for the fact that marine insurance is to-day a comparatively little-known business to the general public. Consult any of our leading insurance journals, and a score or more of pages will be found dealing with other lines of insurance for one dealing with this, the oldest and possibly the most interesting, and, in many particulars, equally important branch. This comparative absence of notice, however, should not cause us to overlook the fact that in this country alone, between six and seven billion dollars worth of property is insured by marine companies, and that it is through this form of insurance that participation in commerce becomes general and continuous. It is not to be supposed that people would risk their fortunes in enterprises surrounded with so many dangers as mercantile ventures, were it not for the indemnifying contract, while in distributing the loss of a few among the many, removes the sense of fear and makes the mercantile industry one of certainty in its results instead of a half-gambling enterprise. As a prominent writer on mercantile affairs correctly states: "Marine insurance bears to commerce the relation of body-guard rather than of mere servile attendant. . . . Of the active forces which influence, control, or forbid the employment of shipping, none have greater effect than the marine insurance power."[1] Marine underwriting may indeed be characterized as just as much an instrumen-

[1] William W. Bates. The "American Marine," p. 219.

tality of commerce and almost as necessary to navigation as the ship itself. It is universally recognized as a most important factor in trade and transportation, and in modern commerce is of the utmost utility. To this may be added that, as the methods of conducting oversea trade are being constantly transformed, marine insurance is becoming an increasingly important adjunct of commerce. As Mr. Gow correctly says: "When large transactions are worked, as is now extremely common, with credits and margins, the amount of the premium of insurance is often the item that decides whether some venture will be attempted or not. The protection which marine insurance affords is now usually regarded as an absolute necessity to the oversea merchant; and thus by degrees marine insurance has become in one shape or another an integral, almost an essential, factor in oversea commercial transactions."[1]

The practice of marine insurance may be regarded as the earliest form of indemnity, antedating other kinds of insurance by many hundred years. Even centuries before the introduction of marine underwriting as we know it to-day, the commercial nations of the ancient world secured the benefits of insurance through the so-called "loans on bottomry," *e.g.* loans made on the security of the ship and cargo at high rates of interest, and with the understanding that the principal with interest was to be repaid only in the event of the safe arrival of the vessel, and that the lender was to forfeit both principal and interest in case of loss. Instead, then, of paying a premium before starting the voyage, as is now the case, and receiving the indemnity after a loss is incurred the insured under the bottomry loan received the indemnity in advance, and only returned the same plus a premium after safe termination of the voyage.

Such loans on bottomry, we are told, were especially sought after and entered into by members of the Roman

[1] Willam Gow. "Marine Insurance," p. 2.

nobility, who, too proud to interest themselves directly in commerce, and yet desirous of obtaining large interest returns, could here find a convenient method of investing their funds profitably, and at the same time avoid engaging personally in mercantile pursuits. That such loans were prevalent among the commercial peoples of early history is attested by the numerous references concerning such transactions which are found in the judicial and other literature of the Romans. In an edict of the Roman Emperor Justinian of A.D. 533, for example, the rate of premium on such loans was fixed at 12 per cent., implying at least that the practice must have been very general at that time. Though indirect in form and partaking merely of the nature of quasi-insurance, this method of indemnifying loss by means of loans was nevertheless real insurance in its results. It should be borne in mind, however, that this method of indemnification is the only one approximating modern insurance of which antiquity furnishes us any clear and direct evidence. It might seem remarkable, indeed, that nations so far advanced in their legal systems as were the Mediterranean countries, and with such extensive commercial interests, should have left us no direct and conclusive evidence to show that they at all understood marine insurance as it is now practised.

Marine insurance as it exists to-day originated at a much later date than the loan on bottomry. Evidence seems to show that it had its start in Italy, especially among the Lombard merchants, at the close of the twelfth and the beginning of the thirteenth century. From thence it spread to Flanders, Portugal, and Spain during the fourteenth and fifteenth centuries, and was finally carried to England by the Lombards in the early part of the sixteenth century. As early as 1601 the British Parliament declared marine insurance to have existed from time immemorial (43 Elizabeth, C. 12), and described it as a means "whereby it cometh to pass that upon the loss or perishing of any ship there followeth not the undoing of any man, but the loss lighteth rather easily upon many than heavy upon few, and rather upon them that adventure not than upon those who do adventure; whereby all merchants, especially those of the younger sort, are allured to venture more willingly and more freely."

Following its introduction in England, marine insurance spread to the various commercial centers of Europe, its application becoming very general, if judged from the consideration given to the subject in the numerous commercial codes and ordinances of the fifteenth, sixteenth, and seventeenth centuries. Finally, there followed the epoch-making Ordinance de la Marine of 1681, which became the model for practically all the modern codes of commercial law on the continent, including the law of marine insurance. In England, on the contrary, the development of the law concerning sea insurance did not begin to assume such clear and definite form until almost the middle of the eighteenth century. It was then that Lord Mansfield, in his efforts to formulate the commercial law of England, began to draw his legal principles very largely from the commercial ordinances and codes of the continent with a view of applying them to English conditions. His decisions practically constitute the foundation of marine insurance law in England, and in turn have become the basis of American decisions. As supplementing this lengthy and continuous legal development, it is important to note that the Lloyd's policy prevailing in England to-day is very similar to the policy which was in use in the early part of the seventeenth century, and that many features of the English policy have in turn been incorporated in the policies used in America. In other words, we have in marine insurance several centuries of usage and judicial interpretation relating to the signification of a single document.

Turning now to the financial development of the business as distinct from the legal, marine insurance has naturally reached its highest efficiency in the United

Kingdom. Its history in that country, whose merchant marine for many decades comprised nearly half of the ocean-going tonnage of the world, has been rendered famous by the close identification of the business with the world renowned corporation of Lloyds. This gigantic institution had its origin in a mere seamen's coffee house, established by an Edward Lloyd near the middle of the seventeenth century. This enterprising and energetic man, besides making his coffee house a convenient place of meeting of merchants and seamen, also created an elaborate system of home and foreign correspondents to supply him with news from all the leading ports of the world concerning the movements and character of vessels for the information of his patrons. In fact, at first the underwriting of marine risks was a subordinate feature of his business. The systematic manner, however, in which maritime information was collected and disseminated soon won for him a large following, and made his coffee house, among the many others existing in London, the principal meeting place for merchants and professional underwriters who, unhampered by any rules or regulations, assembled there and transacted a general marine business. Thus it came to pass that Lloyds soon outgrew its early usefulness, was transferred in 1692 from its original location in Tower Street to Lombard Street, and finally, in 1774, to the Royal Exchange of London, and there developed into the chief center of marine insurance in the United Kingdom, and, for that matter, in the world.

From this account it is not to be inferred that marine insurance in the United Kingdom is confined to Lloyds or to British shipping. Prior to the beginning of the eighteenth century the business was, it is true, confined almost entirely to the plan of Lloyds, according to which individuals assumed risks upon the strength of their personal honesty and financial standing in the community. Indeed, it was the practice of various individuals subscribing their names to the insurance contract for a certain portion of the total risk that gave rise to the familiar term "underwriter." But gradually companies began to participate in the same business that Lloyds was pursuing. The movement seemed to gain strength rapidly, when, in 1720, the British government in return for a payment of £300,000 to the Exchequer limited the privilege of insuring marine risks to only two companies besides Lloyds, namely, the London Assurance Corporation and the Royal Exchange Assurance Corporation. Shortly after, however, this monopoly was removed and since then, especially during the nineteenth century, numerous corporations in London, Liverpool, and Glasgow, with vast accumulated assets and far-reaching importance, have risen alongside the unique and unrivaled corporation of Lloyds, and, like that institution, have extended their influence to all corners of the earth. So effective, in fact, has the competition of the powerful insurance companies become that Lloyds, although yet the center of attraction in the marine business, has largely ceased to possess the dominating influence of former days. It is estimated that Great Britain to-day transacts about six-eighths of the sea insurance of the world, a proportion so large that one can look for an explanation only to the preponderating importance of Great Britain as a shipping nation.

The supreme importance of Lloyds in marine insurance from an international standpoint justifies a brief explanation of its organization and purposes. Until quite recently, Lloyds was an unincorporated body where underwriters assembled and transacted business at will, subject to few or no regulations. In the year 1871, however, Lloyds became an incorporated organization, and, according to the act of incorporation, now exists for the three-fold purpose of conducting an insurance business, of protecting the commercial and maritime interests of its members, and of collecting and disseminating information pertaining to shipping.

To obtain a clear view of how this three-fold purpose is

realized, it is essential to study the institution of Lloyds from two points of view, namely, the intelligence department and the corporation of underwriters. For the sake of convenience we may consider the intelligence department first, since the collection and diffusion of maritime information is a prime prerequisite to successful underwriting. Briefly described, this department consists of numerous agents situated in every part of the world, whose position is considered one of the highest honor and importance, and whose duty it is to forward promptly information to headquarters concerning the arrival and departure of vessels, the occurrence of wrecks and accidents, or any other events which vitally affect shipping. As representatives of Lloyds, these agents are also required to render aid to masters of vessels in distress, to take charge of a wrecked vessel's stores and materials in order to avoid unnecessary loss, to adopt precautionary measures against dishonesty when it becomes necessary to repair ships, and in a general way to protect the interests of the underwriters. To supplement the efforts of these agents, Lloyds also desires the masters of vessels to report to the nearest Lloyds' agent any information of interest concerning other ships which they might have seen or spoken with while on their voyage.

All the information thus obtained by Lloyds from agents and shipmasters from all parts of the globe is next analyzed and distributed for the benefit of underwriters and subscribers. This brings us to the next important feature of Lloyds, namely, its publications. These are five in number, namely:

(1) *Lloyds' List.* The official daily publication of the corporation containing all shipping news as currently received, and generally recognized as the most reliable among the various sources of maritime intelligence.

(2) *Lloyds' Register of British and Foreign Shipping.* An annual publication founded in 1834, and designed to indicate the general character of all vessels in the British

marine of not less than one hundred tons, besides numerous vessels in foreign fleets. Among other items, this publication states the name, materials of construction and state of repairs of the ship, its dimensions, registered tonnage, and general equipment, the date and place of construction and by whom constructed, the name of the owners, the port to which the vessel belongs, and the date of the last survey, and, finally, the name of the master and the date of his appointment. To keep the shipping world informed of any variations which may occur, supplementary lists are published monthly in connection with the annual edition of the *Register*. In other words, this annual register may be likened to a catalogue of nearly all the important vessels of the world, from which the underwriter may ascertain by a hurried reference the general fitness of a specified vessel to make a given voyage or carry a certain cargo. To render such reference on the part of the underwriter still easier, both iron and wooden vessels are each divided into separate classes, and these classes into grades, each grade being designated by a conventional symbol.[1] *Lloyds' Register* is thus the handbook of the underwriter: but it should always be kept in mind that while it is of the greatest service to those who accept marine risks, it

[1] Since the classification of vessels is fundamental in the shipping and insurance business, the importance of a publication like *Lloyds' Register* can not well be overestimated. Its influence became so potent a factor in British shipping that other nations were obliged to adopt a similar system, until to-day *Lloyds' Register* constitutes the standard after which all other maritime nations have modeled their own registers. To such an extent has classification of vessels become a necessary adjunct to the shipping industry, that practically no vessel of any importance in any nation is without a regular classification in some standard register. Chief among the registers now published in addition to Lloyds are the *Register of American Shipping* and the *American Lloyd* of the United States, the *Bureau Veritas* of France, the *Germanische Lloyd* and the *Stettiner Register* of Germany, the *Austro-Ungarian Veritas* of Austria, the *Nederlandische-Werienigung* of Holland, the *Norske Veritas* of Scandinavia, and the *Veritas Hellinque* of Greece.

is controlled by authorities of its own, and is an institution entirely distinct in its organization from the corporation of underwriters.[1]

(3) *The Index.* A list of all British mercantile vessels, together with numerous foreign ships, showing their condition and location according to the latest reports. This publication is not only open to inspection at Lloyds, but members and subscribers, wherever situated, may upon request obtain the latest news concerning any particular vessel.

(4) *A Register of Captains.* A biographical dictionary containing a record of the service, proficiency, and character of the twenty-five thousand or more certified commanders of the British marine, and

(5) *A Record of Losses,* frequently called the Black Book.

Turning now to the corporation of underwriters, as distinct from the intelligence department, it is of interest to note that its membership consists of two classes: (1) the underwriting members who write insurance for their own profit, subject, of course, to the rules and require-

[1] In the modern system of classification, as Professor Gambaro explains, "Ships are divided into three classes, according to the degree of confidence to be placed in their seaworthiness. A vessel recently and strongly built, well rigged and equipped, is assigned for a number of years to the first class, and may, therefore, during such period be employed with full confidence in any voyage, for the conveyance of any kind of merchandise; provided, of course, that she suffer no deterioration or damage as may render her unserviceable, and be maintained in good state of repair, which is ascertained by periodical surveys. A second term of the same class is often granted to ships proving still strong, and in a good state of preservation after the first period. A special distinction over and above the highest classification may be obtained for a ship, provided, such materials be used in her build as directed by the committee. Vessels which have gone through this first class term are assigned to the second, and lastly, to the third class; the latter embracing vessels in very poor condition, considered fit only for short and easy voyages, and to carry cargoes not to be damaged by sea-water, such as timber, salt, etc.". — Gambaro's "Lessons in Commerce," p. 137.

ments imposed by the managing committee of Lloyds, and (2) the non-underwriting members, who, as brokers and merchants, transact business through the underwriting members either for themselves or others. In addition to these two classes, there are also numerous subscribers to Lloyds for the information received at the Royal Exchange, many of whom are British and foreign insurance companies. Here it remains to be said that practically all the great marine insurance companies of the United Kingdom (and they number some thirty or more), even though their marine business in the aggregate far exceeds that of Lloyds, must nevertheless be represented on its floor, and must necessarily and continually receive the assistance of that organization in the prosecution of their business.[1]

As a corporation Lloyds resembles our stock exchanges in many particulars. It assumes no responsibility whatever for the solvency of its members. It seeks only to provide proper facilities to its members for the conduct of their business, and to limit admission to men of recognized honesty and financial standing. As a guarantee for the fulfilment of contracts, each underwriting member is required to deposit with the committee of Lloyds securities to the value of £5000. Aside from this requirement, the corporation does not concern itself as to the nature or the volume of the business transacted by its members. They are free to do as much underwriting as they like, and may pursue any kind of insurance they choose, only they must do it honestly. As a consequence Lloyds, although marine insurance and the furnishing of maritime intelligence is the fundamental character of its business, is a place where one may insure against all sorts of contingencies — against fire, epidemics, sickness and all sorts of accidents, against the risks of journeys and business

[1] For a concise account of the organization of Lloyds and an excellent description of its system of classifying vessels and distributing marine intelligence, see Professor Gambaro's "Lessons in Commerce."

ventures, against the loss of works of art and valuable possessions, or to avoid loss from the unforeseen stoppage of games and races, or to meet contemplated changes in foreign tariffs, or to provide against the risks of war during periods of political excitement, and a hundred and one other contingencies of every conceivable kind, many of them nothing more than betting arrangements. Combining all these different forms of indemnity with the marine business, authorities place the total amount of risk carried at Lloyds at approximately $2,500,000,000, while the total deposits paid in by members as a guarantee for the performance of contracts are placed at not more than $20,000,000, or about only 1 per cent. of the risks assumed.

In its daily routine of business Lloyds affords an interesting and instructive spectacle, and illustrates the complexity and arbitrary nature which surrounds a good share of the business. On the Exchange, for example, are several hundred underwriters, unincorporated and unable thus to act jointly. To describe the manner in which these members transact business, I can do no better than cite from Mr. Samuel Plimsoll's concise and picturesque account. "There are seldom," he says, "less than fifty underwriters on a policy, frequently over one hundred (the three policies before me show an average of seventy-two subscribers), not bound together at all, each individual can only act for himself, and accepts just so much of the whole risk as he pleases; he seldom, almost never, accepts for any large amount, always for a very small proportion indeed of the whole amount covered. The way of it is this: a member of Lloyds (underwriters' room) first gives evidence or security as to his ability to pay losses; then he has a desk allotted to him (they are very numerous — between three hundred and fifty and four hundred in London alone, where, however, the bulk of underwriting is done); the proposals of insurance are handed around by the insurance brokers' clerks all day long; these proposals, called slips, give the name of the ship, amount to be insured, and rate per cent. offered. Perhaps sixty or seventy of these slips, or even more, are laid before each underwriter daily. After reference to Lloyds' List of Ships, he either passes it on or, if he decides to 'take a line' upon it, he subscribes or 'underwrites' his name, together with the amount he is willing to guarantee for at the rate specified; this varies much and generally goes as low as £200 or £100, frequently £50, and sometimes even less than that — never an amount large enough to warrant his disputing his liability in case of loss.[1] "

As a result of the procedure thus described by Mr. Plimsoll, it follows that the underwriter at Lloyds has practically no opportunity to examine the risk as he would do in other leading forms of insurance. The only sources of information which he might use as a guide are, as a rule, the publications of the corporation, like the *Annual Register*, the *Captain's Register*, and *Lloyds' List*. From these he may obtain useful information concerning the age, size, structure, equipment and management of the vessel as based on frequent surveys by expert surveyors. But naturally such classifications have their limits, and do not purpose giving more than a general description of the vessel in question. Concerning many factors like stowage, the amount of load, the size and efficiency of the crew, and numerous other factors equally vital to the safety of a vessel and cargo at sea, these publications can offer no assistance. It is here that the insurer must use his judgment, and where success is largely dependent upon the specialized ability of the underwriter. Nor would it be to the interest of the insurer at Lloyds to make such an examination, assuming that he could do so. Not only will his limited time and the large number of proposals made to him daily render this impossible, but the mere fact that probably half a hundred other persons have

[1] Samuel Plimsoll. *The Nineteenth Century*, Vol. XXV, p. 329.

underwritten the same policy will make it seem foolhardy that he alone should undertake the examination. To retain his business he must be quick in accepting or rejecting proposals on the spot, and can not afford to tarry, since it is the brokers' business to secure insurance for his patrons as quickly as possible. Moreover, the amount of the total risk, to which he has subscribed is, as we have seen, comparatively small and limited to an amount which will not make it worth his while to contest a claim or pursue an examination. And even if the underwriter be a subscriber for a large amount it does not necessarily follow that he will be actually liable for the amount underwritten, for as soon as he fears having sustained a loss he will endeavor to transfer his risk. This he does by offering a higher premium as an inducement for some one else to take all or a share of his risk. One underwriter fearing a loss thus transfers part of his risk to another, who expects the early and safe arrival of the vessel. If uncertainty concerning the vessel continues, this second underwriter by offering a still higher premium may transfer part of his risk to another, who again has good hopes, and so on until, if it is finally learned that the vessel and cargo are lost, the risk has been so widely diffused that the loss incurred by any one individual is comparatively small. Lastly, it is interesting to note that collectively the underwriters at Lloyds have no interest in examining risks because they have no interest in diminishing loss. On the contrary, strange as it may seem, they express a preference for a high rate of loss to a low one. Individually they all desire and expect to avoid the payment of claims, but collectively they all wish and expect to profit by high rates. Hence it is that they prefer the increase in premiums which accompanies an increase in losses.

A review of marine insurance in the United States shows that its development as well as its present status is radically different from that in England as just described. In the first place, the business has been conducted almost altogether by corporations, the Lloyds system of underwriting, though often tried, having never obtained a prominent foothold in this country. Secondly, while British companies have had a long and prosperous career, the companies of the United States, with few exceptions, have either failed or changed the character of their business. If we are justified in fixing definite limits, the development of the business in this country seems to divide itself into four main epochs, each with distinctive characteristics of its own. The dates of these periods may be roughly placed at 1793 as marking the end of the first period, 1793 to 1840 as indicating the limits of the second period, 1840 to 1860 the third, and 1860 to the present time the final period.

During the first period, extending to the end of the eighteenth century, the only form of insurance upon goods or vessels of which we have definite knowledge was by personal underwriters. Resort was had at first to the private underwriters of Great Britain, frequent mention being found in early colonial correspondence concerning London indemnity for American shipping. Even as late as 1721 there was as yet no insurance office in Philadelphia, dependence being placed mostly upon foreign underwriters. In that year we find a Mr. John Copson advertising in the *American Weekly Mercury* of May 25, the opening by him of an office of public insurance on vessels, goods, and merchandise, because, as he announced in the advertisement, "the merchants of this city of Philadelphia and other ports have been obliged to send to London for such insurance, which has not only been tedious and troublesome, but ever precarious, and for the remedying of which this office is opened." Four years later Mr. Francis Rawle, of Philadelphia, advised the establishment of a marine insurance office under colonial legislative sanction, and the pamphlet embodying his ideas was, according to report, the first work issued from Benjamin Franklin's press. Following Mr. Copson's and Mr. Rawle's pioneer attempts to establish insurance offices, few efforts were made to follow in their footsteps. Mr. Fowler, in his history of insurance in Philadelphia, informs us that for seventy years afterwards Philadelphia merchants still looked to the Old World as the chief source from which to obtain their insurance. Likewise in New York City it was not until 1759 that the first marine insurance office was opened, and not until 1778 that the New Insurance Office was established. The underwriting in all these cases continued to be by individuals or partnerships only, who generally represented wealthy citizens of the community.

It was not until near the close of the eighteenth century that a number of citizens of Philadelphia succeeded in inducing the General Assembly of Pennsylvania to charter a marine insurance company, capitalized at $600,000. The reasons assigned for this step by the legislative committee reporting in favor of granting the charter were: (1) That an incorporated company of this size could conduct an insurance business on a safer and more staple basis than could individuals; (2) that from a legal point of view justice could be secured more readily in the case of a corporate organization, since it would obviate the expense and loss of time required to sue separately all the different underwriters to a policy; (3) that the number of persons underwriting in Philadelphia was insufficient for the needs of its commercial interests, thus occasioning a drain of money for insurance to Europe and neighboring states; and, lastly, that since the company did not ask for a monopoly, the granting of the charter would simply mean the bringing about of a wholesome competition, and would enable the business to be conducted on an enlarged scale to the great benefit of commerce. In view of these reasons thus offered, the Assembly, in the year 1794,[1] chartered the Insurance Company of North

[1] The Insurance Company of North America began business as an association in 1792, and was incorporated in 1794.

America, the first stock company of its kind upon the continent whose name it bore. Fortunately this pioneer company was launched at a time when Philadelphia was still the commercial metropolis of the country, with its ship-owners and merchants trading in all the remote quarters of the globe, and, therefore, large purchasers of insurance. Indeed it was not long before the brokers, who previously had had the American business to themselves, found that their patrons preferred the stability of corporate underwriting on a large scale to the underwriting of individuals. In the very first year of active business the company refused to write for private offices, and "realizing its strength, made public advertisement of their rules, and invited orders to be addressed directly to the company." [1]

This important step toward the establishment of corporate underwriting with all its advantages was soon to serve as a model for similar undertakings in other parts of the country, and before another decade had passed the Insurance Company of North America was to have active associates in its own home as well as in New York, Boston, Baltimore, Charleston, and other places. In 1796 was established the Insurance Company of New York in New York City, followed by the Associated Underwriters of the same city in 1797, the United in 1797, Columbian in 1801, Washington Mutual in 1802, Marine in 1802, Commercial in 1804, Phoenix in 1807, Fireman's in 1810, Ocean in 1810, and others. In Philadelphia there followed the Insurance Company of the State of Pennsylvania in 1794, the Phoenix in 1803, the Philadelphia in 1804, Delaware in 1804, Marine in 1809, and the United States in 1810. Boston also came into the field at an early date, the Massachusetts Fire and Marine Company being organized in that city in 1795, and the Boston Marine in 1799; while among other early companies of importance may be mentioned the Charitable Marine Society of Baltimore,

[1] "History of the Insurance Company of North America," p. 56.

organized in 1796; the New Haven Insurance Company, of New Haven, in 1797; the Charleston Insurance Company, of Charleston, S. C., in 1797, and the Newburyport Marine, of Newburyport, Mass., in 1797. So rapid, in fact, was the movement of incorporating insurance companies that prior to 1800 thirty-two insurance companies had been established in this country, of which ten were doing a marine business. By 1811 there existed in Philadelphia alone eleven companies, seven of which were marine companies and one a fire-marine company, while by 1825 there were twelve marine stock companies in New York, and at least a dozen in Boston.

Prior to 1830 the history of these companies may be characterized as one of periodical prosperity and depression. If judged by the experience of the largest company (and this is typical of most other companies) the business exhibited the greatest fluctuations. Thus during the first decade of its history ending with December, 1802, the Insurance Company of North America collected premiums of $6,037,456 and paid losses of $5,500,887, leaving a margin of less than 9 per cent. for expenses. During this decade the premium receipts rose from $213,465 in 1793 to $290,656 in 1794 and $1,304,208 in 1798. This large income, received by an American company prior to the beginning of the nineteenth century, it is interesting to note, is equal to three-fourths of the marine premiums received by the same company to-day, and exceeds the marine premium income of any other American company at the present time except one. Then began a decline, until in 1802 the premium income amounted to only $103,902 which sum, however, was trebled in 1805, and again trebled in 1806. Then came the Embargo Acts, and premium receipts suddenly fell to the mere pittance of $5,483 in 1808, while losses continued as high as $108,568. Even in the years 1809 to 1812, inclusive, the average annual receipts equaled but $45,449, as compared with $1,304,000 in 1798. If the decade ending in 1802 is compared with that ending in 1812, it appears that the first shows premium receipts of $6,000,000 and losses of $5,500,000, while the second shows premiums of only $1,364,637, or only one-fifth the income of the first decade, and losses of $1,583,836.

These remarkable fluctuations, as also the decrease in the annual premium receipts and the increase in the ratio of loss to income, are to be explained partly by the growing competition arising from the numerous rival institutions which were springing up everywhere; partly because insurance managers had not yet mastered the lesson of a solid surplus and very imprudently distributed all profits to stockholders without making provision for the heavy losses of the immediate and stormy future; but mainly to the heavy losses connected with the Napoleonic Wars. This series of bitter struggles, with its blockades and counter-blockades, affecting practically all of commercial Europe, subjected American commerce to unusual risks and losses. Insurance was consequently in great demand and came for the first time to be regularly adopted by all ship-owners, and at rates which averaged as high as twelve per cent. But while the business of marine insurance received a strong impetus during this period of strife, the business was, nevertheless, of uncertain tenure, being constantly subject to the heavy losses arising from capture, detention, and litigation which frequently resulted, owing to the absence of a large surplus, in severely impairing the capital of the companies. Mr. Seyfert, for example, in a list compiled from a report of the Secretary of State, shows that the total captures of American vessels by the British, French, Neapolitans and Danes during the years 1803 to 1812 aggregated nearly 1600 vessels, the major portion of which were condemned, and most of the others detained. At the same time we have the statement made in the House of Peers that 600 American vessels were seized or detained in British ports within a period of less than five months from November 6, 1793, to March 28, 1794.[1]

[1] Adam Seyfert. "Statistical Annals of the United States," pp. 79-81.

Such extraordinary losses by capture and detention were bound to prove a heavy drain on the resources of the companies. And in those days of slow communication it would often happen that they might be incurring heavy losses at the hands of foreign cruisers without being able to obtain knowledge of the same for months, in the meantime assuming new risks equally exposed to the attacks of the enemy. To obtain a clear conception of the losses thus sustained one need only examine the proceedings of a few companies of this period. On February 12, 1801, the directors of the Insurance Company of North America "ordered that an account of all illegal captures made by the British and French be made out for the purpose of representing the same to the United States Government."[1] No better evidence can be advanced to indicate the severity of the struggle which the early companies were undergoing than the account of the committee entrusted with this work. Its report stated that "the number and amount of the companies' claims on the British Government for spoliation on property which they (the committee) think that nation ought to refund is about $981,355; other losses occasioned to this office by capture of the British, and for which there is no expectation of reimbursement, is about $78,800. With respect to the captures made by the French, your committee can only state that they amount to $1,952,730."[2] Many of the claims thus incurred were later adjusted by international arrangement. Others, however, were not, and numerous attempts were made in later years to recover losses sustained during this period. No less than twenty-two reports of committees, all favoring the claimants, were made in Congress between the years 1827 and 1846 for an indemnity of $5,000,000. Twice, in 1846 and 1855, did the bills pass through all stages of enactment except the President's signature, and even as late as 1885 we find the matter still before Congress.

[1] "History of the Insurance Company of North America," p. 56.
[2] *Ibid.*

With the cessation in 1815 of the widespread Napoleonic Wars of twenty-three years and the introduction of a period of profound peace one might have supposed that the business would have immediately revived. But such was not the case. The high war rates gradually gave way before low peace rates, and by 1820 these were the general rule. By this time, too, personal underwriters had been almost entirely displaced by underwriting corporations whose number had greatly multiplied in all the leading seaports. To make matters still worse, in view of the rapidly declining rates, these numerous corporations began to wage a fierce and incessant competitive war against each other. The elimination of the personal underwriter meant the establishment of the broker as middleman, and soon the numerous companies in the various leading commercial centers no longer confined their business activity to their own locality, as they had done heretofore, but began to solicit risks from the outside by correspondence and otherwise. As a result of this rate war, many of the younger companies were brought to the verge of insolvency, and most of the older ones were unable to pay dividends on their capital equal to the current rate of interest. So great was the competition that at the close of 1825 the stock of only four of the twelve stock companies in New York was quoted at or above par. Beginning with 1828 marine insurance companies were also obliged to pay extraordinary losses occasioned by fraudulent wrecks on the Atlantic, Gulf, and West India coasts. Estimates place the losses incurred in this way at one-third of the total loss sustained by companies during the twenty years preceding 1840.[1] It was not till 1844 that the companies of Philadelphia, for example, managed to organize a protective association through whose action these heavy losses by fraud could be averted.[2]

[1] Albert Bolles. "Industrial History of the United States," p. 820.
[2] *Ibid.*

Beginning with the fifth decade, the business again showed signs of gradual revival, and the twenty years following 1840 may be justly characterized as the "golden period" of American marine insurance. It was during these years that the American clipper ship received its highest development, and became probably the most efficient carrier in the world. Our tonnage in the foreign carrying trade increased from 762,838 registered tons in 1840 to 2,496,894 tons in 1861, the highest point ever reached in our history, and a tonnage nearly two and one-half times as large as the largest tonnage registered for any single year prior to 1840. Along with this remarkable increase of 1,734,056 tons in twenty years, American vessels continued during these two decades to carry on an average 70 per cent. of the combined imports and exports of the country, the proportion in some years running as high as 81 to 83 per cent. It was also during this epoch that American trade with the Far East and other remote parts of the globe became more prominent than ever before. Unlike the practice in modern commerce, the merchants in those days were largely the owners of the ships which carried their cargoes, and naturally they insured both in American companies. The voyages, as a rule, were long, extending in many cases over six or nine months before the vessel was heard from. The risk was thus very considerable, insurance was an indispensable necessity greatly desired, and rates ranged as high as five to six per cent. We are told that even between New York and Liverpool the rate on dry goods was as high as 2 per cent. compared with the existing rate of between one-eighth and one-tenth of 1 per cent. on our modern steamers. All these factors — increasing commerce under American ownership, long voyages of a risky nature, and high rates — combined to give to marine insurance during this period an impetus such as it had never experienced before.

But this period of unparalleled growth proved to be

but temporary, and was followed by an epoch, extending to the present, as disastrous to the business as the preceding period had been beneficial. For many years marine insurance had kept in the forefront of our commercial life, and could indeed be ranked with fire insurance in importance. It began to show unmistakable signs of decay, for reasons to be mentioned shortly, when the American flag began to vanish from the sea. This decline has been continuous and unchecked. In fact, during the last thirty-five years marine insurance by native companies has had to struggle for its life. How severe this struggle has been, and how severely the business has suffered may be inferred from the fact that since the organization of the first company in New York, in 1796, some thirty companies have been chartered in that state, and of this number only three, the Atlantic Mutual, the Home, and the Greenwich Insurance Companies, still continue to do business. To recite the history of the business in our other commercial states is merely to repeat its history in New York. In all marine insurance once flourished, but in all it has largely disappeared.

But why this decline? it will be asked. The answer is that two main causes have contributed, namely, competition of foreign companies, and changed business conditions. Owing principally to the introduction by England during the fifth and sixth decades of the last century of iron as ship-building material and coal as fuel, just at the time when the United States had not yet developed its iron and coal resources, and when the attention of the country was turned away from the sea to the development of the interior, the American wooden ship, which up to this time had been an important factor in international trade, began for the first time to feel seriously the effects of foreign competition. Immediately following the introduction of the iron steamship by England came the Civil War, with its heavy losses for marine companies, with its heavy taxation of American commerce, with the almost complete cessation of the important cotton trade and the trade with the Southern States, with the capture and destruction of Union ships by Confederate cruisers, with the transfer by sale of a large portion of American tonnage to foreign countries, and, in general, the complete demoralization of American shipping. The direct effect of these various factors, growing out of the Civil War, upon our marine insurance companies can scarcely be over emphasized. To illustrate how the prosperity of the business in the preceding period vanished shortly after the commencement of hostilities, we can do no better than consult the annual reports of the New York Insurance Department, since the experience of the companies here is but typical of that in other states. In the report of 1862 the superintendent of insurance states "that the disorders and complications resulting from the insurrection of several states during the last year have necessarily affected to a considerable extent the business of our marine companies; but an examination of their statements will show that the well-established reputation of our marine underwriters is enhanced by their successful transit over this ever memorable year. With the single exception of the Anchor no failures have occured among the companies." In the report of 1863 we again find that "not a single company is blotted out." But the companies could not continue to fight successfully against overwhelming misfortunes. In 1864 we note that two important companies failed; and in 1865 occurred the failure of the Columbian, with outstanding unpaid losses of $3,470,000. According to the report for 1865 the incomes of the marine insurance companies in New York showed that only one of the eleven companies in the state received more than it expended during the year, the total net excess of expenditures over income being $1,458,309, not counting the heavy losses of the Columbian. While the ratio of marine and inland losses paid to premiums received in the United States in

1904 amounted to but 47.43 per cent., that ratio rose to 71.64 per cent. in 1865 (not including the losses of the Columbian), and to the extraordinary ratio of 83.13 per cent. in 1866. Although the premiums in 1866 were increased $3,223,199 over the year 1865, the losses exceeded those of 1865 by $3,938,606; while the gross expenditures of the companies exceeded the gross income in the sum of $1,243,000, thus causing the superintendent of insurance to report that "the present fearful percentage of loss is too excessive and must in some manner be reduced, and not merely covered by insurance." Before business conditions could again become stable, the number of marine insurance companies in New York had been reduced by failures from fourteen (the number in 1861) to nine in 1867, while nearly all which survived were no longer the prosperous companies of the preceding decade.

But there were also indirect effects growing out of the Civil War and the competition of the iron steamship quite as important as those just mentioned. All the factors enumerated above, coming in close succession and at a most critical time, gave Great Britain the opportunity, which she was only too quick to seize, to monopolize the construction and operation of the world's shipping. As a consequence, the tonnage of the United States engaged in foreign trade has gradually declined to 888,628 tons in 1904, or only one-third of what it was in 1861. While the United States carried 75 per cent. of our total imports and exports in its own ships during the two decades from 1840 to 1861, that proportion has steadily declined until it is less than 8 per cent. to-day.

Now, hand in hand with the steady decay of our merchant marine after the war, there followed a corresponding decline in the magnitude and prestige of the marine insurance business. Great Britain was capturing the carrying trade of the world, and British merchants and shipowners were just as naturally giving their patronage to their own underwriters, as American merchants and ship-owners had insured in American companies while our trade was still in its glory.

But British underwriters were doing more than merely acquiring business which formerly had gone to American companies. They were consciously pursuing a policy, whether justly or unjustly it is not our purpose to state, which aimed to give preference to their own flag on the sea through inspection and classification at Lloyds, and through these channels the fixing of insurance rates. The essential features of this policy may be enumerated as follows:

(1) To grade vessels not so much with reference to their design and sea-going capacity, as according to their intrinsic quality as measured largely by the cost of construction and repairs. This meant discounting the sea-going worth of the American clipper ship.

(2) To favor British-built vessels and British ship-building materials in the matter of inspection and classification. One writer even goes so far as to state that "nothing 'foreign' has ever received the highest rating from Lloyds."[1] Especially in the rating of timber for ship-building purposes has this policy manifested itself most clearly. At no time has American timber been graded the same in years as timber of British origin, the best white oak of the United States being allowed but two-thirds of the time given to British oak. From the beginning, too, Lloyds has observed the rule not to grant a full class to any vessel unless the date and place of building is announced, and the construction has taken place under survey. At the same time, even before iron ship-building began in England, Lloyds never appointed surveyors to inspect the construction of foreign wooden vessels.

(3) To protect and foster metal and steam tonnage and to make the British iron steamship, the construction of which was for many years practically monopolized by Great Britain, the standard in international trade. Such

[1] William W. Bates, "American Navigation," p. 303.

a policy was bound to hasten the decline of American shipping. Underclassing the American wooden ship by Lloyds meant in actual practice a very considerable decrease in the chances for speedy and profitable employment. In 1870, Lloyds refused to classify and register foreign wooden vessels except on special survey and for a period not exceeding one year. The object was to encourage the chartering of British vessels in preference to wooden ships, and the effect of the rule was to obtain for Great Britain a large part of our carrying trade.

Evidence seems to show that marine underwriting has not declined in the United States because American companies have failed to meet the rates of foreign underwriters. Instead, the decline must be attributed to the decay of our merchant marine engaged in foreign trade, and among the numerous causes mentioned as instrumental in bringing about this result, the policy of Lloyds must be classed as one. As Mr. Bates says: "It was rare indeed that a British policy covered an American hull. The purpose was to mark the American ship with *inferiority* in the *Register*, thereby to prevent ready employment and full rates of freight. And yet, in order to get cargoes that were bound to be covered by British insurance, it was necessary to hold a class of some grade in Lloyds' *Register*."[1] Whatever the purpose of the various regulations adopted by Lloyds may have been, whether based justly on the relative merits of vessels or not, they did, at a most critical period in the history of our merchant marine, represent American ships to the world as an inferior type, did contribute toward the decline of the American marine by decreasing its chances of profitable employment, and by helping thus to transfer the carrying trade from the United States to Great Britain, did contribute to the growth of marine insurance abroad and toward its decline here.

Foreign underwriters, however, were not satisfied with

[1] William W. Bates, "American Navigation," p. 305.

getting the American business that came to them at home, but began in the early seventies to invade American territory itself. To ascertain the rapidity of this movement we may again consult the insurance reports of New York, the experience here being typical of that in other leading commercial states. In the report of 1868 the superintendent of insurance states that "no foreign marine insurance companies have ever been admitted by this department to transact business in the State of New York"; while the report for 1871 shows only one foreign company as compared with nine New York companies. By 1872, however, there were four foreign marine companies transacting business in New York; while by 1874 the number had increased to seven. This increase in the number of foreign companies has continued, so that while to-day there are only three New York companies of any importance transacting marine insurance in that state, there are fifteen foreign companies.

In entering American territory foreign companies were materially assisted by the lenient laws of some of our states requiring of foreign companies, as a prerequisite for admission, a deposit equal only to the minimum capital demanded of domestic companies. They began their onslaught by cutting rates, and the American companies, probably too few in number by this time or otherwise unable to effect an efficient combination in opposition, were compelled to follow suit. Then began a period of the most active competition between domestic and foreign companies, the result of which, in view of the other unfavorable attending circumstances already mentioned, meant the gradual forcing of American companies out of existence.

In this competition the foreign competitors had the advantage of the much better organization and the much greater financial strength acquired at home during their much longer existence, and could, therefore, afford to assume much larger risks based on their home capital.

The small American companies, on the contrary, though their assets might be considerably in excess of the assets actually held by foreign companies in this country, were, nevertheless, for the reason mentioned above, limited to a much smaller aggregate of risks. To distinguish between the efficiency of the two classes of companies in this respect one need only examine the data concerning foreign companies as given in the Insurance Year-Book. Of twenty-seven leading British marine companies mentioned here in 1902, twenty, or three-fourths, confine themselves solely to the writing of marine risks, while in the United States nearly all companies transacting a marine insurance business place their greatest reliance upon the fire insurance branch of their business. Moreover, most of the early American companies have ceased doing business and only a few (the leading ones) have had a long and continuous existence. In the United Kingdom, on the contrary, of the twenty-seven companies referred to, eight were organized prior to 1837, three considerably before the beginning of the nineteenth century, and all except four have had an existence of at least a quarter of a century, and most of them much longer. During this long and, on the whole, prosperous existence these companies have accumulated enormous assets, thus giving them an advantage over American companies, a fact which becomes clear when we reflect that the eight principal English companies doing business in the United States to-day have assets at home exceeding $50,000,000. "The financial position of nearly all the British marine companies," according to the Insurance Supplement to *The Statist*,[1] "is of such strength that even an unusually long period of adversity could be faced with equanimity. By a long process of limiting dividends they have acquired funds so large that policy-holders are most adequately secured, while at the same time the interest earnings are sufficient, or nearly sufficient, to provide for the main-

[1] Supplement to *The Statist*, May 6, 1905, pp. 27 and 28.

tenance of the present rate of dividends. Thus even very moderate trading profits are amply sufficient steadily to increase the financial security. . . . To show the great and increasing financial strength of the marine insurance companies it should be noted that the accumulated funds have increased 38 per cent. during the decade 1893–1903, the premium income has only risen 14 per cent. and the proportion of the former to the latter has risen from 177 to 217 per cent. Thus the invested funds represent over £2 for every £1 annually received from policy-holders, an exceedingly satisfactory position from all points of view. . . . In fact, the financial position of most of the offices is so strong that temporary profit fluctuations may be disregarded, and in many cases present dividends could be maintained even if the companies undertook no more business whatever."

The truth of the above summary is borne out by a consideration of the dividends paid and the interest earnings of the thirteen principal British companies (nearly all of which operate in the United States) during the years 1901 to 1904. The last three years of this period have been marked by a severe depression in the shipping industry, and consequently marine profits have been below the average. Yet the annual dividend of only two of these companies averaged as low as 6 and 7.5 per cent., respectively, during the period; in six companies it averaged between 10 and 20 per cent.; in four between 20 and 40 per cent.; and in one 44.5 per cent. In eight companies the average annual interest earnings on the accumulated funds exceeded the large dividends paid, and in the remaining five were nearly as large. Moreover, the average annual surplus of these companies, after deducting from the net premium income of the year the actual losses paid, all expenses, dividends, and appropriations to the suspense account, aggregated $1,708,000. A financial showing of this kind is especially significant since fluctuations in income are inevitable in a business like marine insurance where the rates and the amount of business, roughly speaking, rise and fall with the prosperity or depression of the shipping industry, the most sensitive to changing industrial and political conditions of any large industry in the world. English companies are to-day our main competitors, but companies of other countries, notably Germany and Canada, are entering the ranks against us. Even on the Pacific coast nineteen foreign companies, unknown to other sections of the country, are doing business, representing England, Germany, France, Italy, Switzerland, China, and Japan.

The extent to which foreign companies have acquired control of marine insurance in the United States becomes especially clear if one examines the annual financial reports of the various companies. If a compilation is made of the statistics as found in these reports, it will appear that for the year 1903 the total net marine risks assumed by all the foreign and domestic companies operating in the United States aggregated approximately $6,877,006,221, the net premiums received nearly $18,000,000, and the admitted assets $112,912,000. Of these amounts the American branches of the twenty leading foreign companies (to say nothing of the large number of foreign companies operating on the Pacific coast) wrote $3,723,000,000 of the risks, or 54 per cent. of the total, received $7,160,335 of the net premiums, but possess only $21,733,958, or less than one-fourth of the admitted assets. Most of these foreign companies also confine themselves solely to the writing of marine risks, only six of the above twenty companies transacting a fire business in addition to their marine business.

Strikingly different is the situation as revealed by the statistics collected from the reports of American fire and fire-marine companies. Thus, there are at present thirty-one domestic marine and fire-marine companies operating in the United States, writing approximately $3,153,000,000 of net risks, collecting $10,703,000 of net premiums, and possessing $91,178,000 of admitted assets. Yet of this large number of companies, it must be remembered that the two largest, the Insurance Company of North America and the Atlantic Mutual of New York, write over one-third of the total risks assumed by American companies ($1,220,000,000), collect nearly one-half of the total premiums ($5,180,682), and possess one-fourth of the total assets ($23,285,000). Considering the eleven largest domestic companies, comprising only one-third of the total number, it appears that they write 82 per cent. of the total risks, and own 83 per cent. of the total assets. The remaining companies are of so little significance from a marine insurance standpoint that they may be eliminated for all practical purposes, a fact which becomes apparent when it is remembered that fourteen of these companies combined collected only $83,592 in premiums in 1904.

Unlike the foreign companies operating in the United States, the domestic companies depend much more largely on a fire insurance business in conjunction with their marine business. Only five of the thirty-one domestic companies devote themselves exclusively to marine insurance, and of these five companies only two can be classed as important. All the other companies combine a fire insurance business with the marine business, and almost without exception place much greater emphasis upon the former than upon the latter. Thus of the twenty-six domestic fire-marine companies only two do a larger marine than a fire insurance business; in two other companies the marine and inland business is only 34 per cent. and 45 per cent. as large as the fire insurance business; in three only 22 per cent. to 27 per cent. as large; in two only 11 per cent. and 16 per cent.; and in all the remaining companies less than 7 per cent. Combining the business of all the domestic marine and fire-marine companies, it appears that they carry nearly three times as much fire risk as marine and inland risks, and receive nearly four times as much in premiums from their fire as from their marine and inland business. Indeed, there are many fire insurance companies in the United States to-day whose names clearly indicate that they were at one time fire-marine companies and whose charters originally entitled them to transact a marine insurance business, but which have ceased altogether to underwrite such risks. Moreover, upon inquiry, it was learned from a considerable number of companies that their marine business has been and is decreasing in volume owing to the fact that large foreign marine companies insure entire ship cargoes, leaving only small amounts to be picked up by the smaller companies. Other companies continue to carry each year a small amount of insurance of from several hundred to a few thousand dollars in premiums for the sole purpose of keeping alive that part of their charter which permits them to write marine insurance.

Continuing our investigation still further, it appears that the business of the foreign companies operating in the United States is by no means limited to any particular section of the country, but is general throughout. In the Eastern coast states of Massachusetts, New York, Pennsylvania, and New Jersey, where over one-half of the country's total marine insurance is transacted, the business is divided nearly half and half between domestic and foreign companies. Domestic companies wrote in 1903 54 per cent. of the total risks and earned 65 per cent. of the net premiums, the greater part of the insurance being for hulls and cargoes of American vessels engaged in the coastwise trade. The business of foreign companies, on the other hand, representing 46 per cent. of the risks and 35 per cent. of the premiums, consists in very large measure of insurance on the cargoes of foreign vessels engaged in our foreign trade.

But foreign companies have by no means confined their activity to our Eastern coast, as might at first be supposed, but have boldly extended their business into the interior of the country, until to-day they control the greater part of the marine insurance business of the Great Lake region. This becomes apparent upon an examination of the insurance statistics as published by the insurance departments of Ohio, Michigan, Illinois, Wisconsin, and Minnesota. A tabulation of these statistics shows that the nine principal American companies operating in these states (and they transact nearly all the business done by American companies), wrote $160,345,676 of marine risks in 1903; the local companies of these five states wrote only $5,394,358; while the thirteen foreign companies which have entered these states wrote $249,711,561. In other words, of the $405,450,000 of marine risks assumed by all companies in the Lake region, foreign companies wrote 61.5 per cent. and received 53 per cent. of the total premiums collected.

In the Gulf region the influence of foreign companies is still more apparent, judging from the experience of the three leading commercial states of Alabama, Louisiana, and Texas. In 1904 the marine insurance business transacted by all companies in these states aggregated $308,508,895 of risks and $1,648,000 of premiums. Of this business the local companies wrote only 4 per cent., while all American companies combined represented considerably less than one-fourth. Foreign companies, however, representing England and Germany, wrote over 75 per cent. of the risks and received nearly 83 per cent. of the total premiums.

What has been said concerning the gradual control of marine insurance by foreign companies on our Eastern coast and in the Lake and Gulf regions is true to an even greater extent on the Pacific coast. As illustrative of the situation here, California may be taken as the example, since over four-fifths of the insurance on the Pacific coast is written in this state. Thus a review of the last report issued by the insurance department of California shows that in 1903 forty-six companies were transacting a marine insurance business in that state, and that of this large number only seven were American companies, while thirty-nine represented foreign countries, nine being located in London, seven in Liverpool, seven in the leading ports of Germany, four in Hong Kong, three in Switzerland, two in Australia and New Zealand, two in Canada, two in Shanghai and one each in Paris, Tokio, and Milan. Of the $210,500,000 of marine risks written in California in 1903, only $31,500,000, or 15 per cent. of the total, was written by California companies, and only $11,500,000 or 5.5 per cent. by companies of other states. On the other hand, the companies representing foreign countries wrote $167,499,372 or 79.5 per cent. of the total risks, and collected 73 per cent. of all the premiums paid. Even in the State of Washington where the aggregate risk assumed by marine companies is as yet very small (only $18,069,683[1] in 1903), and where two Western companies,[2] the only American companies in the state, have had control of most of the business, eight foreign companies, representing England, Germany, Switzerland, and Canada wrote nearly one-third of the business in 1904. These statistics show conclusively that the vast bulk of the marine insurance business on the Pacific coast is now controlled by foreign capital, and that American companies have gradually been forced out of business through undue competition. Local insurance capital and earnings have always been invested in buildings, mortgages, bonds, etc., of the state, subject to taxation, while foreign capital for many years, as President Fowler, of the Insurance Company of San Francisco, said in substance in 1891, "entered the State of California without any deposit or security to protect the policy-holders, sending its earnings to the head office, and not contributing one dollar toward the expenses

[1] In addition to this amount marine brokers transacted $3,591,485 of business for unauthorized companies during the year 1904, thus giving $21,661,168 of net risk for the State of Washington in that year.

[2] Fireman's Fund Insurance Company (of San Francisco) and St. Paul Fire and Marine Insurance Company.

of the state and national government, thus transacting business in California upon more favorable and advantageous terms and conditions than local capital."[1] Under such circumstances, President Fowler points out, that it is not to be wondered at that by 1891 twelve California companies, with a paid-up capital of $5,600,000 and with annual fire and marine premiums of $10,000,000, had either failed or retired from business;[2] and this decrease in the number of local companies, be it noted, has continued so that while there were five California companies still in operation in 1891, that number has declined to only two in 1903. Moreover, most of the companies to which President Fowler referred had reinsured in foreign companies with the result that upon their retirement their business simply helped to increase the large volume of business already transacted in the state by foreign companies.

But while the number of foreign companies on the Pacific coast and the volume of their business has increased at the expense of domestic companies, it should be noticed that, despite the increasing importance of San Francisco and other Pacific ports, marine insurance as transacted by insurance companies, has, as a whole, shown little tendency to increase for the last twenty years for the reason, as pointed out by the Insurance Commissioner of California, "that nearly all of the steamship companies owning vessels plying in and out of San Francisco are organized and controlled outside of the state, and the tendency of these corporations is either to carry their own insurance or place it outside of the State of California, while the coasting fleet is running practically without insurance. In addition much of the Oriental business is from and with Atlantic ports and is insured on the Atlantic side."

[1] For President Fowler's remarks, see William W. Bates' "American Marine," pp. 290–291.

[2] *Ibid.*

Viewing the marine insurance business of the United States in its entirety, it is clear that domestic companies are to-day entirely unable to meet American requirements. On the Eastern coast foreign companies claim nearly one-half of the business. The same is true to an even greater extent in the Lake region; while in the Gulf States and on the Pacific coast approximately four-fifths of the business is controlled by foreign capital. Even in our coastwise trade, the one branch of our commerce from which foreigners have been excluded by statute for nearly a century, the largest buyers of insurance place it almost half and half between domestic and foreign companies. Evidence before the United States Industrial Commission tends to show that the home market soon becomes exhausted, and that it is the practice of the principal shipping companies to take all the American insurance they can obtain, and to depend upon foreign underwriters for the rest.

Recently there has also been a marked tendency toward self-insurance. The International Mercantile Marine Company, for example, embracing some of the largest steamship lines leaving the port of New York, announces in its report of December 31, 1903, that "the company has inaugurated a system of insuring its own ships to a large extent, it being deemed that this could be done advantageously and safely with such a large fleet as the company commands." (138 ships.) Under this system an insurance fund has been established into which gross premiums were paid in 1903, amounting to $2,100,523 and against which all losses and premiums paid for additional insurance are charged. The insurance department of the company insures the vessels owned by the company against all the marine risks usually covered by insurance companies, at the market rate for the various services. It also insures the risks on freight and passage money in connection with its own business, and follows the custom of underwriters in placing with regular insurance companies for its own protection a portion of certain large risks which it has assumed. The premiums paid in by the various steamship lines are placed on separate accounts with two banking houses, one in London and one in New York, and thus kept distinct from the company's operating transactions.

While this is the most notable recent example of self-insurance, it should be remembered that this method was practised on a large scale many years ago. As early as 1867, we are informed by Mr. Hopkins, in his work on marine insurance of that date, that the Peninsular and Oriental Steamship Company possessed not only an insurance system for its fifty-three large steamships, but also insured its passengers, baggage and effects, and issued policies on goods. I am informed by the managers and officers of the largest steamship lines that self-insurance is practised extensively by their companies in one form or another. While the coastwise lines and the smaller trans-oceanic lines depend almost entirely upon marine insurance companies for their insurance, it is a fact that in the case of such lines as the great German steamship companies nearly all the insurance is carried by the companies themselves. It is the general rule, however, followed by the German lines as well as the International Mercantile Marine Company, that they refrain from insuring the cargo, and permit this risk to be covered by marine insurance companies.

CHAPTER XVIII

THE POLICY CONTRACT IN MARINE INSURANCE[1]

THE more direct introduction of marine insurance in the British Isles was by the Lombards, who settled in that country in the fourteenth century. In London they were the great money lenders, and were then known as usurers. They combined with their business of banking the practice of marine insurance. The form of "policy" now used appears to have been introduced by them from Italy. The name denotes Italian origin and is supposed to mean a promise. The policy, being thus brought down from mediæval times, partakes largely of the quaint language of an early period. An English judge pronounced it "an absurd and incoherent instrument. But it has obtained a clear and definite meaning through a prolonged series of judicial decisions." Almost every word of it has been weighed in the judicial balance and assigned its proper value. Reference is made to the remarks made by Mr. Justice Blackstone in his celebrated Commentaries: "The learning relating to marine insurance has of late years been greatly improved by a series of judicial decisions which have now established the law in such a variety of cases that if well and judiciously collected they would form a very complete title in a code of commercial jurisprudence."[2]

Some changes have been introduced into the form of policy used in the United States, but the original enumera-

[1] By A. A. Raven, President of the Atlantic Mutual Insurance Company, New York. Reprinted from pp. 177–203 of the "Yale Lectures on Insurance, Fire and Miscellaneous."

[2] Martin on the "History of the Lloyds."

tion of the perils insured against has been retained and, I believe, is used by all marine insurers. Too much time would be required to give a complete analysis of the policy, but a few reflections may be necessary to throw light upon the part relating to the risks assumed by the insurer. As respects that part of the contract, the policy reads:

"Touching the adventures and perils which the said insurer is contented to bear and takes upon itself, in this voyage, they are of the seas, men of war, fires, enemies, pirates, rovers, thieves, jettisons, letters of mart and counter-mart, reprisals, takings at sea, arrests, restraints and detainments of all kings, princes, or people of what nation, condition or quality, soever, barratry of the master and mariners, and all other perils, losses, and misfortunes that have or shall come to the hurt, detriment or damage of the said goods and merchandise or any part thereof." The perils thus enumerated are used synonymously with the losses arising from them.

The originators of the policy evidently had in mind serious perils to which maritime ventures were exposed from the violence of man, both as a marauder and in the exercise of warlike operations which in early times, in the latter case, were almost perpetual. It is not to be wondered at that they were thus apprehensive. Piracy and buccaneering did not cease with the dawn of a higher civilization, nor were such practices restrained, but continued even when the mediæval spirit had given way to nobler purposes in other respects, for we find that as late as in the reign of Queen Elizabeth of England, that sovereign recognized the exploits of a noted marauder and conferred upon him the honor of knighthood.

Letters of Mart and Counter-mart. — The first is authority to make reprisals on an enemy's property. Commissions were given by governments at war to private vessels to make such reprisals on the high seas, and the practice is commonly designated privateering. Letters of counter-mart represented a similar authority to private expeditions to resist those empowered to make captures through letters of mart. Both of these came under the risk of war. By the declaration of maritime law adopted at the Congress of Paris in 1856, this system of preying upon an enemy's property upon the high seas by privateers was abolished. The United States and Spain, however, did not concur in the declaration.

Barratry of the Master and Mariners. — The word barratry appears to have been derived from the Italian "barratatore," meaning fraudulent dealing, fraud, etc., and represents all dishonest practices whereby the ship-owner or others interested are defrauded. The ship may be wrecked, fired, or abandoned with fraudulent intent. It is to be observed that to constitute barratry under an insurance the owner must not be privy to nor cognizant of the act. Formerly barratrous acts were quite common, but in recent years they have become rare in their heinous form.

The scope of the policy, it will be noticed, is exceedingly broad and the terminal expression, "and all other perils, losses, and misfortunes, that have or shall come to the hurt, detriment, or damage of the said goods, and merchandise of any part thereof" would indicate a further broadening of the contract, so as to include all possible perils; but the real intent and meaning of the policy does not include any other perils than those of the sea, and the losses for which the insurer assumes liability are those which are caused from those perils through fortuitous or overpowering circumstances and not by any inherent defect in the subject insured. This latter is legally termed "vice propre," as for example, any article that during the ordinary course of transportation necessarily becomes deteriorated by the inevitable result of defects in itself. Such losses are not recoverable in marine insurance. It will be observed that hazards named "perils of the sea," and which are contemplated as a marine venture, are those resulting from the violent action of the elements, — all casualties as distinguished from the ordinary undisturbed prosecution of the voyage. The original form of policy did not provide any limit as to the liability of the insurer. In the course of time, experience demonstrated the necessity of limiting his burden and excluding from the policy liability for losses arising from natural causes as before referred to. In the year 1479 a committee of Lloyds, London, decided upon the introduction of a clause in the policy known as the "memorandum." In this clause, the various articles which were then more particularly subjects of insurance were divided into classes, each of which was subject to special limitation. The first class was composed of articles peculiarly susceptible to damage, viz.: corn, fish, salt, fruit, flour, and seed. With respect to these articles, claim for damage or partial damage was excluded, unless the vessel stranded. The second class consisted of articles less liable to damage, such as sugar, tobacco, hemp, flax, hides, and skins. As to these goods, liability for damage was excluded unless amounting to 5 per cent. The third class included all other goods as well as the vessel and freight. These were insured excluding liability under 3 per cent. unless the vessel stranded. A similar clause was introduced in their policies by American insurers in 1840, but the articles excluded as to damage were considerably increased. At that time the importations into the United States were made up of articles, some of which were regarded as peculiarly susceptible of damage. More recently these conditions have been materially modified, and changes have been made to conform to the requirements of commerce, and extra premiums to cover the increased liability have been charged.

In the early practice of marine insurance, the applicant prepared the policy on a form furnished to him and submitted it to the insurer and, if accepted by the latter, he signed it, and thus he became what is now known as "the underwriter." The contract is signed by the underwriter only, but the assured also assumes certain obligations. It is quite manifest that good faith is an essential element in negotiating all contracts, but peculiarly so in one involving such exceptional obligations and so complex in its character as a contract of marine insurance. Everything material to the risk must of necessity be frankly imparted to the underwriter and he, in turn, should carefully consider the interest of the assured when he accepts the risk. In the matter of valuation, the assured is entitled to insure his full interest in the venture, but he is not warranted in placing an excessive value on the property. If, however, the underwriter agrees upon a specified valuation, it is binding unless there be fraud. Misrepresentation or withholding anything vital to the risk vitiates the insurance.

An insurance may be made by the party in interest or through an agent. The practice is to submit particulars of the venture on which insurance is desired to the underwriter. A formal application is then prepared, outlining the details. This preliminary paper is signed by the applicant, and if the risk is accepted by the underwriter, he also signs it, and thus the contract is binding and the policy is subsequently issued, but, as before intimated, the policy is signed by the underwriter only.

There are also implied warrantees, three in number, binding on the assured, although not incorporated in the policy. The first is that the ship or vessel is seaworthy; second, that she is to proceed without unnecessary delay from the port of departure direct to the port of destination; third, that she is not to engage in any illicit trade and conforms to all the requirements of law as respects her credentials.

As to the first of these, that is, the warranty of seaworthiness, the owner is under obligation to prepare her in all respects for the contemplated voyage, that is, on sailing, she must be tight and stanch in her hull, properly rigged (if a steamer, her machinery must be in good working condition); she must have an ample supply of fuel, she must be stored with provisions and provided with competent master and crew, with all things necessary for the intended voyage. Her cargo also must be properly stowed and not in excess in weight over what she can prudently carry. In fine, everything pertaining to the ship, her equipment, and cargo, must be on the line to insure safety, thus recognizing the obligation the ship owner has to the public, either as shipper of cargo or as passenger.

A careful consideration of these implied warrantees as required by the common law will suggest to us both the wisdom and justice of them. It is proper to observe that the original form of bills of lading used in the shipment of cargo gave no immunity to the ship-owner for loss or damage to the property shipped, except in respect of losses caused by perils beyond the control of man to prevent or overcome, but in recent years attempts (as expressed by [1] a United States judge) have been made to limit as far as possible the liability of the vessel and her owners by inserting in bills of lading stipulations against losses arising from her unseaworthiness, and stowage and negligence in navigation, and other forms of liability which have been held by the courts of England, if not of this country, to be valid as contracts and to be respected even when they exempted the ship from the consequences of her own negligence.

As decisions were made by the courts from time to time, holding the vessel for non-excepted liabilities, new clauses were inserted in the bills of lading to meet these decisions, until the common law responsibility of carriers by sea had been frittered away to such an extent that several of the leading commercial associations, both in this country and in England, had taken the subject in hand and suggested amendments to the maritime law

[1] Justice Brown of U. S. Supreme Court in case of "The Delaware," 161, U. S., 471.

in line with those embodied in the Harter Act. The act referred to bears the name of its author and was passed by the Congress of the United States in February, 1893. It renders null, void, and of no effect any clause, covenant, or agreement, whereby the ship-owner shall be relieved from liability for loss or damage arising from negligence, fault, or failure in proper loading, stowage, custody, care, or proper delivery of any and all lawful merchandise or property committed to his charge.

The same act provides, that if the owner of any vessel transporting merchandise to or from any port in the United States shall exercise due diligence to make the vessel in all respects seaworthy and properly manned, equipped, and supplied, that he shall not become or be held responsible for damage or loss resulting from faults or errors in navigation or in the management of said vessel.

It will be observed that the common law requirement as to seaworthiness, in other respects, is not abridged nor affected by the act, but much greater latitude is given in Great Britain to what is termed "special contract" in bills of lading. While this immunity from obligation certainly protects the ship-owner, it can hardly be said to be in the interests of the public.

As to the second warranty, namely, making a direct passage, since the introduction of steam the modern form of bill of lading which is alleged to be a special contract gives liberty to deviate to any extent, so that with respect to steamers, at least, that warranty is largely modified.

As to the premiums charged for the various risks, the rate in each case is dependent upon,

1. The character of the vessel; this is deemed an important factor.

2. The nature of the cargo.

3. The dangers peculiar to the ports of loading and destination.

Any underwriter is supposed to be familiar with the physical conditions of the different commercial ports of the world, as well as the nature of their products, the means employed in loading and unloading the vessel, the direction to be taken by the vessel in her voyage and the time consumed in making it. These are the elementary features of his qualifications. To say that he should also possess a discriminating mind and the power of discerning occult conditions would be but the corollary of his required attainments.

The word "average" frequently occurring in connection with marine insurance may be here explained. It is difficult to trace the origin of the meaning as now applied, but the use of it in maritime affairs, particularly in insurance, doubtless suggests a contribution in a sea venture. Particular average in marine insurance is damage to or partial loss of particular goods insured for which a contribution may be due from the underwriter. As, for example, A insured ten cases of dry goods. On arrival at destination, one or all the cases are found to be damaged by perils of the sea; that would be "particular average"; or, if any number of the cases short of the whole were totally lost, that would also be particular average, but, in the latter case, under certain conditions, it might be considered a "constructive total loss." This will be hereafter explained.

"General average" is a contribution due from all interests in the venture, and if insured, recoverable from the insurer. General average occurs under the following circumstances: If during the voyage sacrifice be made of any part of the ship or cargo, or any extraordinary expense incurred to prevent loss of the whole or to rescue the whole adventure from unusual peril, of if the ship be on fire and water is poured into the hold to extinguish the fire, the cargo damaged by the water would be general average, but the cargo damaged by fire only would be particular average, because the damage from that cause was accidental.

Likewise, if the ship should be thrown on her beam ends by shifting of her cargo, or from any other cause, and her spars are cut away to right her, or the hatches are opened and part of her cargo is jettisoned, *i.e.*, thrown overboard to relieve her, the sacrifice so made, including the attending loss or damage in making it, would be contributed for in general average.

The form of sacrifice termed "jettison" is more frequently resorted to than any other, and is perhaps the one that can more readily be made. When the hatches are opened for that purpose, if any of the cargo is damaged by water getting in to the hold, such damage is also contributed for in general average. There is particular interest attached to sacrifice by jettison, as it is one of the earliest recorded in maritime ventures and was at first probably the only one recognized in the system of general average.

The principle of sacrifice enjoins that when made it shall be the most weighty and of the least valuable of the cargo, but in an emergency requiring such prompt action the proper selection cannot always be made. If the goods sacrificed are insured, the assured can recover from his underwriter, assigning to him his right for contribution in general average. The underwriter also is liable for the general average contribution on property insured by him according to the sum insured, unless specially excluded in the policy. Cargo laden on deck, if jettisoned, is not, as a rule, contributed for in general average.

General average, as before mentioned, is a part of maritime law, and all commercial nations have endeavored to bring its practice within the highest rules of equity, adapting it to various principles as they are unfolded from time to time. Several international congresses have been held for the consideration of the subject, notably, those at York, England, in 1864; and at Antwerp in 1877. At the latter congress a new code was adopted and designated York-Antwerp Rules. This code is frequently referred to as a basis of agreement in general average questions. But the practice as respects minor details varies somewhat in different countries.

Salvage is also a charge upon the property saved. The word salvage has a dual meaning. The dictionaries give the definition as "the compensation allowed to persons by whose voluntary exertions the vessel or cargo or the lives belonging to her are saved from danger or loss in case of wreck, capture, or other marine misadventure"; and also that "which is saved from the wrecked or abandoned vessel." It will be noticed that both the compensation for saving and that which is saved is termed salvage.

As an illustration of the operations of salvage, various cases might be cited, but one quite illustrious, and which has, to some extent, been made the subject of romance, may be mentioned.

The brig "Mary Celeste" sailed from New York on November 7, 1872, destined for Genoa, Italy, with a cargo consisting of 1700 barrels of alcohol. The captain was accompanied by his wife, and his child, and the vessel had a crew of seven persons. There were two passengers on the vessel. On the 27th of November, in latitude 38 north and longtitude 17 west, the brig was sighted by the brig "Dei Gratia," and when boarded by a part of the crew of that vessel, no one was found on the "Mary Celeste," although under full head of sail she appeared to have been sailing that way for three days. The last entry in the log book was made on the 24th of November. Her fore hatch was off, and, with the exception of the boats being missing, everything denoted perfect order. The indications were that the people which were on her had left suddenly in the boats. She was towed into Gibraltar, the nearest port, and there the Admiralty Court awarded a salvage of £1700 — the equivalent of about $8300. This was a moderate compensation, being only about 18 per cent. on an aggregate value of $47,000 for vessel, freight, and cargo. It is not unusual when derelicts, *i.e.*, abandoned vessels, are picked up at sea, for a salvage award of more than twice that percentage to be made to the salvors. No tidings have ever been received of the people who sailed in this vessel, although the government used every means in its power to ascertain what had become of them.

Savings of property from shipwreck are also termed salvage.

We will now revert to the policy. The conditions in it are frequently changed by written clauses conforming to what is specially agreed upon between the assured and the underwriter. In order to reduce the cost of insurance, or for other reasons, the merchant may request the insurance made "free of particular average," which means that the underwriter will be relieved from liability for damage or partial damage to the goods. An insurance so made covers total loss and general average contribution. General average is payable by the owner even though the goods be not insured. If insured the underwriter is liable for it, because the sacrifice or expense was incurred to save the venture from a total loss. The condition, "free of particular average," is now qualified in most insurances by adding "unless the vessel be stranded, sunk, burned, or in collision." It is a form of clause introduced in the English policies. Some American insurers use the words, — "unless caused by the perils enumerated," that is, stranding, etc., thus eliminating the uncertainty as to the cause of damage.

The difference between the two forms may be explained as follows: If cargo be insured under the English clause, free of particular average unless the vessel be stranded, etc., and while the vessel is proceeding out of her port of loading, touches bottom and remains ashore, even for a brief period, without sustaining any injury, it would be deemed a case of stranding, and although the cargo might not be damaged or injured in any form by such stranding, yet the fact of that innocuous stranding would cause a change in the policy, and the cargo insured would then be subject to, instead of free of, particular average, and for any damage sustained by heavy weather on the passage, the underwriter would be liable.

Any writing in the policy takes precedence of the printed part to which it is opposed, and sometimes printed clauses in red are introduced in the policy to nullify certain printed conditions in the body of the policy. For example, the risk of capture and other warlike measures, are named as perils insured against, but a side clause, when inserted in the policy, exonerates the insurer from liability from such losses, risks of war and all losses incidental to war, and when by reason of the actual existence of war the merchant deems it necessary to have that risk covered, when agreed upon with the underwriter the exonerating clause is waived, thus restoring the policy to its normal condition and covering the war risks. When that risk is assumed by the underwriter, a large premium is added to the ordinary marine premium. The risk of war is deemed greater than all the other perils enumerated in the policy, thus showing that the winds and waves and the raging of the sea do not equal the destructive tendencies of man when his frenzy is aroused. During our Civil War one insurance company paid nearly $2,000,000 in losses for war risks, and the Confederate cruisers destroyed by burning at sea 18 ships, 7 barks, 4 schooners, 1 brig, and 1 steamer — 31 vessels in all, and about the closing of the war one of the same cruisers proceeded to the Arctic Ocean and destroyed 15 whalers. It is estimated that the amount of property destroyed on the high seas by Confederate cruisers aggregated over $20,000,000.

The printed form of policy insuring vessel, freight, cargo, or profits is essentially the same. It differs only as it is adapted to apply to the character of the respective interests insured. There is, however, a special name given to each policy, corresponding with the risk it is designed to cover. For example, the policy insuring a risk for a single voyage, as from New York to Liverpool, is called a voyage policy.

A time policy insures a vessel for a specified time, usually for one year. In Great Britain, no insurance can be legally made for a longer period than one year at a time. No such legal enactment prevails in the United States.

A valued policy is one giving a definite value to the property insured. An open policy is one where the value is left open to be determined when ascertained upon receiving the shipping documents. A floating policy covers by vessel or vessels, either sailing or steam, and insures the goods as soon as shipped. Details of each shipment, when received by the consignee, are reported to the insurer and premium is charged thereon. This latter class of policy is rendered necessary in the business of importers, who frequently order their goods several months in advance of the time of shipment, and they are not usually advised of the shipments until the goods arrive.

A wager policy is one that shows on the face of it that the assured has no interest in the property. This class of insurance, that is, one without interest, has been quite common in England, but during the reign of George III., under statute 19, insurance without interest was declared illegal, but such insurances are still made on the basis of what is termed honor transactions. In the United States it would be difficult, indeed, to recover in any of the courts under a policy where the principals had no interest in the property insured. It is to be observed that an interest in the property is an indispensable condition of all modern insurance.

As touching the duration of the various classes of risks, the policy reads: "Beginning the adventure upon said goods and merchandises from and immediately following the loading thereof on board of the said vessel." The goods thus insured are covered from the time that they are loaded on the vessel, but, in some cases, the ships are not lying at the wharf, and therefore the goods so insured are transported in lighters to the vessel. In such cases the risk of lighterage is included. As to the termination, it says: "And so shall continue and endure until the said goods and merchandises shall be safely landed at the destination," so that, if the goods are lightered from the vessel to the shore, that part of the risk would also be covered. The risk of lighterage is by no means an immaterial one. Losses on lighters are not infrequent.

The great advance made in the construction of ships as well as the improved condition in navigating them has materially minimized maritime risks, but one dreaded cause of disasters on the ocean is that of collision. The construction of large steamships, commonly known as "greyhounds," has added immensely to the attractions and speed of modern travel. We can hardly realize the progress made in naval architecture nor can the advance in the science of navigation be fully estimated. Not unlike everything else in modern life, we have obtained these at the cost of increased danger. The experienced navigator may be serene in a terrific storm, when the violence of the wind and the waves may appall the affrighted landsman, for the sailor knows his ship and has faith in her power to overcome all. When, however, he is beset by fog, there is no escape but to pass through it, and in doing so he knows not what he will encounter. His experience and skill are of no avail in this emergency. He may carefully observe all the rules and requirements of maritime law, as well as those enjoined by experience, but the mistakes and omissions of others he cannot foresee. He is plunging in the dark, and how frequently it has happened that, when thus enveloped in apparent darkness, dire disaster has been the consequence, through the faults of others, when he himself has made all the sacrifices within human power to prevent the possibility of such a fatal result. Collisions at sea are therefore regarded as one of the great perils of modern navigation. It was not until within the past half century that the question assumed a legal form as to the liability of a ship-owner for damage inflicted on other ships or vessels through collision. Rules of the road have been clearly defined and the requirements in cases of fog have been very carefully outlined, but it can readily be seen that the consequences of disaster to a valuable ship would result in immense loss to the shipowner, whose vessel had sunk another. Therefore legislation has come to his assistance, and in Great Britain the following statutory law has been enacted:

"Where any loss or damage is caused to any other vessel, or to any goods, merchandise, or other thing whatsoever on board any other vessel, by reason of the improper navigation of a ship in respect of loss or of damage to vessel, goods, merchandise, or other things, whether there be in addition loss of life or personal injury or not, an aggregate amount not exceeding £8 — for each ton of their ship's tonnage, £7 — addition for loss of life or personal injury. The tonnage of a ship shall be her gross tonnage, without deduction on account of engine-room, and the tonnage of a sailing vessel shall be her registered tonnage." (Merchants' Shipping Act, 1894.)

The law of the United States on the same subject reads as follows:

"The liability of the owner of any vessel for any embezzlement, loss, or destruction by any person of any property, goods, or merchandise shipped or put aboard of such vessel, or for any loss, damage or injury by collision, or for any act, matter or thing, loss, damage or forfeiture done, occasioned or incurred without the privy or knowledge of such owner or owners, shall in no case exceed the amount or value of the interest of such owner in such vessel, and her freight, then pending." (Revised Statute 4283, Bureau of Navigations, 1903.)

It will be noticed that in the English law the liability is defined according to the size of the vessel, that is, her tonnage, while in the United States it is her entire value, which is to be determined when the legal proceedings have resulted as to the liability of the owner for the loss. The ordinary form of policy does not cover liability of the owner for damage inflicted to other vessels by collision, through the fault of his vessel. In order to protect himself, special insurance is made, which in some cases has been coupled with the policy insuring the vessel against ordinary risks. In most cases such insurance covers only three-fourths of the owner's liability for loss, leaving him to assume one-fourth of it, so that he will exercise diligence and care in the selection of competent and suitable navigators for his vessel.

It will be noticed that the foregoing relates to the damage inflicted on the other vessel. The damage received by the insured vessel comes under the liability of the underwriter on that vessel. When it is legally determined which of the colliding vessels is at fault, the liability for loss will fall upon the one found to be at fault. By the rules of law administered at the Court of Admiralty, when both vessels are to blame, even though not in equal degrees, the whole loss sustained by their owners is apportioned equally between the two. Each party becomes liable to pay to the other one-half of the damage which he has sustained.[1]

Next to collision and probably the greatest menace to ocean navigation is fire. This peril is so subtle and difficult to overcome that it assumes an appalling character. It is not only the direct cause of heavy marine losses, but is frequently attended with serious loss of human life. In recent years means have been employed through skilful inventions to locate fire in the hold of a vessel and to smother it, but these means have not always proved effective.

An insurance made free of general and particular average reduces the liability under the policy to total loss only, but there are various conditions in which the property may not be absolutely lost and yet be regarded a total loss under the policy. There might be what is technically termed "constructive total loss." An actual total loss

[1] Carver on "Carriage by Sea."

is when the property insured is actually lost or destroyed by the perils insured against. Constructive total loss may arise when, by any of the perils named in the policy, the voyage cannot be performed or the property is so damaged as to be of little value, or the expense to forward it to destination would be equal to or exceed the value of the property, necessitating its sale at an intermediate port. In such a case the assured can claim a total loss under his policy. The same principle applies to insurances on the hulls of vessels. If an insured vessel is seriously damaged through perils insured against and the cost of repairing her exceeds her value, the assured may abandon her to the underwriter and claim as for a total loss under his policy.

Insurance on a vessel for a voyage only commences after it is made, the vessel being then in port, either loading or ready to load, and terminates twenty-four hours after her arrival at the port of destination and being moored therein in good safety. Insurance on freight (this interest represents the earnings of the vessel for carrying the cargo) begins at the port of loading and runs simultaneously with the insurance on the cargo so laden, that is, until actually discharged from the vessel.

Charter is an agreement to hire the vessel, either to load at the port where she is, or to proceed to another port to take in a cargo for the ultimate destination. Insurance on such an interest covers from the time the same is made binding, even though the vessel has to proceed to another port to load the cargo, and terminates upon the discharge of the cargo.

Reference has been made to profits as an insurable interest. This may occur under the following conditions: If a merchant should purchase certain articles of merchandise which have not arrived at destination, and there be an advance in the market so that he has a profit in the goods, he has an insurable interest in such profit, and may insure it, even though the property itself was originally insured by the seller. An insurance thus made would represent an insurable interest, even though a subsequent change in the market might have resulted in there being no profit in the goods on their arrival.

We will now refer to the methods of settlement of losses. As respects total losses, the method is simple. It requires the ordinary proof, such, for example, as the protest of the master. Immediately after the loss of the ship, it is the duty of the master to repair to the office of the United States consul, if at a foreign port, and if in a port of the United States to a notary public, and he, together with a part of his crew, sets forth the circumstances under which the vessel was lost, and protests against the perils which resulted in the loss. This document is called a protest. The circumstances, as recorded in the log book of the ship, are noted in the protest under oath or affirmation, and the consul then furnishes the master with an authenticated copy. This is termed "proof of loss." If the insurance be on the ship, the proof of interest would consist of the register of the vessel recorded in the custom house, naming the owner and the extent of his interest in the ship. If the insurance be on the freight, a manifest of the vessel, setting forth the cargo laden and the freight thereon, or, if a charter, the charter party, giving the interest. As respects insurance on cargo, to distant ports, underwriters have, as a rule, representatives at most of the maritime ports of the world whose agency is called into requisition in case of damage to cargo. The agent agrees on a compromise, or, if that cannot be reached, a sale at auction may be resorted to. The agent then gives the consignee an appraisement, detailing the nature of the settlement, with a certificate of the market value of the goods. If the sale at auction be made, the sum realized on the goods, deducted from the market value, represents the loss sustained by the merchant. The percentage of loss thus determined is applied to the sum insured. An example of such an adjustment is herewith presented:

100 bbls. flour, insured for and valued at $5.00 per barrel ...		$500.00
Flour being insured subject to 5 per cent. particular average, necessary for a claim, $25.00		
Sound value at port of destination, $7.00 per barrel ..	$700.00	
Being damaged, sold for, say, $3.50 per barrel	350.00	
Deterioration, 50 per cent.	$350.00	
Insured value, $500.00, at 50 per cent. loss		$250.00
Add extra charges:		
Auctioneer's commission, 2½ per cent.	$8.75	
Surveyor's fee	5.00	
Advertising	1.25	15.00
Loss		$265.00

It will thus be noticed that the underwriter pays the percentage of loss ascertained as above, applied to the amount on which he has received premium, and, while the percentage is ascertained on a higher basis than the sum insured, yet it must be borne in mind that freight has been paid on the flour from the port of importation, likewise duties, and other incidental expenses, in placing the goods where a higher market of necessity prevailed.

As respects particular average on the hulls of vessels: Should an insurance be made of $10,000 on a wooden ship valued at $50,000, the vessel being what is termed, "subject to 5 per cent. particular average," which means that the underwriter will be liable for loss if amounting to 5 per cent. on the entire value of the vessel, that percentage is ascertained after deducting one-third new for old; that is, the repairs being made upon the vessel, the underwriter pays only two-thirds of the cost, and the adjustment would be as follows:

$10,000 insured, valued at $50,000; required, necessary for a claim, $2,500.

Repairs	Particular Average	Net
To Hull	$3,000.00	
Rigging and sails	800.00	
Masts and spars	1,200.00	
	$5,000.00	
Cr. for old materials	500.00	
	$4,500.00	
Off, ⅓ new for old	1,500.00	
		$3,000.00
Protest and surveys		50.00
Particular average		$3,050.00

Policy for $10,000 as above will pay, $610.

Ships are now mostly built of iron or steel, and when repairs are made upon vessels so constructed no deduction of one-third new for old is made unless the vessel be very old.

In most of the American policies provision is made for the payment of loss thirty days after presentation of proofs of loss. Time is thus given to the underwriters to have an opportunity to examine the papers and make the necessary adjustment of the loss, but, as a rule, these payments are made much sooner than the time indicated. Cases are not infrequent where an assured presents his papers, and, the loss being a simple one, as stated in case of a total loss, in the course of two or three hours the adjustment is made and the loss paid that day.

CHAPTER XIX

Steam Boiler Insurance [1]

That there is a legitimate field for steam boiler insurance is shown by the statistics of steam boiler explosions that have been kept for the past forty years by the Hartford Steam Boiler Inspection and Insurance Company. From these it appears that from October 1, 1867, to December 31, 1908, there were no less than 10,051 such explosions in the United States and adjacent parts of Canada and Mexico, resulting in the deaths of 10,884 persons, and in more or less serious injury to 15,634 others. No data as to the loss of property caused by these explosions are available, but there is no doubt that it was very large indeed.

Sir William Fairbairn, in 1854, founded the first association for the systematic inspection and general supervision of steam boilers, his association being now known as the Manchester Steam Users' Association, with headquarters in Manchester, England. The Hartford Steam Boiler Inspection and Insurance Company, organized in 1866, was the first company formed in the United States for a like purpose, though it differed from the Manchester association from the start, in offering a large indemnity, in case the boilers placed under its care should explode. There are now (1909) some thirteen companies doing steam boiler insurance in the United States, though the Hartford Company is still the only stock company that confines its activities to this one line of work alone.

[1] By A. D. Risteen, of the Hartford Steam Boiler Inspection and Insurance Company, Hartford. Reprinted with additions from pages 250–271 of the "Yale Insurance Lectures, Fire and Miscellaneous."

In boiler insurance the fundamental object ought to be, to *prevent* explosions so far as possible. The life insurance companies cannot guard themselves in this manner, save in the most general way. The fire companies can do much more, and they do aim to prevent fires so far as possible by a system of inspection which is designed to detect and remove special sources of danger. The boiler insurance companies can go even further in this direction, however, and experience has shown that it is possible, by thorough inspection, to prevent explosions in a very large measure. Prevention, then, is the key-note of successful boiler insurance; and a very large proportion of the income of a boiler insurance company is expended in the making of inspections, and in other similar services to the assured, which tend to lessen the likelihood of an explosion. The Hartford Company maintains a chemical laboratory, for example, in which troublesome feed waters are analyzed, and appropriate methods discovered for the treatment of these waters, so that they may be used successfully in the boilers in which they have been found to give trouble. It also maintains a department of design, in which plans and specifications for boilers and boiler settings are prepared for the assured, no charge being made for these unless the labor involved is considerable; and in that case the charge is merely nominal, and is intended simply to cover the actual expense to which the insurance company is put.

I imagine that you will want to know something about the way in which the premiums that are received by the boiler insurance companies are expended. I cannot answer this for others, but so far as the Hartford Company is concerned, it may be said that the premium receipts are divisible into a maximum portion of about 80 per cent. of the whole, and two minimum portions of about 10 per cent. each. One of the 10 per cent. portions stands for the profit of the business, and the other represents what may be regarded, roughly, as the amount set aside to provide for the payment of losses due to explosions. The 80 per cent. portion represents what is expended in procuring the risks, and in inspecting them with such care as to keep the losses within the 10 per cent. limit. Experience has shown that it is good business policy to expend a very large portion of the total premiums in the making of inspections, and it is hardly necessary to say that the insurance company is also under moral obligation to its patrons to maintain an inspection service of the highest order of excellence.

The general method of conducting the business of boiler insurance at the present time will best be made clear, perhaps, by tracing the steps by which an insurance contract in this field is made and consummated.

The boiler owner being assumed to be persuaded of the wisdom of taking out a policy, the next questions to be determined are these: (1) The term, or duration, of the policy. (2) The amount for which it shall be written. (3) The premium that shall be paid.

First, as to the term of the policy. This happens to be a very simple matter, for nearly all boiler insurance policies are written for three years, and it is only under exceptional circumstances that this practice is modified. I may as well explain, once for all, that what I shall have to say relates to the great mass of the business of the company with which I am connected; and it is to be understood throughout that when a statement is made, it merely represents this general practice. Reasonable persons may nearly always be expected to do reasonable things; and boiler insurance companies are always willing to take account of any exceptional conditions that a given case may present, and to modify their practice accordingly; — provided the proposed modification does not interfere with the desirability of the risk. The general rule of the business is, then, to write policies for three years.

Second, as to the amount for which the policy is to be written. This problem and the third one, — namely, the amount of the premium, — are intimately connected. For it is evident that the total amount of the premium must be sufficient to repay the insurance company for the expenses incurred in obtaining the risk, and for those incurred in inspecting the boiler periodically while it is insured; and there must also be an excess, over and above these sums, to be set aside for the payment of such losses as may be incurred by explosion. In the early days, it was customary to fix the rate to be charged by means of a sort of sliding scale, the rate being higher for high pressures than for low ones, and higher for boilers that had been in service for some time than for those that were just out of the maker's shop. At the present time, however, it is not the practice to vary the rate in this manner; and the great bulk of the business is now written at a uniform rate of 1 per cent. for the three years, provided the face of the policy is great enough for this rate to yield a premium sufficient to cover the three items just noted; — that is, the expense of obtaining the risk, of inspecting it periodically, and of insuring it. It is not profitable to insure isolated boilers at this rate for a smaller sum than $5000 each; the rate of 1 per cent. for three years yielding, in this case, the sum of $50 for the three years, or an average premium of $16.67 per annum.

In large plants, where there are many boilers, a smaller sum than $5000 per boiler may be sufficient; for in such plants the inspectors can usually arrange to examine several boilers on each trip, and thus reduce the expense of inspection per boiler. A battery of ten boilers, for example, might reasonable be insured for $40,000, at a rate of 1 per cent. for three years; this yielding a total premium for the three years of $400, which is at the rate of $133⅓ per annum for the ten boilers. The business should be good at this figure, if several of the boilers can be had for inspection at the same time, and if the plant is not too far removed from the ordinary routes of travel. In general, therefore, the face of the policy is computed by allowing, for each boiler in the plant, something like $5000 if the plant is a small one, or somewhat less than this if it is a large one; and the total premium to be paid for the three years that the policy is to run is then computed by taking 1 per cent. of the face of the policy as so determined. It will be readily understood that when the risk is of an unusual character, this general rule has to be modified accordingly. For example, a single high-pressure boiler, bursting in the basement of a factory whose product or machinery is especially valuable, might easily do far more than $5000 of damage; and if numerous workmen were employed in parts of the building near to the boiler, the likelihood of a considerable loss of life and personal injury would have to be considered specially. The face of the policy would then naturally be increased, so as to take account of the probable gravity of the results of an explosion. The *rate* charged for the insurance would not ordinarily be raised in such a case, however; for the standard rate of 1 per cent. for three years, would yield a larger gross premium, and the expenses of solicitation and inspection being fixed, it is evident that that part of the premium which would be available for the payment of *losses* would be proportionately greater with the large premium than with the smaller one; and the insurance company therefore has a larger proportionate sum that can be set aside to provide for the increased possibility of a serious explosion.

I cannot emphasize too strongly the fact that there is *no* rate at which a boiler is insurable, when there is any reason to doubt its safety. In fire insurance an extra hazardous risk may be provided for by an increase in the rate of insurance; but in boiler insurance this practice is not followed. It is considered that the ordinary hazards that are necessarily attached to the use of high pressure steam are quite great enough; and a boiler that is not regarded as safe for the pressure to be carried, is not considered to be a fit subject for insurance *at any rate whatso-*

ever. Moreover, I may add that experience has shown that in boiler insurance the moral hazard is negligible. Men doubtless burn their own property occasionally, for the purpose of recovering the insurance upon it; but it is doubtful if they ever intentionally cause their own boilers to explode.

It being assumed, now, that the agent and the boiler owner have agreed upon the term of the insurance, and upon the sum for which the policy is to be written, and upon the premium that is to be paid, the next step is to make out a formal application for the insurance. Suitable blanks are, of course, provided for this purpose, and the agent fills them in by specifying the number, type, and location of the boilers, the name of the person or corporation owning them, the face of the policy desired, the term for which the policy is to run, and the premium that is to be paid. The owner then signs this application, and his signature completes his relations with the agent.

The application, thus made out, is then forwarded to the home office, or to the branch office to which the agent is accredited. The next step is analogous to the corresponding one in life insurance. In life insurance, after the application is made out, the question arises, whether or not the medical examiner will accept the risk; and this point is determined by making a careful physical examination of the applicant. So in boiler insurance, the next step after the delivery of the application is for the insurance company to send, to the mill or factory, one of its experts in steam boiler construction and management, to pronounce judgment upon the condition of the boilers, and to give his opinion as to whether they are or are not in insurable condition. This expert is technically known as an "inspector." After having made arrangements with the owner to have the boilers cool and ready for examination, the inspector proceeds to the plant where they are located, and examines them with great care. I think that I may safely say, that his examination is even more searching than that which is given in the case of life insurance. If the boilers are of a type that will admit of it, he enters them, crawling all about them internally, and noting the dimensions and the actual present condition of every essential part. He also makes a corresponding examination of the external surfaces, recording the thickness of the plates, the pitch of the rivets, and many other items that have to do with the strength of the boiler, and its ability to withstand safely the working pressure that the owner desires to carry. The numerical data that he thus obtains are entered in blank spaces that are provided upon the inner pages of the same application that the owner has signed. To give some idea of the minuteness of his examination, I may say that the blanks that he has to fill out contain forty-two main questions, many of which have several subquestions under them, so that in all he has to answer perhaps as many as seventy-five different questions. I cannot give the exact number, because it naturally varies a little, with the type of boiler. Questions relating to water tube-boilers, for example, are passed over when the boilers under consideration are of the fire-tube type.

It sometimes happens that the boilers are of such small size, or of such a type, that they cannot be actually entered by the inspector. In cases of this kind, he has to infer their internal condition by making an examination through the several small openings that should always be provided in such boilers, and which are technically known as "hand-holes." In such cases he also applies a "hydrastatic pressure" to the boilers. This consists in filling them entirely up with water, and then forcing a small additional quantity of water into them by means of a pump. By this means a considerable stress is easily brought upon the boilers, and when they are thus under pressure, the inspector notes, carefully, whether or not they show signs of distress. The distress may make itself manifest by leakage from the joints or tube ends, or by the breakage of some essential part, or by the bulging, collapse or rupture of some portion of the boiler, or in other ways that I do not need to mention specially.

Having made a thorough examination, the inspector fills out the blanks provided for this purpose upon the inner pages of the original application, and then transmits the application to the chief inspector of the office from which he comes. He also gives his judgment, based upon the construction, age, and condition of the boilers, and upon his previous experience with boilers of the same type, as to the working pressure that the boilers can safely withstand. And, finally, he submits a written report to his office, describing in detail the condition in which he found the boilers; a copy of this report being subsequently forwarded to the boiler owner. It often happens that a thorough inspection of this sort results in the discovery of some defect or structural weakness, which may even be imminently dangerous, and which had not been previously suspected. In such a case the fact is, of course, immediately reported to the boiler owner, and definite recommendations are made as to the alterations or repairs that are required in order to put the boilers into safe condition again. The owner is also informed that the negotiations can proceed no further until the suggested alterations have been made, and the inspector has subsequently satisfied himself by a second inspection, not only that they have been made, but that they have been made properly and well.

It sometimes happens, too, that the preliminary inspection discloses the fact that the boiler is in such bad shape that it would be impossible, or at least unprofitable, to try to repair it; and in this event the inspector condemns it; — or, which is the same thing, he pronounces it uninsurable. I should like to state, however, that wholesale condemnation is not favored by the boiler insurance companies. They would indeed like to insure nothing but ideally perfect boilers; yet in condemning boilers that are already in service, the inspector is expected to exercise his best judgment, in accordance with safe rules, for the benefit of all concerned; — that is, on behalf of the insured, as well as of the company that employs him. His judgment is a disinterested one, so far as he is concerned personally, for his compensation is the same whether he accepts the boiler or rejects it. His company will not insure a boiler that is believed to be unsafe, nor does the owner desire to replace a boiler that is really safe and satisfactory, merely because the inspector would like him to have a somewhat better one. The task of the inspector who condemns a boiler is therefore seen to be a delicate one, involving a number of important considerations; and he is required to give his superior officers in the insurance company full and sufficient reasons for his condemnation, so that the prospective insurer may be really satisfied, in his own mind, that the condemnation is justifiable from his own point of view, as well as from that of the insurance company. I may say that in our own practice we rarely find the boiler owner dissatisfied with the reasons for condemnation that are furnished to him. We cannot force him to replace a defective boiler with a new one; but we almost invariably find him ready to give proper attention to our criticism; and when he really ought to have a new boiler, it is seldom difficult to convince him of that fact.

Assuming, now, that the inspector has satisfied himself that the boilers upon which insurance is desired are really in good condition, the next step is the review of the opinion of the inspector by the chief inspector of his department. This corresponds to the medical director's review, in life insurance, of the opinion given by the examining physician. The chief inspector takes in hand the various measurements and other data obtained by the inspector's examination, and by the aid of them he carefully computes the safe working pressure that his company would be willing to allow the boiler to carry. Usually the estimate so obtained will be found to agree satisfactorily with that given by the inspector; but it sometimes happens that this careful calculation reveals a source of weakness at some point, whose importance the practical eye of the inspector did not perceive; and in such a case the owner of the boiler is notified of the finding, and he must see that the error of construction is remedied before the insurance company will take any further steps towards the issuance of his policy.

If the inspector and the chief inspector are both satisfied of the safety of the boiler at the time that it is offered for insurance, the policy is issued to the owner, who is thereafter protected, up to an amount equal to the face of the policy, against loss of property from the explosion, rupture, or collapse of his boiler or of any part of it, owing to the pressure of steam. He is also protected (always within the amount for which the policy is written) for any loss or damage to which he may be subjected, from the same cause, by reason of the destruction of his neighbors' property, or by reason of loss of life or of personal injuries to any persons whatever. The damages from loss of life, or from personal injuries, are determined, in this line of insurance as well as in other lines, by the earning capacity of the victims; and also, in the case of personal injuries, by the time during which the unfortunate ones are incapacitated. It is usual to specify in the policy, however, that the liability of the insurance company shall not exceed $5000 in the case of any one death.

After the issuance of the policy, the insurance company, primarily for its own protection, but also incidentally in the interest of the assured, regularly makes a certain number of inspections of each boiler, per annum (usually four); and it reserves the right of access, at any time, to the boilers that are insured, and to any and all machinery that may be concerned in the safe operation of the boilers. Of the four inspections that are made per annum, at least one is a complete internal and external inspection, similar to that which is given at the outset, except that it is not necessary to repeat the measurements, these being made once for all. The inspector making these complete inspections prepares a detailed written report in each case, stating in full the condition in which the boilers were found; and a copy of every such report is transmitted to the owner of the boilers.

In these routine inspections, it often happens that the inspector finds that defects or weaknesses have developed, in the course of the service of the boilers; for boilers, like all other structures that are put to constant use under trying conditions, wear out, and develop troubles of various kinds. In fact, the number of different ways in which steam boilers can go wrong would surprise any person not familiar with the general facts of the case. Many of the defects that are discovered in this way, and pointed out to the owners, are of such a nature that they would be overlooked by the regular attendant. For the regular attendant, even although he has been in charge of boilers for many years, and may be an unusually competent engineer or fireman, has at most seen but few boilers, and so far as his actual experience goes, he cannot be expected to be familiar with many different kinds of defects. The inspector of the insurance company, on the other hand, has seen hundreds and perhaps thousands of boilers, and has watched many of them from year to year, under the most varying conditions; and his training has fitted him to detect and forsee intelligently the consequences of defects whose importance the man in immediate charge of the boilers would probably never adequately appreciate.

Defects that develop in use, and which are detected in the course of the regular periodical inspections, are pointed out to the owner of the boilers in the written reports that are submitted to him. If they are considered trivial, that fact is indicated, and he is requested to bear them in mind, so that any tendency that they may manifest towards increase may be promptly noted. If they are considered to be bordering upon danger, his attention is similarly directed to them, and he is requested to have the necessary repairs made at his earliest convenience; the fact that they have been properly made being subsequently verified by the inspector in person. If they are still more serious, and are considered by the inspector to be immediately dangerous, the owner is notified of this fact also, and he is warned not to put the boiler into service again until it has been made safe. Of course, the insurance company has no way in which to enforce its recommendations; but if compliance with them is refused, the company reserves the right to cancel the insurance at once, and few owners care to incur this penalty. For it is universally admitted that the inspectors are, as a class, men of wide experience and good judgment; and if an explosion should occur after the owner has refused to comply with their suggestions, and has had his policy canceled in consequence, he will lose not only the insurance, but he will also be liable to be subject to heavy suits for damages, on the ground of culpable negligence in refusing to act upon the advice that the inspector gave him, before the accident.

When policies are discontinued in this manner, it is customary for the insurance company to return to the assured a certain fraction of the total premium that has been paid. The amount so returned is fixed by deducting from the premium a sum sufficient to compensate the company for the actual expense to which it has been put, and then returning a pro rata fraction of the balance. That is, of the balance remaining after deducting expenses, the assured receives an amount which stands to the whole balance in the same proportion that the unexpired part of the term of the policy bears to the whole term.

In order that you may have some idea of the scale upon which boiler inspections are now made, I may say that in the year 1908 the Hartford Company (which constantly employs more than 200 inspectors) made 124,990 complete internal and external inspections of steam boilers, and detected 151,359 defects, of which 15,878 were considered to be dangerous. In the same year it condemned no less than 572 boilers as unsafe for further use, good and sufficient reasons for such condemnation being given in every case. From the beginning of its business down to January 1, 1909, it had similarly condemned 19,700 boilers; and when it is remembered that in most of these cases the owners had no idea of the danger of their boilers until the inspector had visited them, you will see that there is some substantial ground for our claim that boiler insurance is (or should be) very largely *preventive.*

I have said that it is customary to make at least four inspections of each insured boiler per annum, and I have also said that at least one of these is a complete internal and external inspection, of which the owner is notified in advance, and for which he has his boilers cooled and emptied and otherwise prepared. The remaining inspections are technically known as "externals," since they are made while the boiler is in service, and must therefore be confined to the examination of such conditions as can be observed or inferred without entering the boilers. No notification is given in advance of these visits, and consequently no preparation is made for them. The intention is that the inspector shall have the opportunity of viewing the plant when his coming was not expected, so that he may see it under the ordinary running conditions. He examines the safety valve to assure himself that it is working freely, notes the pressure that is being carried and compares it with the limit that the policy fixes, observes the height of the water in the boiler, and tries the gauge cocks to see if they and the water glass are free. In short, he looks about him generally, to make sure that the boilers are in safe hands, and that they are being cared for properly.

To illustrate the importance of these "external" inspections, let me cite one instance that came under my notice.

One of our inspectors from the Hartford office visited a cotton-mill in Massachusetts for the purpose of making an "external" examination under ordinary running conditions, and found that nobody was present. The attendant had doubtless been there within a short time, but he had vacated the premises for some purpose.

The inspector had hardly entered the room when his experienced ear detected a noise of escaping steam, which he felt assured was not due to any ordinary leakage about a pipe joint. Passing to the rear end of one of the boilers, he opened a door in the brick setting, and speedily satisfied himself that serious trouble was imminent. In an emergency of this kind, the first thing to do is to draw the fire from under the boiler, and (when there are several boilers running together) shut the valve in the steam pipe that connects this boiler to its neighbors. By this means the pressure in the suspected boiler is caused to fall gradually, so that the boiler becomes every moment safer. The inspector was just finishing this operation when the attendant returned and, not knowing who he was, challenged him for interfering with the plant. Explanations followed, and when the boiler had cooled sufficiently to permit of examination, it was found that the brick arch over the rear end of the furnace had fallen down, allowing the incandescent products of combustion to strike directly against the upper part of the rear head; and this, being unprotected by water, had become overheated to such a degree that the back head had bulged out, and the brace rivets had drawn through their holes, permitting the steam in the boiler to escape and make the sound which had first attracted the inspector's attention. I do not know how many of you will find this technical description intelligible; but permit me to say that the accident was of a very serious kind, and that it is probable that in a few minutes more the entire back head of the boiler would have blown out, with a consequent sudden liberation of energy sufficient to destroy the boiler house, and perhaps a considerable part of the main mill adjoining it.

In conclusion, let me state the methods that are followed in the settlement of losses when, in spite of the care taken by the inspectors, a boiler explodes and entails loss of property, and probably also loss of life and injury to person, the assured is supposed to notify the insurance company of the loss as promptly as possible. The insurance company then sends its adjuster to the scene of the explosion, and he performs two duties. One of these consists in looking over the ruins in the interest of the insurance company, so as to learn the cause of the explosion, so far as possible. The information obtained in this way has been found to be very serviceable in the prevention of other explosions from similar causes; so that in this way all the patrons of the insurance company derive an indirect benefit from every explosion upon which the insurance company loses. The adjuster also looks over the damaged property in company with some representative of the owner, and together they attempt to reach a fair estimate of the amount of the loss. It usually happens that an agreement of this sort can be reached without trouble; but in case of an irreconcilable difference of opinion, some third and presumably disinterested person is agreed upon as an arbitrator. The loss or damage to which the assured has been subjected being determined, the insurance company forwards its draft in settlement at the earliest date possible, in order that the assured may not be embarrassed any more than necessary in the repairing of the damage to his plant. The compensation to be awarded by the assured to the injured and to the legal representatives of the killed are determined in a similar manner, and the award agreed upon is included, of course, in the draft that is forwarded to the insured.

The usefulness of the boiler insurance company should not cease with the payment of the loss; because the representatives of the insurance company have seen so many cases of destruction from boiler explosions that they are usually capable of giving valuable advice as to the best methods of clearing away the wreckage, and of restoring the plant to its original condition of efficiency. Services of this kind are freely rendered, and no charge is made for them; for it is understood, throughout the relations of the insurance company and the assured, that the interests of the assured are to be safeguarded and promoted in every way possible.

You will see, from what has been said, that boiler insurance differs in many respects from insurance of other kinds. It does not involve statistical studies to any considerable extent, and the problems that arise in it are mainly those relating to constructive engineering, and to the practical management of boilers, and to the detection of such defects as the boilers may develop in the course of their operation.

Every boiler owner will naturally ask himself, before he takes out insurance, whether the chance that a given boiler will explode is great enough to warrant him in paying the premium that is asked by the company that proposes to insure it. Most of the boiler owners of the country have already answered this in the affirmative, as is shown by the fact that they have accepted the insurance. It is helpful, however, to look at the matter from the following point of view. I have told you that experience shows that a rate of 1 per cent. for three years is sufficient to enable the insurance company to carry on its business soundly and with profit. This corresponds to an annual charge of one three-hundredth part of the face of the policy. Hence if the face of the policy fairly represents the damage that an explosion would be likely to cause (including death claims and claims for personal injuries), it is plain that the insurance company's rate is equivalent, from the standpoint of the theory of probabilities, to an even bet that an insured boiler, when inspected and cared for as the insurance company actually does inspect and care for it, would not blow up in three hundred years, if the natural and inevitable deterioration of the boiler through use would permit of its being kept in service for that length of time. I think I need hardly say that a rate which is based upon a probability of this sort cannot be considered to be in the least degree exorbitant. An even bet that a given boiler would not explode if run continuously from the death of Queen Elizabeth down to the present day, under the stated conditions, appears to be quite a reasonable one from the standpoint of the owner; and in addition it should be remembered that he has the advantage of expert inspections during this whole period, these alone being worth more than the entire sum that he pays, because they tend to lessen his repair bills, and to increase the efficiency of his boilers.

CHAPTER XX

EMPLOYERS' LIABILITY INSURANCE[1]

It is perhaps pertinent to a discussion of this subject to trace the cause for the establishment of this form of insurance. The necessity for such insurance has for its foundation the burdens imposed upon employers by the workings of that branch of the law relating to negligence, so-called. Negligence law, however, existed in some form as far back as there is any definite record, no one having yet been able to determine clearly just when and where it commenced. Employers' liability insurance, on the other hand, is a comparatively new institution, its introduction in the United States dating back to less than twelve years ago, although it had been in operation in Europe for a short period prior to that time.

It may be well, therefore, to trace in outline what is very aptly termed the "evolution of negligence law" down to the time when the employers' liability insurance was adopted as a means of protection against its application.

In early times there were no such fine distinctions as respects negligence as exist to-day. Suits for damages were rare and the plaintiff was usually obliged to prove the damage to have been the result of wilful act.

But while employers' liability insurance is distinctly a modern need, due to the great growth of negligence actions in the past twenty years, the law of negligence has been at least three centuries in building. Its begin-

[1] By W. F. Moore, President of the New Amsterdam Casualty Company of New York. Reprinted from pages 929–971 of "Insurance, a Text-Book."

ning is lost in the obscurity of feudalism, in which the master, as the owner, virtually, of the body of his servant, answered upon the field of arms to those outside his household who were injured by the wrong of his servants or henchmen. Under the feudal régimé there was, of course, no recognition of any right of the servant against the master for the latter's negligence. A feudal master in his own household, like a king, could do no wrong.

The statute of Westminster II (1295 A.D.), allowing the chancellor to grant a new form of action for injury to person or property, marks perhaps the first recorded recognition of a legal remedy for negligence. In the reign of the Plantagenet kings the year-books record no cases of this character. In Comyn's Report (1695–1740) is found the first collection of negligence cases.

Blackstone, whose now classic "Commentaries" afford us the earliest authoritative exposition of English law in its formative stages, refers only briefly to the master's liability to third persons for his servant's negligence and does not even mention the idea of a master being liable to his employee for his own negligence.

Blackstone says: "If a servant by his negligence does any damage to a stranger, the master shall answer for his neglect; if a smith's servant lames a horse while he is shoeing him, an action lies against the master and not against the servant, but in these cases the damage must be done while he is actually employed in the master's service, otherwise the servant shall answer for his own misbehavior. Upon this principle, by the common law, if a servant kept his master's fire negligently so that his neighbor's house was burned down thereby, an action lay against the master."

How great the contrast between the servant's position in that day and in this is emphasized by the further statement of the same author, that if a fire occurs in the master's house through the negligence of any servant, such servant shall forfeit one hundred pounds to be distributed among the sufferers, and in default of payment shall be committed to some workhouse and kept to hard labor for eighteen months.

Somewhat later we find the earliest recorded attempt by an English judge to formulate the law of negligence. After an exhaustive analysis of the Roman law, Lord Holt in the celebrated case of Coggs *v.* Barnard (2 Lord Raymond, 909), in the year 1704 defined three degrees of negligence, viz., gross, ordinary, and slight, varying in proportion to the degree of care assumed by the person with negligence in the act or occupation involved.

The growth of that spirit of individual responsibility which characterizes and animates all Anglo-Saxon jurisprudence soon led the English judges to lay down one broad rule of duty which has since been the basis of the law of negligence, and which, after many modifications, is crystallized in a modern definition as follows: "Negligence, constituting a cause of civil action, is such an omission, by a responsible person, to use that degree of care, diligence and skill which it was his legal duty to use for the protection of another person from injury as, in a natural and continuous sequence, causes unintended damage to the latter."

The early cases recognized the liability of the master only to the public or to third persons. The great mass of law from which has been evolved the employer's liability to his own servants for his negligence or for the negligence of one representing him in the pursuance of the employer's duty is the product of the present century. The master's duty, so elaborately presented in the employers' liability acts of four of our states and in many state constitutions, with its intricate modifications, is the product of the present generation.

It is a striking fact that more suits for negligence have been tried in the supreme court of New York in the last ten years than in all the previous experience in that tribunal.

Following Old World history, therefore, we may look upon the evolution of the law of the master's or employer's liability as an ever-growing tendency of the times, due, doubtless, in large measure, to the changes in the social and industrial condition of the working classes as well as their greater demands and their increased political importance.

The changes in law thus far, however, have been gradual. New rules and tests have been from time to time adopted until the conditions reached a point where the responsibilities of the employer became so burdensome that he was obliged to look about him for some means of protection in addition to the exercise of ordinary care and foresight in the actual conduct of his work. The employer with a limited amount of capital was in constant danger of disaster to his business by reason of exorbitant verdicts obtained because of some technical negligence for which he might not be actually and morally responsible, but for which the law might construe the liability against him.

This contingency seemed to be a proper subject for insurance, and without going into the details of the specific Parliamentary acts which finally caused the organization of companies for the issuing of policies of insurance providing indemnity for loss by reason of the legal liability of the employer, it has perhaps been pointed out with more or less clearness that, while there was no recognized necessity for such insurance in early times, the evolution of the law of negligence brought about a demand which was finally met by employers' liability insurance.

But let us not lose sight of the fact that while this demand was met when the want was most felt, the introduction of insurance as a protection has by no means stopped the march of progress in negligence law.

The premium rates originally charged are found now in many cases to be totally inadequate, not in every case because of faulty judgment in the beginning, but because the cost to the insurance company has been vastly increased by a continued disposition on the part of courts and legislatures to draw the lines closer and place greater burdens on the employer, which burdens, by reason of insurance, fall upon the companies.

As an indication of the trend of public opinion in the direction of "reform" in the relationship between employer and employed, the following quotation is made from a volume entitled "Workingmen's Insurance" recently published by Mr. William Franklin Willoughby, of the United States Department of Labor:

"Step by step we have seen almost all of the European nations abandon the position that employees have no claim for damages except when they can prove negligence on the part of their employers, in favor of the one where their compensation by the employers should be compulsory in all cases except where they are wilfully and seriously at fault. The indemnification of injured workingmen has thus been made one of the normal items in the cost of operation, to be taken account of as any other charge. At the same time, the efforts to enforce this system through the law courts has been abandoned, and the position taken that adequate and prompt compensation can only be secured where the amount of the compensation is determined in advance by a fixed scale of indemnities. It is only as thus organized, moreover, that employers are able to take account of the risks that they run and provide against them by means of insurance.

"While this movement has been going on in Europe, the United States has stood practically still. Scarcely a beginning has been made toward modifying the unjust provisions of the old common law. It is quite beyond our field to attempt any description of the state of the law regarding employers' liability in the United States at the present time. The subject is one of great complexity, and here we are concerned with the principle rather than the details of legislation. It is sufficient to say that the United States is in the position where the injustice of the common law in this respect to this question is more or less recognized, and attempts are being made to bring about a reform through legislation and judicial decisions. The states are thus still in that primitive stage where a solution is sought in the timid modification of the doctrine of common employment, of what constitutes negligence, and other subtilities of the law. They are thus attempting a method of reform long since abandoned by European nations as one which not only does not do justice to the workingman, but is thoroughly inadequate to solve the difficulties of the question. It would be difficult to think of another field of social or legal reform in which the United States is so far behind other nations.

"The most depressing feature of the situation lies in the fact that the very principles involved in this gradual evolution — from the limited liability of employers to that of the compulsory indemnification by them of practically all injured employees — are as yet not even comprehended in the United States. Evidently it is useless to expect any decided legislation until the people generally are made to see the justness and correctness of the position for which we are contending and which has so recently been assumed by Great Britain. The first step, therefore, consists in the education of public opinion. This once accomplished, legislation will inevitably follow."

Mr. Willoughby writes from the standpoint of the philanthropist, having in mind only the protection of the workingman and his family against want and suffering occasioned by loss of work or support; but there is a close relationship between the movement for bettering the condition of the workmen at the expense of the employer and the insurance of the employer against unmeritorious claims, especially when the movement comprehends a practical removal of all the defenses of the employer and by so much increases the hazard assumed by the insurance company.

It is not likely that any such radical change will be

made at once in this country, but we cannot fail to observe the rapid strides made by European countries in the direction of an improvement in the condition of the working classes and to note that wherever such movements are taking place the difficulties of employers' liability insurance increase and its operations become more complicated.

Employers' liability insurance in the United States is, however, now an accomplished fact and a recognized necessity among employers of labor, and, whatever may be its final development, we are able at least to take a retrospective view and profit by past experience so far as it may be of value as a guide for the future.

The year 1887 was the first year in which liability insurance was written in this country to any extent. While some few policies had been issued prior to that time, it was not until 1887 that the business was taken up and prosecuted in any appreciable degree. In that year the premiums received on employers' liability insurance policies in this country amounted to about $150,000. From that time on the increase in business has been marked.

Every year some new requirement for such insurance appears, and it is fair to assume that we have not by any means reached the limit of the scope of this class of insurance.

While employers' liability insurance is permitted to be transacted in every state in the Union, there is not in every case an exact definition of this feature of insurance. Where a definition is given at all, it runs as a rule closely to the definition used in the laws of the State of New York, which is as follows:

"Insuring any one against loss or damage resulting from accident to or injury suffered by an employee or other person and for which the insured is liable."

It will be seen from this definition that it was the intention to provide for insurance, not only of employers as against claims made by employees, but of "any one" as against claims made by employees or any other persons, so that under the feature of employers' liability insurance nearly all of the states provide for insurance against liability for personal injuries in its broadest sense. In some of the states there has been an effort to divide liability insurance into its component parts and to treat each part as a separate branch of insurance, but up to this time the whole field covered by liability insurance is accepted in all of the states as under one head.

The hazards other than employers' liability commonly underwritten by companies engaged in this line are, the liability of a manufacturer or other employer of labor for injuries sustained by persons other than employees, caused by the operations of the business upon which the insurance is granted — this is called public liability insurance; the liability of the owner of horses and vehicles for injuries sustained by pedestrians or others in the public ways — this is called teams insurance; the liability of the owner or tenant of a building where elevators are used for passenger or freight service, for injuries sustained by any person or persons — this is called elevator insurance; the liability of the owner or lessee of any building (except such as may be used by the assured for manufacturing purposes) for injuries sustained by any person or persons by reason of defects in the building or in the ways adjacent thereto or by reason of defective elevators or negligent operation thereof — this partakes of the nature of employers' liability, public liability, and elevator insurance combined, and is called general liability insurance.

The hazards heretofore named are not the only risks taken by the companies under this head. There are other directions in which liability insurance is tending. Proprietors of theaters and other places of amusement may now obtain policies of insurance protecting them against claims for injuries to their patrons or employees. Owners or tenants of private dwellings may protect themselves against the dangers of icy sidewalks, open coal chutes, loose shutters, etc. Owners of ships and other vessels, tugs, barges, and scows used for freighting purposes, may also take advantage of liability insurance. And so also in connection with the insurance of steam boilers against explosions, a feature of liability insurance is introduced. Steam boiler insurance has been carried on for many years in this country and for a longer period in Europe, but it is only of late years that the policies have been so extended as to cover the liability of the owner or operator of the boiler for damages by reason of personal injuries in consequence of boiler explosions.

As the theory becomes better understood the possibilities broaden. New lines are suggested by actual claims that arise and which are not contemplated by any policies now in vogue and it may be predicted with safety that the principle of liability insurance is here to stay in one shape or another, but, as this paper endeavors to show, surrounded by such difficulties and complications always that it will require more care in its supervision and management than any other branch of insurance, because of the constantly changing factors in its underwriting and its claim adjustments.

The first underwriters of employers' liability insurance had practically no basis upon which to work. A scale of rates was adopted, based largely upon the experience of accident insurance companies in this country. This scale was amended from time to time as it became clear that a risk hazardous for personal accident insurance might be non-hazardous for liability insurance and *vice versa.* For a number of years, however, this original scale of rates was used by most of the companies as their published rate schedule. As a matter of fact, however, until three years ago there was no actual scale of rates, each company accepting business according to its judgment, which in many cases proved to be bad. Within the last three years, however, all of the stock companies in the country, with perhaps one exception, became associated for the purpose of determining the actual cost of insuring the many different hazards to which liability insurance is applicable. It was deemed to be wise to collate the past experience of all companies — not with regard to the amount of premiums received, but with regard to the actual expenditure for losses based on the wages of employees or otherwise as the case might be — to determine the actual cost in loss payments as against actual exposure. This work has been and is still going on, and certain important information has been compiled from time to time, resulting in many changes in rates. After computing the actual cost of any given class of business, it is a comparatively easy matter to add a sufficient "loading" to cover expenses and arrive at a premium rate adequate for the hazard, assuming that the conditions will remain the same in the future as in the past. Difficulties, however, have presented themselves in arriving at a system of rates for the reason that, as stated elsewhere in this paper, the hazards differ materially in the several states by reason of the difference in laws and the difference in social conditions. The attempt, however, is a step in the right direction, and while the results thus far have not been entirely satisfactory, there is no doubt that rate-making for employers' liability insurance is being gradually reduced to a science. In almost any other line of insurance the scale of rates once established in this way would be a true guide for the future. In liability insurance the same rule does not apply, because a scale established and found to be correct for to-day might be absolutely incorrect for the future. The only safe rule appears to be the making of a scale by past experience, and adding to it the necessary factor of safety for legislative and other changes each year.

Environment is a serious factor in liability underwriting. Not, however, from the same cause that governs other lines of insurance. There are about as many people injured or killed in a given occupation in one part of the country as in another, but the social conditions obtaining in the different sections influence matters of adjustment and of suits to a greater degree perhaps than does the actual difference in statutory provisions.

In the comparatively new states the population is not as homogeneous as in the older and more conservative communities, where whole families for generations have been employed in one industry or mill or factory. Under the latter conditions few claims are made, because the employer is likely to be in close touch with his employees and his kindly treatment for years will always have an influence on his workmen and tend to prevent excessive claims for slight injuries.

On the other hand, in localities where the working classes are made up largely of immigrants from foreign countries, or in any event is of a cosmopolitan character, no such good feeling exists or is likely to exist, and when claims are made for indemnity on account of injuries sustained, the sums demanded assume proportions, which if paid, would be a menace to the successful continuance of a business or trade where mechanical labor is a chief factor; and in such communities when claims are resisted and carried into the courts unreasonable verdicts are frequently the result, presumably because the juries are to a great extent in sympathy with the working people as against corporations and capitalists.

Beyond these factors in environment is the variation of statistics and the application of the law in the several states of the country. In some states the fellow-servant rule is strictly adhered to, while in others this rule is made elastic and decisions are usually favorable to the injured person; and in still others the rule is abrogated altogether. Promise to repair, proximate cause, contributory negligence, presumption of negligence and many other legal subtilities, are also widely divergent in application, to such an extent that in the matter of underwriting and rate-making all these conditions must be considered as having a direct relationship to the selection of risk.

The premium charge on employers' liability insurance is based on the aggregate wages of all employees. The question, therefore, of the average rate of wages has a direct bearing on the hazard. The average annual wages of workmen in the United States is shown by the last census to be something less than $500. The use of the total pay-roll of any establishment as the basis of the premium charge is on the theory that the wage expenditure will be a correct indication of the number of employees actually engaged. Manifestly, then, the *actual* basis of the premium is the number of employees exposed to the given hazard for one year, and the accepted method of computation at a certain rate for each one hundred dollars of wages expended is on the assumption that the general average is always true.

The total amount of pay-roll during the term of the policy, whether it be for a year or a longer or shorter period, indicates the amount of the premium. A pay-roll of $100,000 is taken to be equivalent to the exposure of 200 employees for one year, or 400 employees for six months and so on.

The general average of wages, however, does not always obtain, and it is a notable fact that the nature of employment and the character of workmen in some states decrease the premium per capita, by reason of the low rate of wages, while the hazard is nowise proportionately improved, but, on the contrary, is likely to be worse, because of the lower grade of intelligence of the laborers.

It is a fair assumption that no two states are exactly alike from the standpoint of underwriting, and this sets up another difficulty in the way of establishing any rule of procedure which would be mathematically correct for the whole country. The iniquitous system of taxation in operation in some of the states has an important bearing on the cost of conducting business in such states, and while it is not always wise for insurance corporations to discriminate *against* certain sections they cannot be expected to discriminate *in favor* of places where additional burdens are placed upon them. Each state at least must be rated and underwritten on the basis of the existing or changing conditions to be found in the given locality, and, as the risks are necessarily very much scattered, the statistical information compiled by any one company is not of great value, except in the most populous manufacturing states. The ultimate value, therefore, of a perfect compilation of the statistics of all the companies engaged in the business cannot be overestimated.

In the matter of expenses, it may be interesting to make some comparisons. It may be fairly assumed that the commissions paid to agents and brokers on liability business are far in excess of like expense on other lines, where the premiums are large.

The commission rate may very properly be said to be in the hands of the individual company to control, but it will be well understood that a precedent in this respect having been once established, it is practically impossible to change without uniformity of action on the part of all companies; and as the agencies of many of the companies are, and have been for many years established on a salary basis, equivalent to a high commission rate, there seems to be no likelihood of reform in this direction in the near future.

Personal accident insurance has always been subject to a high commission rate, and, as most of the companies now engaged in liability business established their field agenices originally for personal accident insurance, there seems to be no doubt that the high accident commissions influenced somewhat the rate paid for commissions on liability insurance. The rates of commission on the latter have not, however, reached the average of accident business, and it is generally agreed that the present commission on liability insurance is excessive, considering the size of the premiums involved, and considering also that high commissions on large premiums open the way to the rebate evil which has become a menace to other lines of insurance. The employment also of salaried men at all principal points for purposes of survey and examination of risks on behalf of the companies is no inconsiderable item of additional expense.

The foregoing refers only to the expense of securing the business. The expense of caring for the business after it is once on the books of the company is infinitely greater than that of any other line of insurance known. The clerical staff must be more numerous and more than ordinarily skilled in the business, the various details of the work requiring constant care and oversight. The loss adjusting department must be supervised by men of the highest order of ability and the detail work in this department requires more skill and a higher grade of men than would be requisite in many other lines of insurance. It may be said that every adjuster employed by the company must have a considerable knowledge of the law and at the same time possess the qualifications of a level-headed business man.

It may be stated with some degree of accuracy that for every thousand policies issued there will be in the neighborhood of one thousand notices of accident annually. Under some policies there will, of course, be more than under others, but considering that many of the policies cover work involving the employment of large numbers of men it is not surprising that few, except the very small risks, escape without any accidents.

Each claim that arises must be carefully investigated and is likely to require many visits and continued expense. The claim is not against the company, but it is a demand made on the policy-holder to whom the company stands in the relationship of counsel. It is not, therefore, a matter of ascertainng the amount of the claim and effecting a settlement for the company, but an examination of all the facts with view of setting up a proper defense for the assured in the event of an action at law, or of effecting a compromise on behalf of the assured should it appear that the injuries were caused by his negligence. This necessarily often introduces the services of lawyers into the cases, and, as lawyers are probably the best paid professional men in this country, it may be truthfully asserted that to the lawyer is attributable a large part of the expense ratio of liability insurance companies.

Expert mechanical inspections also add to the expense of the business. Each company must maintain a bureau for the periodical inspection of risks. A staff of inspectors, skilled mechanics, must be employed, and the assured must be afforded the protection of this service in addition to the indemnity provided by the policy.

It is estimated that at the present time about $500,000 is paid out for mechanical inspections by liability insurance companies annually, and for the most part this amount is expended for steam boiler and elevator inspections. The inspection feature in these two branches of insurance is of paramount importance. While it cannot be shown definitely in how many instances inspections have prevented accidents, it is nevertheless true that in many cases serious defects have been discovered and remedied. Certain it is that inspections at stated intervals by practical men who are trained mechanical engineers have a desirable effect upon employer and employee, and tend to good order and method where otherwise there would exist every opportunity for accident.

While the larger part of the expense for inspections is chargeable to the two branches mentioned, general inspections are being extended to all important risks, and the expense of this department of the business is likely to be increased by the addition of new and untried hazards. The original theory of liability insurance was the protection of the assured against heavy financial loss. The practical administration of it, however, contemplates the payment of many small losses which come within the limits stipulated in the policy. If it were possible with safety to the insurer to eliminate the small losses and pay only those beyond a certain stated amount, the expense ratio might be very much reduced, but this does not appear to be practicable. Small losses left to the assured to adjust would grow into large ones, and the only safety, therefore, of the company insuring would be the handling of every claim, even if the assured paid the damages within certain limitations. By this method the companies' losses would be reduced, but the actual amount paid out for expenses would remain the same, while on the other hand, the premiums being proportionately reduced by reason of the lessened hazard carried by the companies, the expense *ratio* would be materially increased.

The reserve on life insurance policies, being computed on the net premium, is easily arrived at, because there is a well defined rule for determining the net cost. In casualty insurance, however, the net cost has not yet been reduced to a science, and until such time as the experience of all companies is collected, and the proper rule established it will be impossible to compute the reserve on casualty policies by any such method as is used by life insurance companies. It is true also, as shown elsewhere in this paper, that there are difficulties in the way of arriving at any true rule for establishing the net cost for liability insurance, on account of the changes that are constantly occurring by reason of new legal decisions and the enactment of new statutes. It is therefore probable that the only available means of computing the reserve on net cost is to arrive at such net cost by taking from the premium the approximate amount of expenses.

It may be added here that this statement is made without any desire to advocate a reduction of proper reserves; but a reinsurance reserve has no relationship whatever to earned premiums, and if the earned premium of six months less *all* expenses of securing business is deemed sufficient to carry the first six months, then certainly the unearned premium of the remaining six months, less *one-half* of such expense should be an adequate provision for the second six months.

If such a reserve be not sufficient, then the difficulty lies with the rate, and it is there the adjustment should be made. This question of rate-making is now being carefully studied by all the companies having any experience to guide them, and many changes have already been made, having always in view the establishment of rates adequate to the various hazards involved. It is to be hoped that the restrictions placed upon fire insurance companies in some states, preventing coöperation in establishing fair and equitable rates, will not be applied to the casualty companies.

The adjusting of losses under liability policies is admitted to be far more difficult than adjustments under any other form of insurance. As an example of this, almost any case may be selected. The assured notifies the company that one of his employees has met with an injury. It is usual for the company to furnish the employer with printed forms for this purpose. The adjusting department of the company on examination of the report may and often does find a lack of detailed information concerning occupation, rate of wages, place of accident, particulars of accident, and description of injury. In very few cases is the information given sufficient to determine whether or not the employer is liable by reason of negligence. It is therefore necessary for the company to send an investigator to make a personal inquiry into the facts. The investigator gathers all information obtainable from the employer and also from witnesses, and makes his report to the company. From this report the company may be able to base an opinion as to the liability of its assured for the accident. Frequently, however, a single accident will require numerous visits to the scene of its occurrence before all the facts can be brought out.

When the company finds there is no liability in the case

against the assured, he is so notified and the injured person is not approached at all. The papers in the case are carefully filed, and all the information is at hand in the event of a future claim on account of the given accident.

If, on the other hand, it appears to be a case of negligence, and a claim is likely to be made, negotiations are at once begun for an adjustment as between the employer and the employee, the company's representative acting as the representative of the employer.

Then the actual work of adjusting begins. Before an actual settlement is accomplished and a release given, one or more representatives of the company have made visit after visit to the employer and the injured person; witnesses have been examined and their sworn statements taken; it has been necessary, perhaps, to employ a physician to make a physical examination of the injured person, and in the meantime the case may have been placed in the hands of a lawyer by the claimant. A case which looked trivial in the beginning may be the occasion of more negotiation and expense in adjustment than a really meritorious claim. Ignorant persons, guided by the pernicious advice of unscrupulous lawyers, will frequently press claims in which there is no merit whatever.

Within the past few years, and particularly since the advent of employers' liability insurance, our court calendars have been filled with accident cases hunted up by a species of lawyer known as the ambulance runner. These men are a great menace to the public and to the employers' liability companies. They keep themselves well posted by frequent examinations of police reports and otherwise as to every accident that happens, and frequently a person who has suffered a trifling injury will be visited by several such lawyers in the endeavor to magnify the injury into important proportions and to encourage the making of an exorbitant claim. Reputable lawyers do not lend themselves to such tactics. It makes little difference to the ambulance runner whether his client has a case or not, so long as he is given an opportunity to bring suit against some one, depending upon the probability that the person sued would in any event be willing to pay him a small sum rather than pay some other lawyer a large fee to defend. He is looking out for himself rather than for his client in nearly every case, and naturally sees in the liability insurance company an opportunity for piracy of this nature which did not exist before such insurance became an established fact in this country. It does not take long, however, in any locality, to ascertain which of the lawyers have this versatile ambulance-chasing propensity and they receive scant courtesy from the companies when discovered.

Under these circumstances it is obvious that the estimating of ultimate cost of outstanding or resisted claims is altogether a matter of opinion, and naturally opinions differ on this subject. Some companies, taking past experience as a basis, assume that all notices or reports of injury received will cost on the average a certain sum in settlement, that all suits brought will average in cost of settlement a certain stated amount, and cases appealed from lower courts will cost a proportionately higher amount. Other companies estimate each case according to the circumstances surrounding it. It is difficult to say which comes nearer to being right.

It appears to be true that in the early years of the business in this country most of the risks written were those that required little or no solicitation by the companies, because the employers recognized the hazardous nature of their work and gladly availed themselves of the opportunity to insure.

Employers, however, did not recognize altogether the necessity of reporting every injury. Those that were considered trifling cases at the time of accident were not reported, but such as were reported proved expensive to the underwriters, because of the hazardous nature of the business. As time went by it was found frequently that a case which appeared to be a trivial accident at the outset grew in proportions, and claims were often made in cases where it was supposed by the employer that the injured employee had no intention of seeking indemnity. As the volume of business increased, too, and employers became more familiar with the insurance that was offered by the companies, its adoption became more general and persons who theretofore had not taken advantage of it applied for policies. In this way through the large staffs of solicitors employed by the various companies and the consequent general education of employers to a knowledge of the value of insurance, the less hazardous risks became insured and the assured became more careful in reporting accidents, so that at this time it is probable that the average number of notices of injury per annum is greater for the same number of workmen than at the inception of this branch of insurance. Many establishments now report injuries of the most trivial nature, which, if estimated on the basis of the experience of earlier years, would indicate a premium rate far in advance of that actually needed, so that at the present time there does not appear to be any sound basis for estimating the actual average cost of each notice. Such a figure may be reached when the business has run over a term of years sufficient to base such an average on an actual earned premium of large amount; but again in this connection appears another difficulty. An employer takes out a policy in a state where the statute of limitations is three years. The company must protect him for any loss occurring during the life of his policy, for which claim is made upon him during the term of the statute, provided, of course, he has given the company notice of such an accident at the time of its occurrence. The statute of limitations varies in different states, from one year in some states to seven years in others, so that it may be said that the premium of any given year cannot be fully earned until the time of the statute of limitations has entirely elapsed. To arrive, therefore, at an actual basis for any given period of years, the time of the statute of limitations must have expired on all risks of the last year of such period in every state where the business is conducted. There is little doubt that the best method of estimating the value of outstanding losses is to compute the average cost per notice, the average cost per suit and the average cost for each appeal, provided this average cost can be correctly determined. Considering, however, the constant changes in laws, considering the inclination of legislators in the direction of providing workmen with indemnity for accidental injuries, and considering the slow but sure progression of public sentiment in favor of laws such as have been enacted in many of the countries of Europe for the protection of the working classes, it would seem almost impossible ever to arrive at a true rule, because every year would be likely to change the conditions. Under these circumstances, it appears as if the estimating of each case on its merits is best, for the reason that when a case is estimated the prevailing conditions are known and are taken into consideration and the company is more likely to adopt a factor of safety for each year's business than if it depended on a complete change of its average estimate each year.

Opinions differ widely as to the wisdom of litigation by companies engaged in liability insurance. It has been said on the one hand that the company's advice to the assured should be exactly that of the assured's counsel under similar circumstances. On the other hand, it will be admitted that the counsel of the assured in advising his client is not by any means in the same position as the insurance company with the function of loss payer as well as adviser. It is reasonable to suppose, of course, that the lawyer will give the best advice that his judgment dictates. It is clear also that the insurance company should give the best advice, not only by its judgment, but by its actual experience in litigation, because it has to pay the judgment for damages, if one is obtained by the injured party. The business in this country has not yet reached that stage where it can be said with any degree of certainty which is the better policy. It is perhaps fair to assume, however, that the more acceptable method so far as the assured is concerned is a prompt settlement and a full release; and, under ordinary circumstances, settlements can be made to better advantage, if negotiated at once, than if allowed to drift into the hands of unscrupulous attorneys whose exorbitant fees immediately swell the amount demanded. There is good reason to believe that some sort of a payment for every claim that arises would result in establishing dangerous precedents in large establishments, but, it is contended, if every claim is settled and put aside at once there is not likely to be danger of claims accumulating later on. There seems to be no doubt, therefore, that the most acceptable plan to the assured is immediate adjustment when a claim arises, and there seems to be no doubt also that with care and good judgment in settlements this method would be the best one for the companies to follow. As has already been stated, however, there is a wide divergence of opinion on this subject, some insurers believing that where a claim is not meritorious, it should be fought to the bitter end, while others contend that even in such cases, if a reasonable settlement can be effected for a sum not far in excess of the cost of litigation, the result as a whole will be less expensive for the company than any system of adjudication through the courts. Time alone will prove which of the methods outlined above is correct; but thus far those insurers who have undertaken by prompt action to clear away liability have shown the best results, while those who have built up a large outstanding liability by reason of suits against policy-holders, are as far away as ever from the final determination. This proposition does not apply equally to all classes of liability business. In pure employers' liability insurance, settlements are more easily made than in some other branches where the factor of public liability enters; but as an offset to this, while public liability cases frequently require liberal adjustments, so do they often result in large verdicts if allowed to go to trial.

It may be well to point out one danger which is likely to be overlooked by beginners who have had no considerable experience in the business.

The result of the first year's operations at the prevailing rates of to-day is likely to indicate so handsome a profit that the inexperienced manager may be misled into the belief that the rates are excessive. There is probably no other line of insurance so deceptive in this respect. The final results of the first year's business will not be known until the time fixed in the statute of limitations has expired, and if business is transacted in states where the statute extends six or seven years it will be seen over how long a period the business must run before the actual loss may be determined. Then, too, in case of accident to a minor, suit may be brought after he reaches his majority, and the company must protect the employer if he held a policy at the time of the accident and fulfilled all its conditions.

It is estimated that the loss shown as having been paid on a given year's business at the end of the second year will be at least doubled before a final determination of the business of that year.

Notwithstanding all the difficulties of conducting liability insurance, it is believed that it has become an established factor in the operation of business in this country and that its scope will broaden as time goes by. Legislation will undoubtdly affect it from time to time, but the principle will still remain, whatever the local conditions, and these conditions will tend rather to regulate underwriting than to discredit the business.

CHAPTER XXI

GOVERNMENT INSURANCE [1]

A COMPLETE survey of this field would involve treating it from a number of different points of view. Thus we might distinguish between the different kinds of government insurance:

(*a*) According to the risks for which indemnity is given, and distinguish fire insurance, life insurance, hail insurance, accident insurance, etc. This would be a mere duplication of the classification adopted for the earlier part of this course;

(*b*) According to the objects for which indemnity is given. We should thus distinguish house insurance, furniture insurance, live-stock insurance, etc.;

(*c*) According to the exclusiveness of the government business, in which case we should treat of insurance under government monopoly and of competitive insurance;

(*d*) According to the compulsion brought to bear upon the persons insured, in which case we should distinguish between voluntary and compulsory insurance;

(*e*) According to the incidence of the burden of insurance. In this case we should distinguish between insurance which is borne entirely by the persons insured, insurance which is borne by other classes of the population, and insurance which is supported by the state from the proceeds of general taxation. Or we might also have any combination of these cases, such as insurance borne partly

[1] By Henry W. Farnam, Professor of Political Economy in Yale University. Reprinted with additions from pages 283–303 of the "Yale Insurance Lectures, Fire and Miscellaneous."

by the insured, partly by the members of another class, and partly by the state.

Such a complete treatment would not only carry us far beyond the limits of time devoted to this subject, but it would also fail to emphasize what seems to be the typical feature of government insurance. And, while a complete historical treatment would involve considering all of these different kinds of government insurance, it seems wiser to concentrate the attention on certain elements and to refer only by way of introduction to the others.

Insurance has been stated by one of the lecturers to be in the nature of a tax. It is a payment made, not under legal compulsion, but under pressure, in order to guard against the consequences of a contingent evil. The converse is also within limits true. Many taxes are a kind of insurance. We pay money to support the police, the courts, the fire department, the army and navy, not because we expect to obtain a positive good from the expenditure of the money, but because we wish to be protected against a possible evil, such as the invasion of our property rights, the burning down of our homes, the attack of a foreign enemy.

The difference between the two lies not so much in the purpose as in the method of determining the amount of individual contributions. In insurance, the premium is based upon a mathematical calculation of the risk. The wooden house pays more than the brick house. In the case of taxes the payment is based upon some entirely different consideration, usually some criterion which is supposed to indicate the ability of the taxpayer, rather than his liability to call upon the government for some service. The strong man pays as much for police protection as the weak man, if his property is assessed at the same value. The rich, strong man may pay very many times more than the poor, weak man, even though he may be much less liable to call for the help, either of the police or of the fire department.

Inasmuch as many, though by no means all, of the functions of the government have so much analogy with the operations of insurance, it would seem to be a very natural thing that the government should go into the business, provided any advantage could be obtained. Among many that might be named there are two advantages in particular that deserve especial consideration:

(1) It may be that the government can command more skilful actuaries or a larger capital than private companies, so that it is in a position to carry on the business as a business with greater efficiency. This hypothesis would hardly apply to our country, and yet it is conceivably true in countries in which the civil service is of a higher grade and the average business man of a lower grade than in the United States.

(2) Another advantage to be gained from government insurance may lie in the fact that the government can make use of its taxing and of its governing power to carry it through. In other words, it need not conduct its business on actuarial principles exclusively. It can give certain classes benefits out of proportion to the premiums which they pay. In other words, it can combine the quasi tax of the insurance company with the real tax imposed by a sovereignty. If it decides to do this, it is not guided by merely commercial considerations. It hopes to influence the distribution of wealth. Moreover, it has one advantage which the insurance company does not enjoy — it can make its insurance compulsory. Thus not only may a real tax be used to pay for the support of insurance, but the premiums based upon actuarial principles may themselves become a tax collected by the authority of the state, and foresight may become compulsory.

What we have to consider in these lectures is, therefore, the effect on insurance, of whatever kind it may be, of this kind of government action. Conceivably this action might be applied to any of the risks of life, fire, accident, superannuation, even unemployment. Practically it has been applied most extensively to the risks to which certain classes are especially exposed, and is known as workingmen's insurance.

To give even a brief history of governmental insurance schemes would carry us far beyond the limits of these lectures. What I shall attempt will be, first to sketch the history of earlier types of government insurance, then to describe in more detail and analyze critically the peculiar combination of tax and premium which I have just described. I shall not base my deductions upon any *a priori* grounds, but I shall endeavor to interpret as well as possible the most exact data which we have. These necessarily cover but a limited field, and a comparatively short time. I do not claim that we can expect any final, incontrovertible results, but I do believe that we have enough data to indicate some tendencies pretty strongly, and thus to pave the way for future and more conclusive investigations.

The prevalence of government insurance depends naturally upon the general policy of states. Those commonwealths which in modern times have tended to elaborate governmental functions in general are those in which we find the greatest prevalence of government insurance. Those, on the other hand, in which private enterprise has been given free scope are those in which government insurance is either entirely absent or reduced to a minimum. In the former class we find two distinct and in some respects antithetical types of government. On the one hand we find the paternal state, of which the ideal is a benevolent despotism — on the other we find the modern socialistic or semi-socialistic democracy. This is one of those numerous cases in which the extremes meet.

In tracing the history of government insurance it is no surprise to find that (barring such hybrid forms as were connected with the guild system, and which seem to carry the origin of insurance back to the thirteenth century and to distant Iceland) modern government insurance may be dated from the seventeenth century, and had its birthplace in lower Germany and in Denmark. Thus there was at this time a governmental insurance agency against fire in Schleswig-Holstein, and another managed by the city of Copenhagen. In the eighteenth century similar insurance institutions arose in Brandenburg on the initiative of the Prussian government. Thus, in 1701 and 1705 several such village insurance agencies were established. In 1706 one was created in Berlin, and towards the middle of the eighteenth century others were established for various Prussian provinces and other German territories.

These agencies existed exclusively for insuring houses against fire and were generally compulsory. The object of introducing them was to prevent the impoverishment of whole villages by fire, and to help rural credit. The contributions were generally made on the principle of assessment, and it was not often that the risks were classified. From this beginning, public fire insurance, often compulsory, has become a common feature of the administration, especially in the states of Teutonic origin in central Europe. Thus, in 1906 there were 53 public fire insurance offices in the German Empire with insurance outstanding of 63,480,156 marks.[1] Similar offices are also found in Austria.

While in most of these cases the state agencies do not enjoy any monopoly, and compete with private insurance companies, it is a very common thing to make insurance, especially of houses, compulsory. This is particularly the case in the southern German states, Bavaria, Wurtemburg, Baden, also in Saxony and in parts of Prussia, particularly in the cities of Berlin, Stetin, Breslau, etc.

In Switzerland, while the federal government has the general supervision of private insurance companies, it has been left to the cantons to establish governmental insurance agencies. In 1898 there were seventeen cantons in Switzerland out of twenty-five which had cantonal insurance agencies for buildings, and two which extended the insur-

[1] "Statistisches Jahrbuch für das Deutsche Reich," 1908, p. 325.

ance to furniture. In most of these the institution is an old one. Fourteen out of the seventeen were established before 1820. The total amount insured under both heads was over 5,967,000,000 fr. or about $1,193,000,000. In many of these cases insurance is obligatory.[1]

While government insurance seems to have begun with fire risks, it has recently been extended to live stock, with the special object of securing peasants against loss through epizootics. The particular reason for turning over this kind of insurance to the government lies in the difficulty of estimating the risks, and of identifying the animals, which die, as well as in the unequal distribution of risks since an epizootic by its very nature tends to bunch the losses. There is also another advantage in making the government responsible for the losses. It is the only agency capable of enforcing on a large scale the sanitary regulations which are necessary to minimize those losses. Thus in Germany the matter was regulated by an imperial law of June 23, 1880, amended May 1, 1894, which was directed against the spread of disease among animals. This law left it to the individual states to provide indemnities for those whose animals were killed, and also to determine how the indemnity should be raised, and in most of them, as in Prussia under the law of March 12, 1881, there is a yearly tax upon the owners of live stock which amounts to a kind of mutual insurance against epizootics.

Insurance against injury by hail is, like the insurance of cattle, important for the farmer, and similar reasons exist for putting it under the control of the state. This has, however, not been done to any considerable extent, excepting in Bavaria, where a state hail insurance department was organized in 1884, endowed with a guarantee fund of 1,000,000 marks (about $250,000), and an annual subsidy of 40,000 marks ($10,000). This department enjoys, however, no monopoly; it simply competes with private companies. Nor is insurance compulsory.

[1] "Statistisches Jahrbuch der Schweiz," 1900, p. 159.

Government insurance against old age has been tried on a moderate scale in England as well as in France. As far back as 1771 a bill was introduced into the British Parliament to provide for old age insurance, but it was not carried, and no positive action was taken until 1833. The act passed in that year permitted the purchase of annuities, either deferred or immediate, of not less than £4 or more than £20 value. This was intended to provide for a kind of old age pension. It was at the time opposed, not only by the private insurance companies, but also by the friendly societies, and it was not until 1864 and 1882 that further acts were passed, making the system efficient. Under the present system immediate or deferred annuities for not less than £1 nor more than £100 can be purchased through a postal savings bank on the life of any person over five years of age. Persons between fourteen and sixty-five cannot be insured for less than £5. The cost varies with the age. Thus a man of twenty-four can, by paying annually 4s. 4d., purchase an annuity of £1 to commence when he has reached his fifty-fourth year, or he can obtain the same sum by the immediate payment of £3. 19s. 10d. This system has had comparatively meager results.

In France the bank for old age pensions was established in 1850. Its benefits were similar to those offered in England. By paying 5 fr., or a multiple of this sum, one could obtain after a certain time a regular pension not exceeding 600 fr. Two forms of insurance were provided — one with alienated capital, the other with reserved capital. In the latter case the pension was lower, but, on the other hand, if the beneficiary died either before or after the beginning of the pension, all sums paid by him, less the interest upon them, were returned to his heirs. Some of the details have been changed by subsequent laws. The law of 1886 fixed 1200 fr. as the maximum pension, and provided that the annual payments should not exceed 100 fr., excepting in the case of benefit societies. A law passed in 1893 provided that the maximum deposited in one year should be 500 fr. The results of this system have been somewhat disappointing. Very few workingmen are directly insured in this establishment. The bulk of the insurance is taken collectively by societies and employers for the benefit of others. The sum paid annually by individuals has shown but a slight increase from year to year and has often fallen off. Thus for the year 1889 it was 9,500,000 fr.; in the year 1905 it was 8,704,062 fr., while collective deposits in 1905 were over 43,000,000 fr.

Of the new individual depositors in 1905 numbering in all 8285, 2949 were minors without profession, 1288 were persons who belonged to the liberal professions or other members of the middle class. The workingmen proper, including domestics, numbered only about 1395.[1]

Since 1868 two other forms of government insurance have been introduced in France — one for accidents, the other for death, but comparatively little use has been made of either. The total receipts of the insurance agency against accidents in 1905 amounted to only 2868 fr., paid by 474 persons.[2] The use of the life insurance bureau has likewise been small. From 1868 to December 31, 1905, only 3565 persons had been individually insured, 524,257, collectively.

Governmental life insurance has been developed in recent times in New Zealand. Facilities for life insurance being poor in the early days of the colony, it was proposed by Sir Julius Vogel that the want should be supplied by the state, and a law was accordingly passed which created a life insurance department in 1870. It began on a small scale with but 463 clients. At the end of 1906 it had 45,981 policies outstanding, and did over one-third of the life insurance business of the colony. Of the total insurance of $29,036,047, the state insurance department had placed $10,667,591.[3] It is said that the New Zealand people

[1] "Annuaire Statistique de la France," 1906, p. 331.

[2] *Ibid.*, 342.

[3] "New Zealand Official Year-Book," 1908, p. 533.

carry more life insurance per capita than those of any other country, the average amount for every European inhabitant of the colony at the end of 1906 being £31, 19s. 1d., or about $160. Accident insurance by the state was introduced by an act passed in 1899, state fire insurance by an act passed in 1903.[1] In all of these cases the government insurance is neither a monopoly nor obligatory, but simply enters the field in competition with private corporations in order to supply a want, and it is stated that state fire insurance, which did not go into operation until 1905, has reduced the rates by 10 to 33⅓ per cent.[2]

Except for the annuity system mentioned above, England and the United States have not formally entered the field proper of governmental insurance. Yet, in our marine hospital service we have something closely allied to government insurance under another name. Under an act of Congress passed in 1798, sailors who fall sick or are injured on vessels sailing under the United States flag are entitled to be cared for at government expense, and down to 1884 were required to submit to a certain deduction from their wages, which corresponded roughly to an insurance premium.[3]

This sketch of government insurance is obviously made up of fragments. Different conditions have led in some countries to the use of one kind, in some countries to the use of another. In some few cases insurance has been compulsory, in most cases it has been voluntary. Nor has government insurance in any of the instances cited been carried out on a sufficiently large scale to furnish us with valuable experiences. Within the past twenty-five years an entirely new set of government insurance agencies has entered the field. Beginning with Germany, a number of

[1] "New Zealand Official Year-Book, 1908, p. 681.

[2] *Ibid.*, p. 682.

[3] A full history of the marine hospital service will be found in an unpublished mongraph, written in 1907 for the Carnegie Institution of Washington by Dr. Alba M. Edwards.

governments have boldly taken up the subject of workingmen's insurance. They have given it a compulsory character. They have aided it by subventions from the treasury, and, while they have not in most cases retained an absolute monopoly of the business for themselves, they have actually taken charge of the greater part of it. Moreover, as this whole mass of legislation has come into existence in an age which hungers and thirsts for statistics, unusually complete records have been preserved and published. We, therefore, have an experience which enables us to test the essential features of government insurance, and, while the experience is not long enough to justify us in reaching confident generalizations, it does supply us with much instructive material.

The beginning of modern workingmen's insurance is to be found in Germany. This is no mere accident. We have seen how at an early day fire insurance was introduced by the public authorities, and was made compulsory in that country, and for several centuries the German states have been preëminently the states of a paternally active administration. There were some special reasons, however, which brought about the introduction of compulsory workingmen's insurance in the ninth decade of the nineteenth century.

(1) Germany has been the nursery of modern scientific socialism. For many years after the death of Lassalle and the exile of Marx, socialism partook largely of a theoretical and revolutionary character. The formation of the German Empire in 1871, which brought with it universal suffrage, also brought the first socialist member of parliament, but he sat alone in the parliament of 1871. In 1874 the number had increased to nine, while in 1877 there were twelve, representing a constituency of 493,000. In 1878 two attacks were made upon the life of the emperor. He escaped without injury from the first; in the second he was seriously wounded, though he ultimately recovered and lived for ten years longer. There was no proof that

either of the would-be regicides had any connection with the socialist party. Indeed, the second one had lately been acting as colporteur for the Christian Socialist Party, whose chief article of faith was its loyalty to the church and to the monarchy. But Prince Bismarck thought the occasion a good one to strike a blow at the Social Democratic Party, and, after the dissolution of the parliament and a new election, succeeded in carrying through in 1878 a law which gave to the police the power to suppress newspapers, confiscate books, and close associations and meetings aiming at the subversion of the state. In the twelve years of the existence of this law 2716 prohibitions were issued. Its first effect was to break up temporarily the regular organization of the party, and only nine socialists were returned to parliament in 1878. But in the next election their number rebounded to twelve, and in the election of 1884 it had grown to twenty-four. It was clear that mere suppression was not effectual against this party. Prince Bismarck decided, therefore, boldly to take the wind out of its sails by introducing a series of measures, calculated to do as much for the working classes as the socialists themselves could have promised. There was, therefore, a strong political motive for introducing these measures at that time.

(2) This movement was aided by the newer tendencies of economic thought in Germany. With the formation of the Empire came a greater aversion to following in the footsteps of English economists, while the introduction of the historical method of research, not only in law, but also in economics, gave scholars a new appreciation of the efficiency of the government in the economic development of Germany. This movement of thought is illustrated by two votes passed by the *Verein für Sozial Politik,* which had been formed in 1872 in order to discuss questions of practical economics, and in which most of the professional economists of Germany were enrolled. In 1875 the question of compulsory insurance for invalidity and old

age was discussed, and the vote stood 28 to 11 against compulsion. In 1882 a similar question was again brought up, and the vote was in favor of compulsion for accident and sick insurance, though against the immediate introduction of insurance for invalidity as well as for widows and orphans. The more advanced thinkers among the German economists were moving steadily towards the idea of compulsory insurance.

(3) Another reason for at least insurance against accidents lay in the failure of the employers' liability act of June 7, 1871, and in the feeling that industries should bear the burden of their own accidents without the litigation and ill feeling connected with suits for damages.

The elaborate legislation for compulsory insurance which Germany adopted was, therefore, not an isolated experiment or merely a shrewd political move. It grew naturally out of the political, economic and social situation which existed in Germany during the decade following the formation of the Empire, and it, in turn, has stimulated a movement towards so-called socialistic measures, which has shown itself more or less in almost all of the advanced industrial countries of the world during the last quarter of a century. In no country, however, could such a radical and extensive scheme have been carried out so successfully as in Germany, with its corps of highly trained officials, its habits of obedience, and the most powerful figure of the nineteenth century for its chancellor. The legislation is so extensive and so complicated that even a summary of its main provisions would occupy more time than is allotted to the whole subject. Fortunately the details of the law are easily accessible, not only in the voluminous German literature on the subject, but also in works published in the English language, and I shall, therefore, content myself with bringing out the salient points which are characteristic of the governmental features of the laws.[1]

[1] See Fourth Special Report of the Commissioner of Labor on Compulsory Insurance in Germany, by John Graham Brooks, Washington,

The first bill, providing for accident insurance, was submitted to parliament early in 1881, but was rejected. When the House convened November 17, 1881, it was greeted with a message from the emperor which created a profound impression, and in which he expressed his desire to leave behind him to the Fatherland "new and lasting pledges of its internal peace, and to the needy greater certainty and abundance of the assistance to which they have a claim." This message, which came as a kind of a political testament of the venerable emperor, created a strong presumption in favor of compulsory insurance. A new bill for accident insurance was introduced as well as a bill for insurance against sickness. The latter, which was the first to be passed, was published June 15, 1883, and went into effect December 1, 1884. The accident insurance bill was passed July 6, 1884, and went partially into effect upon its proclamation, though it was not put fully into operation until October 1, 1885.

Both laws have been repeatedly amended, mainly by laws which have extended or liberalized their provisions, but their fundamental principles have not been altered. The first formal bill for the insurance against invalidity and old age was brought before parliament in 1888, and published as a law July 22, 1889. The provisions with regard to the machinery of insurance were to go into effect at once. The beginning of its business operations was left to imperial ordinance and was finally set for January 1, 1891.

Thus in less than ten years the three-fold plan for caring

1895; W. F. Willoughby: "Workingmen's Insurance," 1898; Report of the Industrial Commission, Vol. XVI., pp. 228–241, Washington, 1901. Excellently compiled statistics may be found in Lass und Zahn, "Einrichtung und Wirkung der Deutschen Arbeiterversicherung," 1900, a volume prepared for the Paris Exposition of 1900; "Die Deutsche Arbeiterversicherung; als Soziale Einrichtung," 1904, a volume prepared for the St. Louis World's Fair of 1904; and in the regular publications of the *Reichsversicherungsamt* and the Imperial Statistical Bureau.

for the working classes was carried through and put into operation.

I. The sick insurance law applies to all cases of sickness, regardless of cause, and to practically all persons employed for wages in any of the mechanical trades or in commerce, as well as to some of those engaged in agriculture. At the end of 1907 there were over 12,000,000 persons who were subject to its provisions. It also applies to ordinary laborers and even to those occupying an official position as far as their salary is less than 2000 M. or about $500. Of the occupations to which the law applies, some are unconditionally subject to it, others conditionally. The principal trades in which the compulsion is general are railroading, mining, manufactures, internal navigation, commerce, the telegraph and postal service, navigation in harbors, etc., though regular seamen are provided for by a special law. Its provisions can, however, be extended by ordinance to certain other classes. Exemptions are allowed for certain classes, such as soldiers and public servants, whose office entitles them to support in sickness, and in some other cases on special application. Voluntary insurance under this head is also permitted to certain classes of persons to whom the compulsory character of the law does not apply, and those who have passed out of an occupation subject to the law are allowed to continue their relations to the insurance agency in which they were inscribed.

The organization of the sick insurance seems at first sight very complicated, since there are no less than eight different kinds of organizations which may be within the operation of the law. The object of this was to adapt compulsory insurance as far as possible to existing institutions, and to the needs of different classes of the people. The following table gives a summary of the number and membership of the different classes of societies concerned in 1907:

	Societies [1]	Members [2]
1. Local Sick Insurance Agencies	4757	5,915,114
2. Establishment Sick Insurance Agencies	7914	3,146,386
3. Building Sick Insurance Agencies	41	15,222
4. Guild Sick Insurance Agencies	761	240,087
5. Registered Benefit Societies	1318	893,330
6. State Benefit Societies	151	36,168
7. Municipal Associations	8290	1,475,489
8. Miners' Associations	168 [3]	806,276 [3]
	23,400	12,528,072

The benefits which are given must come up to a certain minimum, which must supply:

(1) Free medical attendance and medicine from the day of sickness;

(2) A regular allowance beginning with the third day after the sickness has shown itself.

As a rule this sum is equal to one-half of the rate of wages upon which the premiums are based, and it may be given for thirteen weeks. A number of variations are, however, permitted, such as care in a hospital, which may be substituted for medical attendance, allowance, etc. The funds are supplied normally by the insured person and by the employer jointly, the latter contributing one-third of the premiums, the former two-thirds, but the total amount is advanced by the employer, who indemnifies himself by deducting the quota of the insured from his wages. In general the contributions range from 1½ to 4½ per cent. of the normal wages.

II. Insurance against accidents covered from the beginning a large number of different people, and its scope has

[1] Statistik des Deutschen Reichs, Bd. 194. Krankenversicherung im Jahre 1907, p. 1.

[2] *Ibid.*, p. 3.

[3] Vierteljahrshefte zur Statistik des Deutschen Reichs, 1909. Heft 2, p. 92.

been considerably extended of late years, an amendment, which was passed in 1900, actually going so far as to include convicts in prison.

In 1906 over 21,000,000 persons were insured against accident, or over one-third of the entire population of the German Empire.[1] They include, not only industrial employees and those engaged in railroading and internal navigation, but also those engaged in agriculture, forestry, and all kinds of building operations. The organization of this form of insurance is quite different from that of the sick insurance. It rests entirely upon so-called professional associations, in which the insured are grouped according to their occupations. These associations, of which there were 114 in 1906, are virtually unions of employers who are leagued together as far as possible according to the character of their industry. In some cases one association extends over the entire Empire, as in the case of the Iron and Steel Association. In other cases they cover but a limited territory. Each one is, however, in the main self-governing. It elects its own officers and manages its own affairs, subject to the general provisions of the law. The benefits given are in general of two kinds:

(1) In the case of injury, the benefits begin with the fourteenth week, inasmuch as during the first thirteen weeks the injured person is cared for under sick insurance or, failing that, at the direct expense of his employer. Beginning with the fourteenth week he is entitled under accident insurance to the cost of medical attendance, medicine, etc., and to an allowance to continue during the period of his disability. The amount of the allowance is graded according to the severity of the injury, two-thirds of the normal wages being usually given in the case of total disability.

(2) In the case of death, the expenses of burial are to be paid, and an annuity given to the widow until her death or remarriage, or to the children.

[1] "Statistisches Jahrbuch für das Deutsche Reich," 1908, p. 307.

The entire expense of accident insurance is borne by the employers, excepting in as far as the injured person may be a contributor to a sick insurance fund on which his care during the first thirteen weeks rests. The funds are raised according to the assessment principle, that is, the expenses of each year are apportioned among the employers who are subject to the insurance law. The rate of apportionment depends partly upon the amount paid in salaries and wages, and partly upon the risks of the employment. There are, however, some exceptions to this general rule.

III. Insurance for invalidity and old age applies in general to persons engaged in agriculture and industry, in trade, domestic service, and public service. It also includes officials, provided their salary is not over 2000 marks. Certain other persons may take advantage of the law, but without compulsion, while certain persons in the enumerated classes are exempt either by law or on their own application. The former exemption applies mainly to persons who are entitled by virtue of their occupation to a pension, the latter to persons who are already over seventy, or who do not work regularly for wages. The organization of the insurance differs radically from that of both of the other systems. It is in charge of an imperial bureau which has its subdivisions scattered over the country. For this purpose Germany is divided into thirty-one districts, each with its insurance department. In general the place of a person's occupation determines the district in which he is insured. It was estimated that in 1906 about 14,000,000 persons enjoyed the benefit of this form of insurance.[1] The benefits are twofold:

(1) An invalidity pension which is given without regard to age to those whose earning capacity is reduced to less than one-third of the normal.

(2) An old age pension to which every one over seventy years of age is entitled whether infirm or not, provided he has complied with the general conditions of the law.

[1] Statistisches Jahrbuch für das Deutsche Reich, 1908, p. 318.

The principle of these requirements is that the applicant must have been a contributor to the fund for an aggregate of one thousand two hundred weeks, or twenty-four years. The benefit consists in both cases of a uniform contribution of 50 marks (about $12.50) per year from the Empire, and of an additional sum which depends upon the wage class of the recipient and upon the length of time during which he has contributed. The beneficiary is entitled to have a part of his contributions refunded on certain conditions:

(*a*) In the case of women, one-half is refunded upon marriage.

(*b*) In case accident insurance provides for the insured, he may likewise receive back one-half.

(*c*) In case the insured dies before the beginning of the pension, the surviving wife or husband may receive one-half of the amount contributed.

Excepting for the uniform subsidy given by the Empire, the cost of the insurance is divided evenly between the employer and the employed, but is advanced by the former. The financial principle under which the rates are fixed differs, however, from that which applies to either of the other insurance systems. The premiums are based upon the principle that each one is to contribute on the average the capital out of which his own allowances are paid. In the beginning this rate was determined provisionally for a period of ten years, but as it was found that the rates were sufficient for the permanent requirements of the system, they were definitely fixed by the amendment of 1899. As a transitional measure, it was provided that persons over forty years of age when the law went into effect, if they had been occupied in one of the dutiable employments for three years previous, should have the term normally fixed for their contributions shortened by as many years as their age exceeded the age of forty. Thus a person fifty years of age, instead of being obliged to contribute for twenty-four years, would only be obliged to contribute for fourteen.

The enactment and successful execution of the German insurance laws led to a rapid extension of the system in other parts of the world. The first state to follow the German example was Austria, which provided for compulsory accident insurance in 1887, for sick insurance in 1888, and for miners' insurance in 1889. Hungary pasesd a law for sick insurance in 1891. Norway passed a law for accident insurance in 1894, modeled somewhat after the German plan. Sweden, after considerable discussion, accepted in 1901 a law according to which the employers must either give compensation for accidents, or must insure their employees. In 1901 Holland passed a law providing for compulsory insurance against accidents, and even distant Iceland adopted in 1890 a scheme for insurance against invalidity and old age.

In December, 1903, the new Belgian law on accident insurance was published, which, however, is more in the nature of workmen's compensation than of insurance, though it amounts in some of its features to an indirect insurance, and there was a strong pressure in the Chamber to give it the character of insurance.

A number of states which have not formally adopted a scheme of workingmen's insurance have passed laws which are intended to give somewhat similar benefits. Thus Italy, in 1898, passed a law requiring certain classes of workingmen to be insured against accident at the expense of their employers. Workmen's compensation acts were adopted by Great Britain in 1897, France in 1898, Russia in 1903, and Sweden in 1904, under which those who suffer in industrial accidents are indemnified by the employers. Old age is now being provided for in some countries, not by insurance but by state pensions, as in Great Britain by the act of 1908 and in the Australian Commonwealth, and a number of Australian colonies, beginning with New Zealand in 1898. In these cases the funds are obtained from the general revenue of the government without any contributions by the beneficiaries. Even unemployment is now being treated by insurance, and though most of the plans actually tried, like the so-called Ghent System, are local, the subject is being considered seriously by a number of states.[1] In the United States the State of Maryland adopted in 1902 a species of accident insurance, but it was overthrown on constitutional grounds.

The experience of Switzerland with workingmen's insurance has been peculiar and may perhaps in the future prove to be exceptionally instructive. Under the Swiss constitution, as originally adopted, the federal government could do nothing in the way of workingmen's insurance. An amendment was accordingly adopted in 1890, by a popular vote of about three to one, in which it was provided that "the Confederation shall by means of legislation provide for sick and accident insurance, having regard to the existing sick clubs. It can make membership either generally or for special classes obligatory." After considerable debate two bills — one for sick insurance, the other for accident insurance — passed the federal legislature, but, upon a demand being made for a referendum, a vote was taken May 20, 1900, and the whole plan was rejected by 337,000 to 147,000 votes, the majority against these specific bills being greater than the majority of ten years earlier in favor of the general scheme.

For a number of years the subject was dropped, but a new bill has now been worked out by a special commission. It provides for sick and accident insurance, but it departs widely from the German model. Compulsion is applied only in accident insurance, and here the insured may be required to bear one-quarter of the premiums. Sick insurance is to be promoted by a subsidy which the Confederation may pay to voluntary sick clubs and other societies, and is not made general as in Germany.

Some form of workingmen's insurance is now so common

[1] For full data see: "Die Versicherung gegen die Folgen der Arbeitslosigkeit im Ausland und im Deutschen Reich. Bearbeitet im Kaiserlichen Statistischen Amt." Berlin, 1906, p. 1449.

on the Continent of Europe that it is the rule rather than the exception. If we look at accidents alone, more than half of the inhabitants of Continental Europe west of Russia live under a system of accident insurance which is compulsory for large sections of the population.

With these extensions have, however, come new problems, and the pioneer states in this field are now beginning to revise their laws in the light of experience. In Austria a new codification was proposed by the government, November 3, 1908. The bill, in 325 sections bears the significant title, "Sozialversicherung"[1] and includes insurance against sickness, old age and invalidity, and accidents. In Germany, a similar re-codification was proposed, April 2, 1909, under the title "Reichsversicherungsordnung." This bill, while it groups together the three existing branches of workingmen's insurance, does not merge them, as had been proposed, but still retains for each branch its own system. It, however, extends the scope of insurance, especially of sick insurance by including in it workers in agriculture and forestry, domestic servants and those engaged in domestic industries. It also provides in connection with old age insurance for a kind of life insurance for the families of those who die.[2] In view of the changes which are being proposed in the German system, the present time seems a peculiarly good one for a review of its operations during the past quarter of a century.

[1] Separatbeilage zu Nr. 11 der "Sozialen Rundschau," Wien, 1908.

[2] "Die sozialpolitische Bedeutung der Reichsversicherungsordnung," von Professor Dr. Stier-Somlo in "Soziale Praxis" for April 29, May 6, June 3, 1909.

CHAPTER XXII

OPERATION OF COMPULSORY WORKINGMEN'S INSURANCE IN GERMANY[1]

It was explained in the beginning that government insurance, which is supported in whole or in part by taxation or by the contributions of others than the beneficiaries, is not insurance in the strict sense of the word. It is an institution which, while having the form and the immediate purposes of insurance, partakes, as regards its ultimate ends and the means by which it is carried into effect, of social legislation. This is clearly understood, in spite of some differences of opinion, by German authors. One of the first authorities on the purely legal side of the institution, Professor Heinrich Rosin of Freiburg, says that, in spite of the official designation, the great workingmen's insurance institutions cannot be properly classified as insurance. "We are not dealing," he says, "with a single two-sided legal relation, but with two one-sided relations. Of these, one, which is the principal, provides for the working classes assistance on the part of the state; the other, which is secondary and does not necessarily stand in legal connection with the first, has to do with the raising of money by contributions levied from certain persons."[2]

While, therefore, the subject might be an interesting one to consider from the point of view of technical insurance questions, its chief interest lies in its social operations, and

[1] By Henry W. Farnam, Professor of Political Economy in Yale University. Reprinted with additions from pages 304–328 of the "Yale Insurance Lectures, Fire and Miscellaneous."

[2] "Das Recht des Arbeiterversicherung, Vol. I, p. 257.

it is, therefore, from that point of view alone that I shall consider it. Partly for the sake of simplicity, and partly on account of the fulness of the data, I shall confine my analysis to the German laws, although the indications are that the experience of Germany is repeated elsewhere under similar conditions. In the famous message of the Emperor which has already been referred to, we read that "the cure for social maladies is to be found not exclusively in the repression of social democratic excesses but equally by means of the positive promotion of the welfare of laborers. The Fatherland should, therefore, receive new and lasting pledges of its inner peace, and those who are in need should receive greater certainty and abundance of help." Similarly in the preamble to the law for accident insurance, which was presented to the parliament in 1881, it is stated: "That the state should consider its needy members more than hitherto is not only a duty of humanity and of Christianity which should permeate such institutions, but is also a duty of state preserving policy which is to follow the aim of cultivating among the non-property-owning classes of the population, who are at the same time the most numerous and the least educated, the view that the state is not only a necessary but also a beneficial institution. To this end they must be brought, by means of directly recognizable advantages which are given them by legislative measures, to conceive of the state not only as an institution invented for the protection of the better situated classes of society, but also as one which serves their needs and interests." The present Emperor expressed himself in similar terms in 1888, when the bill for invalidity and old age insurance was presented.

Every attempt to influence the structure of society or the distribution of wealth by legislation is like a surgical operation. As soon as the knife is applied, it is liable to produce results different from those which were contemplated, and sometimes decidedly antagonistic to them. In endeavoring to analyze the operation of this legislation, therefore, I shall distinguish the direct and intended results, from those which are incidental and indirect, and I shall furthermore distinguish the strictly financial and economic results which are, as it were, but a means to an end, from the social results which are the real and ultimate purpose of the legislation.

At the time of the Paris Exposition of 1900 the German Government sent as a part of its exhibit a huge, gilded obelisk some forty-five feet in height, which was intended to represent gold of the value of the total amounts paid to the beneficiaries of the insurance laws from 1885 to 1899. This would have weighed 960,000 kilograms, and represented a value of 2.4 milliards marks, or about $600,000,000. That sum has now more than doubled. The total amount paid out for indemnities down to 1906 amounted to 5,682,-000,000 marks or about $1,420,500,000. The total income during that period was over 8,000,000,000 marks and of this sum 3,645,000,000 came from the employers, 3,282-, 000,000 from the insured, 435,000,000 from the Empire and 748,000,000 from interest and premiums.[1]

It is clear, therefore, that through this elaborate organization the government has succeeded not only in turning a stream of wealth, enormous in the aggregate, into the pockets of the working classes, but in drawing this stream in about equal portions from the employers and the beneficiaries themselves.

It has done this at a cost which is on the whole not excessive. The total cost of administration during the period from 1885 to 1897 was but 10.1 per cent. of the total expenditure, and the tendency is downward. The total cost down to 1906 was about 9.1 per cent. In sick insurance alone the cost of management was 5 per cent. in 1904, 4.7 per cent. in 1907.[2]

It might, perhaps, be supposed, and there are some economists who would consider this a necessary deduction from

[1] "Statistisches Jahrbuch für das Deutsche Reich," 1908, p. 318.
[2] "Statistik des Deutschen Reichs," Bd. 177 and 194.

the wage-fund theory, that the rate of wages would have fallen during the same period on account of the burdens resting upon the employers, or, if not, that German industry would at least have suffered a severe blow. Neither of these results appears to have taken place. The period covered by insurance has been on the whole a period of great prosperity for German industry. It has not prevented the growth of large establishments, as is shown by the following table:

	Establishments		Persons		Increase or Decrease	
	1882	1895	1882	1895	Estab.	Pers.
Independent workers.	1,430,465	1,237,349	1,430,465	1,237,349	−13.5	−13.5
Small establishments (2-5 persons)	745,392	752,223	1,839,939	1,953,776	+ 0.9	+ 6.2
Medium establishments (6-50 persons) .	85,001	139,459	1,109,128	1,902,049	+64.1	+71.5
Large establishments (over 50 persons) . .	9,481	17,941	1,554,131	2,907,329	+89.3	+87.2
	2,270,339	2,146,972	5,933,663	8,000,503	− 5.4	+34.8

International trade has progressed at such a rapid rate as to put Germany in the second rank among the great states of the world. The total foreign trade of Germany, exports and imports, increased from 8,000,000,000 marks in 1890[1] to 17,000,000,000 marks in 1907.[2] Looking at the percentage of the total trade of the world which she enjoyed, we find that she passed from the third to the second place as shown by the following table:

[1] "Statistisches Jahrbuch für das Deutsche Reich," 1908, p. 60.*
[2] "Ibid, 1908, p. 67.*

	1890	1900	1906
Germany	11.1	12.1	12.4
France	11.3	10.0	8.9
Great Britian	20.8	19.5	17.4
United States	9.4	10.3	10.0

Of the four countries in question, Germany showed the most rapid rate of increase in her foreign trade. The ratio of growth in her case was 107.4 per cent., in the case of the United States 101.5 per cent.

Wages appear to have risen during this period. But German wage statistics are not very satisfactory, as there are no general figures systematically collected for the whole empire.[1] Some of the trade unions have published figures for the wages of their members. The accident and sick insurance associations have tables of normal wages on which to base the indemnities. Special statistics have also been compiled for the wages of city employees and for other groups of workers. In all of these the upward tendency is so marked, that we are safe in saying that money wages have risen, even though we may not be able to express the rise in a percentage or to correlate accurately the rise of the wages with the rise of prices.

The general well-being is also indicated by the per capita increase in the consumption of commodities used by the masses. The per capita consumption of sugar increased from an annual average of 6 kilograms during the five years 1871–1875 to 16.8 in 1906–1907; the consumption of coffee rose in the same periods from 2.27 kilograms to

[1] On the general subject of wage statistics see "Die Lohnstatistik in Deutschland," Reichsarbeitsblatt, February, 1909, pages 104–109. The statistics for a number of trades are reprinted in "Third Abstract of Foreign Labor Statistics," issued by the British Labor Department, 1906. See also Kuczynski: "Die Entwicklung der gewerblichen Löhne seit der Begründung des Deutschen Reichs," 1909.

3.02; rice from 1.55 to 2.51.[1] The difficulty of getting domestic servants, the migration of people into the cities, and the consequent scarcity of farm laborers, the falling off of emigration from 2.16 per thousand of the population in 1888 to .51 per thousand in 1907 are all indirect evidences of an increasing prosperity of the wage-receiving classes.[2]

Besides the direct transfer of wealth which was intended by the insurance laws, there has been incidently a great accumulation of capital. A report published by the Imperial Insurance Office, and carrying the figures down to December 31, 1903, shows that in the single year 1903 the capital invested by the insurance offices in various public works was not less than 42,825,599 marks, or over $10,000,000, while the entire sum thus applied since 1884 was 336,851,529 marks, or about $84,000,000, and this only represents a part of the entire capital of the insurance bureaus.

The purposes to which this capital has been applied are extremely varied. Thus not less than 67,000,000 marks (about $17,000,000) were put into farm loans, narrow-gauge railroads, the improvement of highways, the improvement of live stock, etc. Some 148,000,000 marks ($37,000,000) were used for building hospitals and other institutions for the sick or the poor, etc. A very large sum was used for workingmen's dwellings — no less than 118,000,000 marks ($29,000,000) being used for this purpose.[3] The total property of the three groups of insurance agencies in 1906 was 1,854,000,000 marks or about $463,500,000.[4]

Great improvements have also been made in the introduction of safety appliances and sanitary measures. Thus

[1] "Statistisches Jahrbuch für das Deutche Reich," 1908, pages 247 and 251.

[2] *Ibid.*, p. 25.

[3] Summary in "Soziale Praxis," February 19, 1904, p. 548.

[4] *Ibid.*, p. 318.

accident stations have been established in Berlin by the accident insurance associations to minimize the cost of accidents which has to be borne by the employers. These places are equipped with bandages, splints, and other surgical appliances, and have physicians on call, both for day and night service. The manufacturers' associations have taken pains to introduce strict rules with regard to the handling of dangerous goods, the introduction of life-saving apparatus, etc. Safety elevators are more generally provided than formerly, the oiling of machinery is being done automatically instead of by hand, the belting is being adjusted by means of a handle, machinery is being fenced in, and premiums are sometimes paid for the rescue of the injured. In order to secure the execution of these regulations some associations have established a regular inspection service.

While accident insurance has provided safety appliances, sick insurance has promoted hygienic regulations. In Munich one of the local sick insurance bureaus has induced the storekeepers to give their employees means for sitting down, a noon day rest, and other advantages. Lectures on hygiene have been given in a number of cities, particularly regarding tuberculosis, dust diseases, etc. The death-rate has fallen steadily in Germany. In 1885 it was 27.2 per thousand, in 1907 it was 18.98 per cent.[1] In the three charity clinics of Berlin the mortality due to consumption fell from fifty-four in 1889–1890 to thirty-four in 1898–1899.

Let us now turn from these physical facts to the political and social changes which have taken place in Germany since compulsory insurance went into operation. It was clearly stated at the beginning that the object of the insurance laws was to counteract the dangerous tendencies of the social democrats, and to preserve inner peace, by which was probably meant industrial peace. And it was also expected, though this was not so clearly brought out, that

[1] "Vierteljahrsheften zur Statistik des Deutschen Reichs," 1908.

insurance would be substituted for and thus ease the burden of poor relief. Let us consider these points one by one.

(1) The political effect on the growth of the social democratic party.

This matter can be dealt with by a very simple table showing the results of successive parliamentary elections from 1871 down to the present:

	Socialist			Socialist	
	Voters	Members of Reichstag		Voters	Members of Reichstag
1871	101,927	1	1887....	763,128	11
1874	351,670	9	1890....	1,427,298	35
1877	493,447	12	1893....	1,786,738	44
1878	437,158	9	1898....	2,105,305	56
1881	311,961	12	1903....	3,010,472	81
1884	549,990	24	1907....	3,259,000	43

This table shows that from 1881 to 1903 the number of socialist representatives increased from twelve to eighty-one, nearly sevenfold, and that though there was a great drop in their numbers in 1907 their constituency showed a gain. As a means of suppressing socialism, insurance laws can hardly be considered a success. It is true that there has been a considerable change in the character of the party. It is less than it formerly was a party of revolution, it has even ceased to be a party of opposition pure and simple, and in some of the more recent amendments to the insurance laws it has at least negatively favored the government measures. How far this is due to the sobering effect of that responsibility which comes with numbers, how far it is due to a change in the theoretical views of the younger socialists, how far it is due to an actual feeling of friendliness towards the existing parties, it is impossible to say, and any discussion of this matter would carry us beyond the limits of our subject. The fact remains that the social democratic party is still the party of discontent, and that its membership has grown very rapidly in spite of what compulsory insurance has done for its working class members.

(2) Social Peace.

A good deal of stress is laid in the official history of the insurance laws upon their conciliatory effect in creating a better feeling between employers and employed. Officially the conditions are described as almost idyllic. "With the improvements in the material and social position of the workingmen which have been introduced through workingmen's insurance there is a spontaneous increase in their pleasure in work, and at the same time in the quality and amount of their product. Therefore the employers are in general quite willing to bear the heavy burdens in money and voluntary service."[1] We are told that, in addition to the burdens of insurance placed upon them by law, many employers have voluntarily introduced additional benefit features for their employees. Thus in 1898, 103 joint stock companies, 90 private employers and 48 other persons spent 27,000,000 marks for the benefit of their employees, while in 1899 the amount contributed by 625 joint stock companies and 349 private persons reached the sum of 39,000,000 marks.[2] Individual examples, such as are found in the establishment of the General Electrical Company of Berlin, in the famous steel works of Krupp in Essen, etc., are not unfamiliar to readers in this country. "This social activity," we are told, "which the employers are unfolding under the standard of our new social legislation, cannot fail in the long run to produce a conciliatory reaction upon the differences existing between employer and employed. A mutual understanding is also furthered by the common consultations and meetings in which the workingmen's insurance unites employer and employed."[3] It is difficult either to prove or disapprove a general state-

[1] "Lass und Zahn," p. 223.

[2] Ibid., p. 224.

[3] Ibid., p. 225.

ment of this kind, but there are some facts which seem at least to cast doubt upon the conclusions just quoted. That the employers have done a great deal for their employees in Germany is undoubtedly true; that this activity is due to any large extent to the insurance laws may well be questioned. It is certainly a fact that Krupp voluntarily introduced vast schemes for the welfare and insurance of his men long before government insurance was thought of. It is likewise true that in other countries such as England, France, and the United States, where no such insurance exists, brilliant examples of this far-sighted interest in the workers on the part of large corporations and large individual employers can be found. In our own country, for instance, the Colorado Fuel and Iron Company has established a regular sociological department which publishes a weekly magazine and superintends very extensive educational and social advantages provided for the people on the company's pay-roll. It would, therefore, be a mistake to attribute this exhibition of social activity entirely or in large degree to the compulsory insurance laws. It would also seem as if the statement regarding the good will existing between employers and employed in Germany was hardly borne out by the few statistics which are available for this purpose. Generally speaking, it is true that sentiments cannot be measured by the statistical method, but when sentiments take shape in action, the actions can be counted and furnish at least a rough index of the prevalence of the sentiments. Any ill feeling between employers and employed is in modern times pretty sure to result sooner or later in strikes, and strike statistics have been collected with more or less regularity in Germany since about 1890. In 1889, shortly after the new laws had gone into effect, there occurred a notable strike among the miners of Western Germany, in which it is said that about 90,000 persons took part. In 1891–1892 there was a very general and disastrous strike of the printers, which ultimately led to a complete change in the character of the principal printers' union. This union had previously been noted for its conservative and peaceful character, but has now become almost entirely identified with social democracy. Another great strike was that of the Hamburg dock laborers in 1896–1897, in which over 16,000 persons took part. A significant fact is that in 1897 a special insurance company called "Industria" was formed with a capital of 5,000,000 marks, with the special province of indemnifying employers for losses through strikes, and though it failed subsequently, its failure was by no means due to the disappearance of strikes from the industrial world. The following table, which is not altogether uniform and therefore not very satisfactory, indicates that strikes still have their ups and downs, and that the tendency throughout the years seems to be more upward than downward:[1]

STRIKE STATISTICS

	Prussia		German Empire	
	Strikes	Strikers	Strikes	Strikers
Summer of 1890......	216	28,643		
Winter " 1890-1....	71	6,573		
Summer " 1891......	118	25,100		
Winter " 1891-2. ..	99	7,787		
Summer " 1892......	99	7,878		
Winter " 1892-3....	116	55,882		
Summer " 1893......	74	4,070		
Winter " 1893-4....	48	2,835		
Summer " 1894......	127	9,764		
Winter " 1894-5....	71	3,861		

[1] The figures for Prussia down to 1897 are taken from "Handwörterbuch der Staats-Wissenschaften," 2d ed., Vol. I, p. 761; the later figures are compiled from "Statistik des Deutschen Reichs," Vols. CXXXIV, CXLI, CXLVIII, CLVII, CLXIV, CLXXI, CLXXVIII, CLXXXVIII. The figures for Prussia give the data for strikes ended in each year; in the case of the Empire, the column of strikes gives those begun, the column of strikers refers to strikes ended in each year.

STRIKE STATISTICS — *Continued*

	Prussia		German Empire	
	Strikes	Strikers	Strikes	Strikers
Summer " 1895......	189	6,365		
Winter " 1895-6....	606	17,349		
Summer " 1896......	304	51,309		
Winter " 1896-7....	158	16,181		
Summer " 1897......	285	25,398		
Year 1899...........	807	58,931	1,336	99,338
" 1900...........	929	82,510	1,462	122,803
" 1901...........	632	36,114	1,071	55,262
" 1902...........	614	33,997	1,084	53,912
" 1903...........	841	51,633	1,405	85,603
" 1904...........	1,190	70,146	1,908	113,480
" 1905...........	1,401	338,675	2,448	408,145
" 1906...........	1,893	152,045	3,378	272,218
" 1907...........	1,204	108,332	2,279	192,430

(3) The effect upon poor relief.

While it was not announced as one of the objects of government insurance to diminish the amount spent on the poor, it was undoubtedly expected that its effect would be to lessen the number of paupers. Investigations made into the causes of poverty in Germany some years ago, some of which were made by Dr. Victor Boehmert and others by the Imperial Statistical Bureau, concur in showing that in the aggregate some 75 per cent. of the cases of pauperism were attributed to sickness, accident, physical incapacity, old age, or death of the bread-winner. Now it so happens that all of these causes of pauperism are provided for in workingmen's insurance, and if the great mass of wage workers, who are the ones most liable on account of their small incomes to become dependent, are forced to insure themselves, and reap the benefit of the contributions of their employers, it would seem natural to expect that fewer would become dependent, and that gradually insurance would take the place of poor relief for all but the worthless or those who are peculiarly unfortunate. This expectation seems the more natural, when we consider the figures in more detail. Unfortunately we have no general statistics giving the cost of poor relief since the investigation of 1885, and it is doubtful if we should place implicit reliance upon the figures gathered at that time. Yet, as we have no others, they may at least furnish us a rough means of comparison. The number of paupers enumerated in the German Empire in that year was 1,592,386, and the amount spent upon them was about 90,000,000 marks, which gave an average expenditure for every one hundred inhabitants of 193 marks. In 1897 the total amount spent on benefits of all kinds under compulsory insurance was 256,000,000 marks, which, with the increased population, gave an expenditure for every one hundred inhabitants of about 474 marks, or about two and one-half times the average expenditure on poor relief in 1885. This did not include the expenses of administration, but only the amount directly spent on the beneficiaries. So large an expenditure of money upon the very classes who are most liable to become dependent might be reasonably expected almost to abolish pauperism, since there must be many cases in which individual members of a family could now be supported with the rest, when they previously were thrown upon the public. That the question has interested the authorities is seen in the fact that the Verein für Armenpflege has twice, namely in 1895 and in 1901, taken the matter up for investigation and discussion, and that the Imperial Statistical Bureau undertook in 1894 and published in 1897 an elaborate investigation into the whole subject. It obtained its material mainly in the form of answers to the following three specific questions, which it addressed to the officials in charge of poor relief throughout Germany:

A. Has the care of the poor been relieved by workingmen's insurance?

(a) Through sick insurance?
(b) Through accident insurance?
(c) Through old age and invalidity insurance?

B. Has the number of those supported and the amount spent upon them since the introduction of the several insurance laws not diminished, and to what is this to be attributed?

C. Has the care of the poor in numerous cases been made supplementary to the benefits of workingmen's insurance and provisionally substituted for them?

The answers received were not complete, and it was not possible statistically to prove either an increase or a decrease in the total amount spent upon the poor throughout the Empire. I have, however, tried to analyze the returns as far as possible, and compared my analysis with the generalizations published by the Bureau. As regards the first question, subdivided into three heads, which asks whether the care of the poor has been relieved by workingmen's insurance, the official summary says "that by far the greater part" of the authorities questioned say that it has been relieved. A careful count shows that of the total number of answers, just 44 per cent. give a simple affirmative, while 19 per cent. more give a more or less qualified affirmative answer. Yet, when we come to ask whether there has been a diminution either in the number of paupers or in the amount spent for them, it appears that 58 per cent. state that there has been no such diminution. In other words, it would appear that in a good many cases those who say that the burden of poor relief has been lessened, mean, not that it is absolutely less than it formerly was, but that it would have been increased much more, if it had not been for workingmen's insurance. When we consider that the period under consideration has been a period of industrial prosperity, commercial expansion, external peace and rising wages, we should naturally expect that the burden of poor relief would tend downwards, as it has been tending in England, and as out-door relief has been tending in many of our American cities under good administration. If there are no general economic reasons for an increase in the needs of the poorer classes in Germany, it would seem as if there must be a social or psychological reason, and there are certainly strong indications of this. While some officials speak of depression in particular trades, the migration of workers to the cities, etc., as causes of the increased expenditure, others speak of the tendency of the poor to demand more. A report from Gotha says that the poor have become accustomed to demand help from the public. It is stated that the shrinking from the eleemosynary character of the poor relief is "disappearing among the needy, so that those who are not insured demand public support more frequently than formerly, and refuse private aid. Then again, those who are not insured, seeing the amounts which are paid to those who are insured, demand a more ample allowance from the poor law authorities, and not infrequently get it." It also happens here and there that, when people have been refused a demand for an allowance under the insurance law for lack of proof, they go to the poor law authorities and demand a larger sum on account of their presumptive demand for an allowance.[1] In a report made to the Verein für Armenpflege und Wohlthätigkeit by Wilhelm Helling in 1901 we learn some facts which seem to indicate that insurance is not having the educational effect upon thrift that was expected. "It is unfortunate," he says, "to be obliged to say that persons who have established a contingent claim upon the benefits of insurance by contributions find it so difficult to make up their minds to maintain this claim by the payment of small voluntary sums, and also that hardly any use has been made of the right of optional insurance. . . . It is positively terrible to notice the number of women who, when they marry, give up the rights, which they have earned, in order to obtain possession of a comparatively small sum of ready money, by having the half of sums already

[1] "Lass und Zahn," p. 229.

paid refunded to them." Even where the burden of poor relief has been diminished, it has not always fallen to an extent equal to the cost of insurance to the employers alone. Thus in the city of Königsberg, in spite of an increase of 20,000 in the population during four years, the expenditure on poor relief actually diminished, but, while they did not claim to have made a saving on this score of more than 130,000 marks, employers paid in 1896–1897 about 380,000 marks, or nearly three times this amount, as their share of the burdens of insurance.[1]

While insurance provides for indemnity only, it does not accomplish its social purpose, unless at the same time it leads to a restriction of the contingencies which give rise to the indemnity. Thus protection against fire has gone hand in hand with fire insurance, and the mere fact that in insurance pure and simple the premiums are graded according to the risk puts a certain penalty upon the encouragement of risk. It is for the interest of the insured as a body to keep down casualties, even though an individual may think that he can profit by them. It is, therefore, somewhat surprising to learn that, since the sick insurance laws have gone into effect, there has been a steady increase in the cost of sickness per member, in the expenditure for each case of sickness, and also in the expenditure for each day of sickness, as shown by the following table:

[1] "Lass und Zahn," p. 231. An elaborate plea for the contention that workingmen's insurance has relieved the burden of pauperism in Germany is contained in two articles by David Grünsprecht under the title: "Die Entlastung der öffentlichen Armenpflege durch die Arbeiterversicherung," (Conrad's "Jahrbücher," 1907, pages 63–88 and 364–378). The author concedes, however, at the outset that the expenses of poor-relief are almost everywhere steadily rising.

COST OF SICKNESS[1]

Year	Marks	Per Member	For each Case of Sickness	For each Day of Sickness
1885	47,400,121	....	26.41	1.88
1886	53,041,099	....	30.99	2.02
1887	55,202,067	....	31.78	2.04
1888	61,561,484	11.40	34.93	2.08
1889	70,975,191	11.55	34.76	2.12
1890	84,040,014	12.77	34.69	2.15
1891	89,166,091	12.96	37.19	2.19
1892	94,258,373	13.55	38.03	2.20
1893	101,971,698	14.35	36.50	2.21
1894	99,588,457	13.67	39.96	2.28
1895	104,822,366	13.93	38.77	2.26
1896	109,722,779	13.81	39.70	2.30
1897	120,487,910	14.45	40.64	2.34
1898	128,057,300	14.60	42.68	2.40
1899	145,324,200	15.87	42 74	2.40
1900	157,865,200	16.58	43.01	2.43
1901	163,355,600	16.94	45.25	2.45
1902	167,801,400	17.02	47.00	2.49
1903	180,841,700	17.69	47.84	2.52
1904	213,931,500	19.97	50.64	2.56
1905	232,243,900	20.76	52.16	2.63
1906	241,793,600	20.68	54.70	2.76
1907	273,887,500	22.56	55.35	2.81

Not only has the expenditure for sickness increased, but also the number of cases of sickness in proportion to the insured, the number of days of sickness in proportion to the insured, and the number of days of sickness in proportion to each case of sickness. On the other hand, the number of deaths has fallen in proportion to the number insured, as is shown by the following table:[2]

[1] This table is taken down to 1897 from "Lass und Zahn," p. 144. The figures for the later years are compiled and computed from "Statistik des Deutschen Reichs," Vols. CLVI and CXCIV.

[2] This table is taken down to 1897 from "Lass und Zahn," p. 139. The figures for the later years are compiled from "Statistik des Deutschen Reichs," Vols. CLVI and CXCIV.

	Cases of Sickness		Days of Sickness			Deaths	
	Absolutely	Per 100 insured	Absolutely	Per 100 insured	Per case of sickness	Absolutely	Per 100 insured
1888 ...	1,762,520	32.6	29,528,770	547.0	16.8	44,500	0.96
1889 ...	2,042,082	33.2	33,428,682	544.1	16.4	48,388	0.95
1890 ...	2,422,350	36.8	39,176,689	595.4	16.2	54,287	0.99
1891 ...	2,397,826	34.9	40,798,620	593.0	17.0	54,002	0.95
1892 ...	2,478,237	35.6	42,756,026	614.7	17.3	56,413	0.98
1893 ...	2,794,027	39.3	46,199,436	650.1	16.5	57,295	0.98
1894 ...	2,492,309	34.2	43,686,440	599.9	17.5	54,343	0.90
1895 ...	2,703,632	35.9	46,470,023	617.5	17.2	55,314	0.89
1896 ...	2,763,757	34.8	47,608,226	599.2	17.2	57,000	0.86
1897 ...	2,964,937	35.6	51,513,783	617.9	17.4	59,432	0.85
1898 ...	3,002,593	34.2	53,201,173	606.6	17.7	60,334	0.82
1899 ...	3,476,067	38.0	60,406,683	659.8	17.4	67,550	0.87
1900 ...	3,679,285	38.6	64,916,827	681.8	17.6	71,349	0.88
1901 ...	3,617,022	37.5	66,652,488	691.3	18.4	67,889	0.83
1902 ...	3,578,410	36.3	67,377,057	683.5	18.8	68,624	0.82
1903 ...	3,782,620	37.0	71,726,598	701.5	19.0	69,785	0.80
1904 ...	4,229,177	39.5	83,259,967	777.4	19.7	73,211	0.80
1905 ...	4,451,448	39.8	88,082,296	787.5	19.8	77,965	0.81
1906 ...	4,423,756	37.8	87,444,605	748.1	19.8	77,237	0.76
1907 ...	4,956,388	40.8	97,148,780	800.3	19.6	82,486	0.78

Curiously enough, a somewhat similar phenomenon shows itself in the case of accidents. Not only has the number of accidents indemnified increased absolutely, but it has increased in proportion to the number of those insured.

"Fortunately," says the report, "not the more serious accidents which result in death or complete inability to work make up the increase in the frequency of accidents. On the contrary these show a digressive tendency . . . only the lighter accidents, that is those with partial continuing, and particularly those with a temporary, inability to work have increased." These facts are shown in the following table:

Number of Injured Persons for Whom Indemnities Have Been Granted for the First Time in All Kinds of Accident Insurance [1]

	Absolute Figures					Per 1,000 Insured				
	In All	Consequences of the Injury				In All	Consequences of the Injury			
		Death	Permanent Incapacity of Support		Temporary incapacity		D	Permanent Incapacity of Support		Temporary incapacity
			Complete	Partial				Complete	Partial	
1888..	21,057	3,645	2,203	11,023	4,186	2.03	0.35	0.21	1.07	0.40
1889..	31,019	5,185	2,882	16,337	6,615	2.32	0.39	0.22	1.22	0.49
1890..	41,420	5,958	2,681	22,615	10,166	3.03	0.44	0.20	1.65	0.74
1891..	50,507	6,346	2,561	27,788	13,812	2.80	0.35	0.14	1.54	0.77
1892..	54,827	5,811	2,640	30,569	15,807	3.04	0.32	0.15	1.69	0.88
1893..	61,874	6,245	2,487	36,236	16,906	3.41	0.34	0.14	2.00	0.93
1894..	68,677	6,250	1,752	38,952	21,723	3.78	0.34	0.10	2.14	1.20
1895..	74,467	6,335	1,668	40,527	25,937	4.05	0.35	0.09	2.20	1.41
1896..	85,272	6,989	1,524	44,373	32,386	4.84	0.39	0.09	2.52	1.84
1897..	91,171	7,287	1,452	46,489	35,943	5.08	0.41	0.08	2.59	2.00
1898..	96,774	7,848	1,109	47,764	40,053	5.30	0.43	0.06	2.62	2.19
1899..	104,811	7,999	1,297	51,240	44,275	5.63	0.43	0.07	2.75	2.38
1900..	106,447	8,449	1,366	51,111	45,521	5.63	0.45	0.07	2.70	2.41
1901..	116,089	8,359	1,416	54,340	51,974	6.15	0.44	0.08	2.88	2.75
1902..	119,901	7,842	1,396	55,264	55,399	6.28	0.41	0.07	2.90	2.90
1903..	127,947	8,236	1,517	58,129	60,065	6.57	0.42	0.08	2.99	3.08
1904..	136,126	8,552	1,578	62,563	63,433	6.85	0.43	0.08	3.15	3.19
1905..	139,787	8,757	1,476	63,530	66,024	6.91	0.43	0.08	3.14	3.26
1906..	138,283	8,970	1,454	60,814	67,045	6.67	0.43	0.07	2.93	3.24

This is a curious phenomenon. The official report says, "From what has been said there is no ground for the claim that obligatory accident insurance itself leads to an increase of accidents, in that it makes the workingmen careless and employers indifferent. That any one should now, having regard to the existing insurance, expose himself more frivolously to an accident; that he should allow a finger to be cut off, or allow his leg to be crushed, is in contradiction, as Boediker well remarks, to the instinct of self-preservation. The fear of pain, the uncertainty of the result, which may be deadly, operate upon the mind more than the prospect of getting an allowance which at

[1] "Statistisches Jahrbuch für das Deutschen Reich," 1908, p. 312.

the most may be equal to two-thirds of the forfeited earnings. Accidents which are brought about intentionally are in any case not indemnified."[1]

This *a priori* reasoning is a plausible answer to the claim that men deliberately injure themselves to get an indemnity, but cases are not unknown in which people have acted in what seems to be an irrational manner, and it still remains necessary to explain why minor accidents should have increased in spite of the very great efforts made by employers to introduce safety appliances and prevent injuries. A number of reasons are, therefore, given for this increase:

(1) It is said that they are more strictly reported, which may well have been the case ten years ago, but it is hardly probable that an increasing accuracy in reporting accidents should continue through twenty years.

(2) The increase in the use of machinery and the concentration of workingmen in large establishments is given as a reason, but this argument seems to be weakened by the fact that the increase in the frequency of accidents is more noticeable in agriculture, where the Germans use much less machinery, than in industry, for while the industrial accidents indemnified increased 378 per cent. in eighteen years, accidents in agriculture increased 492 per cent. in sixteen years.[2] Moreover, it is remarkable that, if the different occupations are ranked according to the frequency of accidents, those which involve the use of comparatively little machinery are near the head, while those involving much machinery are at the foot. Thus the number of persons indemnified per 1000 persons injured is found to be 16.97 per cent. in the case of vehicle driving, 13.51 per cent. in the case of grist-mills, 11.94 per cent. in the case of quarries, while in railroads it is but 5.86 per cent., in metal industries 4.21 per cent., in

[1] "Lass und Zahn," p. 167.

[2] The percentages are based upon the figures given in "Statistisches Jahrbuch für das Deutsche Reich," 1908, p. 312.

textile 3.41 per cent.[1] The claim that machinery is responsible for the increase in accidents would, therefore, hardly seem to hold true.

(3) It is claimed that the great activity of trade has required the appointment of less experienced men. It is impossible to control this statement by statistics, but some light is thrown upon it by the figures which show that accidents are much less frequent in proportion among the younger men than among the middle aged and elderly.

It appeared, for instance, in 1897 that the number of the injured, in proportion to one hundred insured in each class, varied as follows:

Under 16	0.24	20–30	0.54	50–60	1.38
16–18	0.32	30–40	0.92	60–70	1.42
18–20	0.36	40–50	1.23	70 and over	0.85

It is not shown that the inexperienced laborers are necessarily young, but this is not an unfair assumption.

(4) The increased familiarity of the men with the law is given as not the least of the causes, and there seems every reason to consider this true. In other words, the causes of the accidents are not mainly material or mechanical, but to a large extent psychological.

The psychological element in accidents also shows itself in the distribution of accidents according to the day of the week and the hour of the day. We find quite universally that Monday furnishes the largest number of accidents, and Saturday the next largest, and this law applies both to industry and to agriculture. An interesting table bearing upon the same subject is one which shows an increasing percentage of accidents due to the fault of the industrial worker:

[1] Figures quoted in "Lass und Zahn," p. 170, also in the "Report of the New York Bureau of Labor for 1899," p. 769.

	1887	1897
Fault of employer	20.47%	17.30%
" " worker	26.56	29.74
" " both together	4.61	4.83
" " fellow workers, or third person	3.40	5.31
Other causes, such as danger of occupation	44.96	42.82

One is tempted to contrast the German figures with the results of the operations of a mutual fire insurance company in which the beneficiaries also bear the losses, and therefore have a direct motive for minimizing them. The Manufacturers' Mutual Fire Insurance Company was organized in 1850. It was for many years under the management of Edward Atkinson, as president and treasurer. Being mutual, it is similar to the accident insurance associations of Germany, in that those who pay the premiums also have to bear the losses; so that the manufacturers in this company are interested, as the German manufacturers are, in reducing to a minimum the accidents that cause losses. The statistics, running over half a century, are very instructive regarding the effects of this system, especially if we take the figures averaged by decades. The single years show considerable variations, as might be expected. The report issued for the year ending December 31, 1899, gives the rate of loss to the amount written per hundred dollars, as follows:

First decade	1850–1859	0.3631
Second decade	1860–1869	0.2427
Third decade	1870–1879	0.2098
Fourth decade	1880–1889	0.1963
Fifth decade	1890–1899	0.1080

It is difficult to escape the impression that the number of minor accidents has increased under the operation of the insurance laws. Whether workmen have become more careless, or whether they have become more ready to exaggerate their injuries, the effect of giving them under the forms of insurance an indemnity of which they do not bear the burden seems to have stimulated an irresponsibility, which all the efforts of the employers to diminish accidents have not yet overcome.

There are other facts which indicate similarly a relaxation of the spirit of self-help. The deposits in the savings banks, while they show an increase, show a diminishing rate of increase of the smaller deposits, as compared with deposits in general.

DEPOSITS AND SMALL DEPOSITORS IN PRUSSIA

	Total Deposits 1,000,000 M.	Increase		Number Depositors Under 60 M. 000 Omitted	Per Cent. of all Depositors	Increase	
		Absolute 1,000,000 M.	Per cent.			Absolute 1000 Depositors	Per Cent.
1880	1,593	....	....	725	....	....	...
1885	2,261	668	41.	1,214	....	489	69.
1890	3,281	1,020	45.	1,609	29.4	395	32.
1895	4,345	1,064	32.	1,972	28.9	363	22.
1900	5,745	1,400	32.	2,421	28.1	449	22.
1901	6,236	491	8.5	2,514	28.0	93	3.8
1902	6,727	491	7.8	2,624	28.0	110	4.3

Dr. Barthelme,[1] from whose book the foregoing figures are taken, shows that in Germany the savings banks are not used by the poorer classes as much as they should be. He therefore advocates a special system of premiums on savings.

It was stated at the beginning, as one of the chief characteristics of government insurance, that the premium was turned wholly or partly into a tax — a payment, therefore, not borne exclusively by the beneficiary. The German experience with this kind of insurance seems to show

[1] Dr. Georg Barthelme: "Das Deutschen, insbesondere das Preussische Sparkassenwesen," pages 48 and 60.

that it is possible with a highly trained, intelligent administration to carry through a scheme which will compel provision against various contingencies, and that this can be done without checking the growth of industry or lowering wages. The great danger of the system seems to lie in its effects upon the beneficiaries themselves. When we find that, in spite of measures to diminish accidents, and in spite of a diminution in the more serious accidents, the proportion of minor accidents is steadily increasing; when we find that in spite of generally improved sanitary conditions and a diminished death-rate, the cases of sickness are increasing in proportion to the number of the insured, and that the average duration of each case of sickness is lengthened, the conclusion seems inevitable that the working classes as a whole are taking advantage of the insurance benefits to make more of their accidents and ailments than they did in the beginning. If such a thing is possible under an administration which is, on the whole, very strict and punctilious, we naturally ask, what would it be, if the government officials were lax, or corrupt, or subject to political influence? In other words, the indications are that unsuspected and rather insidious evils have developed under the system, which must be taken account of by any country which aims to copy it. As in all legal measures, we must weigh, not only the mechanical operations of the laws, but also their effect on the mind and character of those to whom they apply.

INDEX

A

B

C

D

M

N

S

T

U

V

W